SB
Shojo Beat

Yona of the Dawn

19

Story & Art by

Mizuho Kusanagi

Hey! Hak, stop that!

My whole body...is paralyzed...

POKE

POKE

Yona of the Dawn

Volume 19

CONTENTS

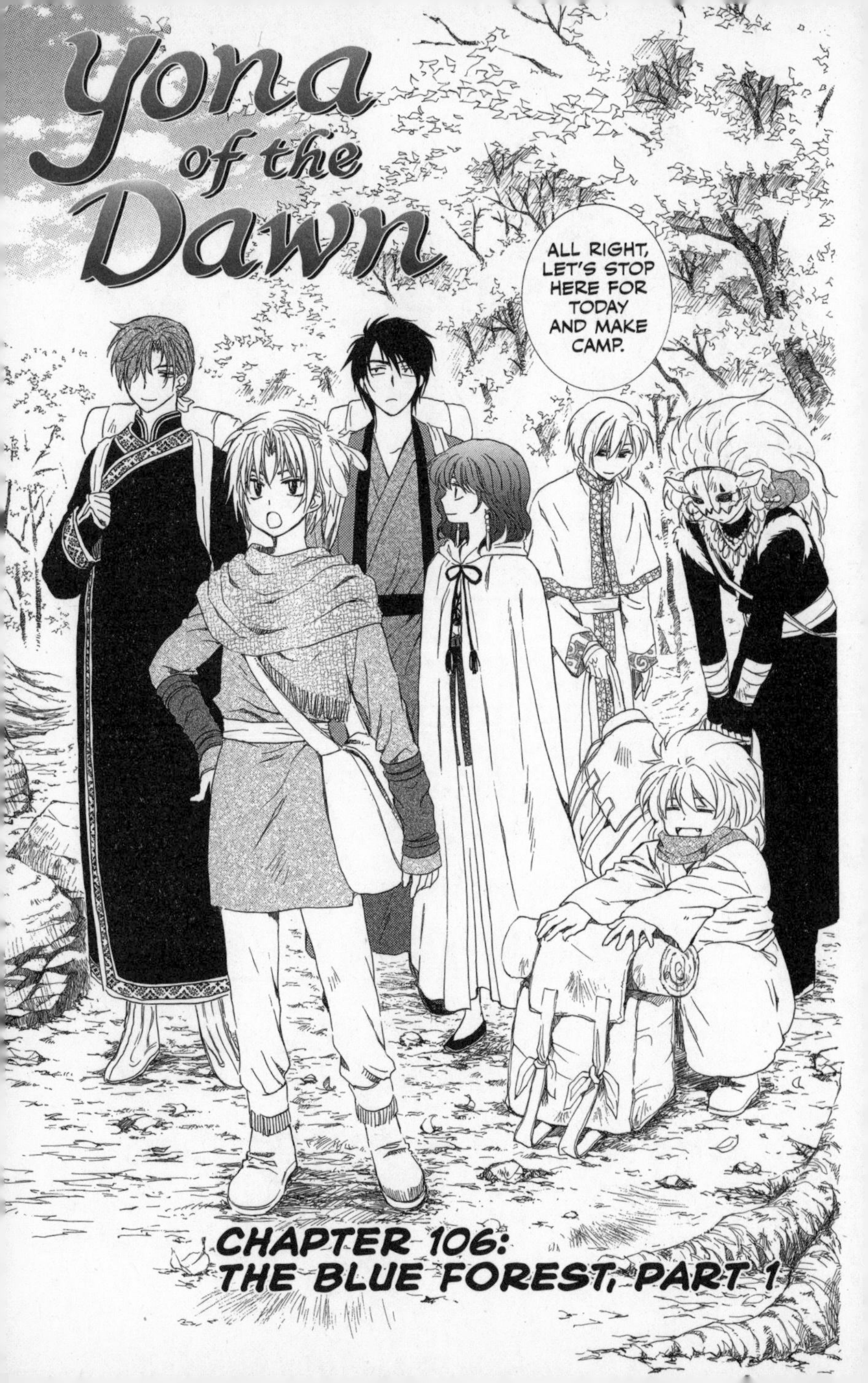
Yona of the Dawn
ALL RIGHT, LET'S STOP HERE FOR TODAY AND MAKE CAMP.
CHAPTER 106: THE BLUE FOREST, PART 1

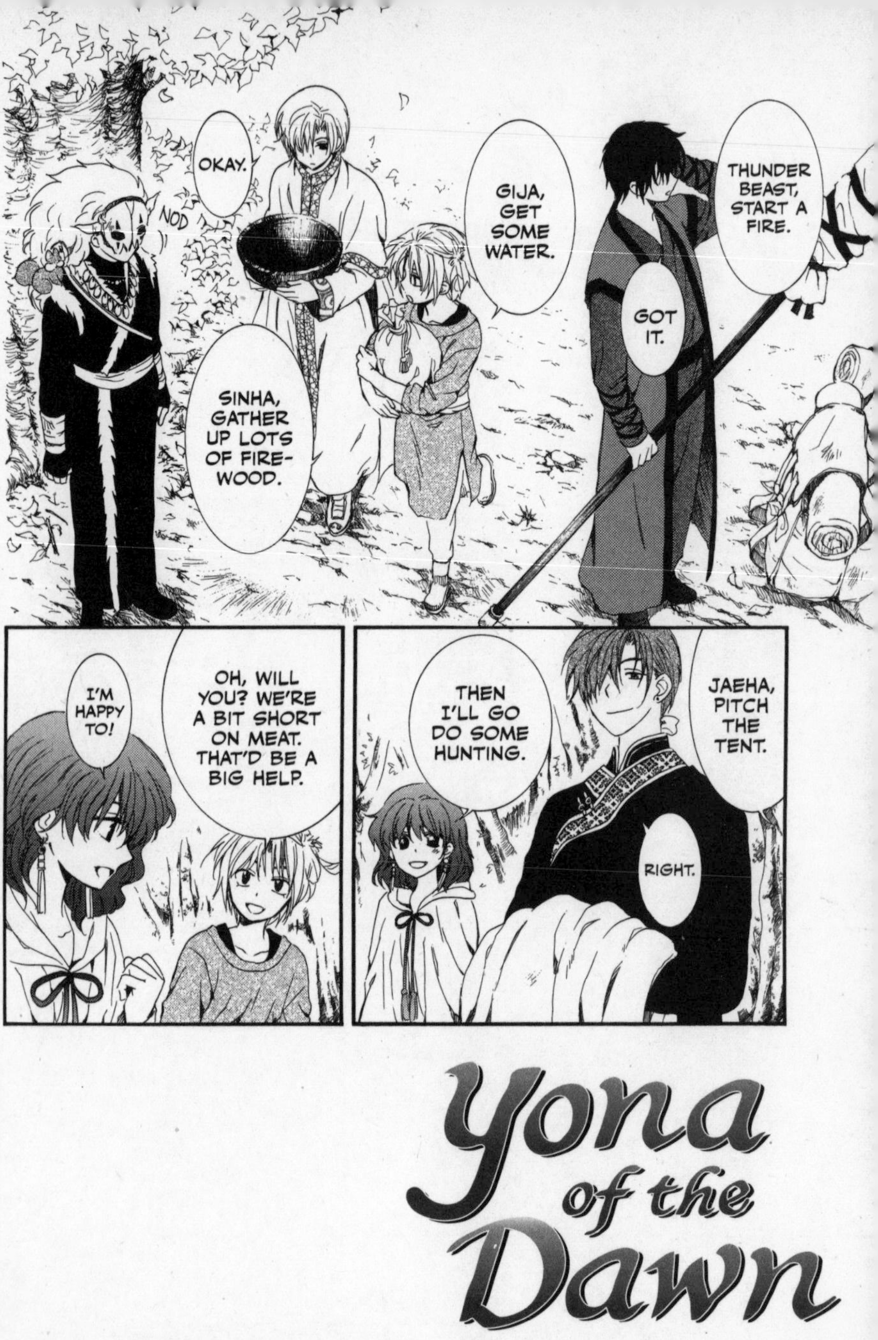
THUNDER BEAST, START A FIRE.
GOT IT.
GIJA, GET SOME WATER.
SINHA, GATHER UP LOTS OF FIRE-WOOD.
OKAY.
NOD
JAEHA, PITCH THE TENT.
RIGHT.
THEN I'LL GO DO SOME HUNTING.
OH, WILL YOU? WE'RE A BIT SHORT ON MEAT. THAT'D BE A BIG HELP.
I'M HAPPY TO!

Yona of the Dawn

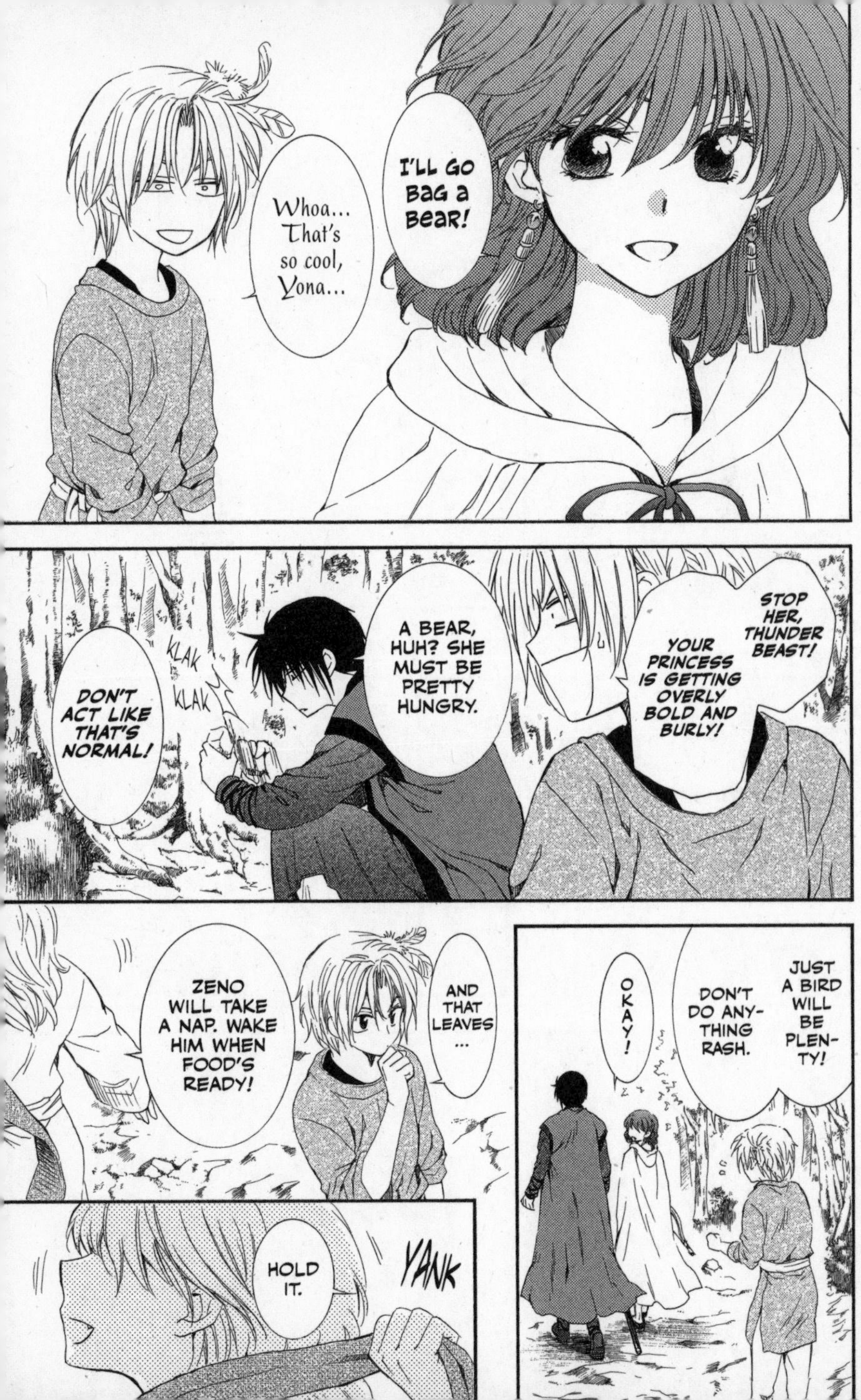
I'LL GO BaG a BeaR!
Whoa... That's so cool, Yona...
STOP HER, THUNDER BEAST!
YOUR PRINCESS IS GETTING OVERLY BOLD AND BURLY!
A BEAR, HUH? SHE MUST BE PRETTY HUNGRY.
KLAK KLAK
DON'T ACT LIKE THAT'S NORMAL!
JUST A BIRD WILL BE PLEN-TY!
DON'T DO ANY-THING RASH.
OKAY!
AND THAT LEAVES...
ZENO WILL TAKE A NAP. WAKE HIM WHEN FOOD'S READY!
YANK
HOLD IT.

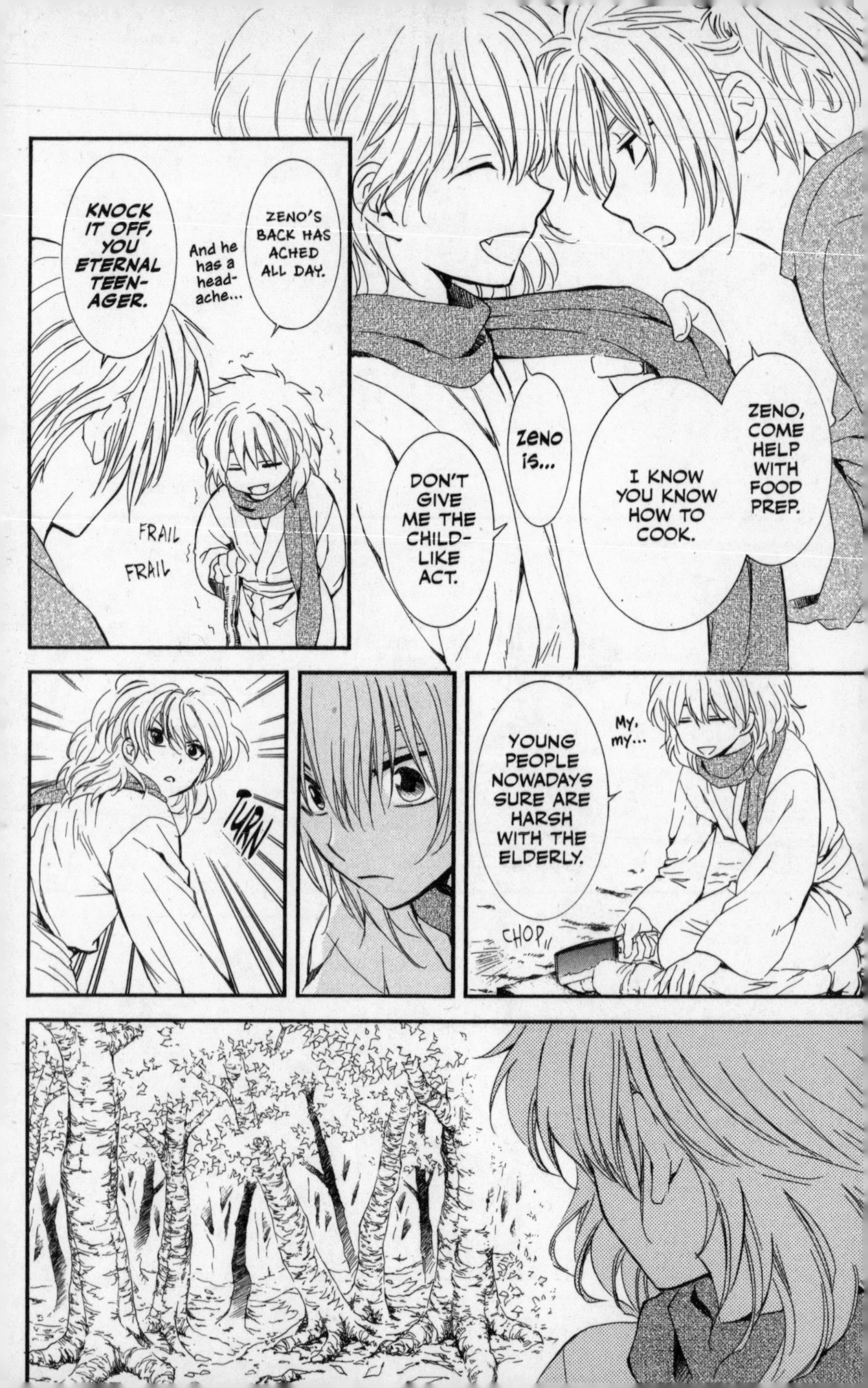
ZENO, COME HELP WITH FOOD PREP.
I KNOW YOU KNOW HOW TO COOK.
ZENO IS...
DON'T GIVE ME THE CHILD-LIKE ACT.
ZENO'S BACK HAS ACHED ALL DAY.
And he has a head-ache...
FRAIL
FRAIL
KNOCK IT OFF, YOU ETERNAL TEEN-AGER.
My, my...
YOUNG PEOPLE NOWADAYS SURE ARE HARSH WITH THE ELDERLY.
CHOP
TURN

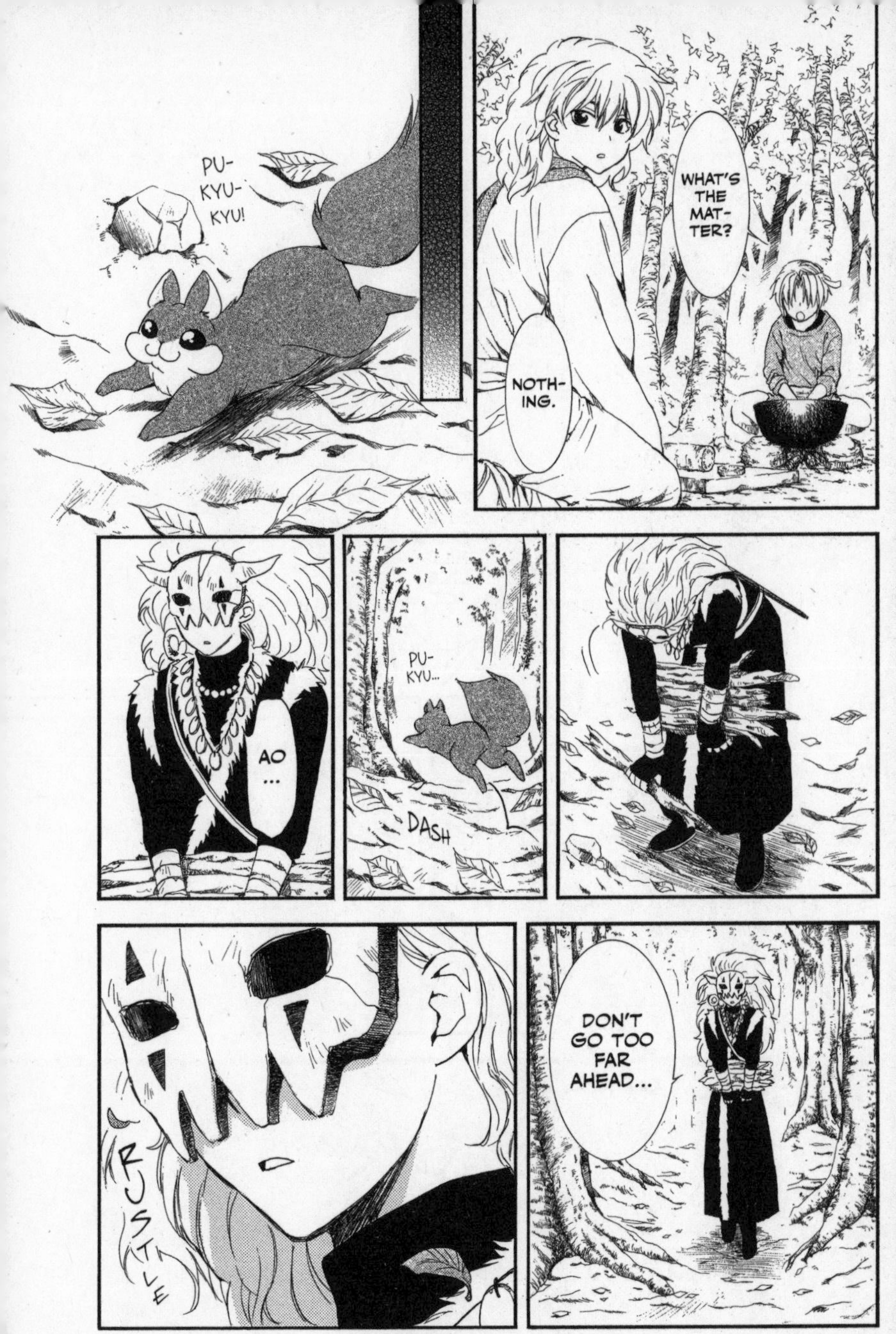
WHAT'S THE MAT-TER?
NOTH-ING.
PU-KYU-KYU!
PU-KYU...
DASH
AO ...
DON'T GO TOO FAR AHEAD...
RUSTLE

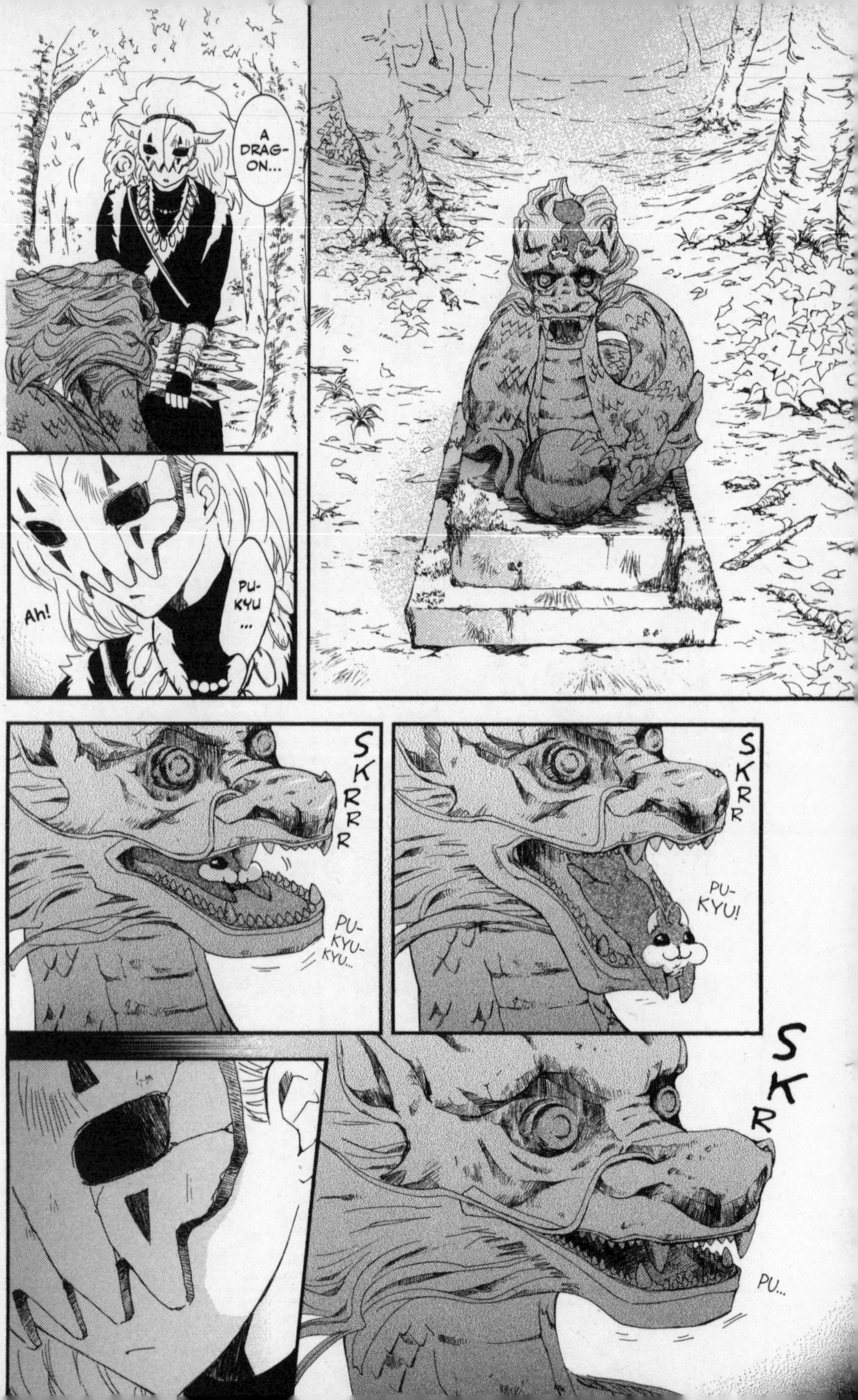
A DRAG-ON...
PU-KYU...
Ah!
SKRR
PU-KYU!
SKRRR
PU-KYU-KYU...
SKR
PU...

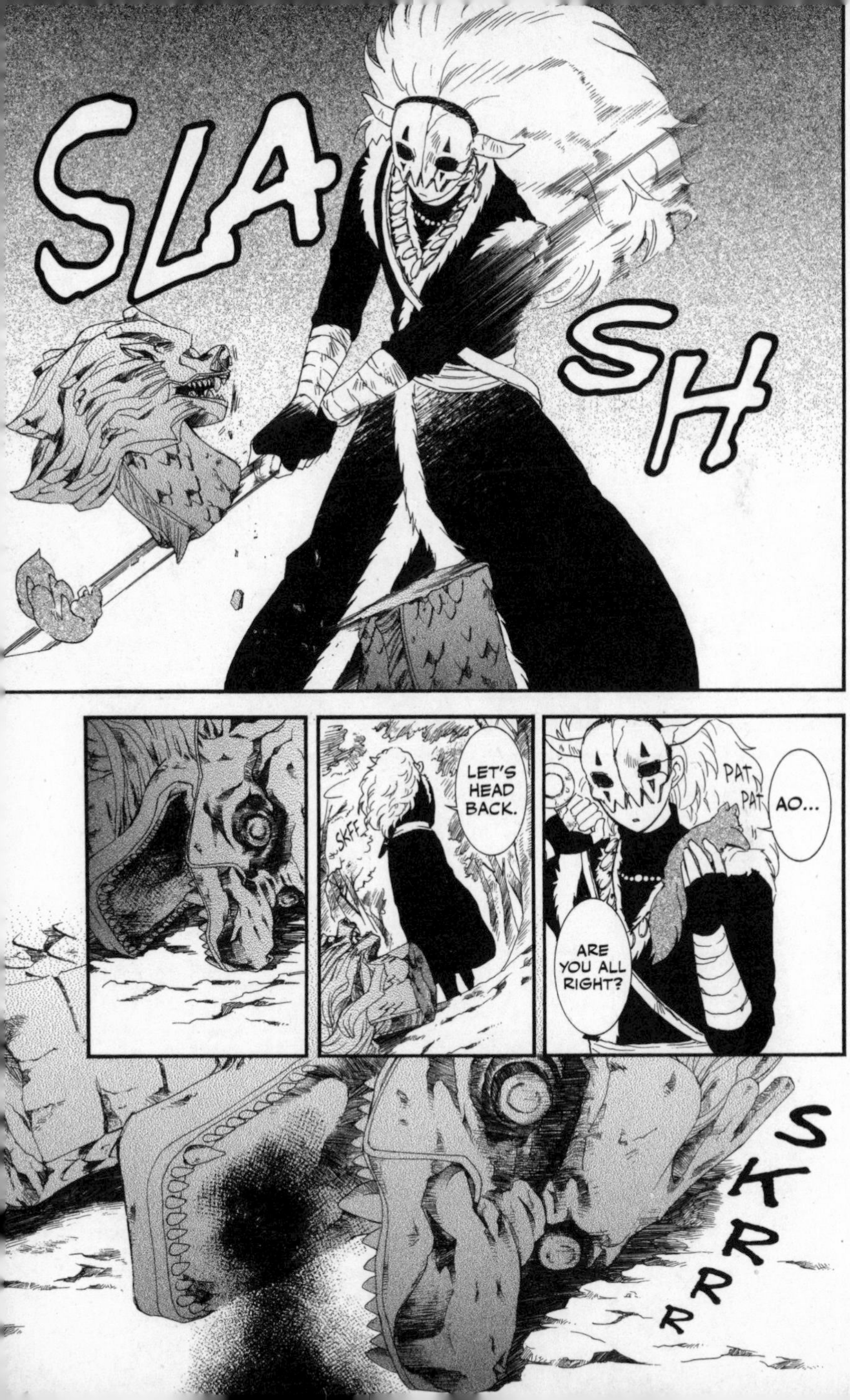
SLASH
PAT PAT
AO...
ARE YOU ALL RIGHT?
LET'S HEAD BACK.
SKFF
SKRRRR

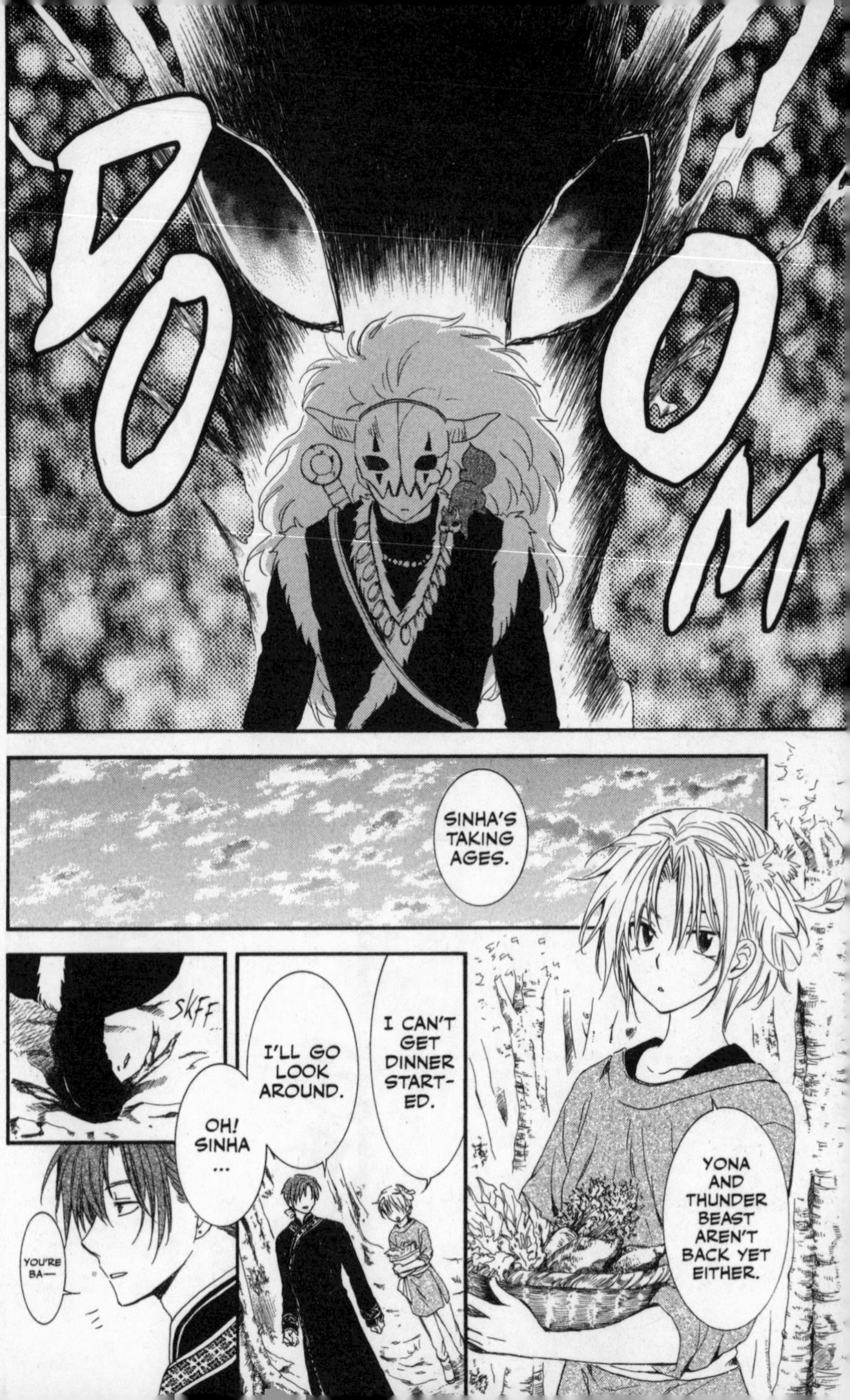
DOOM
SINHA'S TAKING AGES.
YONA AND THUNDER BEAST AREN'T BACK YET EITHER.
I CAN'T GET DINNER START-ED.
I'LL GO LOOK AROUND.
OH! SINHA...
SKFF
YOU'RE BA—

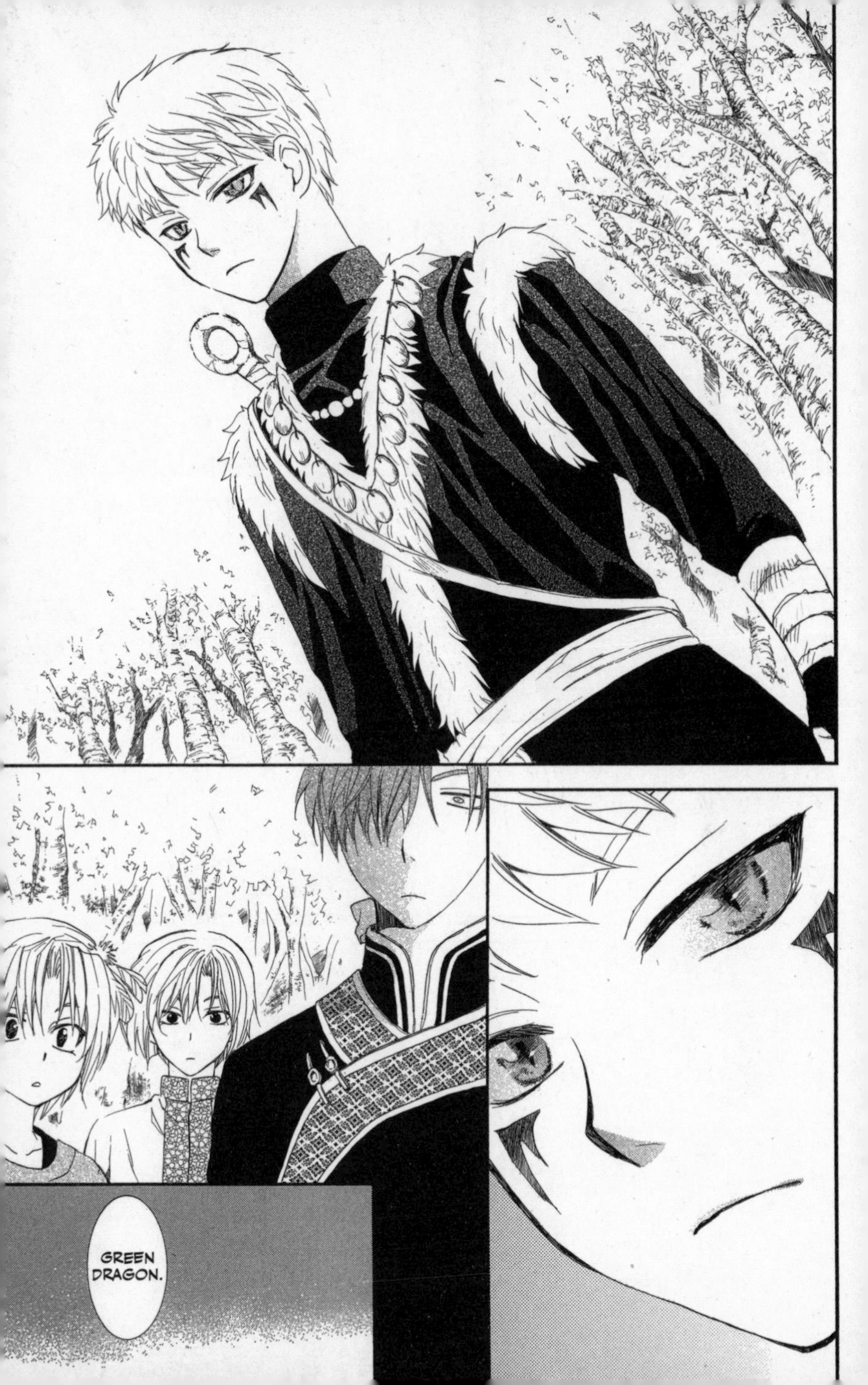
GREEN DRAGON.

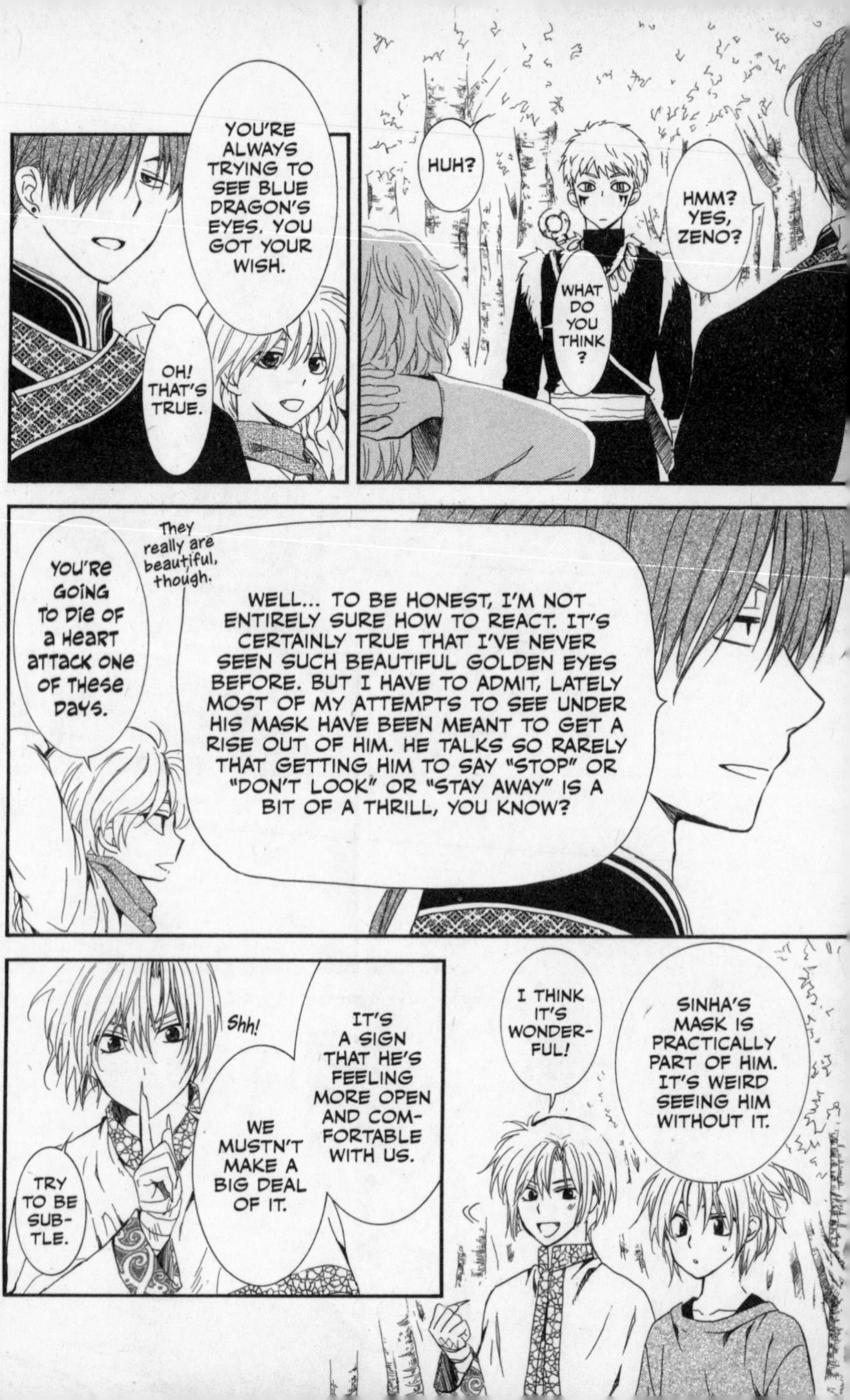
HMM? YES, ZENO?
HUH?
WHAT DO YOU THINK?
YOU'RE ALWAYS TRYING TO SEE BLUE DRAGON'S EYES. YOU GOT YOUR WISH.
OH! THAT'S TRUE.
WELL... TO BE HONEST, I'M NOT ENTIRELY SURE HOW TO REACT. IT'S CERTAINLY TRUE THAT I'VE NEVER SEEN SUCH BEAUTIFUL GOLDEN EYES BEFORE. BUT I HAVE TO ADMIT, LATELY MOST OF MY ATTEMPTS TO SEE UNDER HIS MASK HAVE BEEN MEANT TO GET A RISE OUT OF HIM. HE TALKS SO RARELY THAT GETTING HIM TO SAY "STOP" OR "DON'T LOOK" OR "STAY AWAY" IS A BIT OF A THRILL, YOU KNOW?
They really are beautiful, though.
YOU'RE GOING TO DIE OF A HEART ATTACK ONE OF THESE DAYS.
SINHA'S MASK IS PRACTICALLY PART OF HIM. IT'S WEIRD SEEING HIM WITHOUT IT.
I THINK IT'S WONDER-FUL!
IT'S A SIGN THAT HE'S FEELING MORE OPEN AND COM-FORTABLE WITH US.
WE MUSTN'T MAKE A BIG DEAL OF IT.
Shh!
TRY TO BE SUB-TLE.

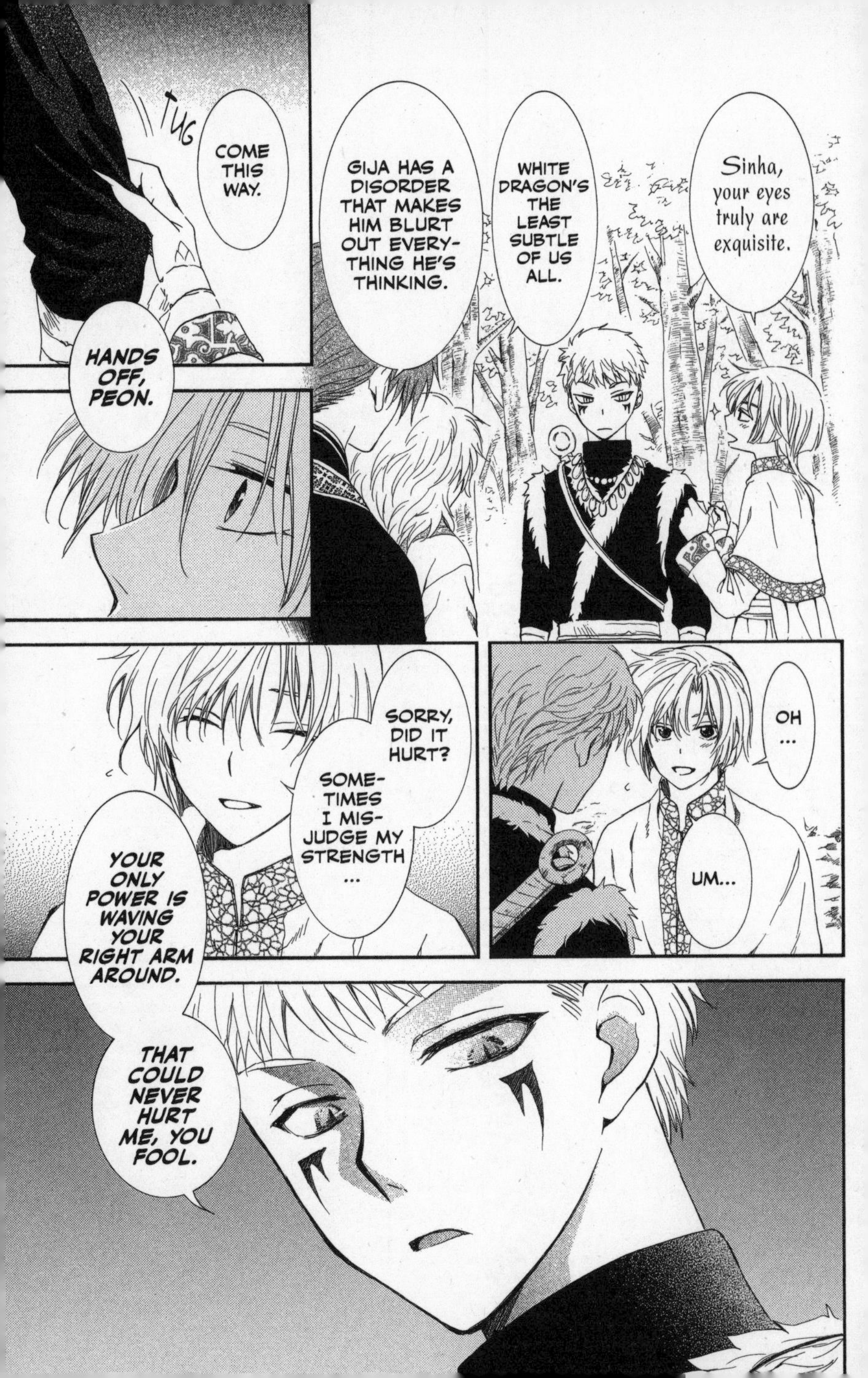

Sinha, your eyes truly are exquisite.
WHITE DRAGON'S THE LEAST SUBTLE OF US ALL.
GIJA HAS A DISORDER THAT MAKES HIM BLURT OUT EVERY-THING HE'S THINKING.
TUG
COME THIS WAY.
HANDS OFF, PEON.
OH ...
UM...
SORRY, DID IT HURT?
SOME-TIMES I MIS-JUDGE MY STRENGTH ...
YOUR ONLY POWER IS WAVING YOUR RIGHT ARM AROUND.
THAT COULD NEVER HURT ME, YOU FOOL.

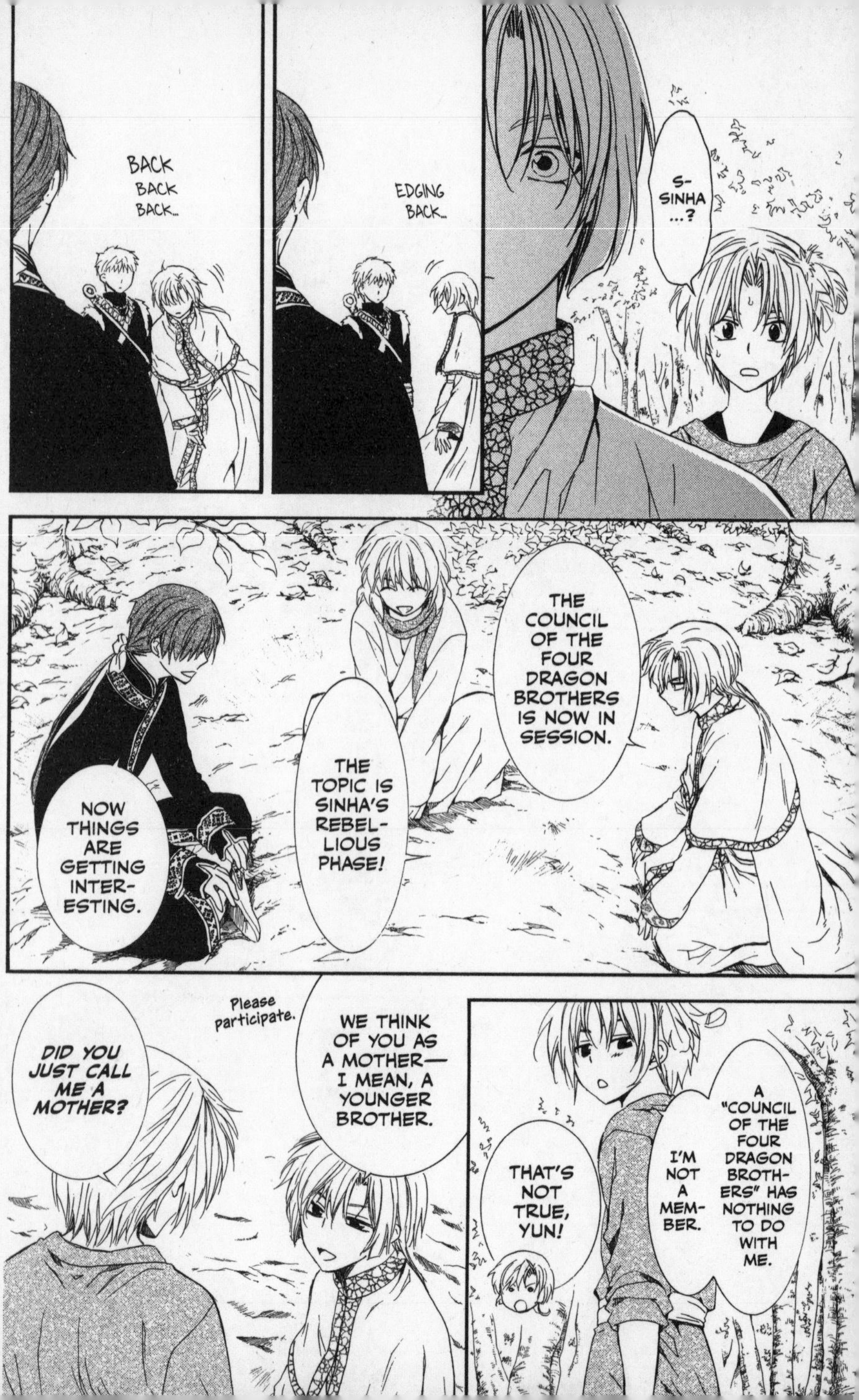
S-SINHA ...?
EDGING BACK...
BACK BACK BACK...
THE COUNCIL OF THE FOUR DRAGON BROTHERS IS NOW IN SESSION.
THE TOPIC IS SINHA'S REBEL-LIOUS PHASE!
NOW THINGS ARE GETTING INTER-ESTING.
A "COUNCIL OF THE FOUR DRAGON BROTH-ERS" HAS NOTHING TO DO WITH ME.
I'M NOT A MEM-BER.
THAT'S NOT TRUE, YUN!
WE THINK OF YOU AS A MOTHER— I MEAN, A YOUNGER BROTHER.
Please participate.
DID YOU JUST CALL ME A MOTHER?

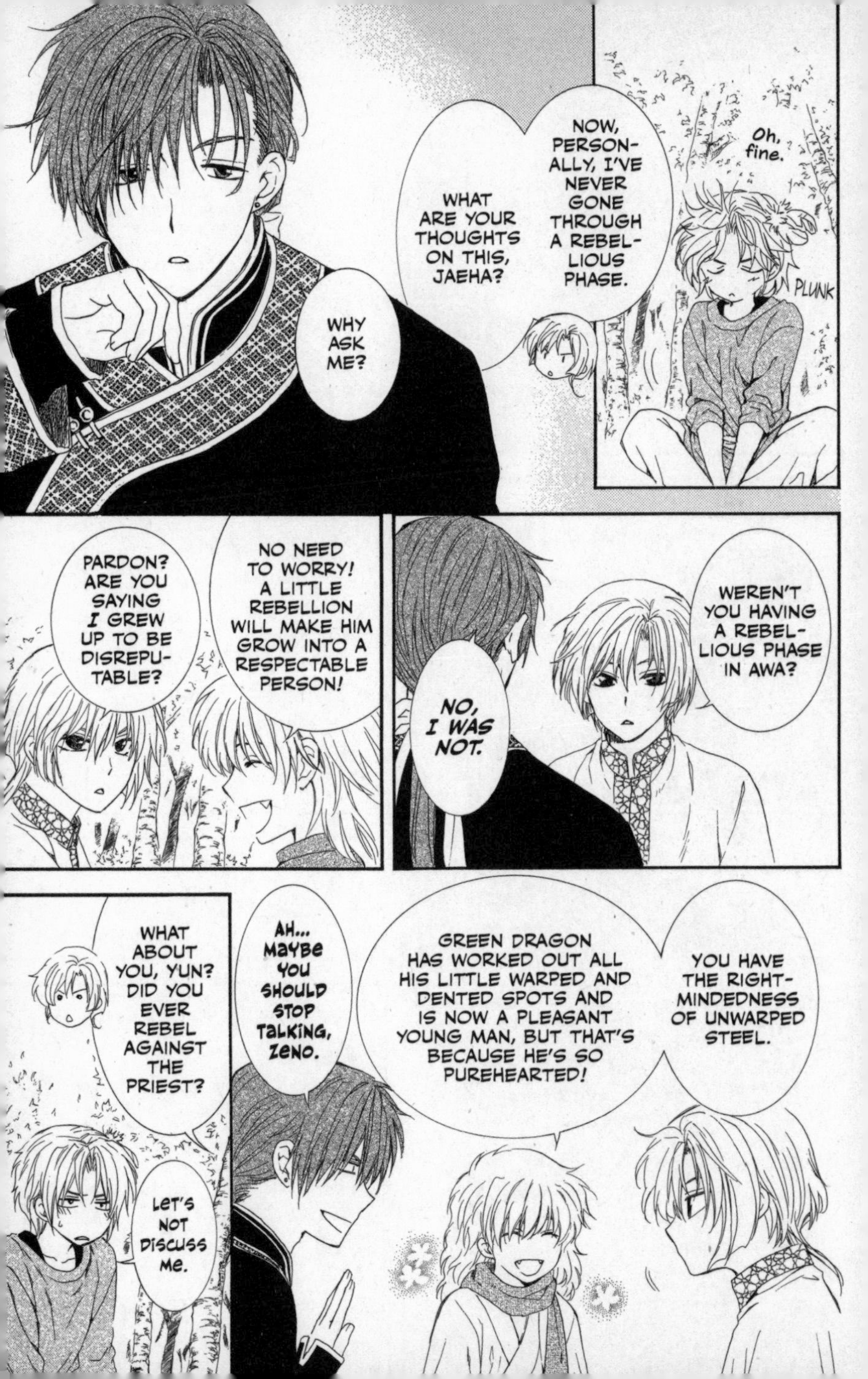
Oh, fine.
PLUNK
NOW, PERSONALLY, I'VE NEVER GONE THROUGH A REBELLIOUS PHASE.
WHAT ARE YOUR THOUGHTS ON THIS, JAEHA?
WHY ASK ME?
WEREN'T YOU HAVING A REBELLIOUS PHASE IN AWA?
NO, I WAS NOT.
NO NEED TO WORRY! A LITTLE REBELLION WILL MAKE HIM GROW INTO A RESPECTABLE PERSON!
PARDON? ARE YOU SAYING *I* GREW UP TO BE DISREPUTABLE?
YOU HAVE THE RIGHT-MINDEDNESS OF UNWARPED STEEL.
GREEN DRAGON HAS WORKED OUT ALL HIS LITTLE WARPED AND DENTED SPOTS AND IS NOW A PLEASANT YOUNG MAN, BUT THAT'S BECAUSE HE'S SO PUREHEARTED!
AH... MAYBE YOU SHOULD STOP TALKING, ZENO.
WHAT ABOUT YOU, YUN? DID YOU EVER REBEL AGAINST THE PRIEST?
LET'S NOT DISCUSS ME.

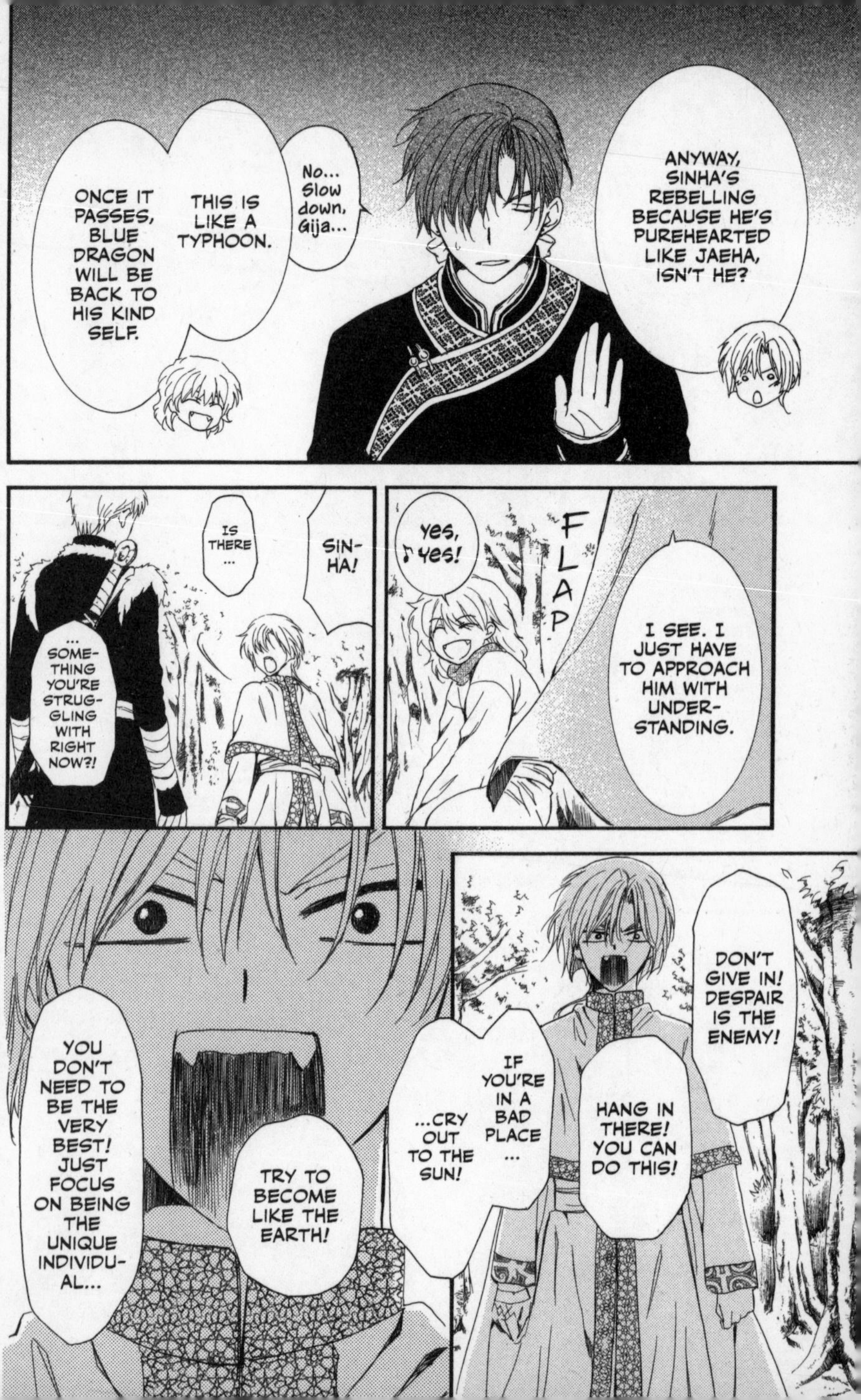
ANYWAY, SINHA'S REBELLING BECAUSE HE'S PUREHEARTED LIKE JAEHA, ISN'T HE?
No... Slow down, Gija...
THIS IS LIKE A TYPHOON.
ONCE IT PASSES, BLUE DRAGON WILL BE BACK TO HIS KIND SELF.
I SEE. I JUST HAVE TO APPROACH HIM WITH UNDER-STANDING.
FLAP
yes, ♪yes!
SIN-HA!
IS THERE ...
...SOME-THING YOU'RE STRUG-GLING WITH RIGHT NOW?!
DON'T GIVE IN! DESPAIR IS THE ENEMY!
HANG IN THERE! YOU CAN DO THIS!
IF YOU'RE IN A BAD PLACE ...
...CRY OUT TO THE SUN!
TRY TO BECOME LIKE THE EARTH!
YOU DON'T NEED TO BE THE VERY BEST! JUST FOCUS ON BEING THE UNIQUE INDIVIDU-AL...

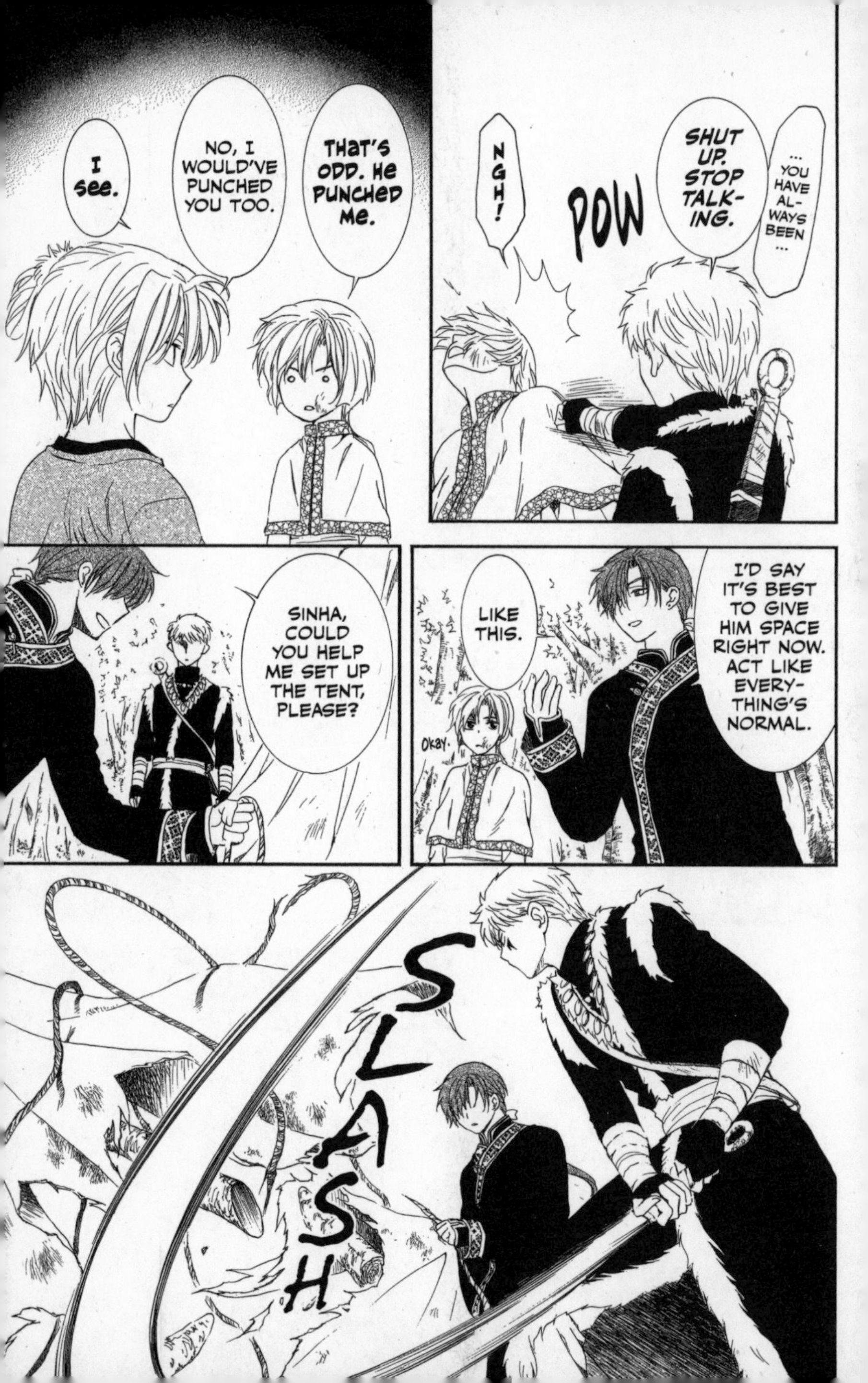
... YOU HAVE AL-WAYS BEEN ...
SHUT UP. STOP TALK-ING.
POW
NGH!
THAT'S ODD. HE PUNCHED ME.
NO, I WOULD'VE PUNCHED YOU TOO.
I SEE.
I'D SAY IT'S BEST TO GIVE HIM SPACE RIGHT NOW. ACT LIKE EVERY-THING'S NORMAL.
LIKE THIS.
Okay.
SINHA, COULD YOU HELP ME SET UP THE TENT, PLEASE?
SLASH

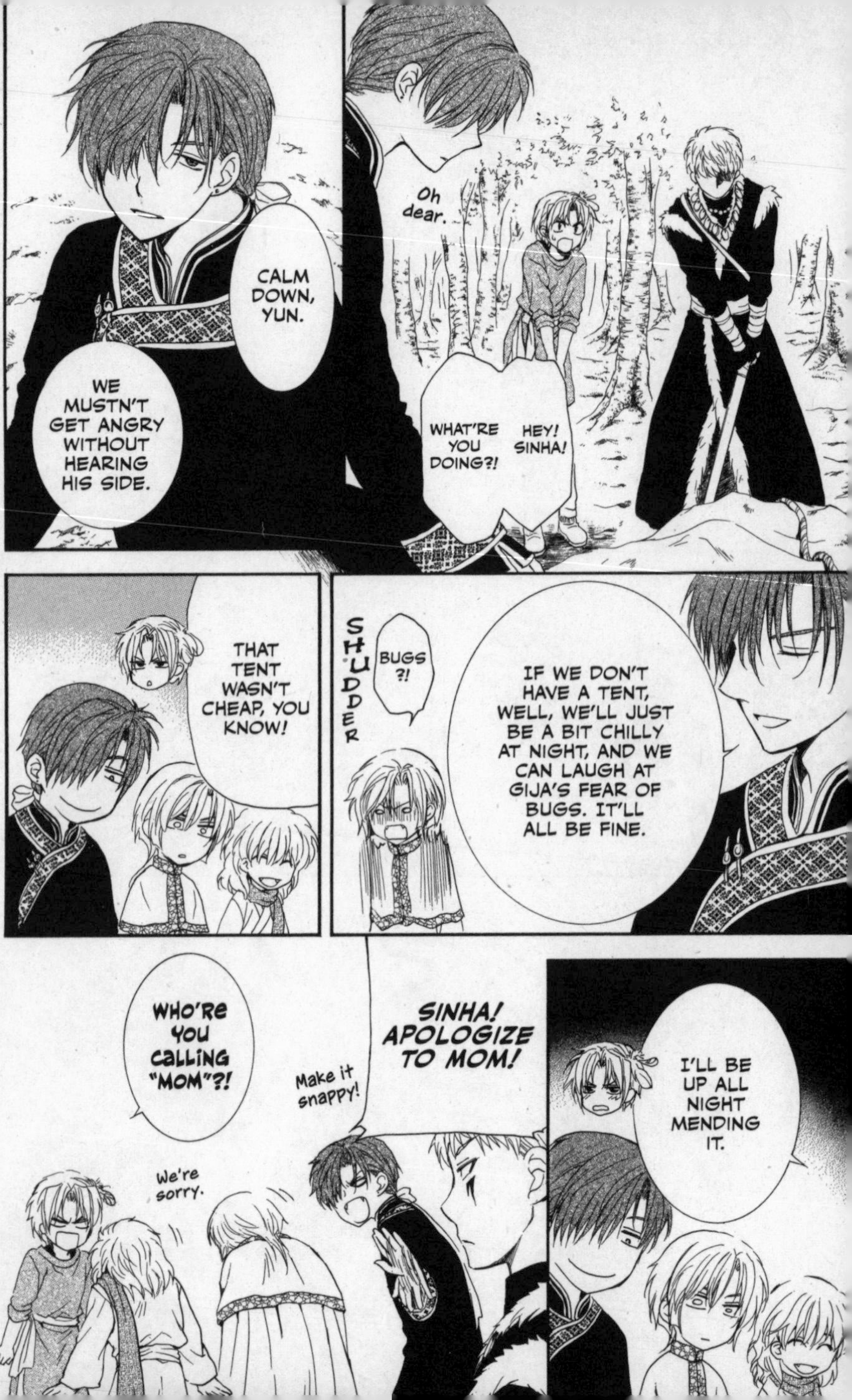
HEY! SINHA! WHAT'RE YOU DOING?!
Oh dear.
CALM DOWN, YUN.
WE MUSTN'T GET ANGRY WITHOUT HEARING HIS SIDE.
IF WE DON'T HAVE A TENT, WELL, WE'LL JUST BE A BIT CHILLY AT NIGHT, AND WE CAN LAUGH AT GIJA'S FEAR OF BUGS. IT'LL ALL BE FINE.
SHUDDER
BUGS?!
THAT TENT WASN'T CHEAP, YOU KNOW!
I'LL BE UP ALL NIGHT MENDING IT.
SINHA! APOLOGIZE TO MOM!
Make it snappy!
WHO'RE YOU CALLING "MOM"?!
We're sorry.

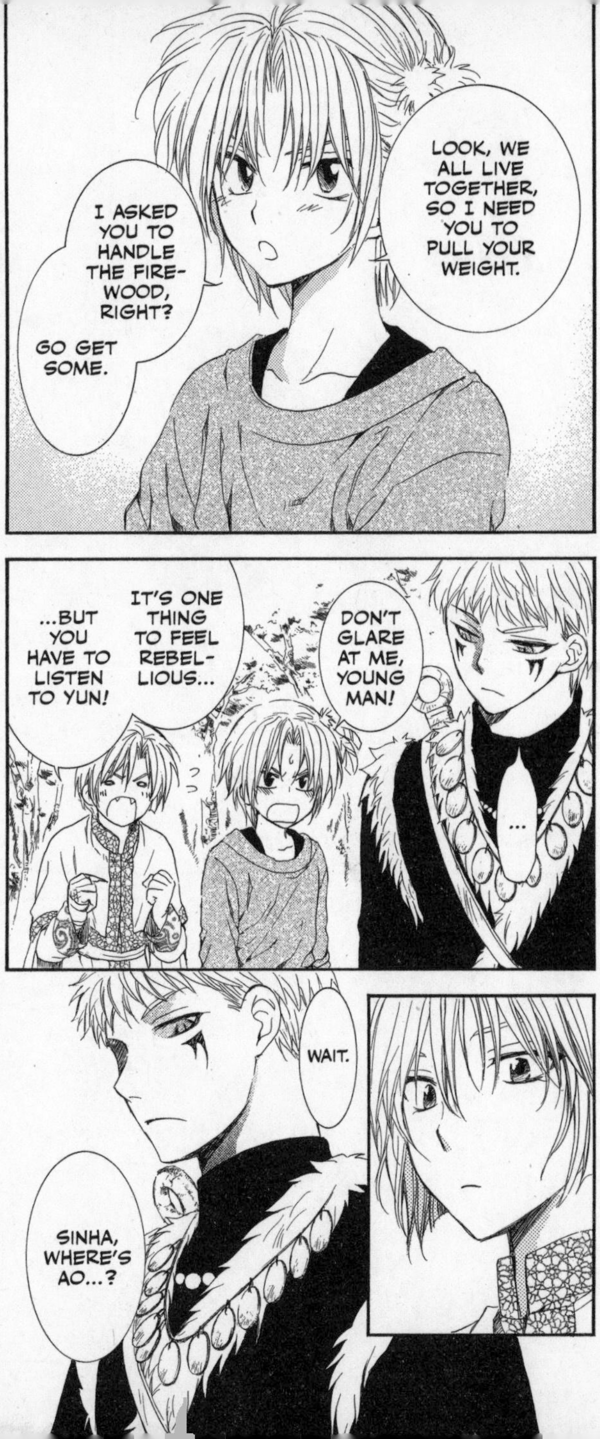
LOOK, WE ALL LIVE TOGETHER, SO I NEED YOU TO PULL YOUR WEIGHT.
I ASKED YOU TO HANDLE THE FIRE-WOOD, RIGHT?
GO GET SOME.
DON'T GLARE AT ME, YOUNG MAN!
IT'S ONE THING TO FEEL REBEL-LIOUS...
...BUT YOU HAVE TO LISTEN TO YUN!
...
WAIT.
SINHA, WHERE'S AO...?

Thank you for picking up volume 19 of Yona!

Yona has entered its seventh year. The time has just flown by! I feel as if it hasn't been that long since I started this series, but I got a message from someone who began reading it in grade school and has since become a member of society. It really hit me that I've been writing this for quite a long time.

Drawing a comic is difficult, but I keep at it because it brings joy to people—that's really important to me.

This has become a long series, but I hope you'll keep reading it for a while longer.

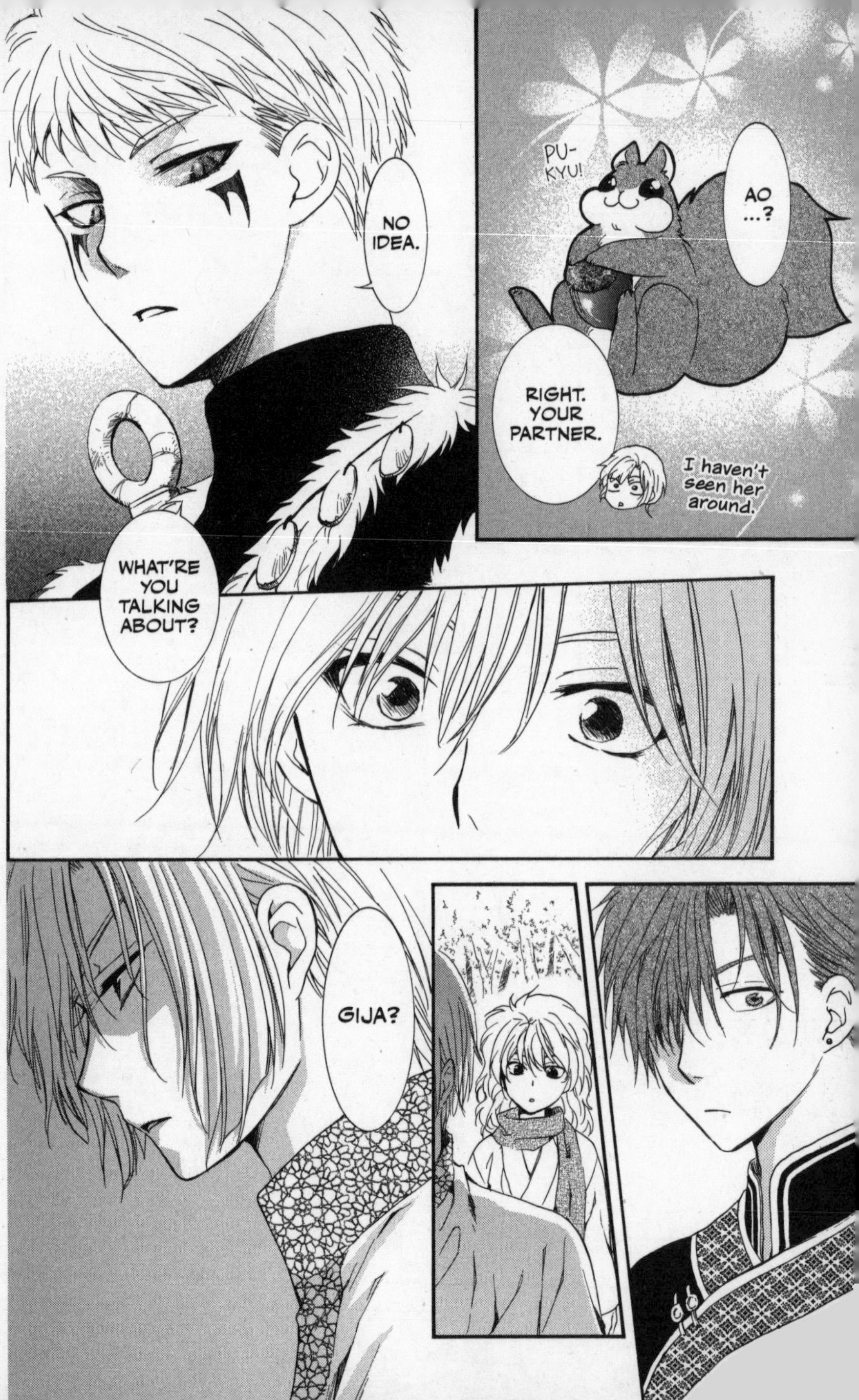
AO ...?
PU-KYU!
RIGHT. YOUR PARTNER.
I haven't seen her around.
NO IDEA.
WHAT'RE YOU TALKING ABOUT?
GIJA?

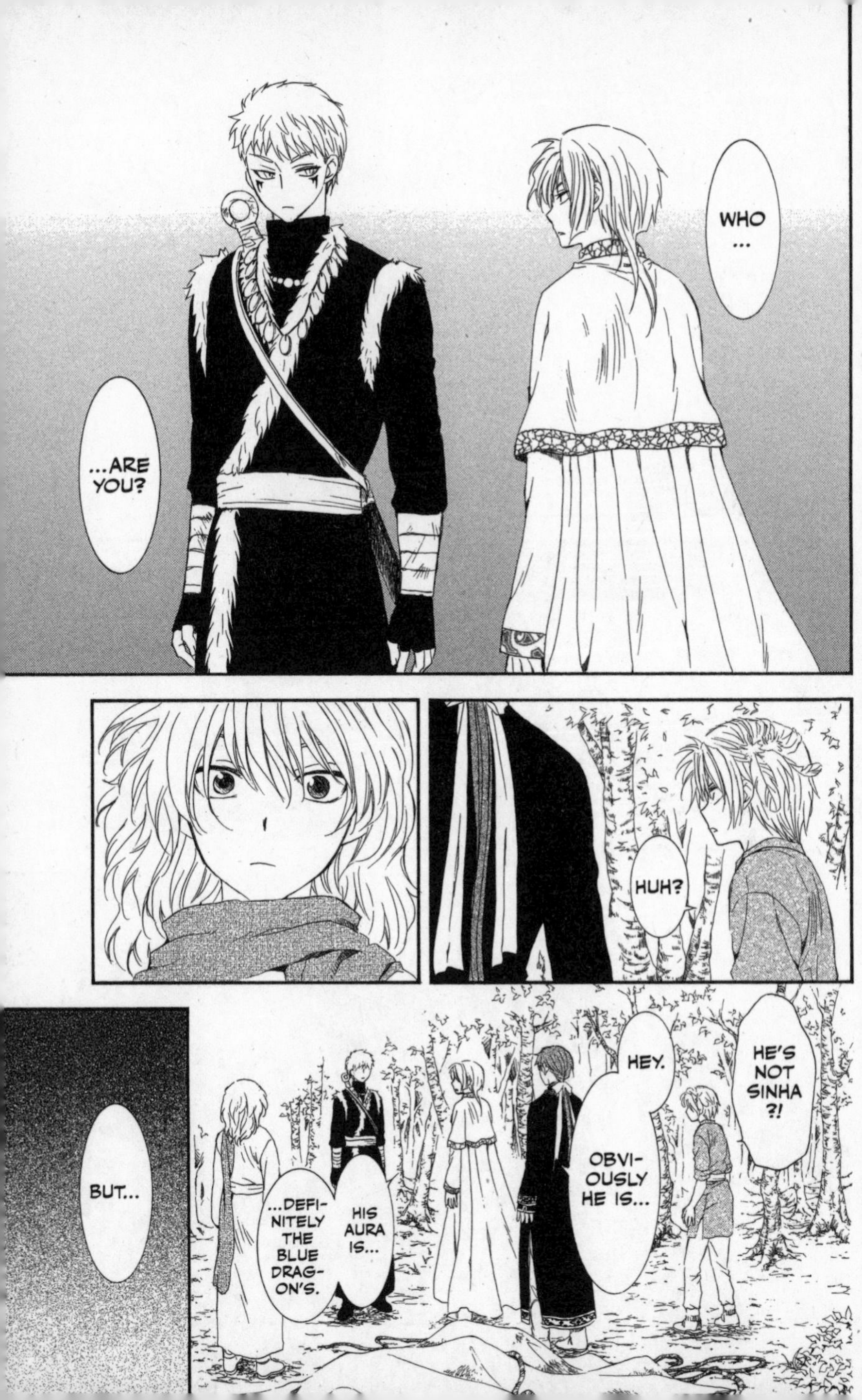
WHO ...
...ARE YOU?
HUH?
HE'S NOT SINHA ?!
HEY.
OBVIOUSLY HE IS...
HIS AURA IS...
...DEFINITELY THE BLUE DRAGON'S.
BUT...

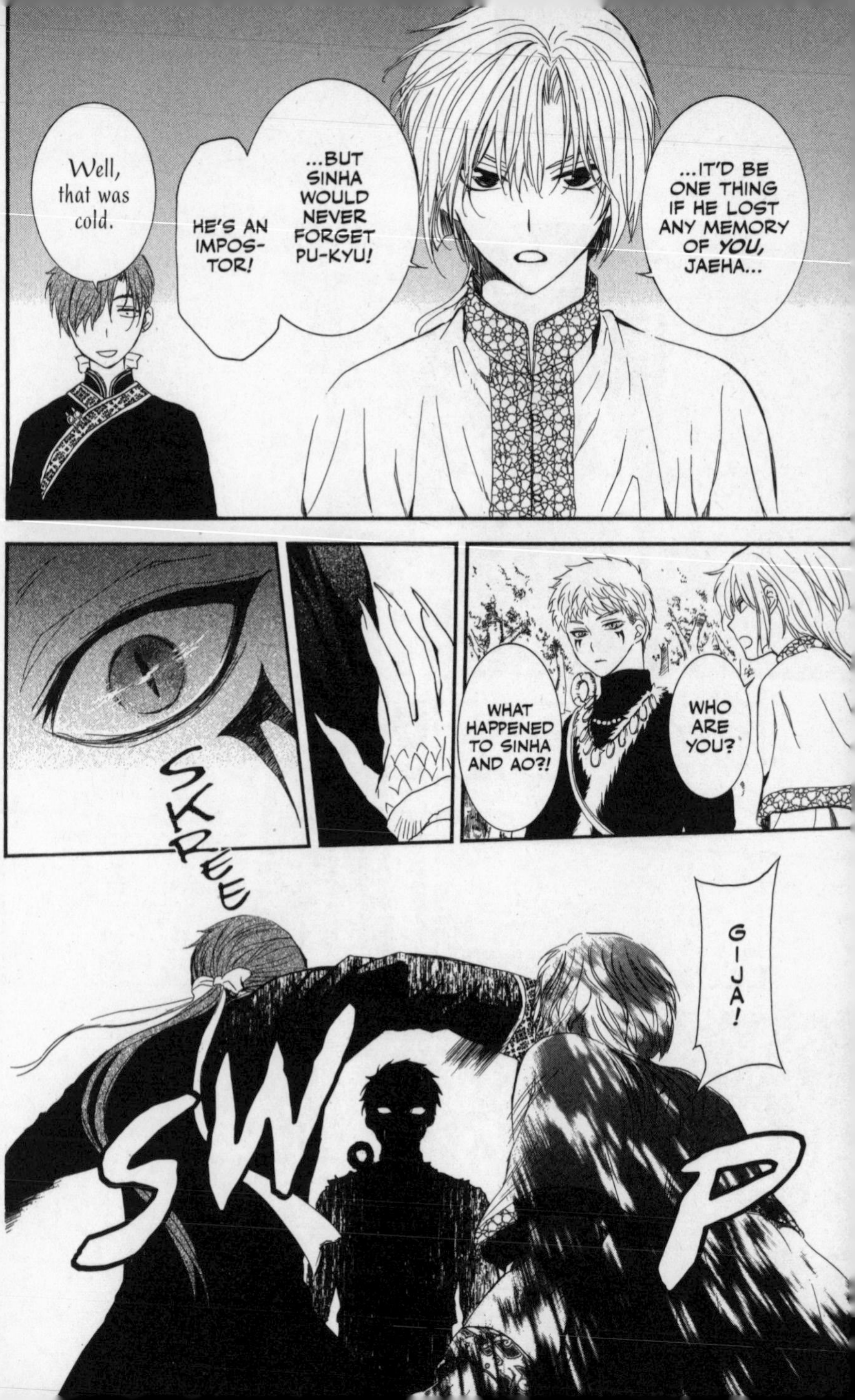
...IT'D BE ONE THING IF HE LOST ANY MEMORY OF *YOU,* JAEHA...
...BUT SINHA WOULD NEVER FORGET PU-KYU!
HE'S AN IMPOS-TOR!
Well, that was cold.
WHO ARE YOU?
WHAT HAPPENED TO SINHA AND AO?!
SKREE
GIJA!
SWP

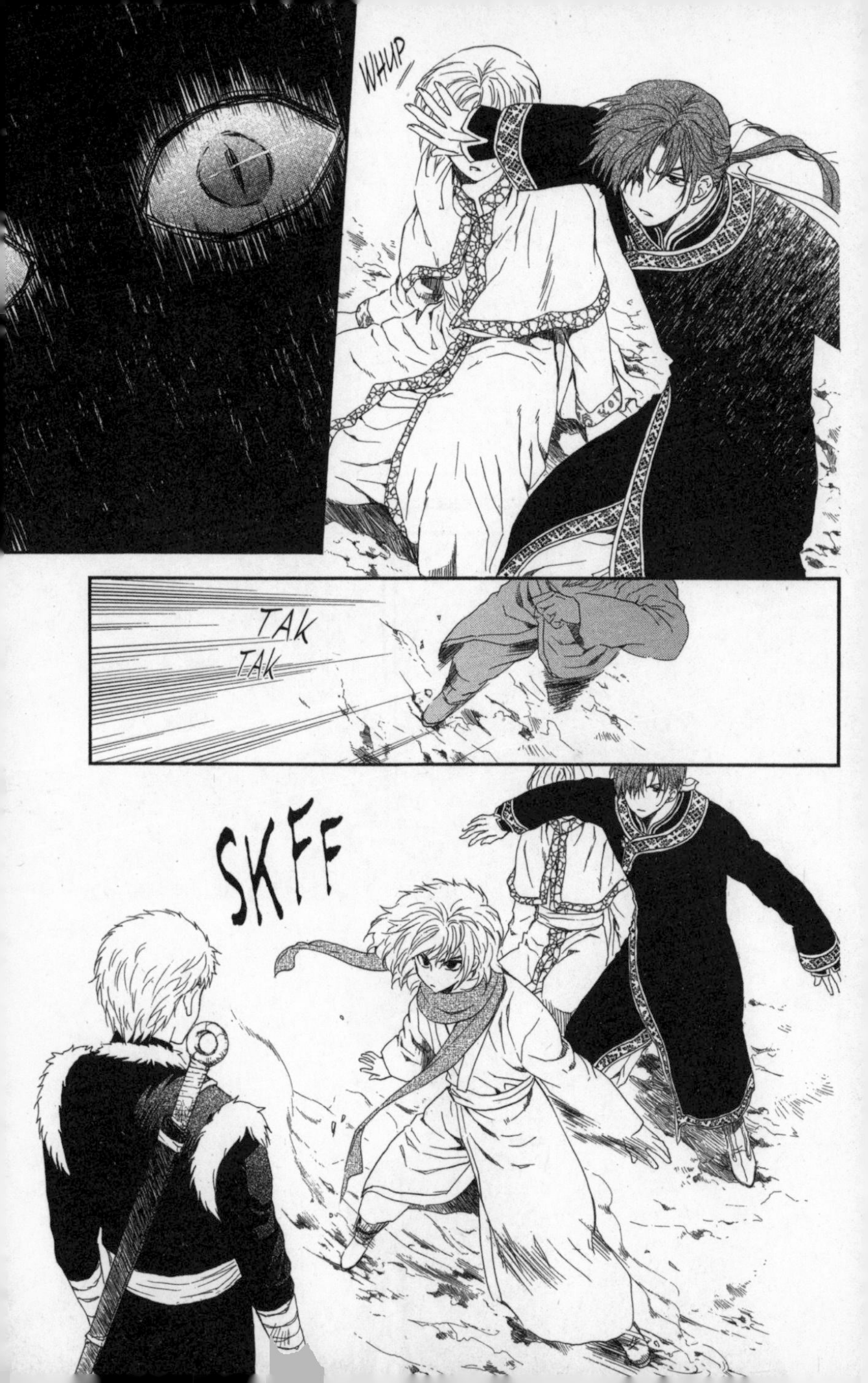
WHUP
TAK
TAK
SKFF

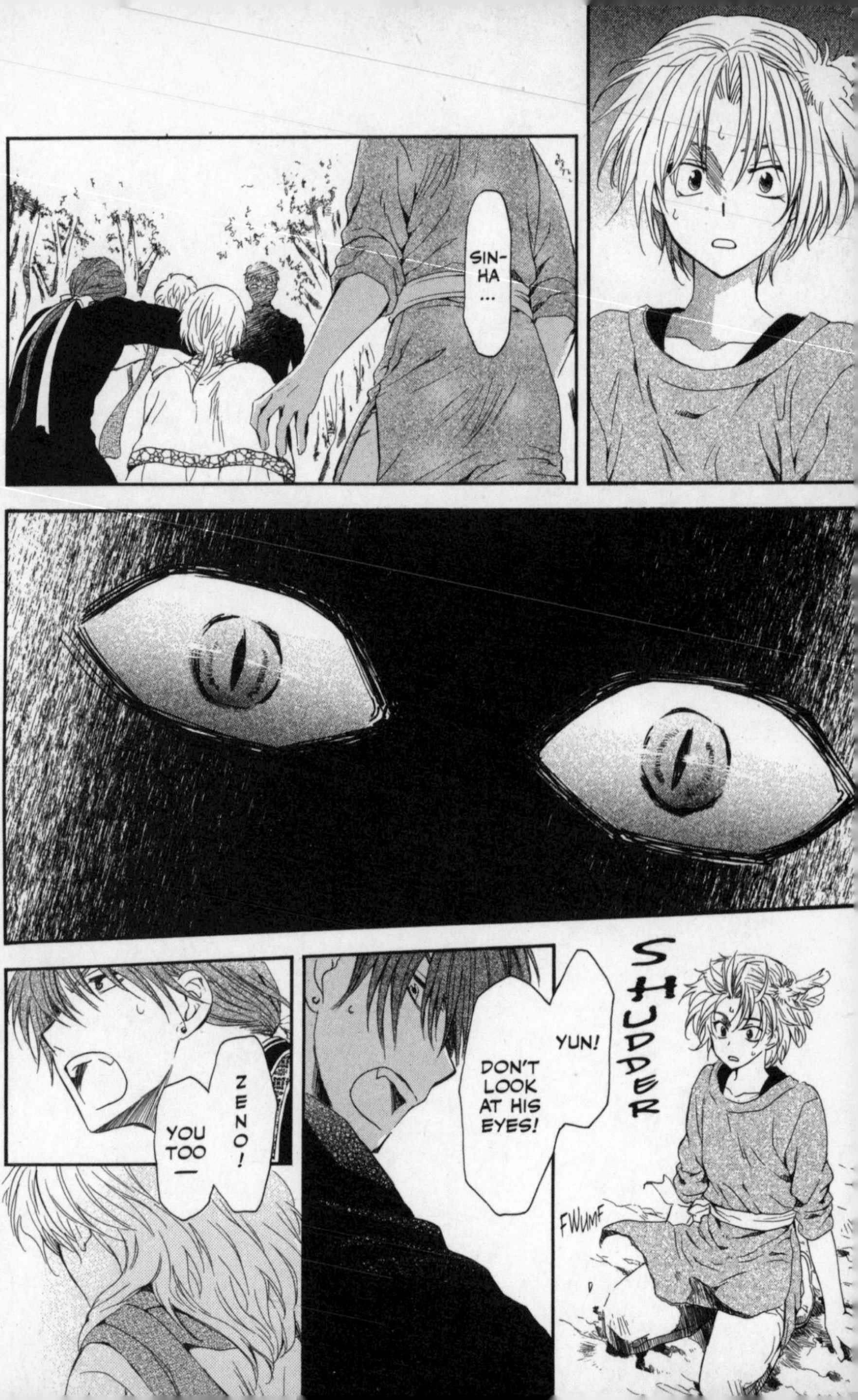
SIN-HA ...
SHUDDER
FWUMF
YUN!
DON'T LOOK AT HIS EYES!
ZENO!
YOU TOO —

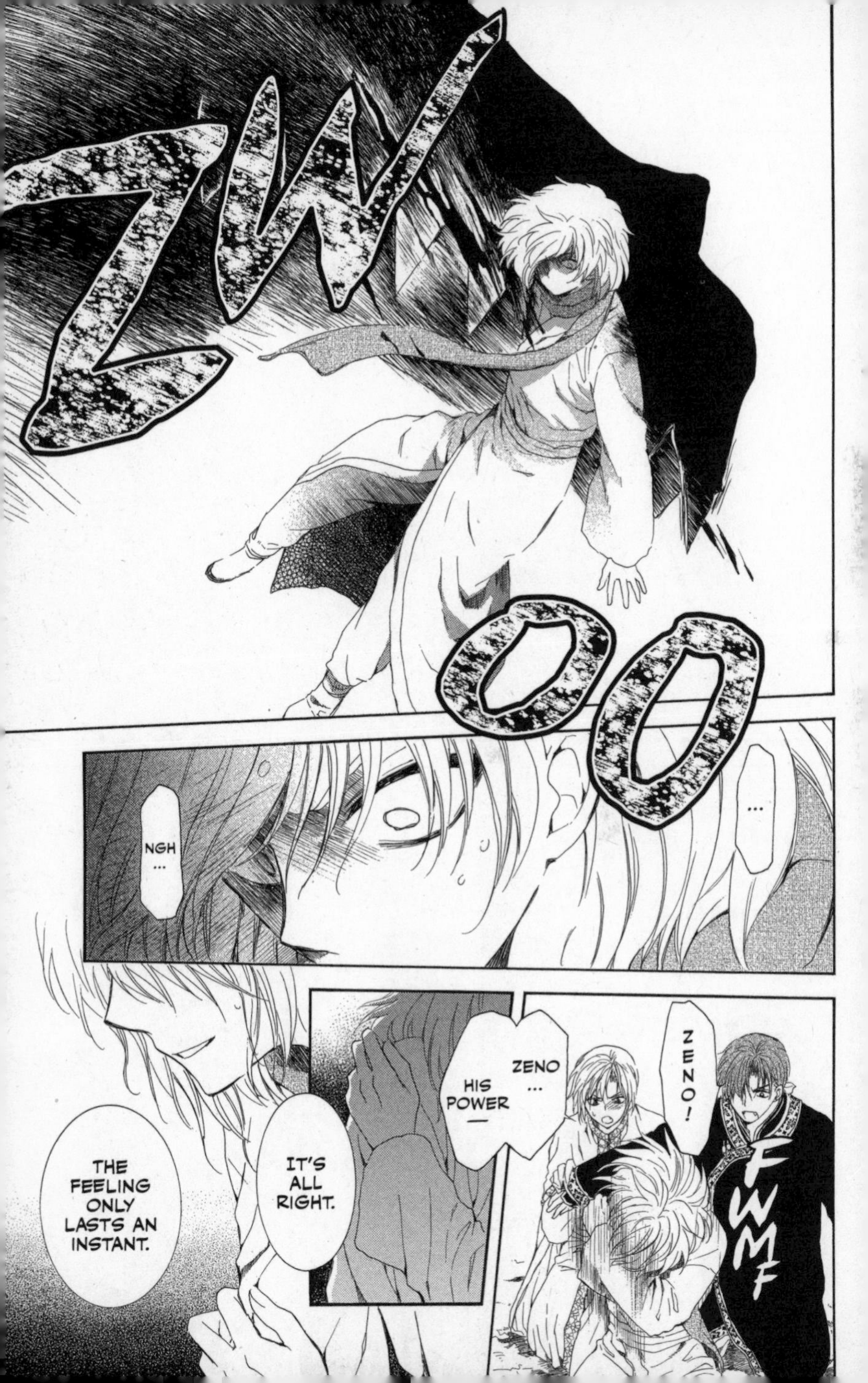

ZWOO
...
NGH ...
ZENO!
FWMF
ZENO ...
HIS POWER —
IT'S ALL RIGHT.
THE FEELING ONLY LASTS AN INSTANT.

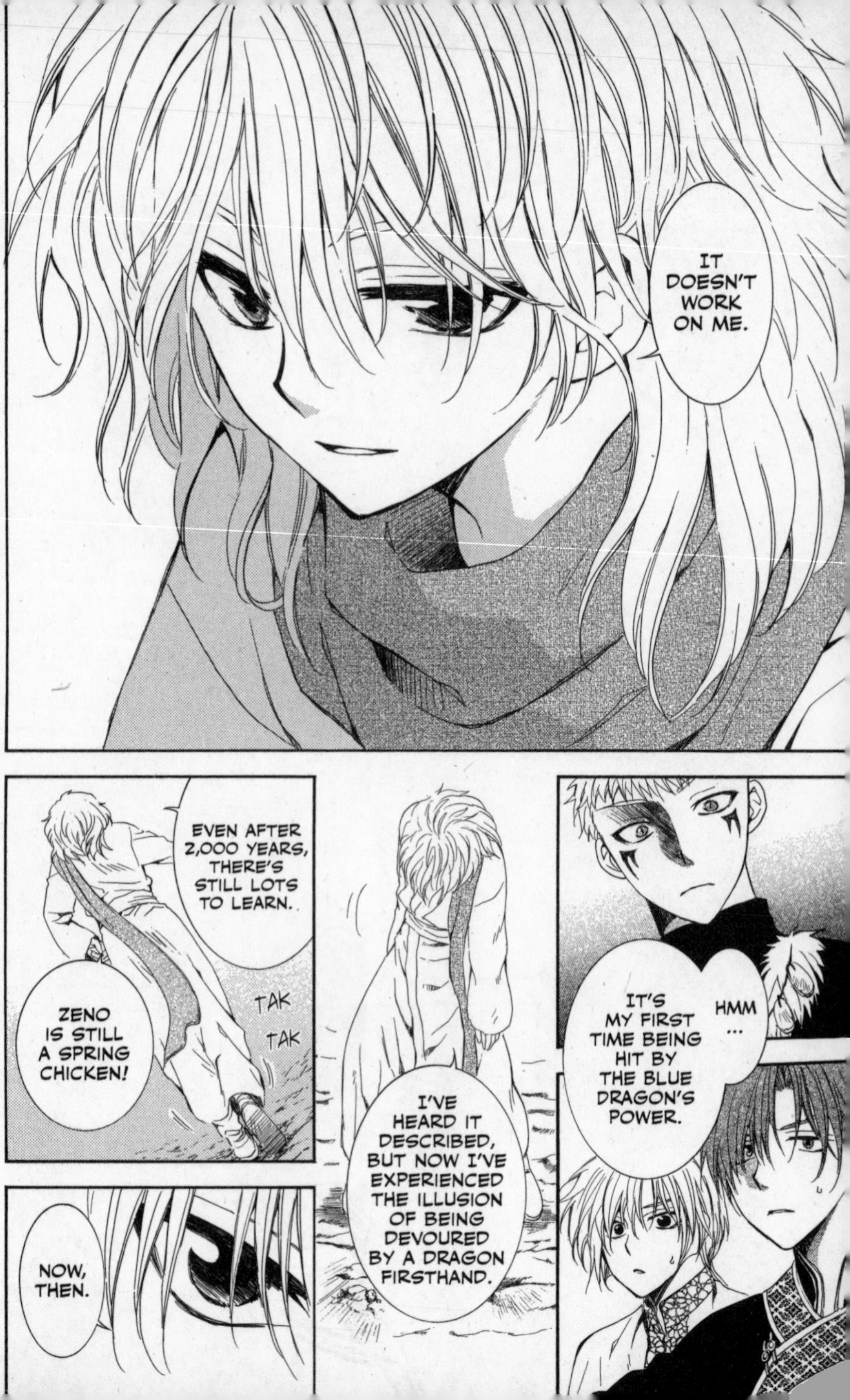
IT DOESN'T WORK ON ME.
HMM ...
IT'S MY FIRST TIME BEING HIT BY THE BLUE DRAGON'S POWER.
I'VE HEARD IT DESCRIBED, BUT NOW I'VE EXPERIENCED THE ILLUSION OF BEING DEVOURED BY A DRAGON FIRSTHAND.
EVEN AFTER 2,000 YEARS, THERE'S STILL LOTS TO LEARN.
TAK
TAK
ZENO IS STILL A SPRING CHICKEN!
NOW, THEN.

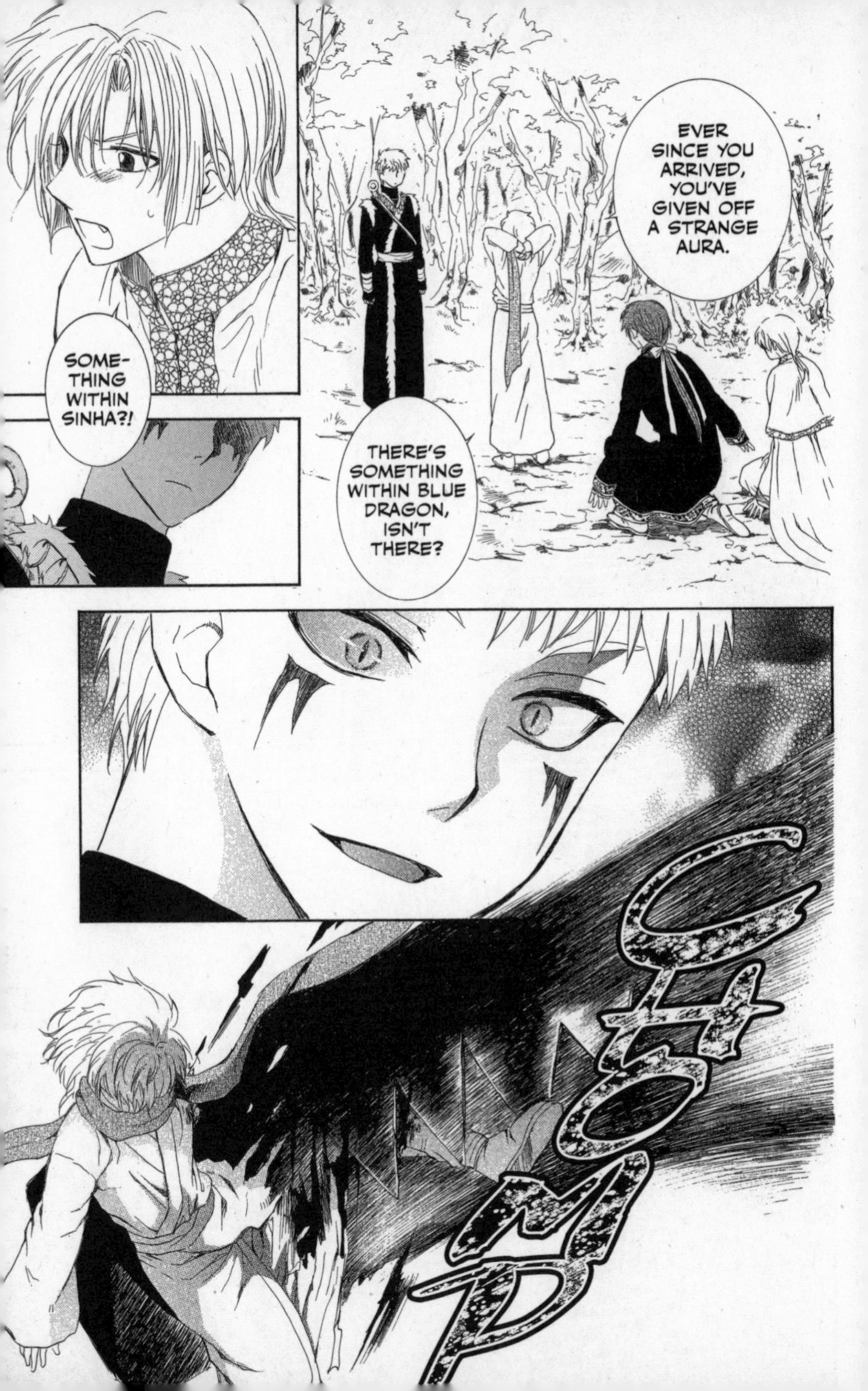
EVER SINCE YOU ARRIVED, YOU'VE GIVEN OFF A STRANGE AURA.
THERE'S SOMETHING WITHIN BLUE DRAGON, ISN'T THERE?
SOME-THING WITHIN SINHA?!
CHOMP

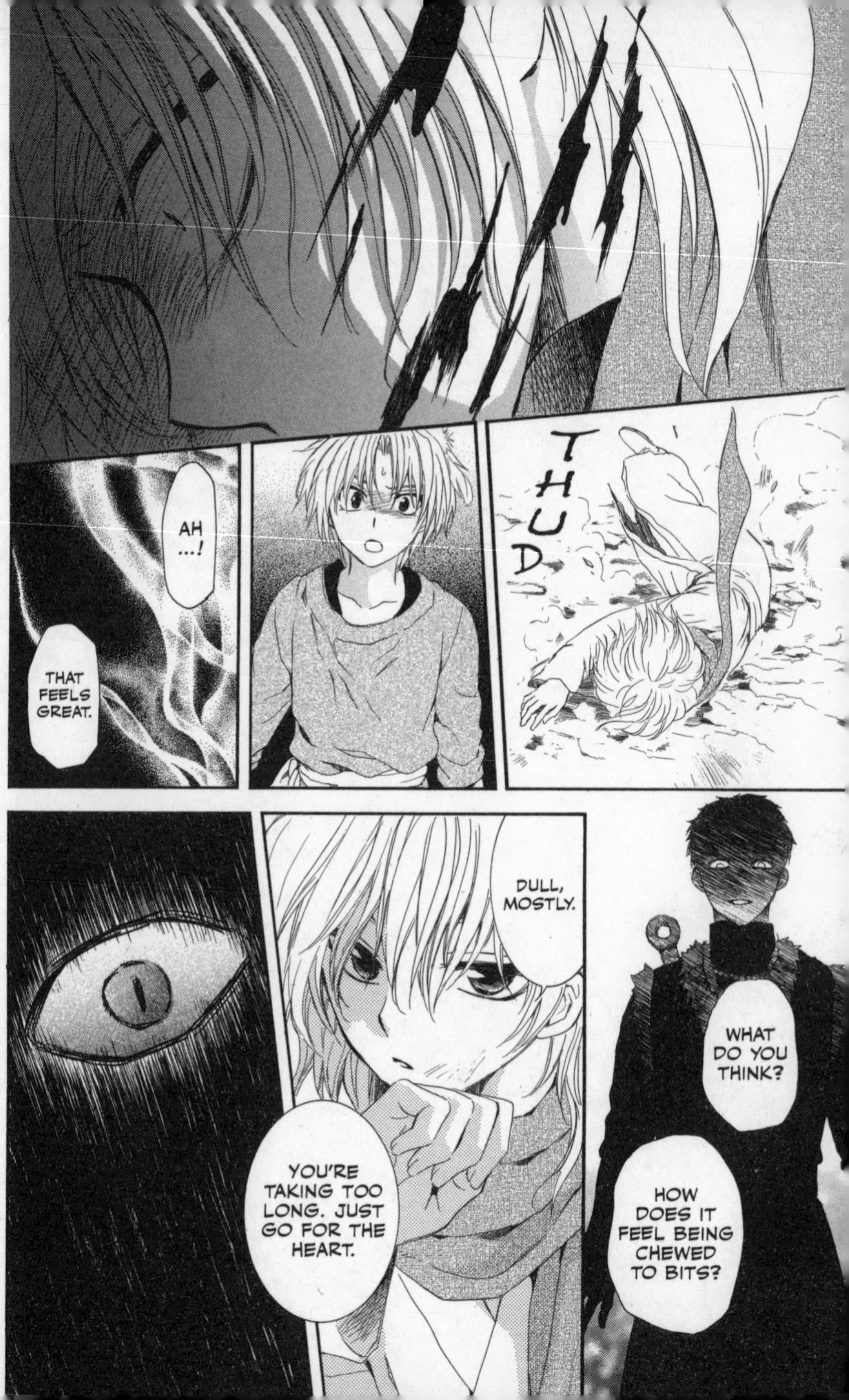
T H U D
AH ...!
THAT FEELS GREAT.
WHAT DO YOU THINK?
HOW DOES IT FEEL BEING CHEWED TO BITS?
DULL, MOSTLY.
YOU'RE TAKING TOO LONG. JUST GO FOR THE HEART.

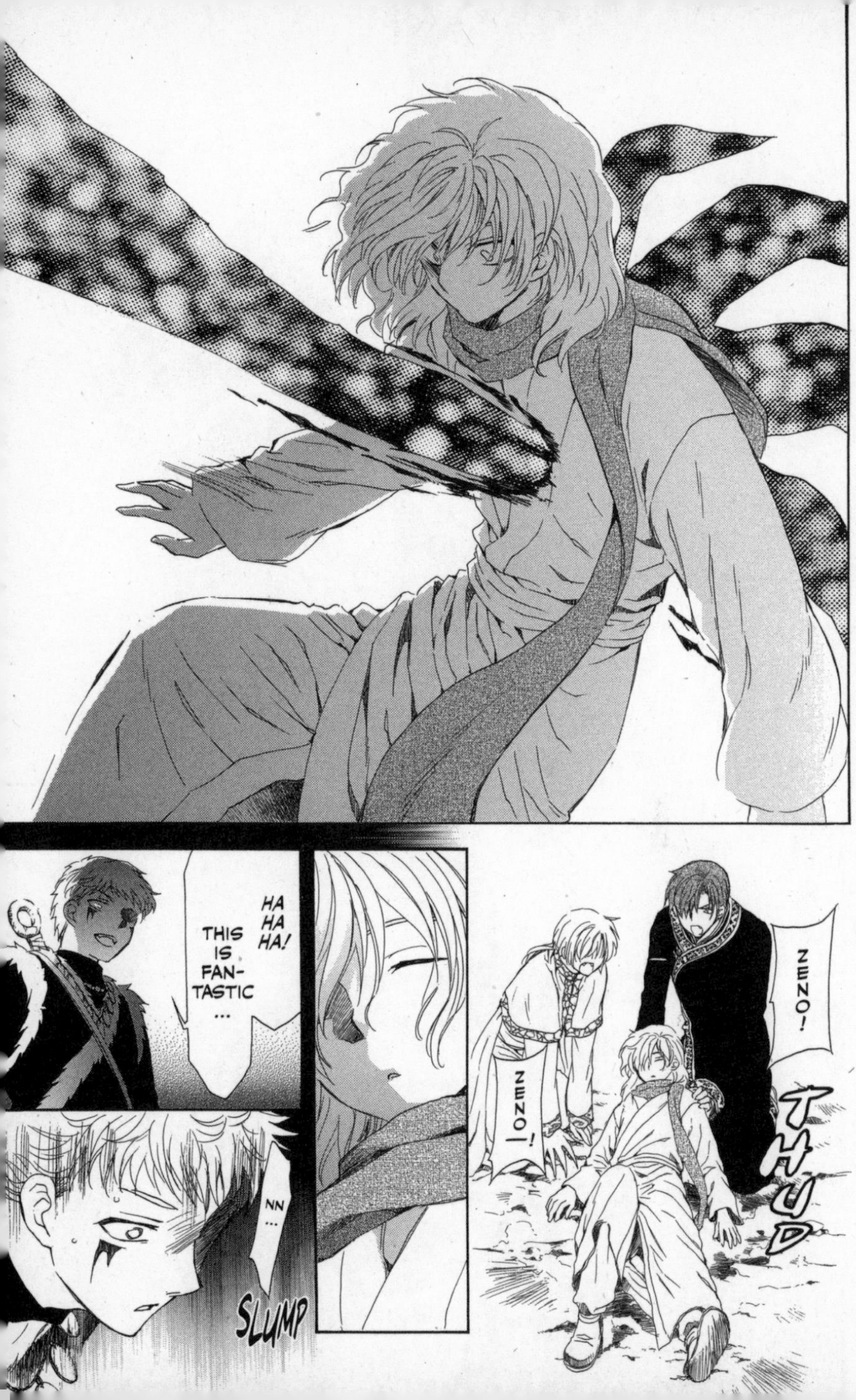
ZENO!
ZENO!
THUD
HA HA HA! THIS IS FAN-TASTIC...
NN...
SLUMP

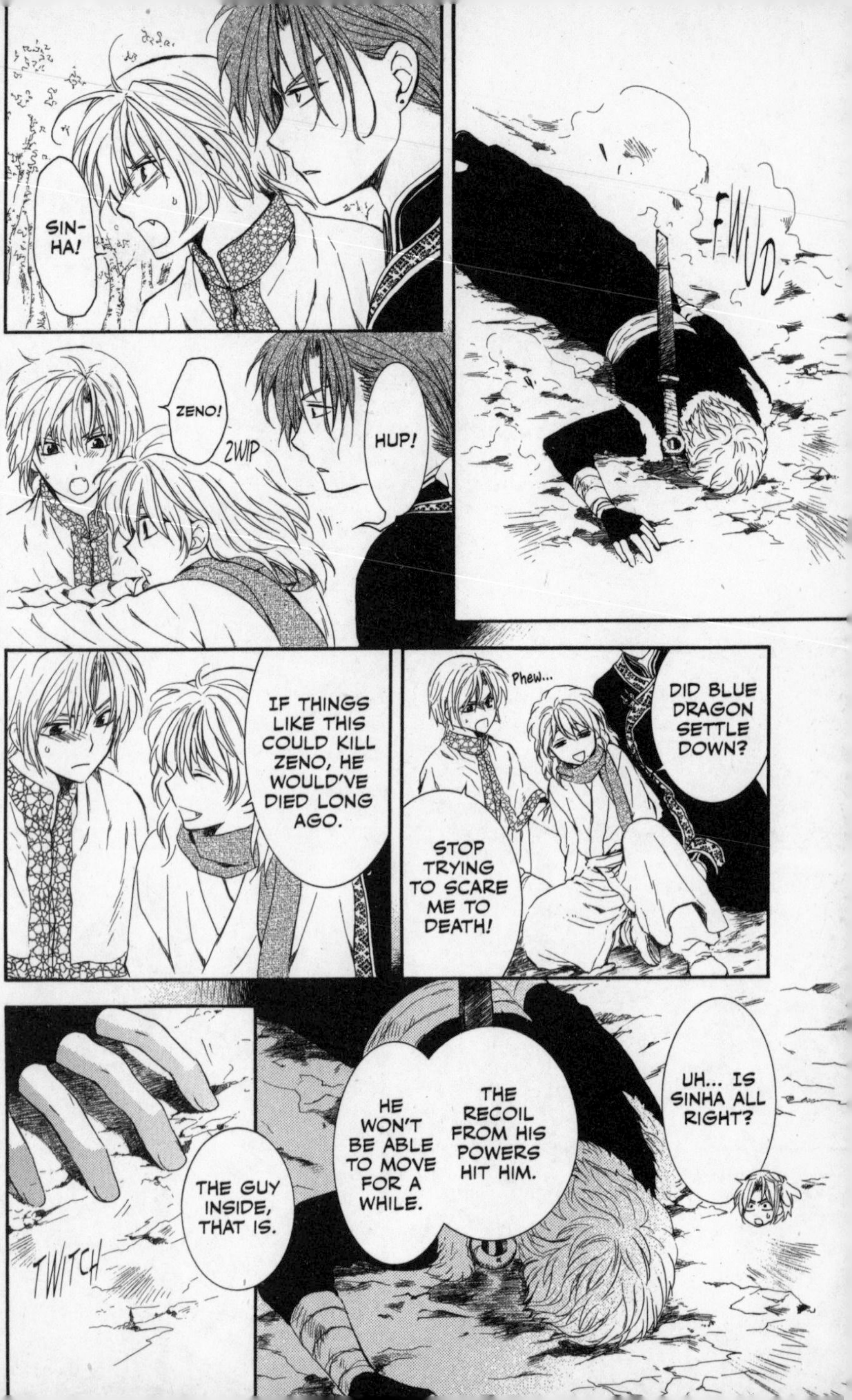
FWUD
SIN-HA!
HUP!
ZWIP
ZENO!
DID BLUE DRAGON SETTLE DOWN?
Phew...
STOP TRYING TO SCARE ME TO DEATH!
IF THINGS LIKE THIS COULD KILL ZENO, HE WOULD'VE DIED LONG AGO.
UH... IS SINHA ALL RIGHT?
THE RECOIL FROM HIS POWERS HIT HIM.
HE WON'T BE ABLE TO MOVE FOR A WHILE.
THE GUY INSIDE, THAT IS.
TWITCH

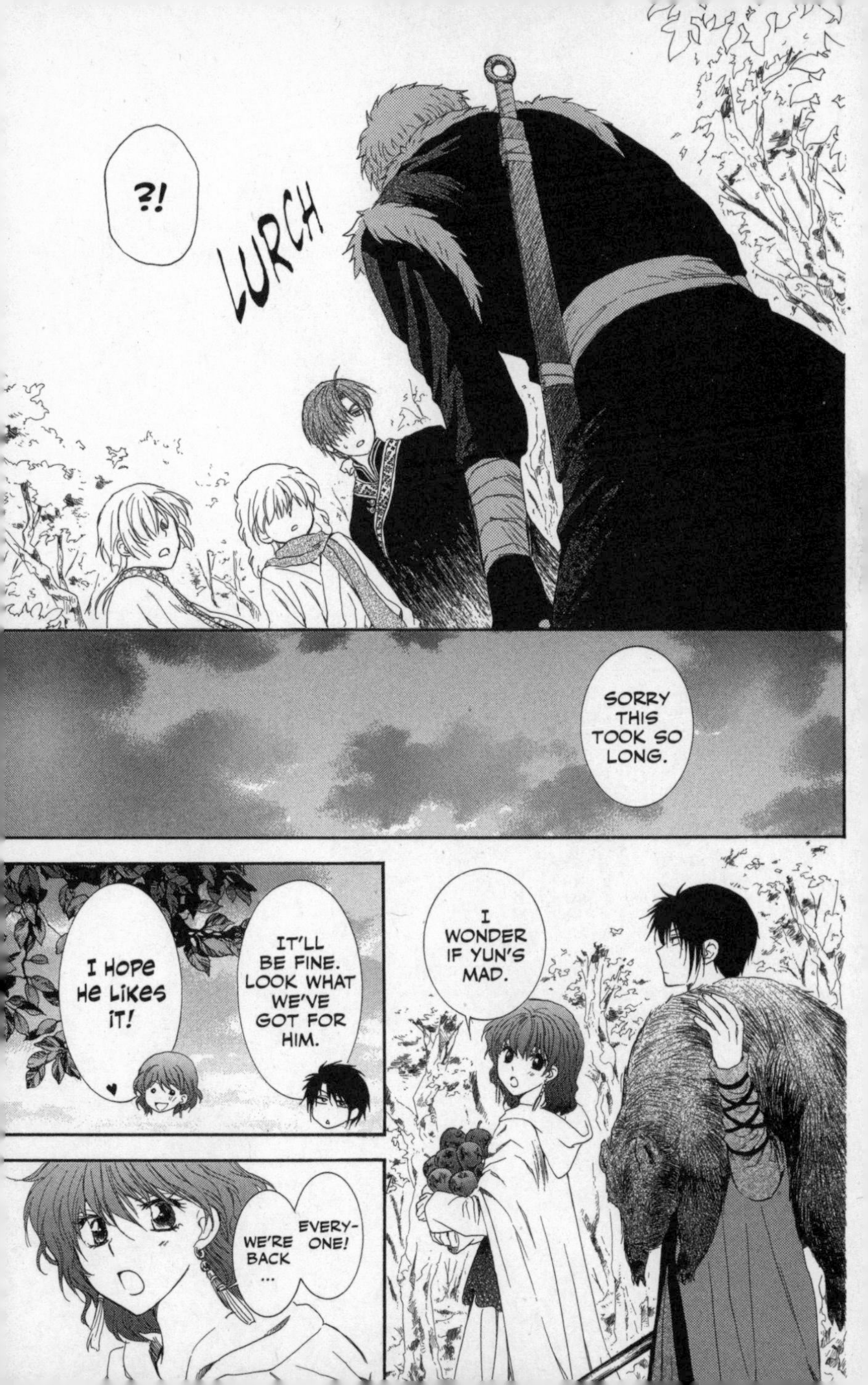
?!
LURCH
SORRY THIS TOOK SO LONG.
I WONDER IF YUN'S MAD.
IT'LL BE FINE. LOOK WHAT WE'VE GOT FOR HIM.
I HOPE HE LIKES IT!
WE'RE BACK... EVERYONE!

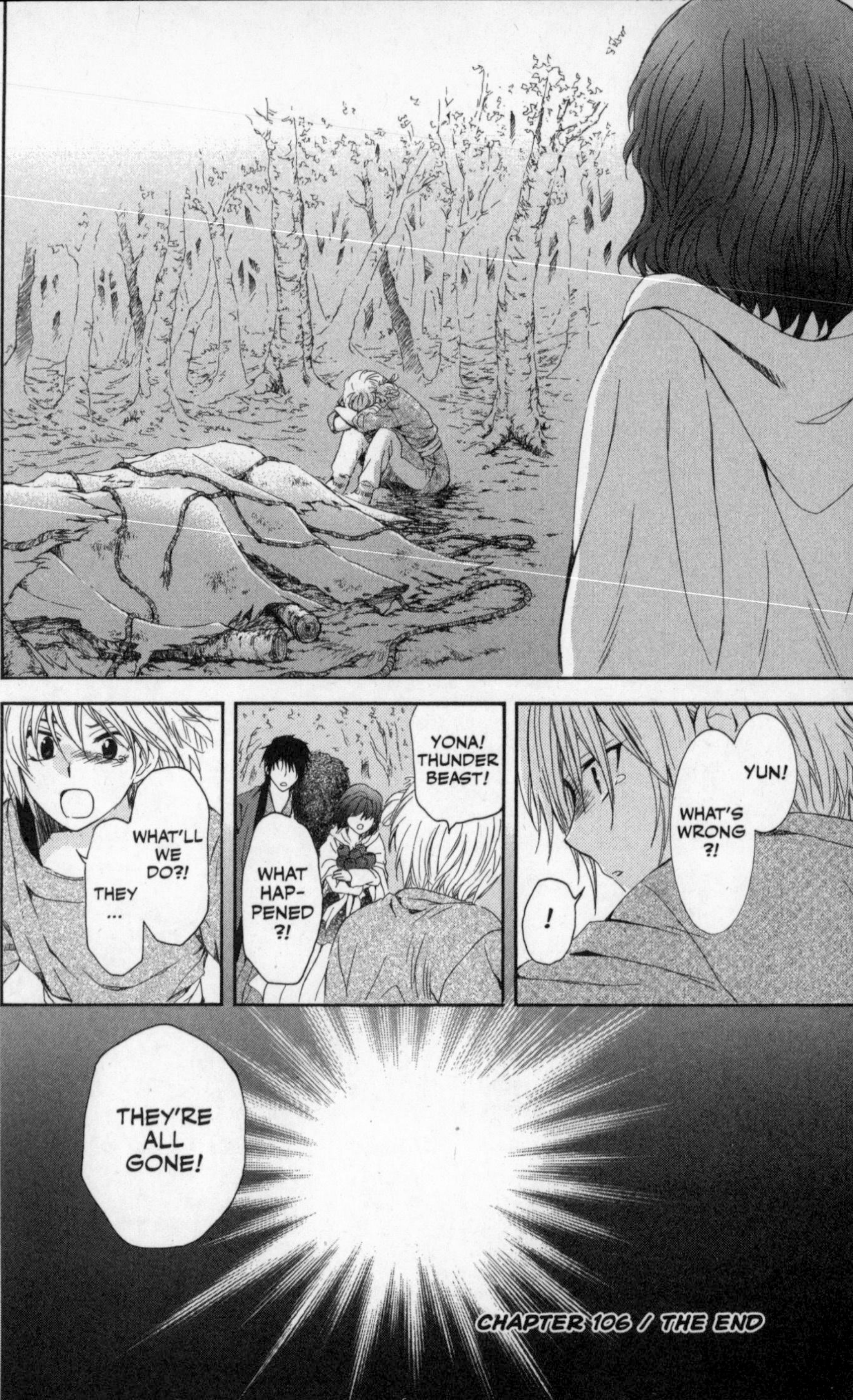
YUN!
WHAT'S WRONG?!
!
YONA! THUNDER BEAST!
WHAT HAPPENED?!
WHAT'LL WE DO?!
THEY ...
THEY'RE ALL GONE!
CHAPTER 106 / THE END

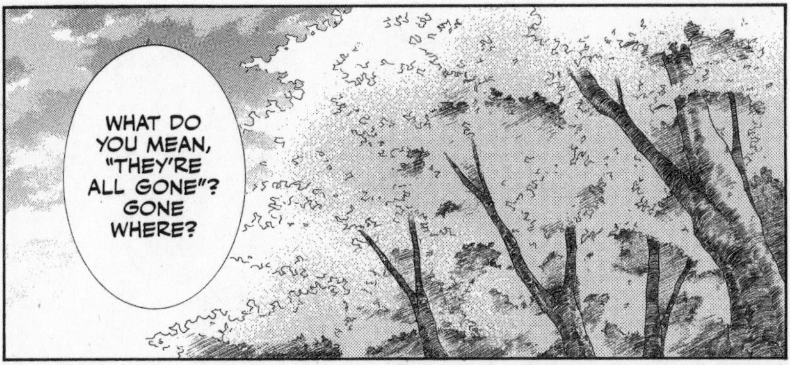
WHAT DO YOU MEAN, "THEY'RE ALL GONE"? GONE WHERE?

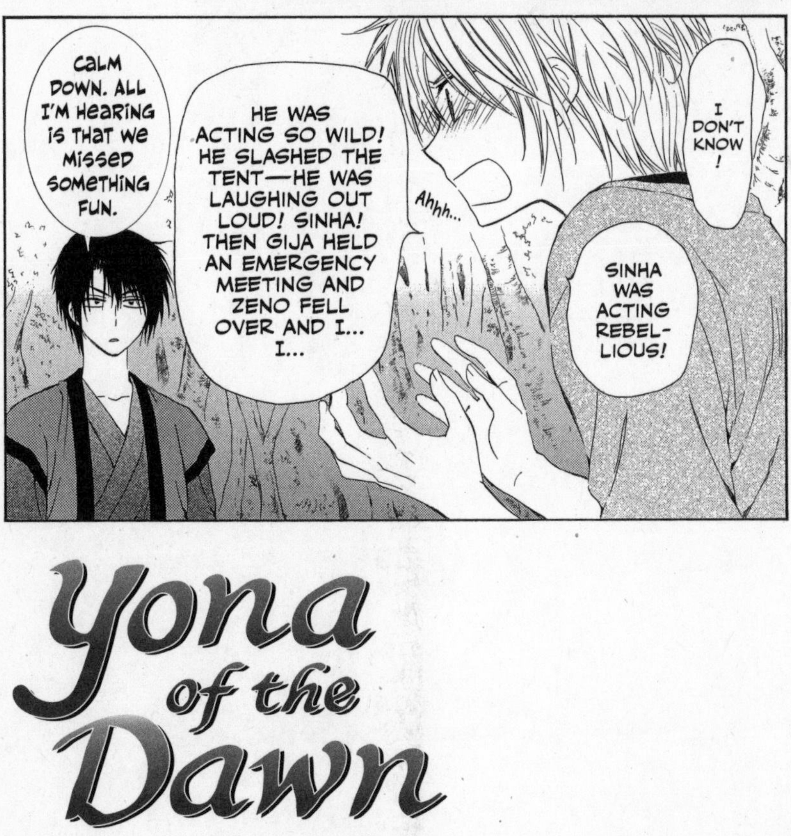
I DON'T KNOW!
SINHA WAS ACTING REBEL-LIOUS!
Ahhh...
HE WAS ACTING SO WILD! HE SLASHED THE TENT—HE WAS LAUGHING OUT LOUD! SINHA! THEN GIJA HELD AN EMERGENCY MEETING AND ZENO FELL OVER AND I... I...
CALM DOWN. ALL I'M HEARING IS THAT WE MISSED SOMETHING FUN.

Yona of the Dawn

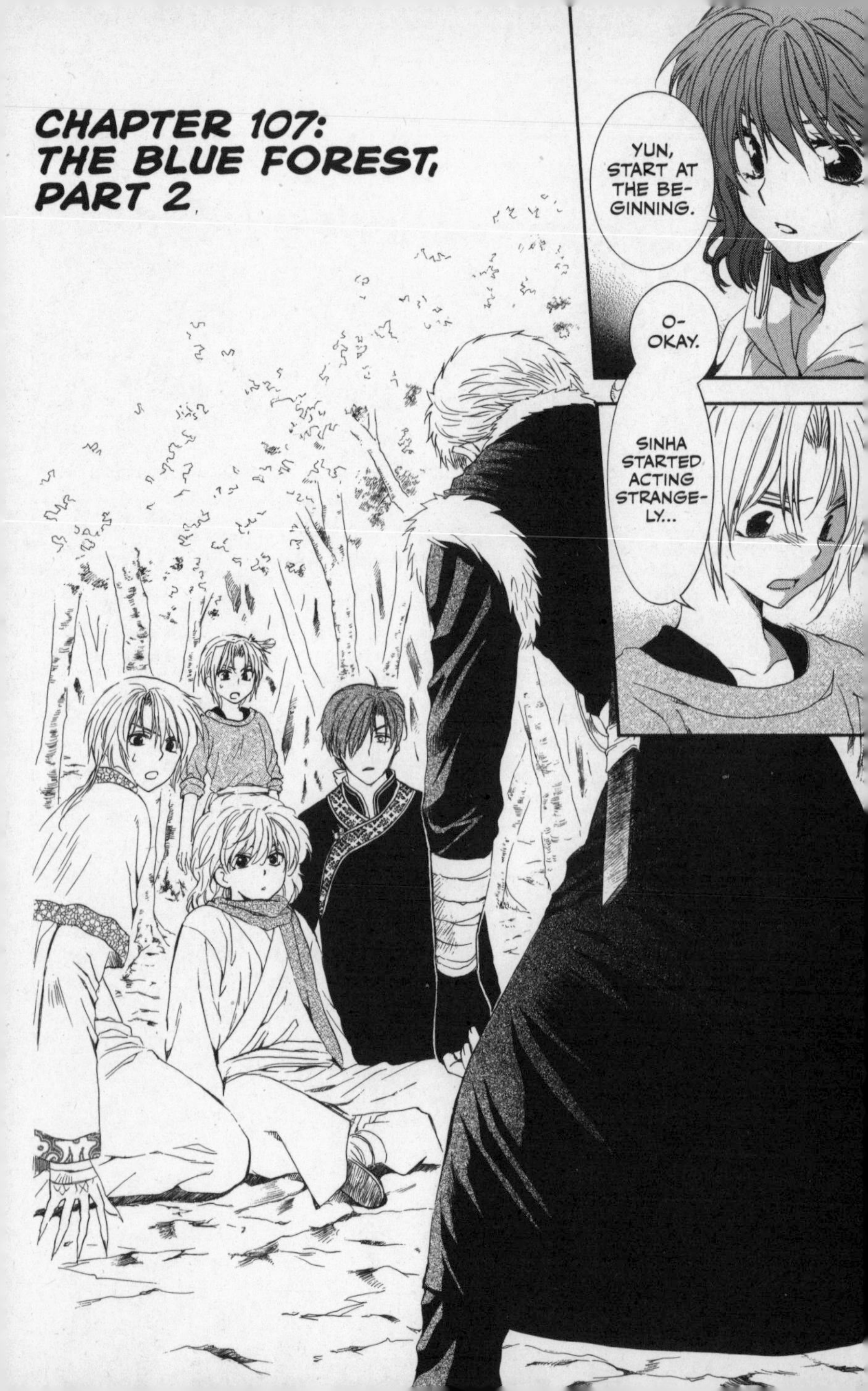
YUN, START AT THE BE-GINNING.
O-OKAY.
SINHA STARTED ACTING STRANGE-LY...
CHAPTER 107: THE BLUE FOREST, PART 2

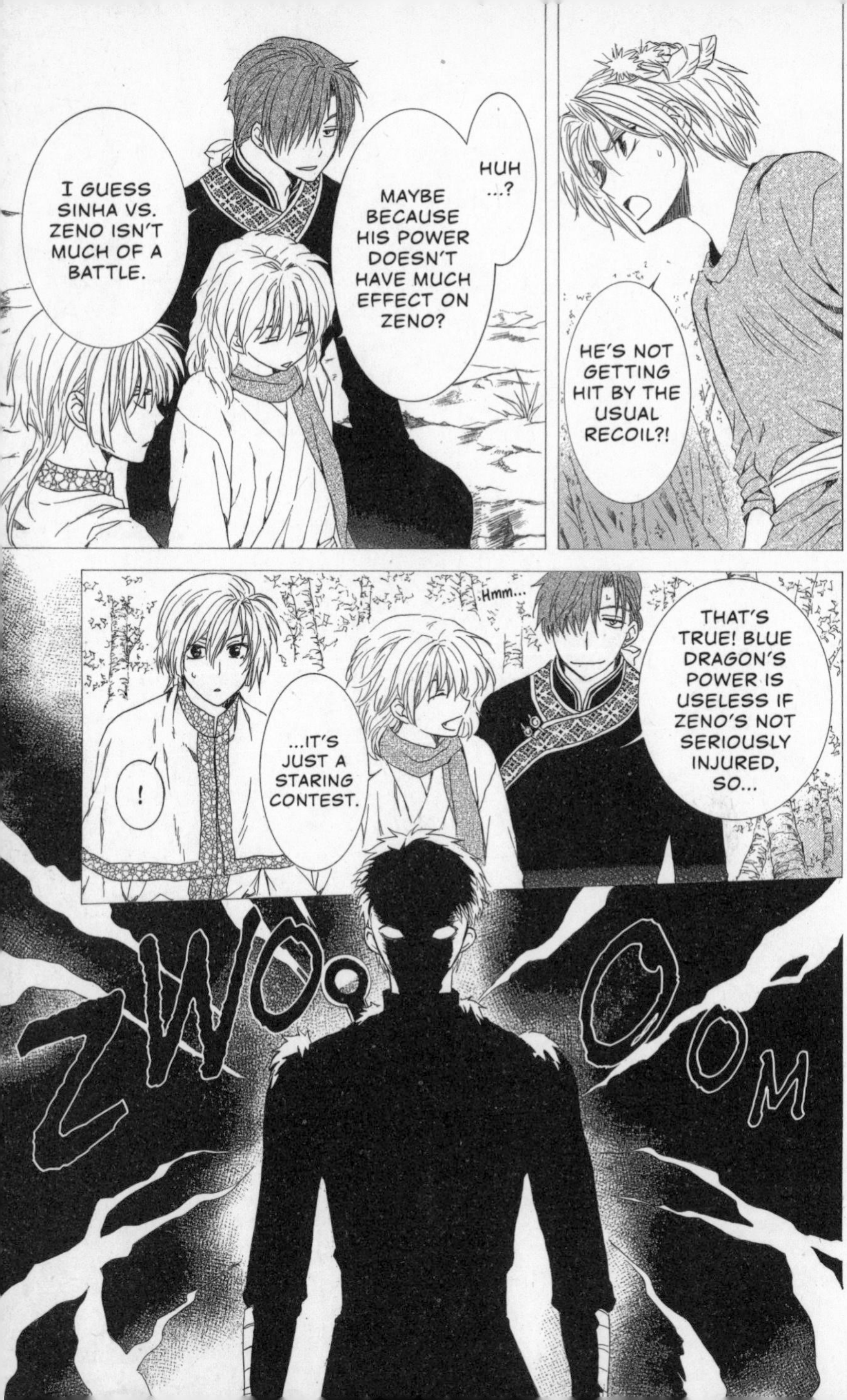
HE'S NOT GETTING HIT BY THE USUAL RECOIL?!
HUH ...?
MAYBE BECAUSE HIS POWER DOESN'T HAVE MUCH EFFECT ON ZENO?
I GUESS SINHA VS. ZENO ISN'T MUCH OF A BATTLE.
THAT'S TRUE! BLUE DRAGON'S POWER IS USELESS IF ZENO'S NOT SERIOUSLY INJURED, SO...
Hmm...
...IT'S JUST A STARING CONTEST.
!
ZWOOOM

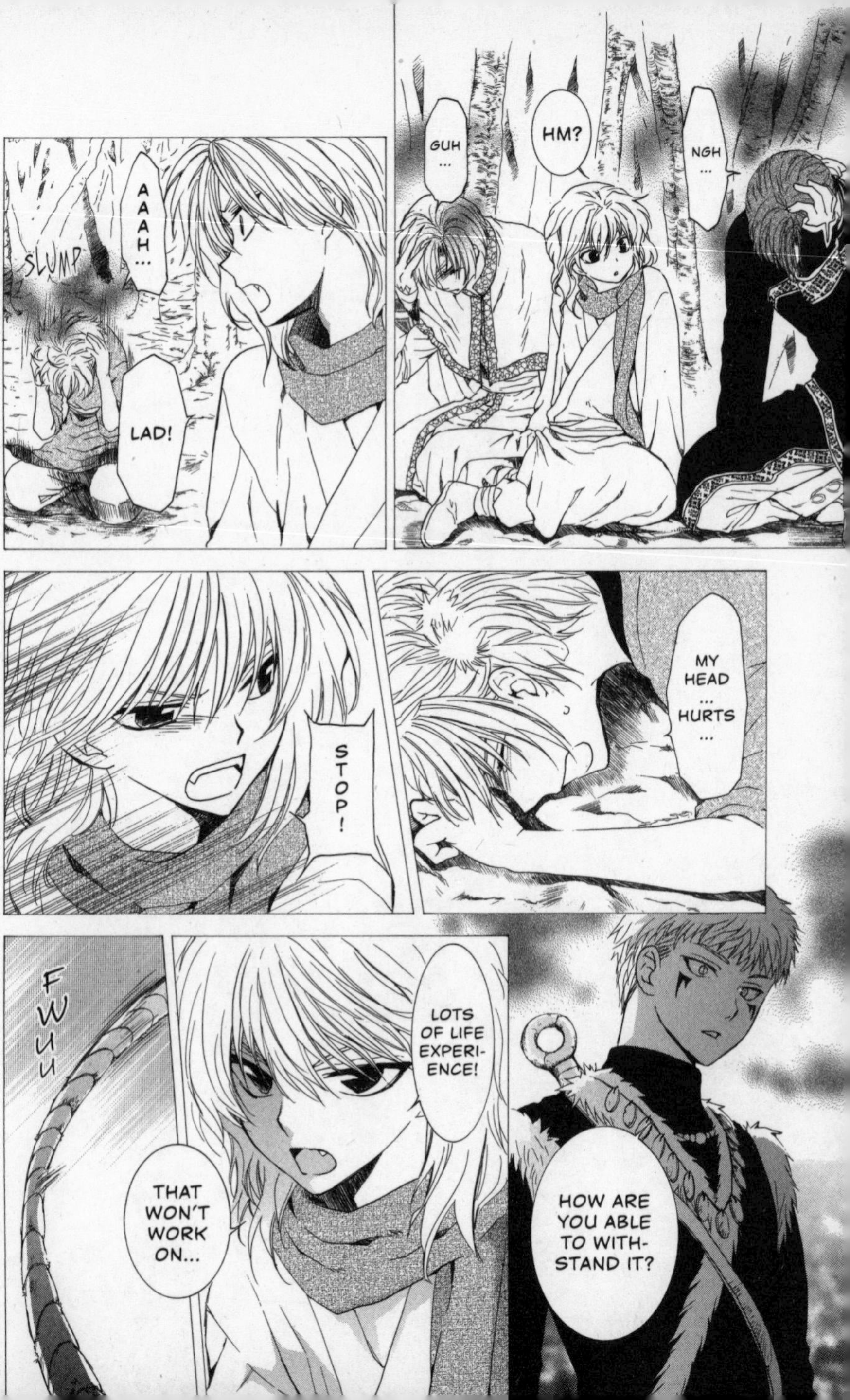
NGH ...
HM?
GUH ...
AAAH...
SLUMP
LAD!
MY HEAD ... HURTS ...
STOP!
HOW ARE YOU ABLE TO WITH-STAND IT?
LOTS OF LIFE EXPERIENCE!
THAT WON'T WORK ON...
FWUU

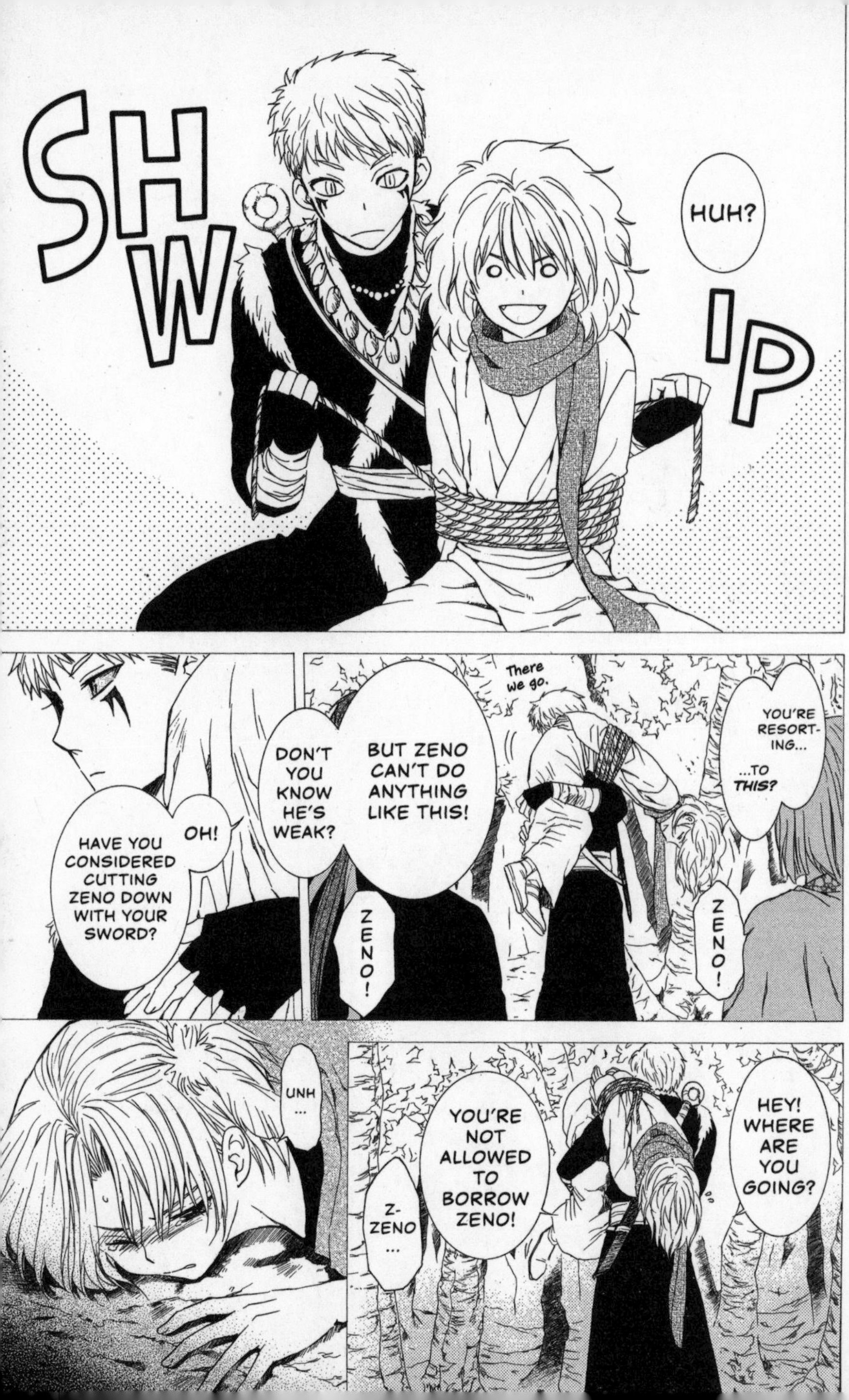
HUH?
SHWIP
YOU'RE RESORTING...
...TO *THIS?*
There we go.
ZENO!
BUT ZENO CAN'T DO ANYTHING LIKE THIS!
DON'T YOU KNOW HE'S WEAK?
ZENO!
OH!
HAVE YOU CONSIDERED CUTTING ZENO DOWN WITH YOUR SWORD?
HEY! WHERE ARE YOU GOING?
YOU'RE NOT ALLOWED TO BORROW ZENO!
Z-ZENO...
UNH...

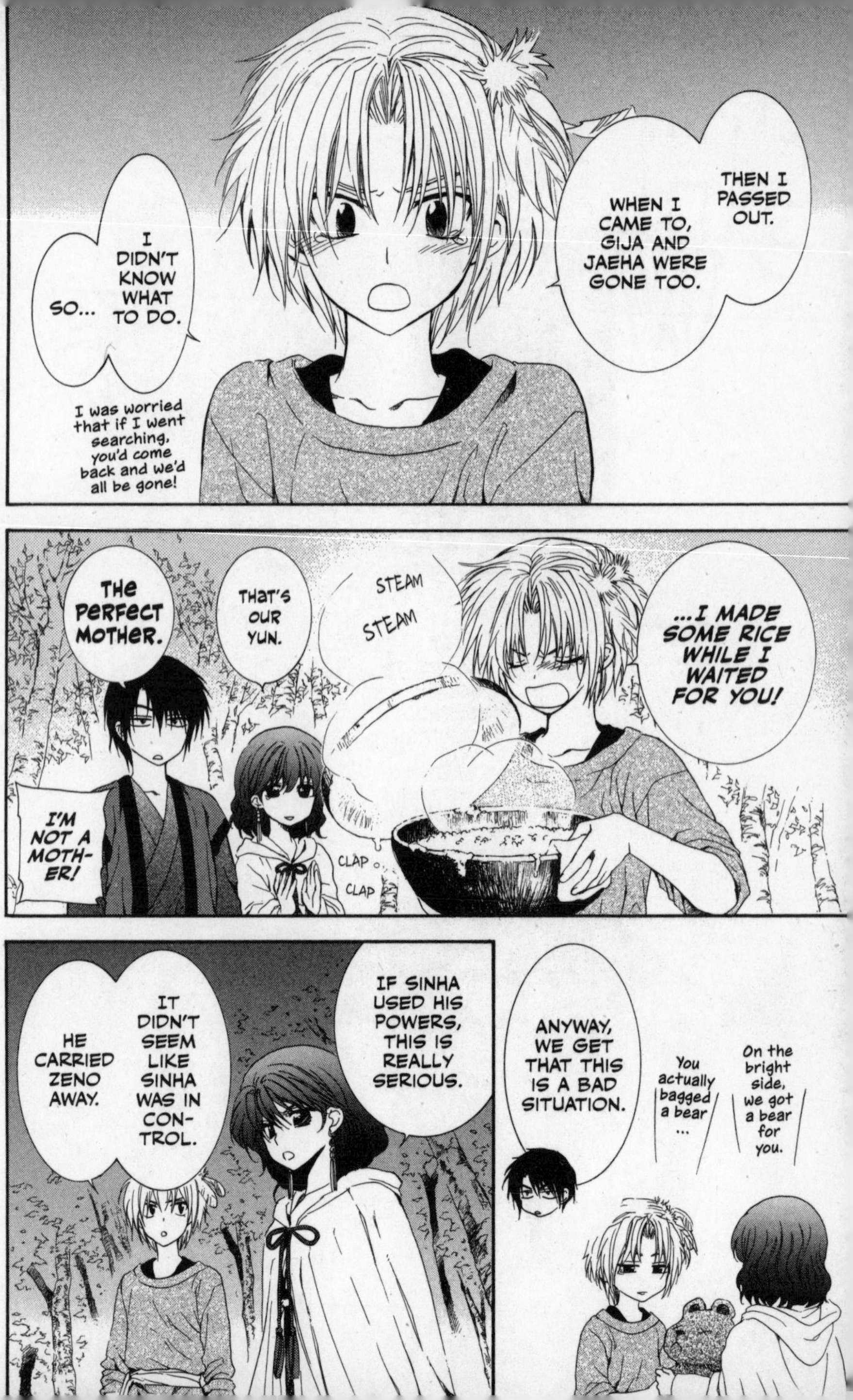
THEN I PASSED OUT.
WHEN I CAME TO, GIJA AND JAEHA WERE GONE TOO.
I DIDN'T KNOW WHAT TO DO.
SO...
I was worried that if I went searching, you'd come back and we'd all be gone!
...I MADE SOME RICE WHILE I WAITED FOR YOU!
STEAM
STEAM
THAT'S OUR YUN.
The Perfect MOTHER.
CLAP
CLAP
I'M NOT A MOTHER!
On the bright side, we got a bear for you.
You actually bagged a bear...
ANYWAY, WE GET THAT THIS IS A BAD SITUATION.
IF SINHA USED HIS POWERS, THIS IS REALLY SERIOUS.
IT DIDN'T SEEM LIKE SINHA WAS IN CONTROL.
HE CARRIED ZENO AWAY.

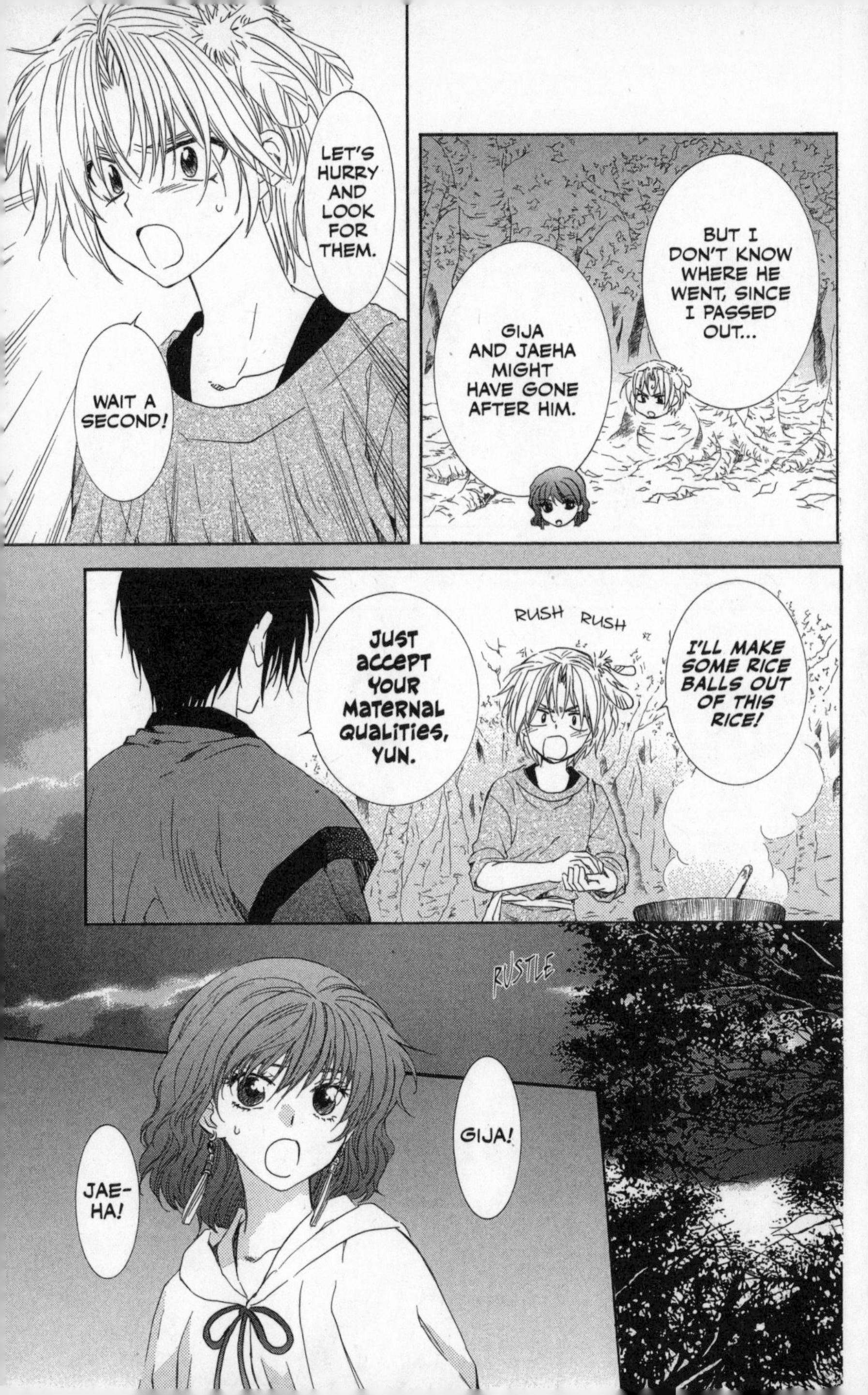
BUT I DON'T KNOW WHERE HE WENT, SINCE I PASSED OUT...
GIJA AND JAEHA MIGHT HAVE GONE AFTER HIM.
LET'S HURRY AND LOOK FOR THEM.
WAIT A SECOND!
I'LL MAKE SOME RICE BALLS OUT OF THIS RICE!
RUSH RUSH
JUST ACCEPT YOUR MATERNAL QUALITIES, YUN.
RUSTLE
GIJA!
JAE-HA!

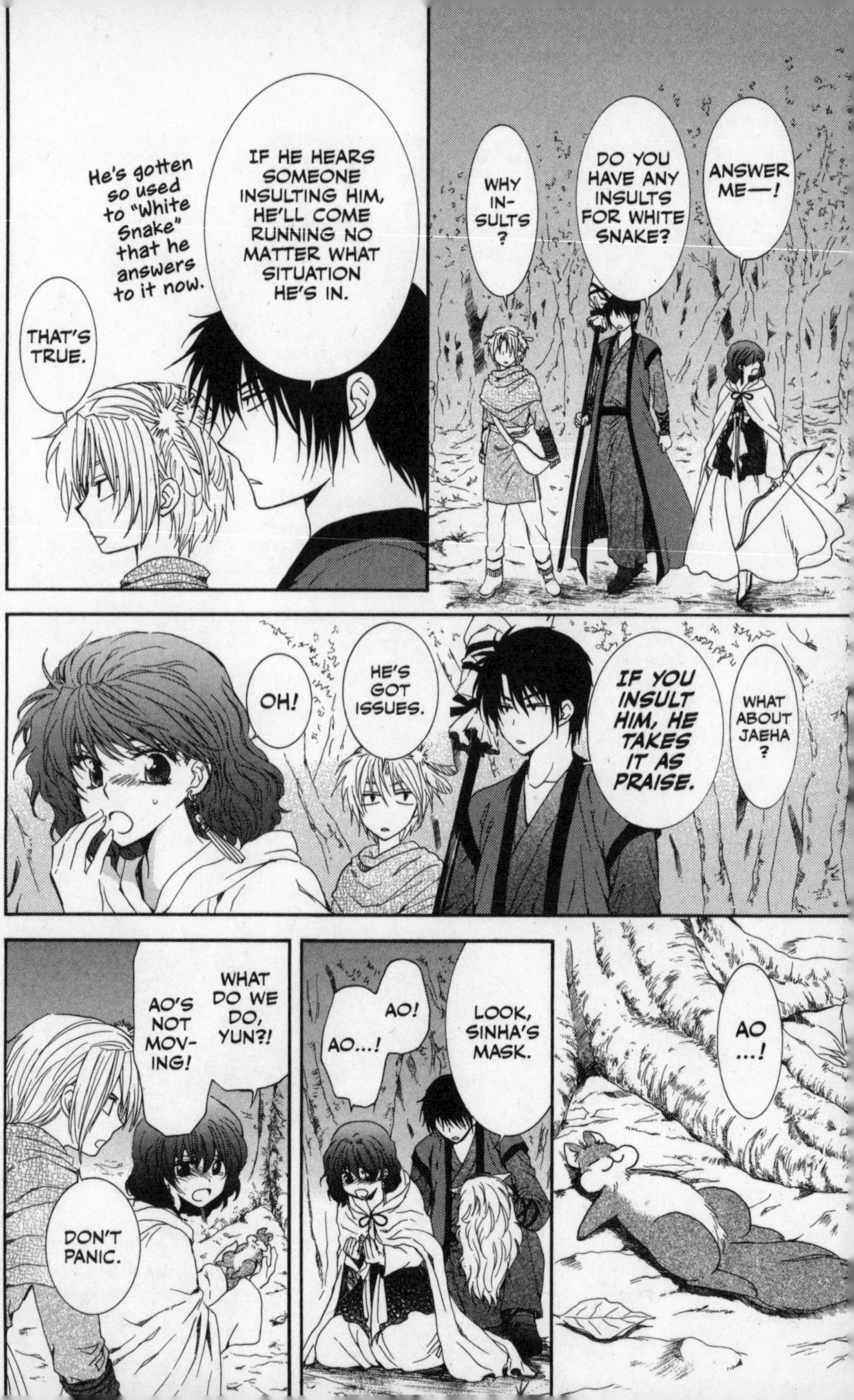
ANSWER ME—!
DO YOU HAVE ANY INSULTS FOR WHITE SNAKE?
WHY IN-SULTS?
IF HE HEARS SOMEONE INSULTING HIM, HE'LL COME RUNNING NO MATTER WHAT SITUATION HE'S IN.
He's gotten so used to "White Snake" that he answers to it now.
THAT'S TRUE.
WHAT ABOUT JAEHA?
IF YOU INSULT HIM, HE TAKES IT AS PRAISE.
HE'S GOT ISSUES.
OH!
AO...!
LOOK, SINHA'S MASK.
AO!
AO...!
WHAT DO WE DO, YUN?!
AO'S NOT MOV-ING!
DON'T PANIC.

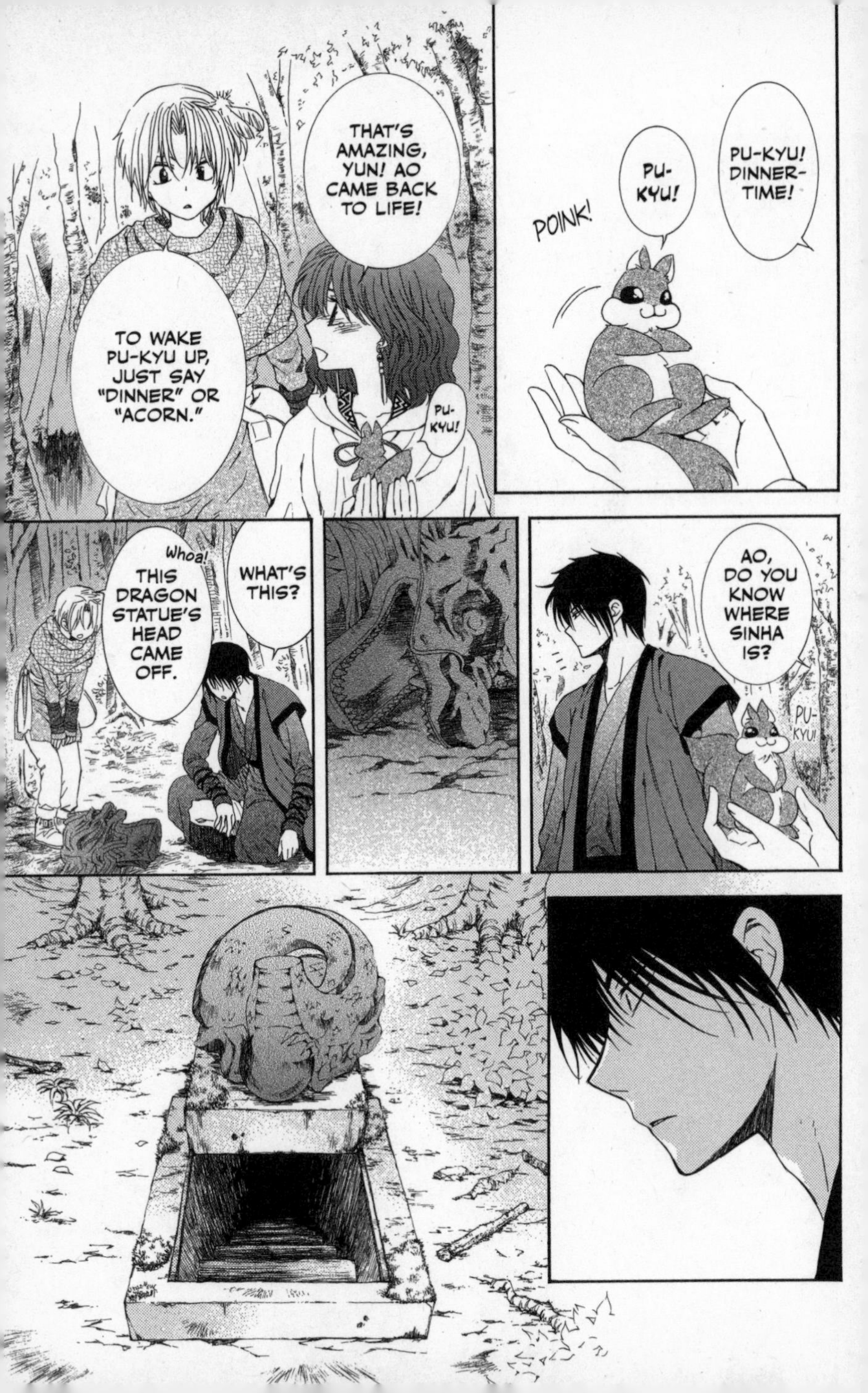
PU-KYU! DINNER-TIME!
PU-KYU!
POINK!
THAT'S AMAZING, YUN! AO CAME BACK TO LIFE!
TO WAKE PU-KYU UP, JUST SAY "DINNER" OR "ACORN."
PU-KYU!
AO, DO YOU KNOW WHERE SINHA IS?
PU-KYU!
WHAT'S THIS?
Whoa!
THIS DRAGON STATUE'S HEAD CAME OFF.

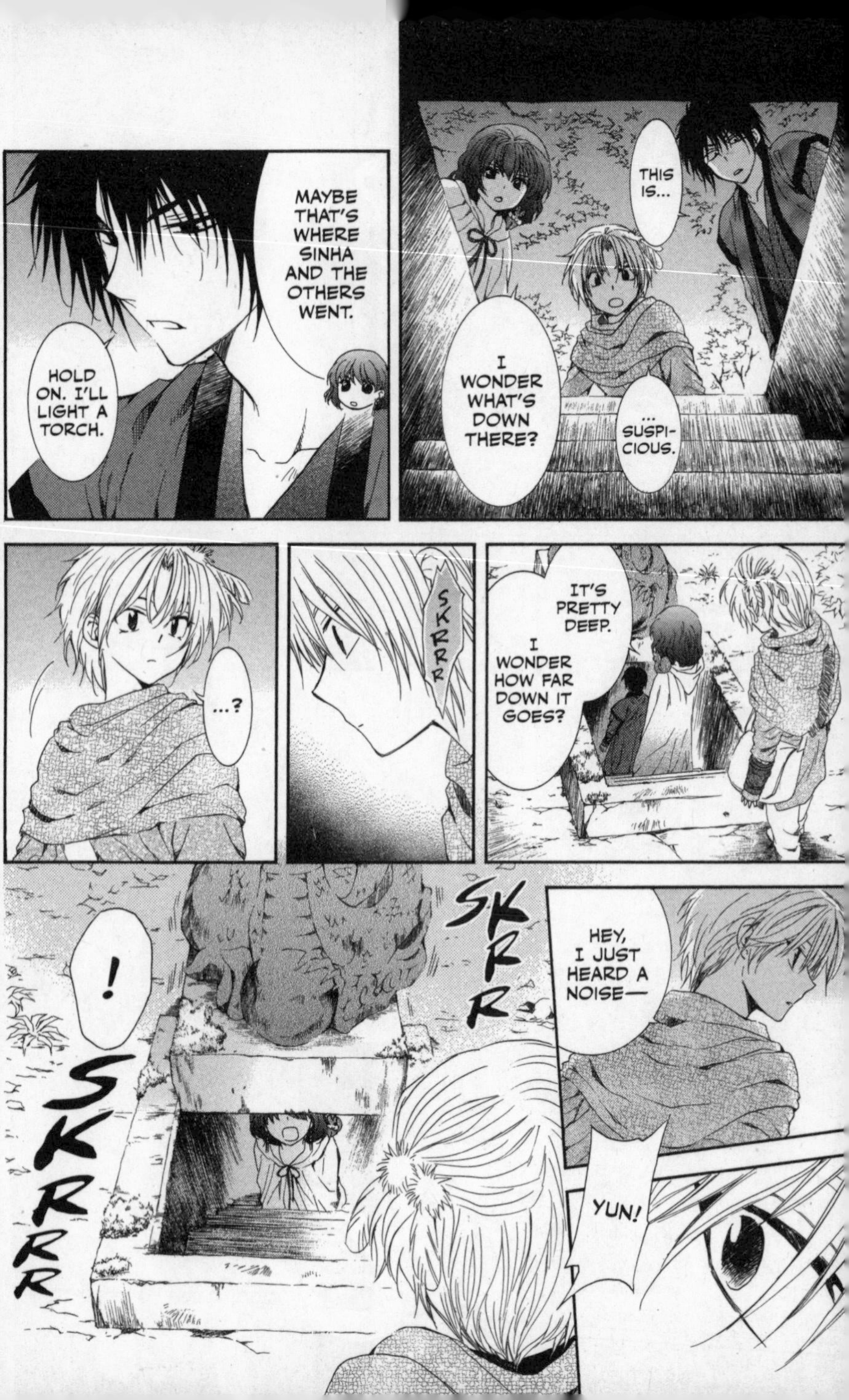
THIS IS...
I WONDER WHAT'S DOWN THERE?
... SUSPICIOUS.
MAYBE THAT'S WHERE SINHA AND THE OTHERS WENT.
HOLD ON. I'LL LIGHT A TORCH.
IT'S PRETTY DEEP. I WONDER HOW FAR DOWN IT GOES?
SKRRR
...?
HEY, I JUST HEARD A NOISE—
SKRR
YUN!
!
SKRRRR

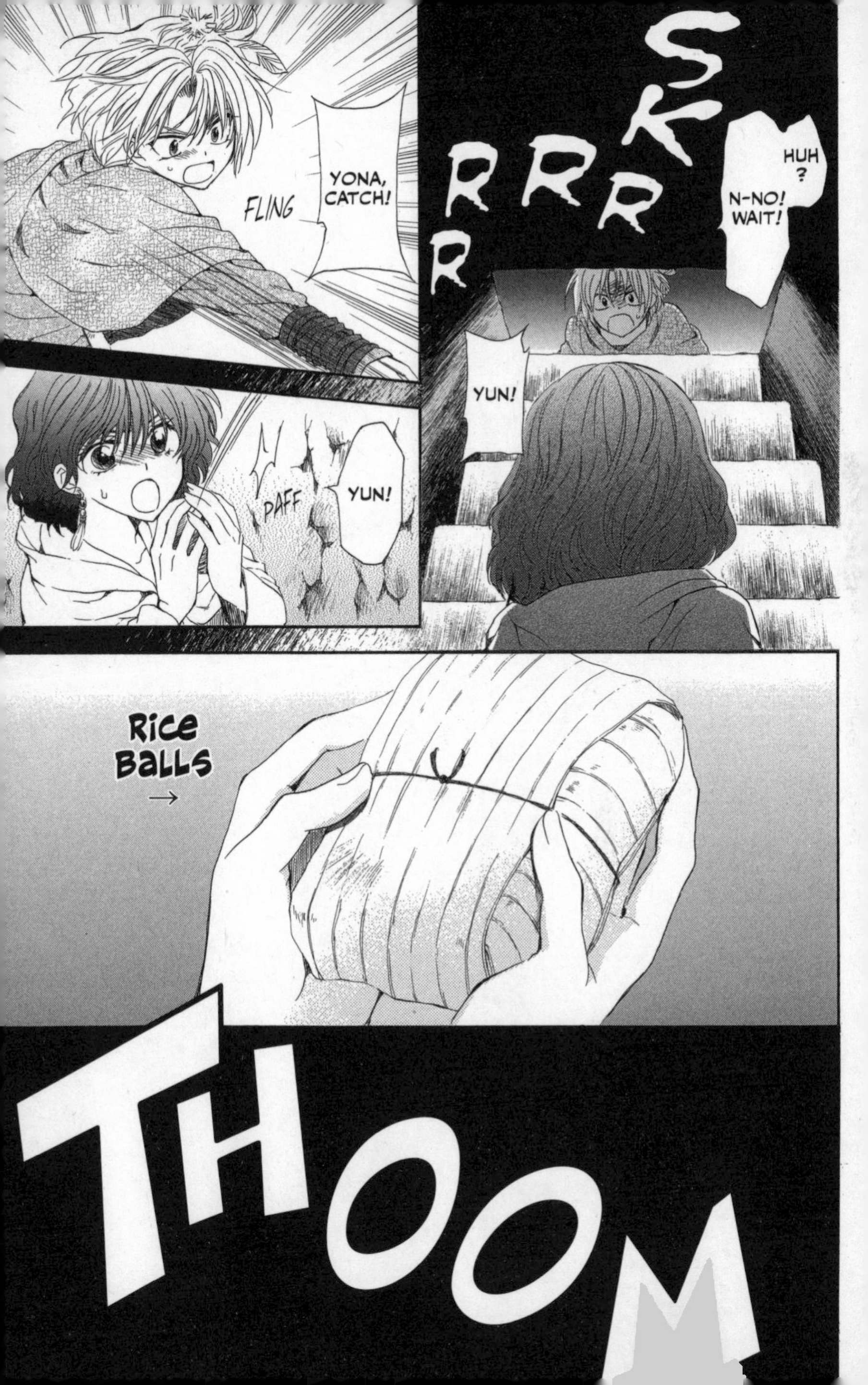
SKRRRR
HUH?
N-NO! WAIT!
YUN!
YONA, CATCH!
FLING
PAFF
YUN!
Rice Balls →
THOOM

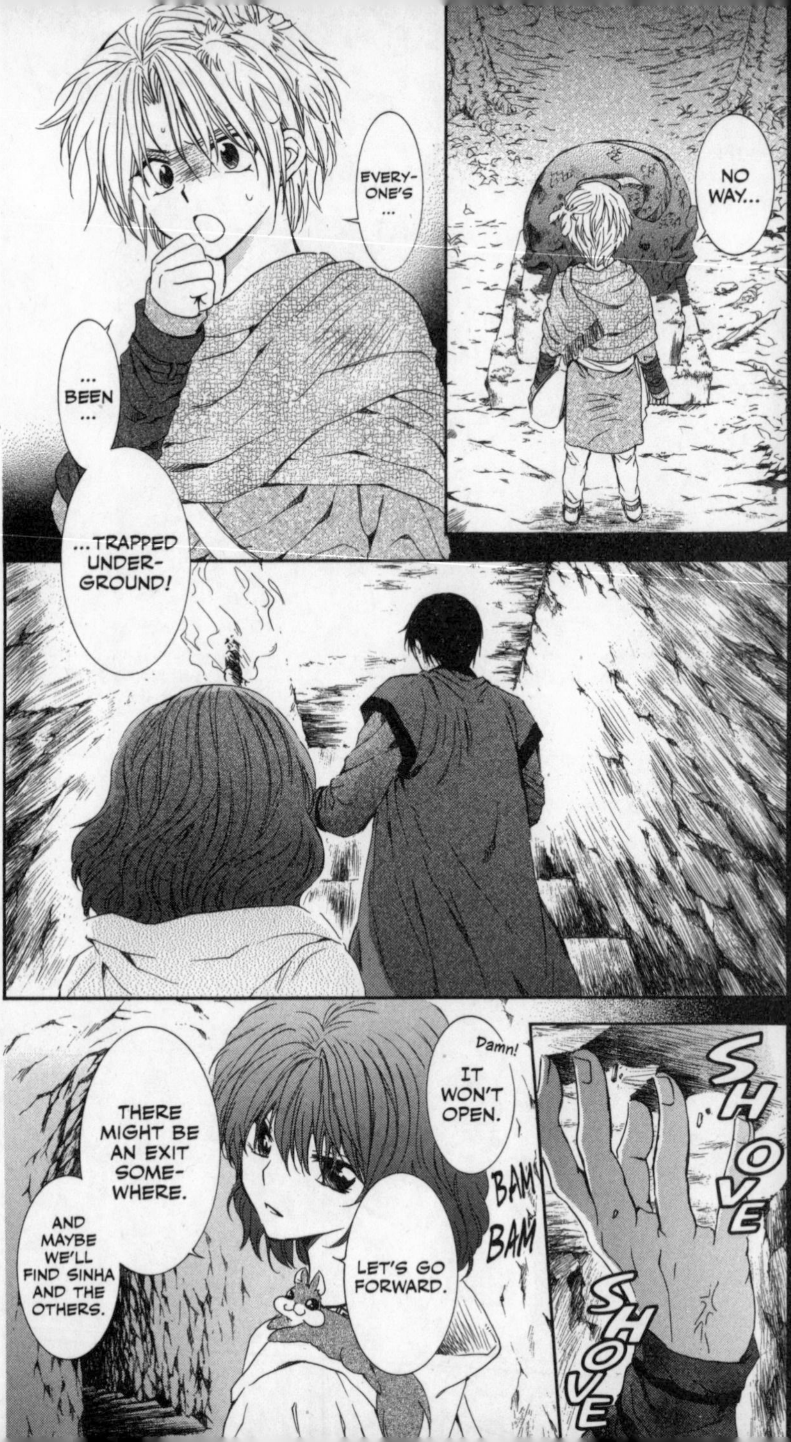
NO WAY...
EVERY-ONE'S ...
... BEEN ...
...TRAPPED UNDER-GROUND!
SHOVE
SHOVE
Damn!
IT WON'T OPEN.
BAM BAM
LET'S GO FORWARD.
THERE MIGHT BE AN EXIT SOME-WHERE.
AND MAYBE WE'LL FIND SINHA AND THE OTHERS.

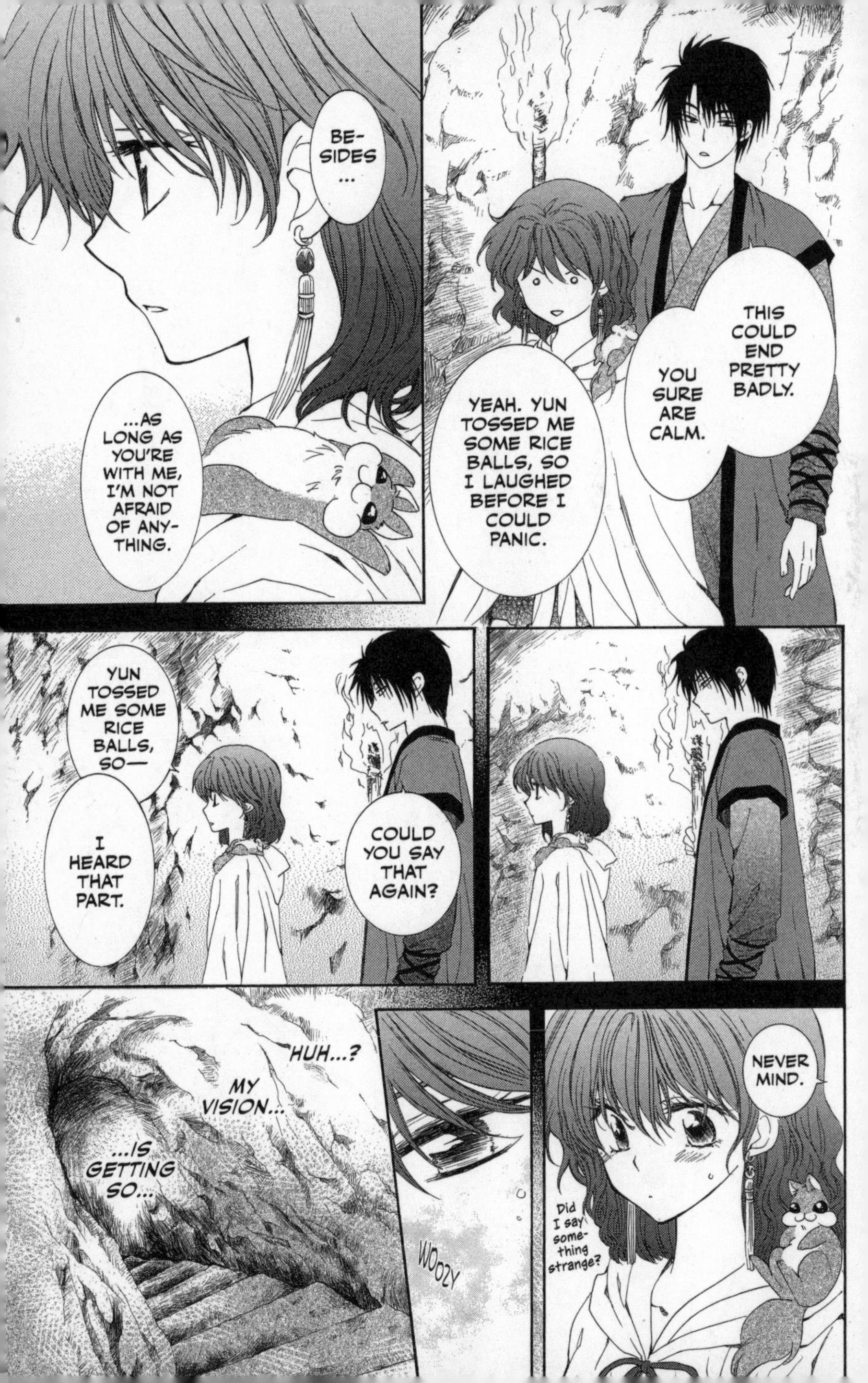
THIS COULD END PRETTY BADLY.
YOU SURE ARE CALM.
YEAH. YUN TOSSED ME SOME RICE BALLS, SO I LAUGHED BEFORE I COULD PANIC.
BE-SIDES ...
...AS LONG AS YOU'RE WITH ME, I'M NOT AFRAID OF ANY-THING.
COULD YOU SAY THAT AGAIN?
YUN TOSSED ME SOME RICE BALLS, SO—
I HEARD THAT PART.
NEVER MIND.
Did I say some-thing strange?
WOOZY
HUH...?
MY VISION...
...IS GETTING SO...

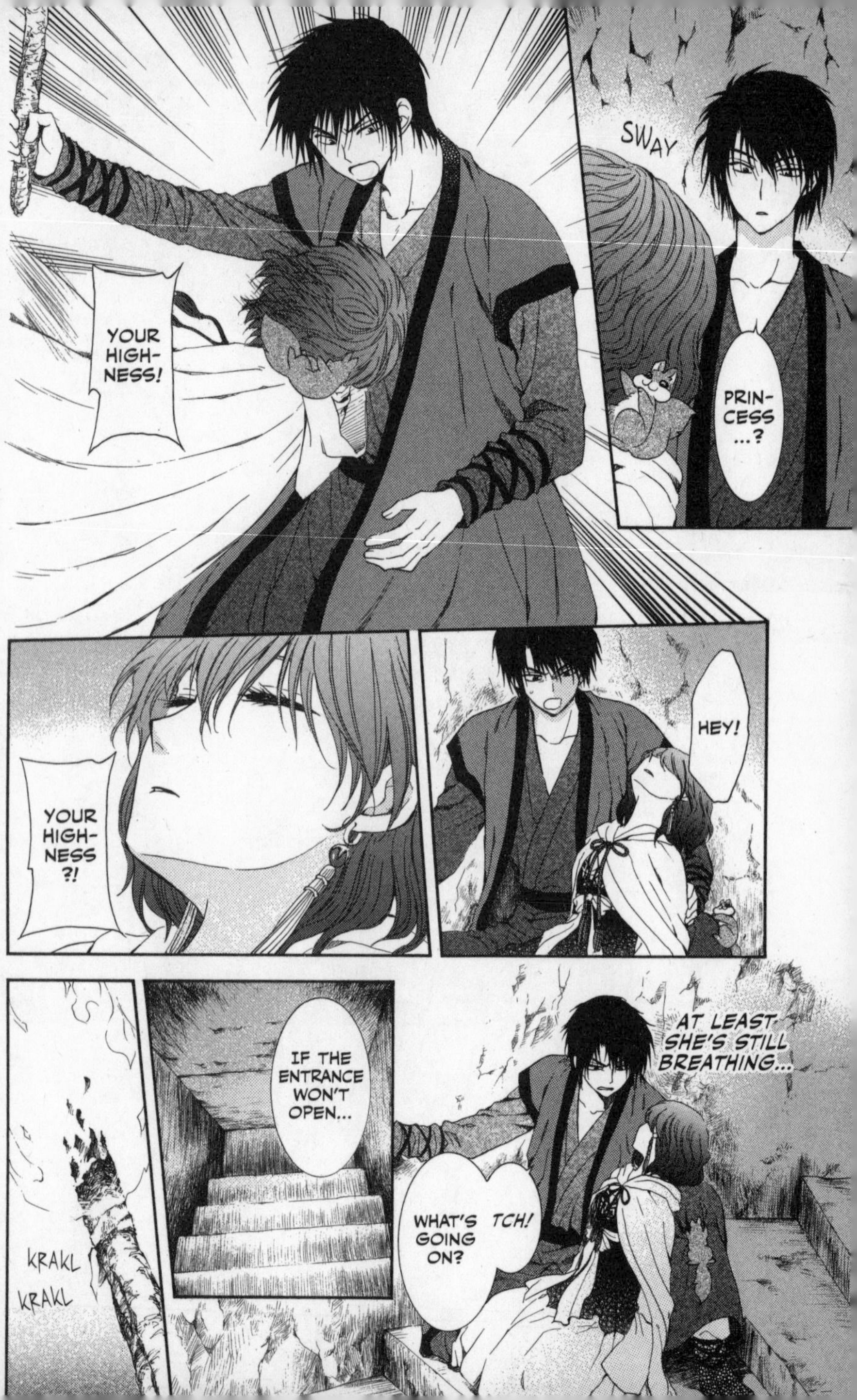
SWAY
PRINCESS...?
YOUR HIGHNESS!
HEY!
YOUR HIGHNESS?!
AT LEAST SHE'S STILL BREATHING...
TCH!
WHAT'S GOING ON?
IF THE ENTRANCE WON'T OPEN...
KRAKL
KRAKL

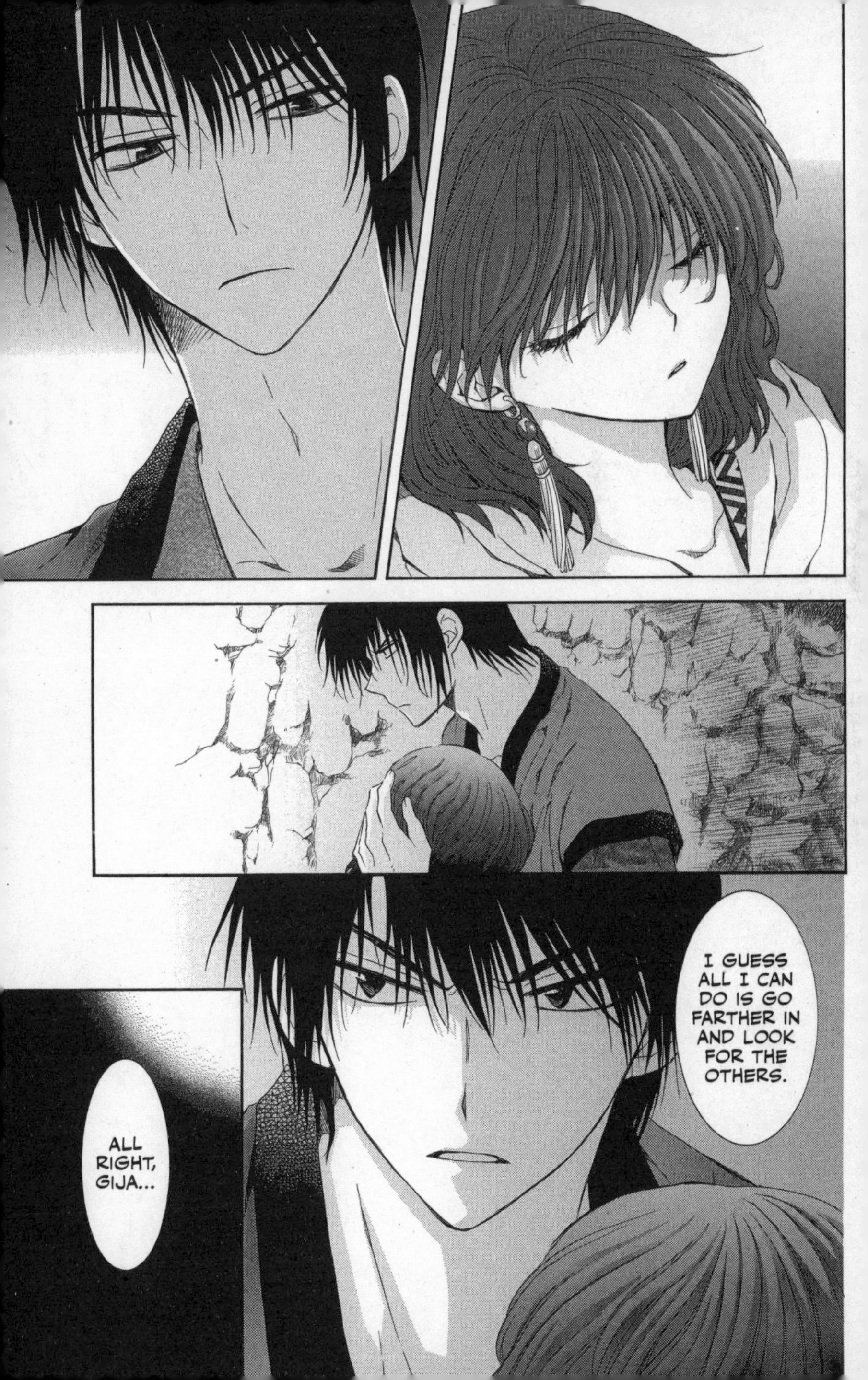
I GUESS ALL I CAN DO IS GO FARTHER IN AND LOOK FOR THE OTHERS.
ALL RIGHT, GIJA...

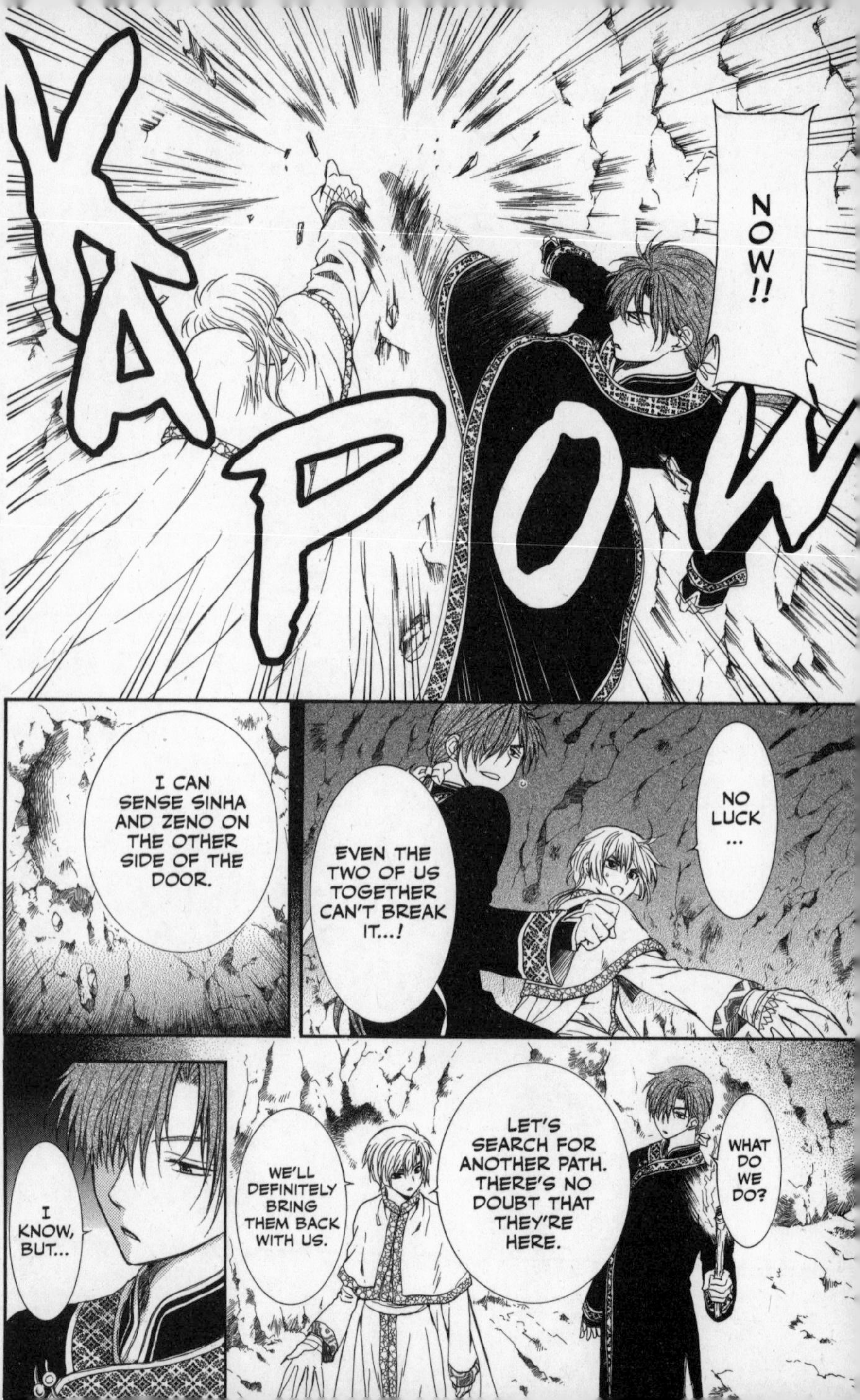
NOW!!
KAPOW
NO LUCK...
EVEN THE TWO OF US TOGETHER CAN'T BREAK IT...!
I CAN SENSE SINHA AND ZENO ON THE OTHER SIDE OF THE DOOR.
WHAT DO WE DO?
LET'S SEARCH FOR ANOTHER PATH. THERE'S NO DOUBT THAT THEY'RE HERE.
WE'LL DEFINITELY BRING THEM BACK WITH US.
I KNOW, BUT...

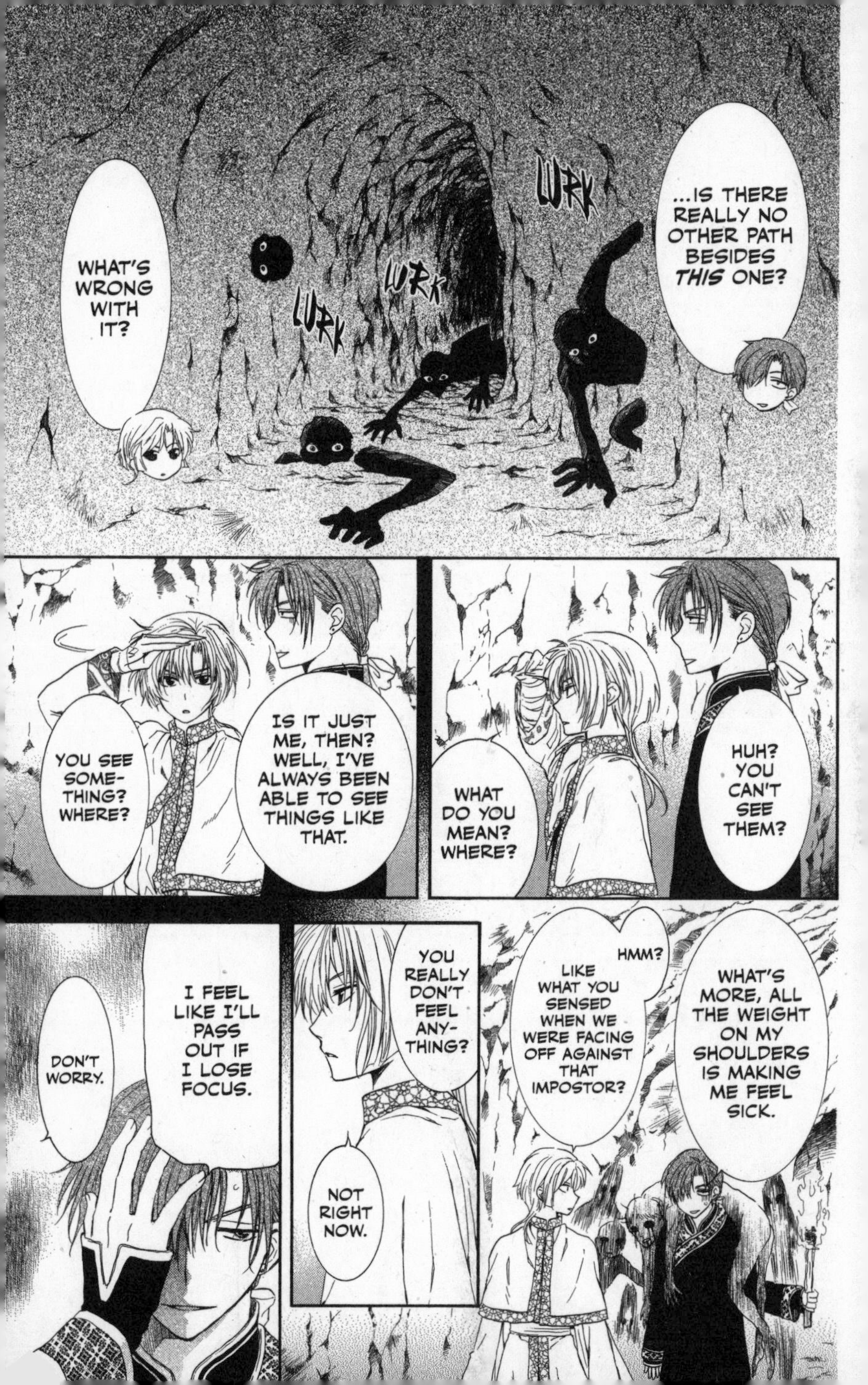
...IS THERE REALLY NO OTHER PATH BESIDES THIS ONE?
LURK
LURK
LURK
WHAT'S WRONG WITH IT?
HUH? YOU CAN'T SEE THEM?
WHAT DO YOU MEAN? WHERE?
IS IT JUST ME, THEN? WELL, I'VE ALWAYS BEEN ABLE TO SEE THINGS LIKE THAT.
YOU SEE SOME-THING? WHERE?
WHAT'S MORE, ALL THE WEIGHT ON MY SHOULDERS IS MAKING ME FEEL SICK.
HMM?
LIKE WHAT YOU SENSED WHEN WE WERE FACING OFF AGAINST THAT IMPOSTOR?
YOU REALLY DON'T FEEL ANY-THING?
NOT RIGHT NOW.
I FEEL LIKE I'LL PASS OUT IF I LOSE FOCUS.
DON'T WORRY.

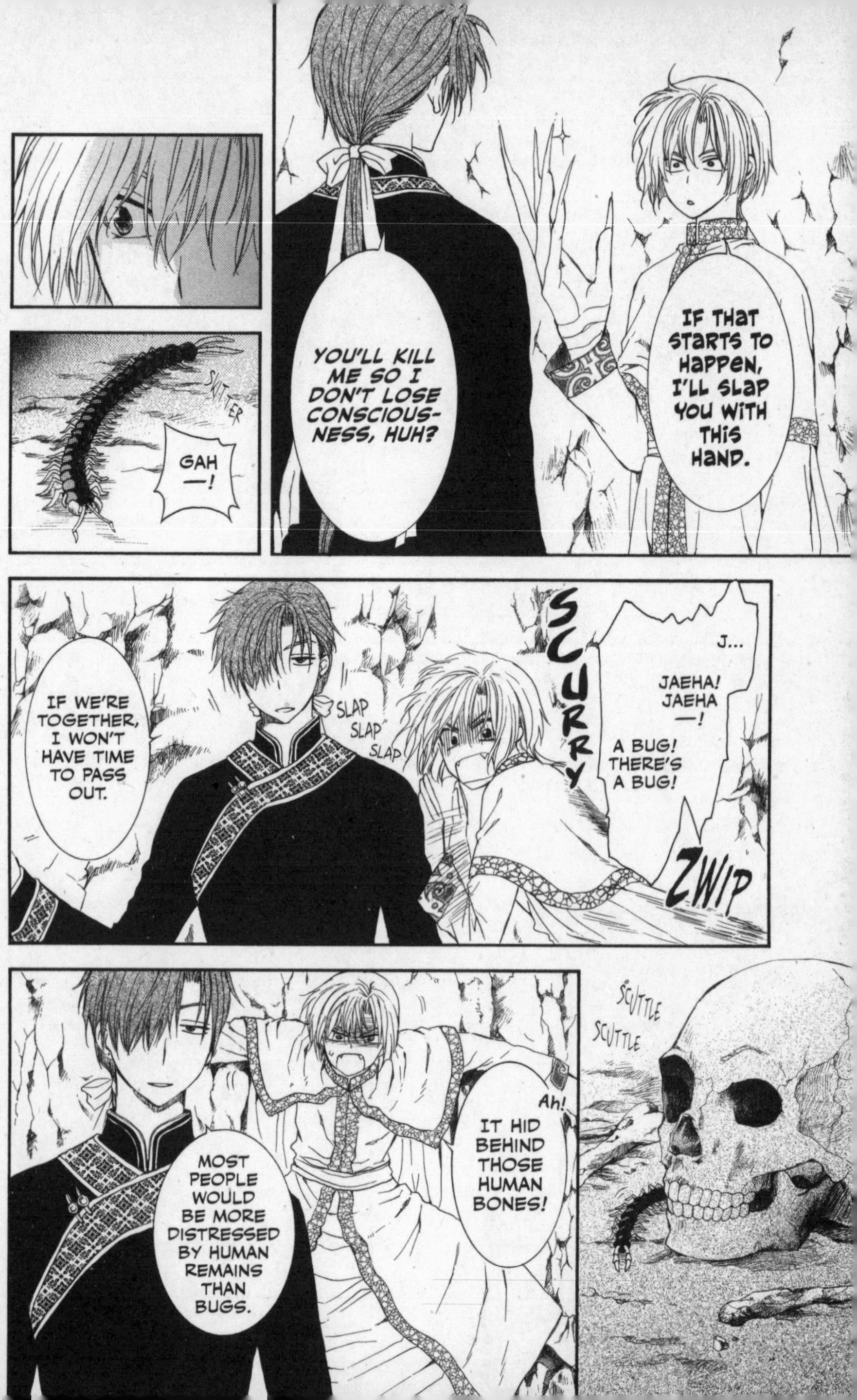
IF THAT STARTS TO HAPPEN, I'LL SLAP YOU WITH THIS HAND.
YOU'LL KILL ME SO I DON'T LOSE CONSCIOUS-NESS, HUH?
SKITTER
GAH—!
J...
JAEHA! JAEHA—!
A BUG! THERE'S A BUG!
ZWIP
SCURRY
SLAP SLAP SLAP
IF WE'RE TOGETHER, I WON'T HAVE TIME TO PASS OUT.
SCUTTLE SCUTTLE
Ah!
IT HID BEHIND THOSE HUMAN BONES!
MOST PEOPLE WOULD BE MORE DISTRESSED BY HUMAN REMAINS THAN BUGS.

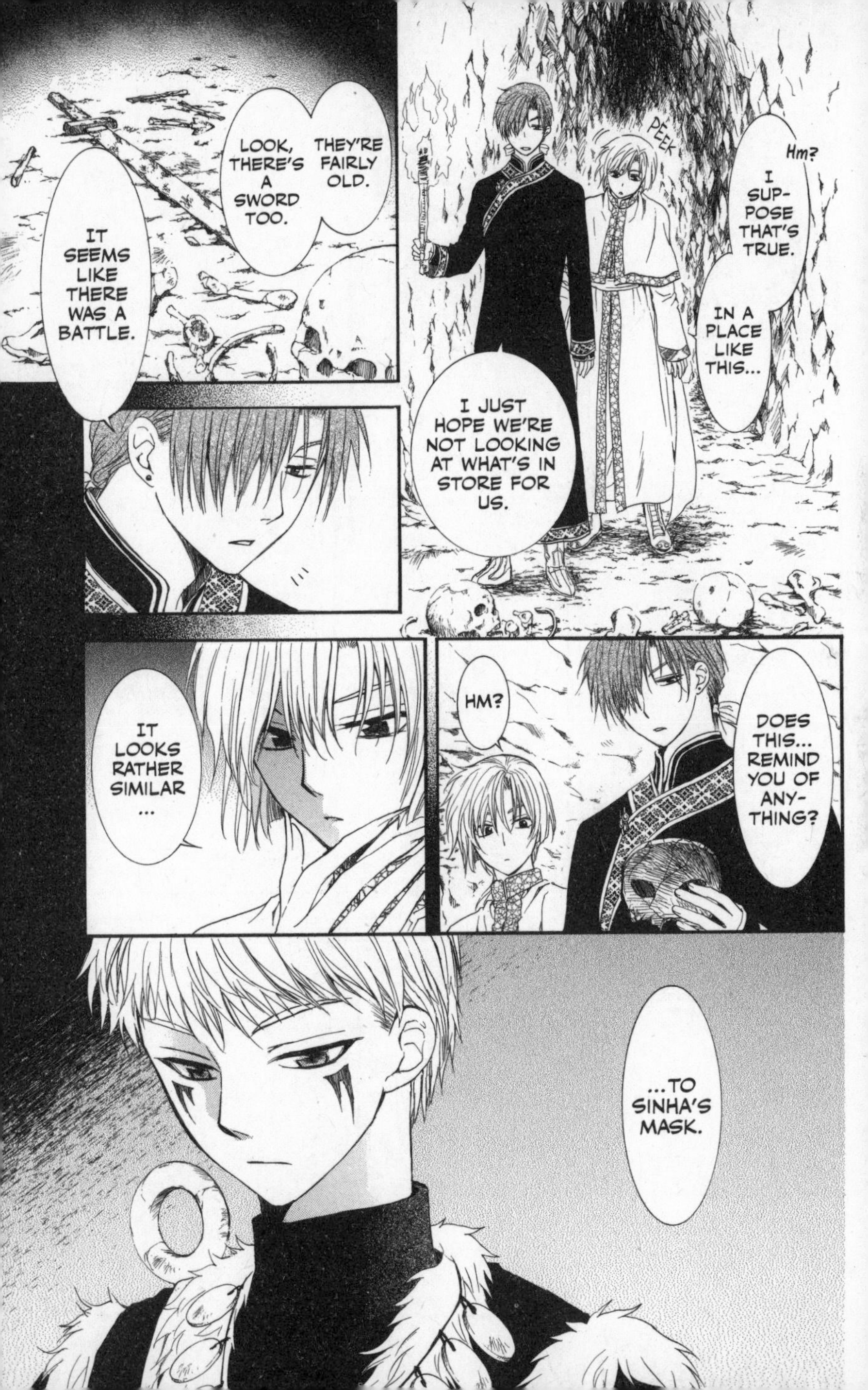
Hm?
I SUPPOSE THAT'S TRUE.
PEEK
IN A PLACE LIKE THIS...
I JUST HOPE WE'RE NOT LOOKING AT WHAT'S IN STORE FOR US.
THEY'RE FAIRLY OLD.
LOOK, THERE'S A SWORD TOO.
IT SEEMS LIKE THERE WAS A BATTLE.
DOES THIS... REMIND YOU OF ANY-THING?
HM?
IT LOOKS RATHER SIMILAR...
...TO SINHA'S MASK.

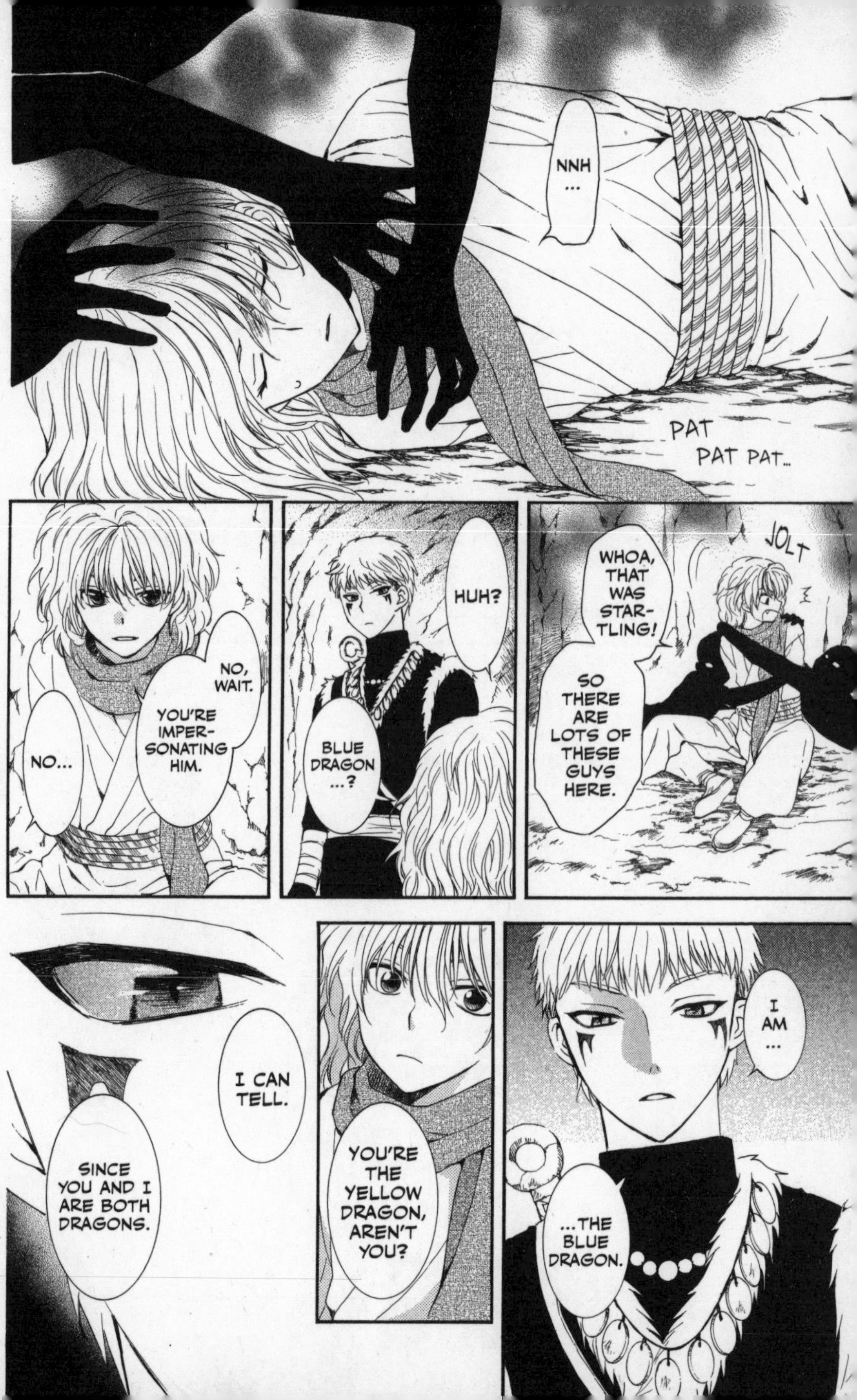
NNH...
PAT PAT PAT...
JOLT
WHOA, THAT WAS STARTLING!
SO THERE ARE LOTS OF THESE GUYS HERE.
HUH?
BLUE DRAGON...?
NO, WAIT.
YOU'RE IMPERSONATING HIM.
NO...
I AM...
...THE BLUE DRAGON.
YOU'RE THE YELLOW DRAGON, AREN'T YOU?
I CAN TELL.
SINCE YOU AND I ARE BOTH DRAGONS.

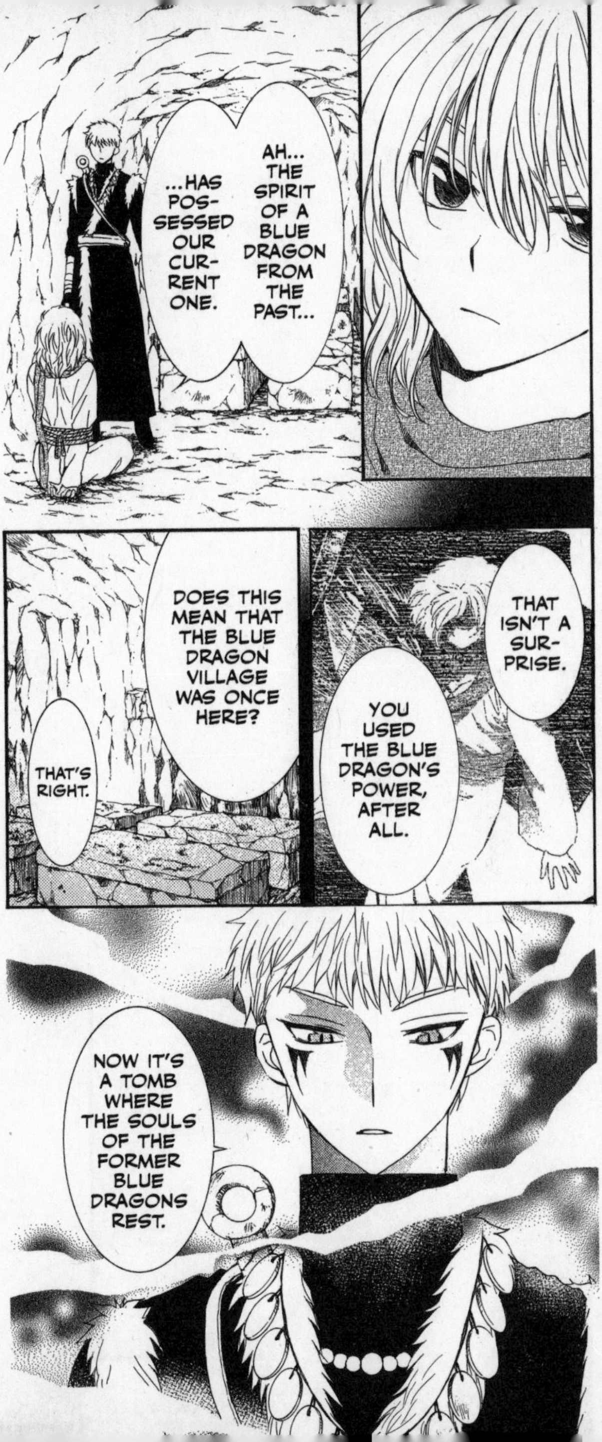
AH... THE SPIRIT OF A BLUE DRAGON FROM THE PAST...
...HAS POSSESSED OUR CURRENT ONE.
THAT ISN'T A SURPRISE.
YOU USED THE BLUE DRAGON'S POWER, AFTER ALL.
DOES THIS MEAN THAT THE BLUE DRAGON VILLAGE WAS ONCE HERE?
THAT'S RIGHT.
NOW IT'S A TOMB WHERE THE SOULS OF THE FORMER BLUE DRAGONS REST.

The preorder special edition of volume 19 comes with an original anime DVD (in Japan)! It includes the animated version of the bonus chapter "Upon His Back" and the special chapter "Gija" from volume 12. I wrote those stories with great care, so I'm really excited to see how they were animated.

Also, issue 20 of *Hana to Yume*, which goes on sale the same day as volume 19 (on 9/18), comes with a Yona drama CD! It includes this story, "The Blue Forest."

Yona and her friends aren't the only ones you'll hear. The first dragons—Guen, Abi and Shuten—also appear in an additional episode! Please give it a listen.

Unfortunately, I wasn't able to do a Su-won story. DU

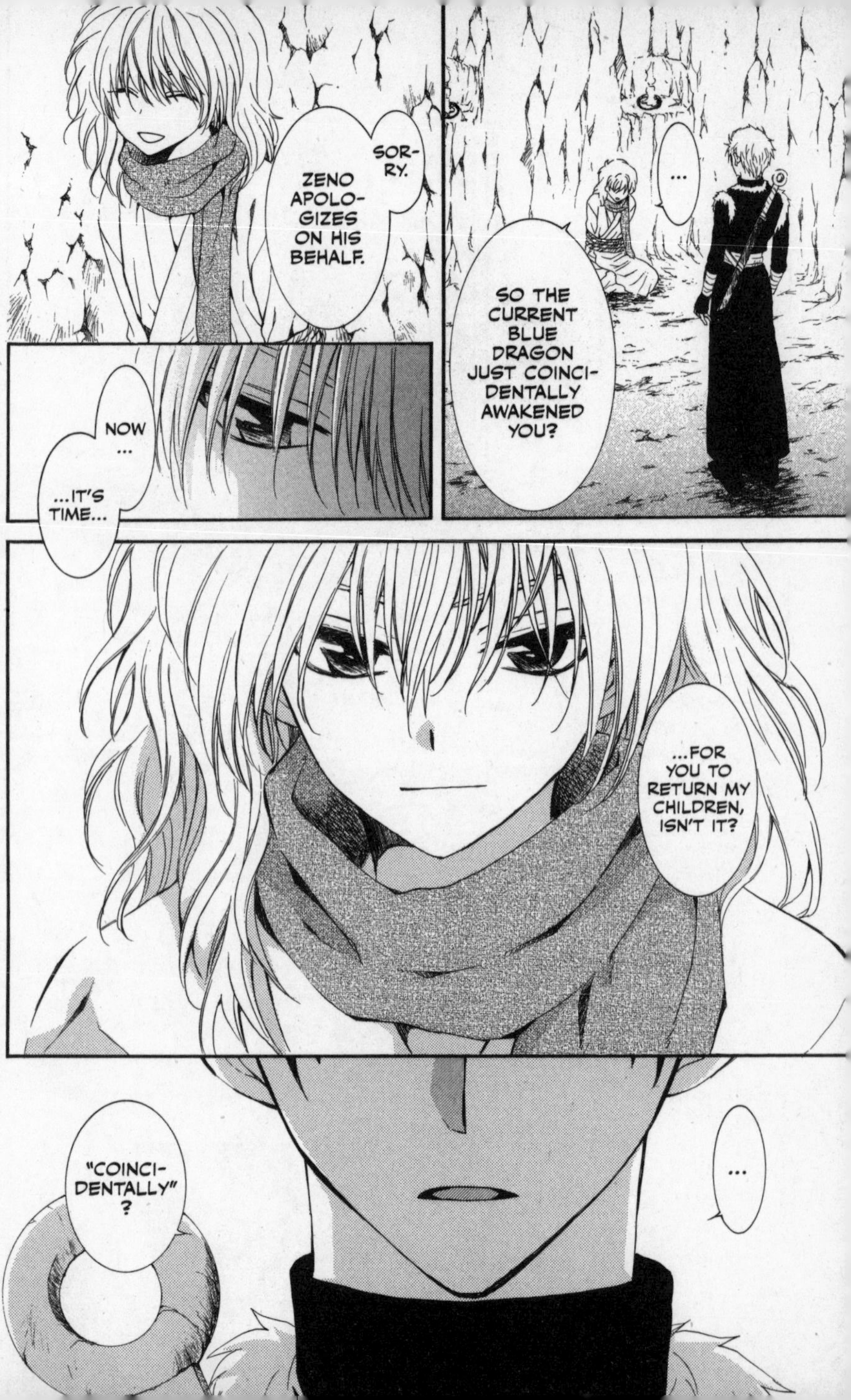
...
SO THE CURRENT BLUE DRAGON JUST COINCIDENTALLY AWAKENED YOU?
SOR-RY.
ZENO APOLOGIZES ON HIS BEHALF.
NOW ...
...IT'S TIME...
...FOR YOU TO RETURN MY CHILDREN, ISN'T IT?
...
"COINCI-DENTALLY"?

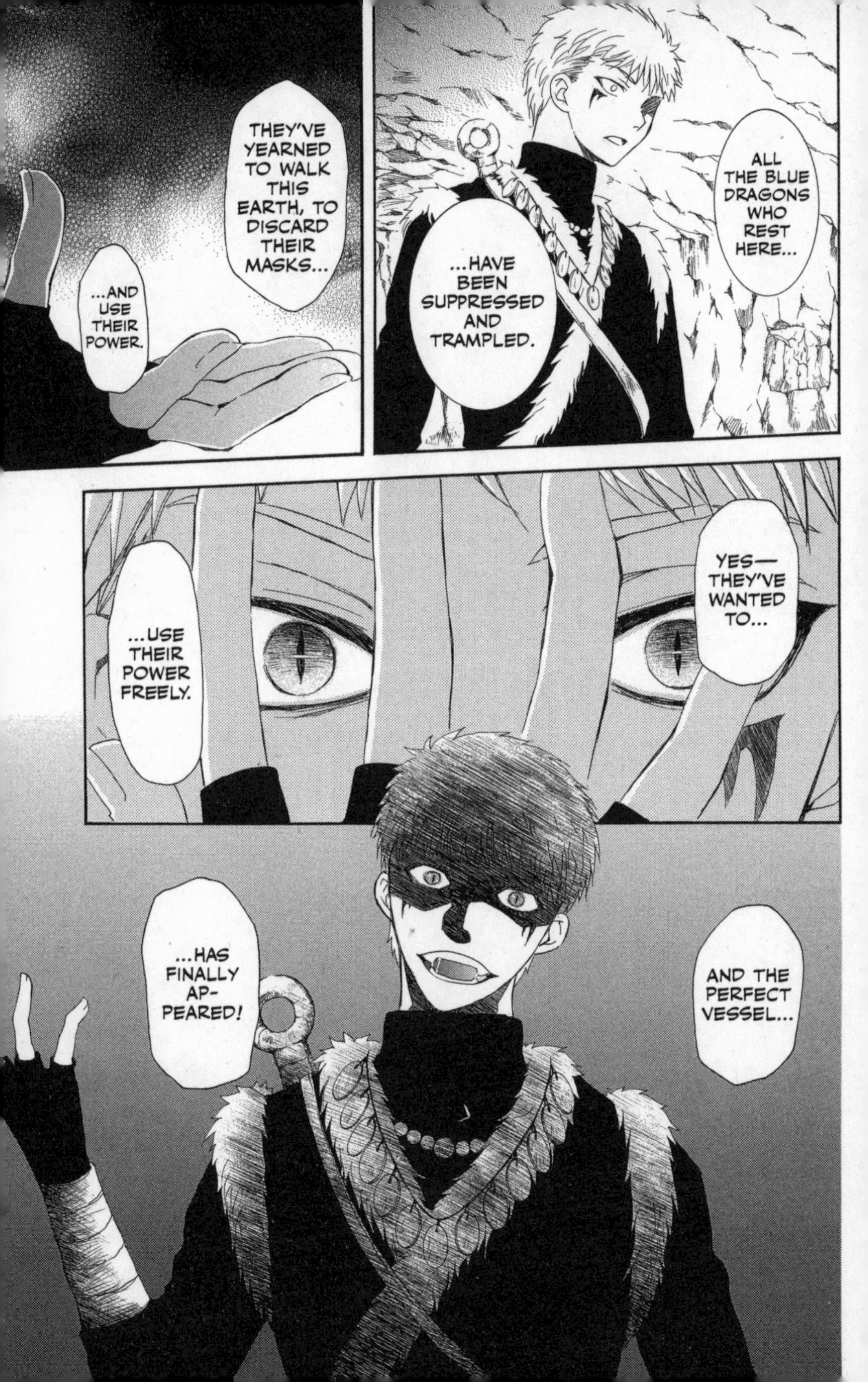
ALL THE BLUE DRAGONS WHO REST HERE...
...HAVE BEEN SUPPRESSED AND TRAMPLED.
THEY'VE YEARNED TO WALK THIS EARTH, TO DISCARD THEIR MASKS...
...AND USE THEIR POWER.
YES— THEY'VE WANTED TO...
...USE THEIR POWER FREELY.
AND THE PERFECT VESSEL...
...HAS FINALLY AP-PEARED!

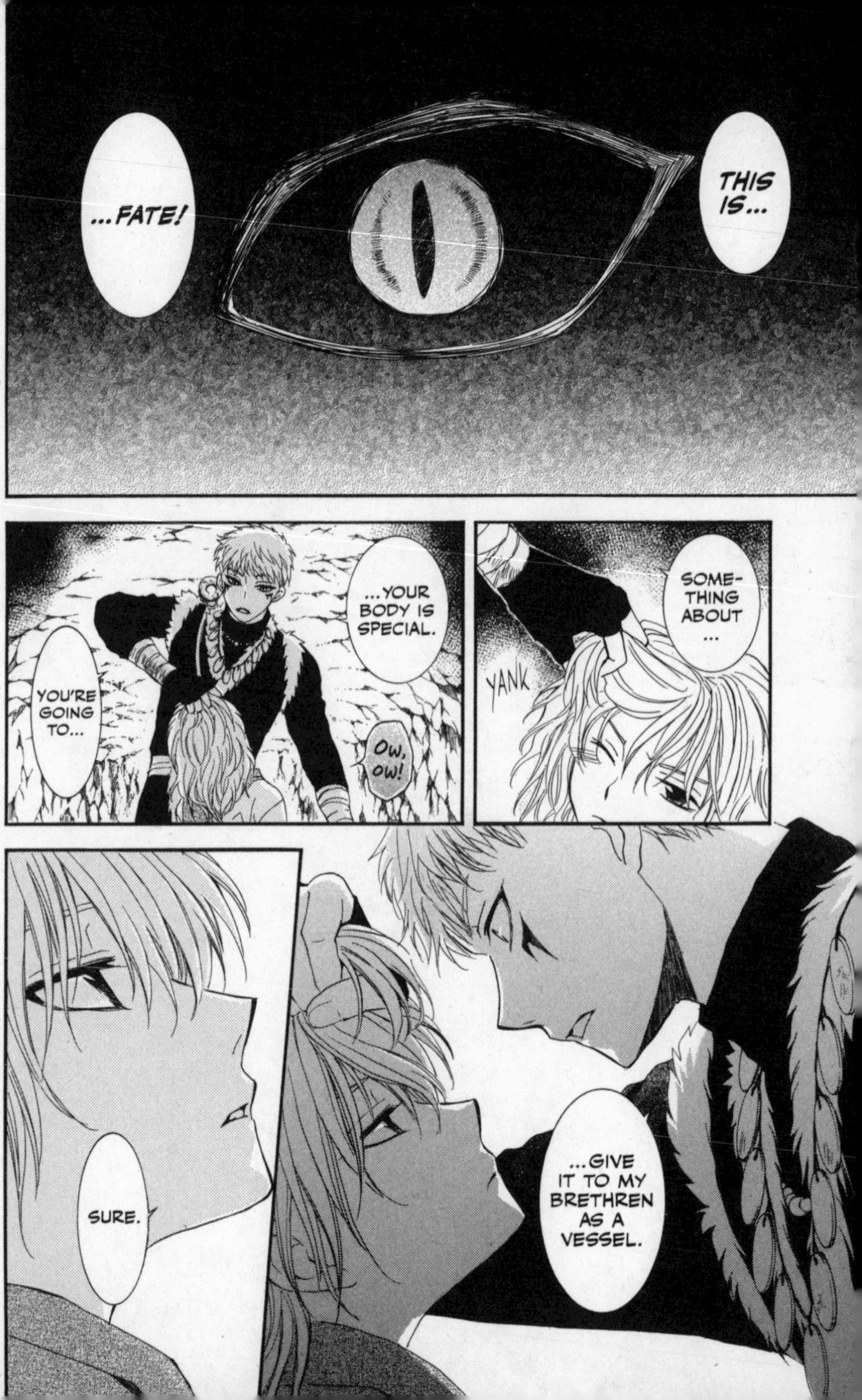
THIS IS...
...FATE!
SOME-THING ABOUT ...
YANK
...YOUR BODY IS SPECIAL.
OW, OW!
YOU'RE GOING TO...
...GIVE IT TO MY BRETHREN AS A VESSEL.
SURE.

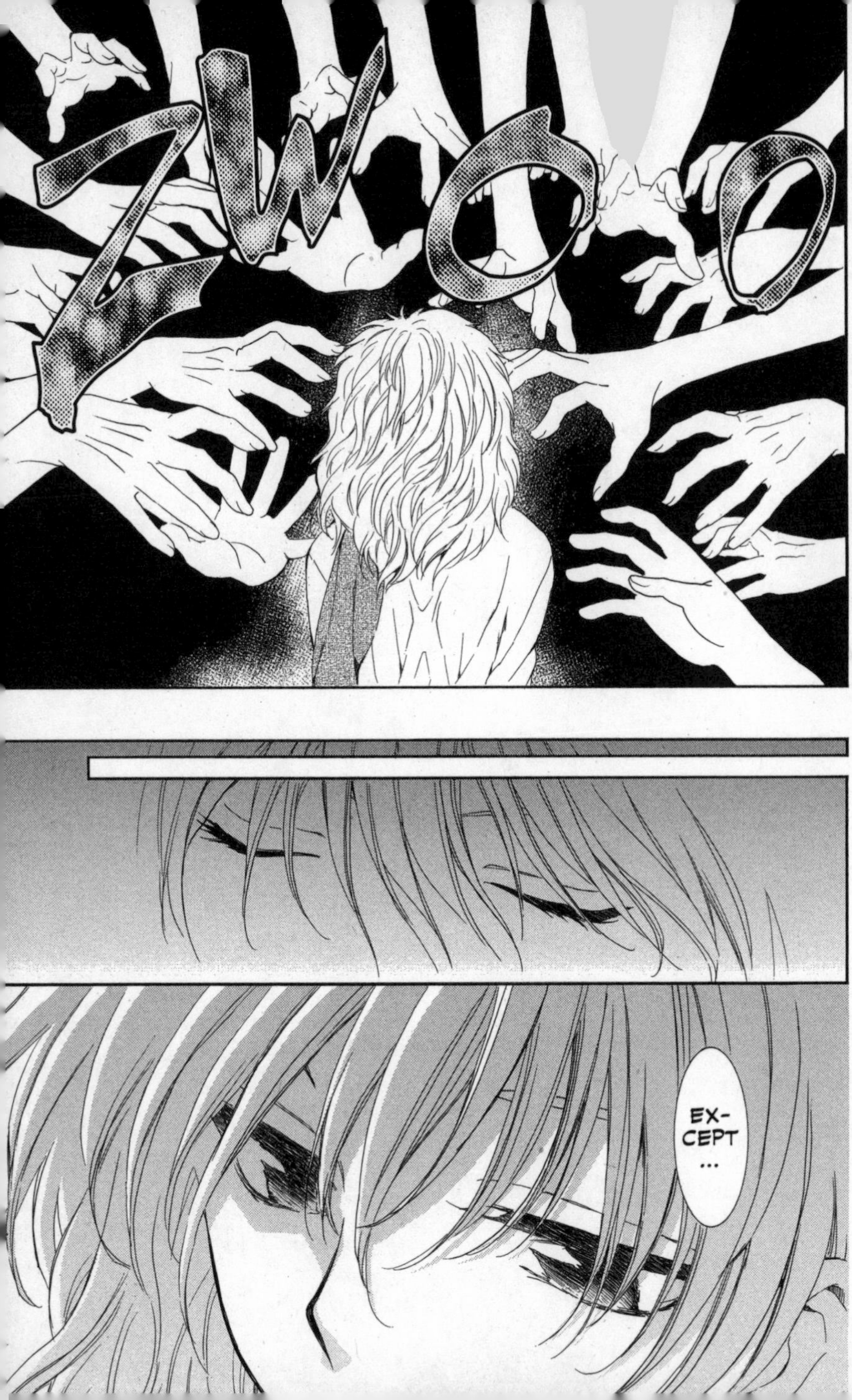
ZWOO
EX-CEPT...

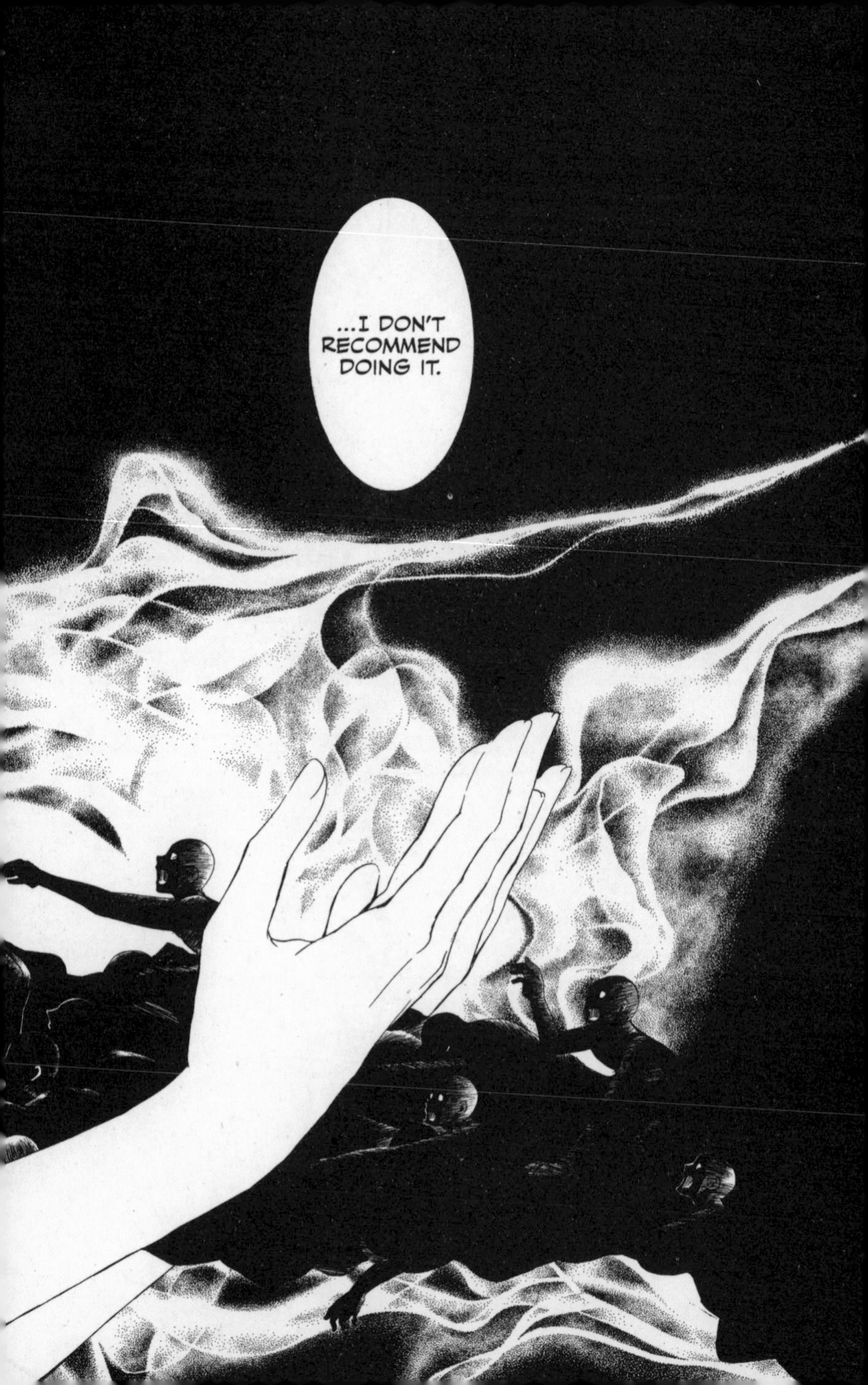
...I DON'T RECOMMEND DOING IT.

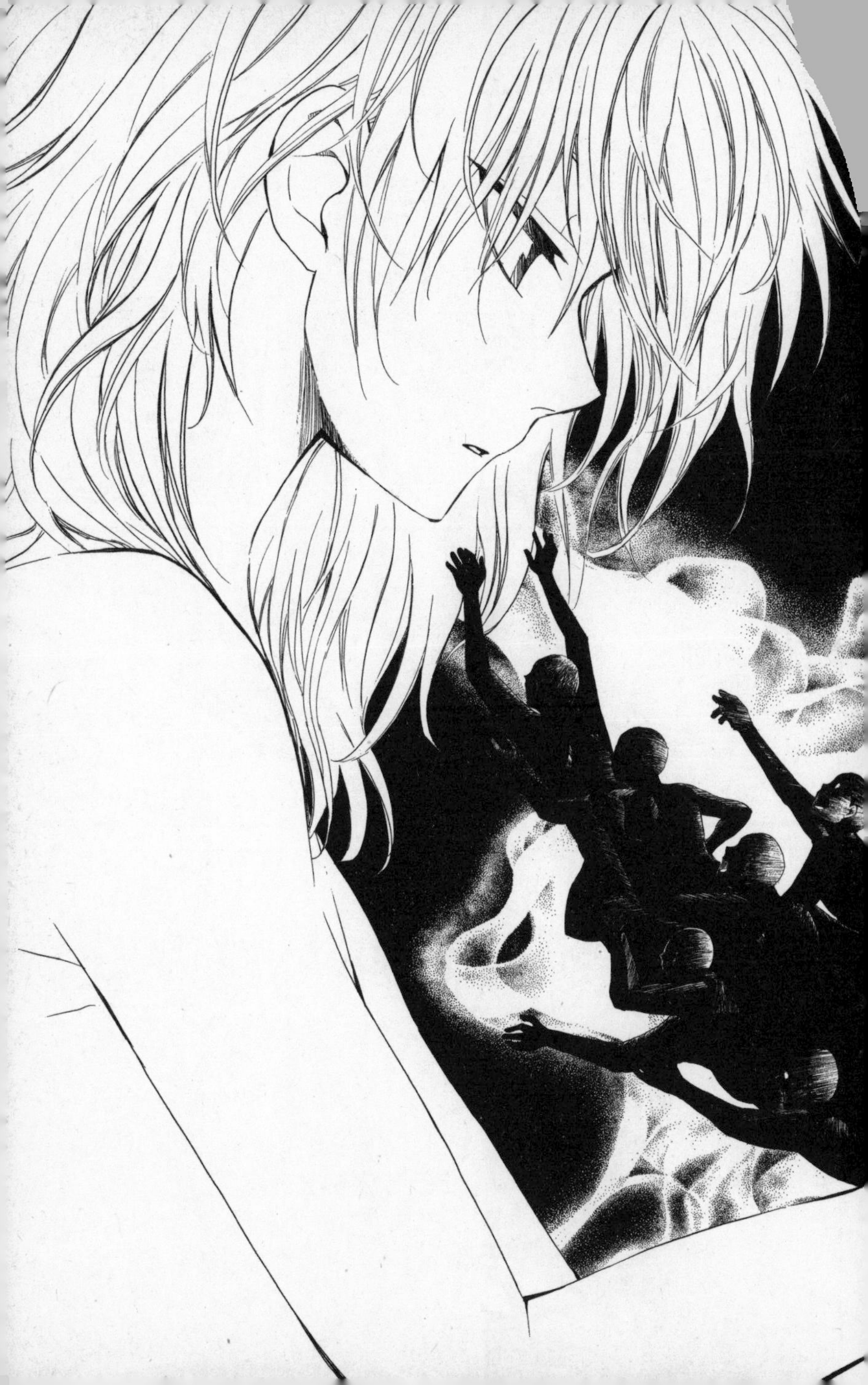

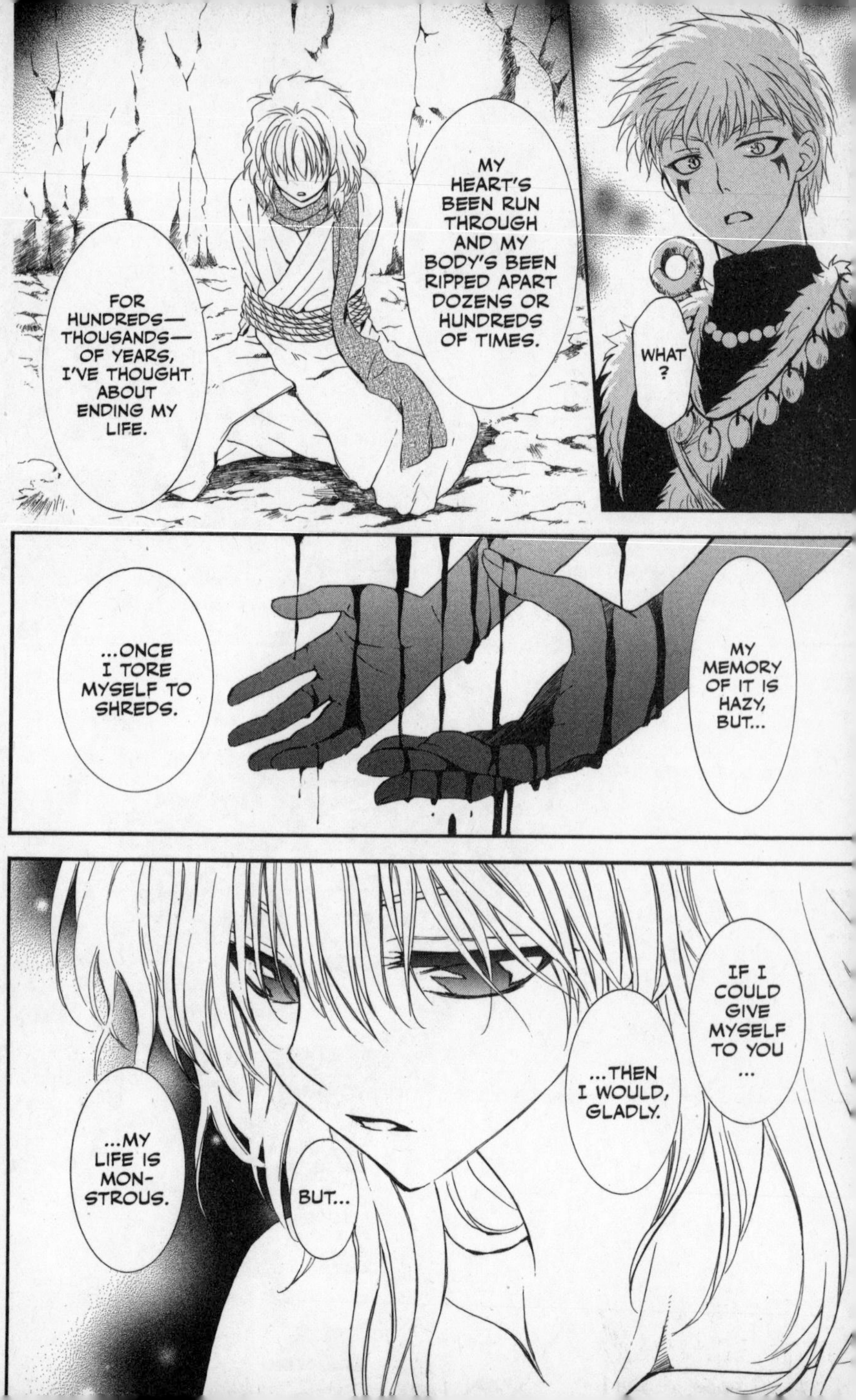
WHAT?
MY HEART'S BEEN RUN THROUGH AND MY BODY'S BEEN RIPPED APART DOZENS OR HUNDREDS OF TIMES.
FOR HUNDREDS—THOUSANDS—OF YEARS, I'VE THOUGHT ABOUT ENDING MY LIFE.
MY MEMORY OF IT IS HAZY, BUT...
...ONCE I TORE MYSELF TO SHREDS.
IF I COULD GIVE MYSELF TO YOU...
...THEN I WOULD, GLADLY.
BUT...
...MY LIFE IS MON-STROUS.

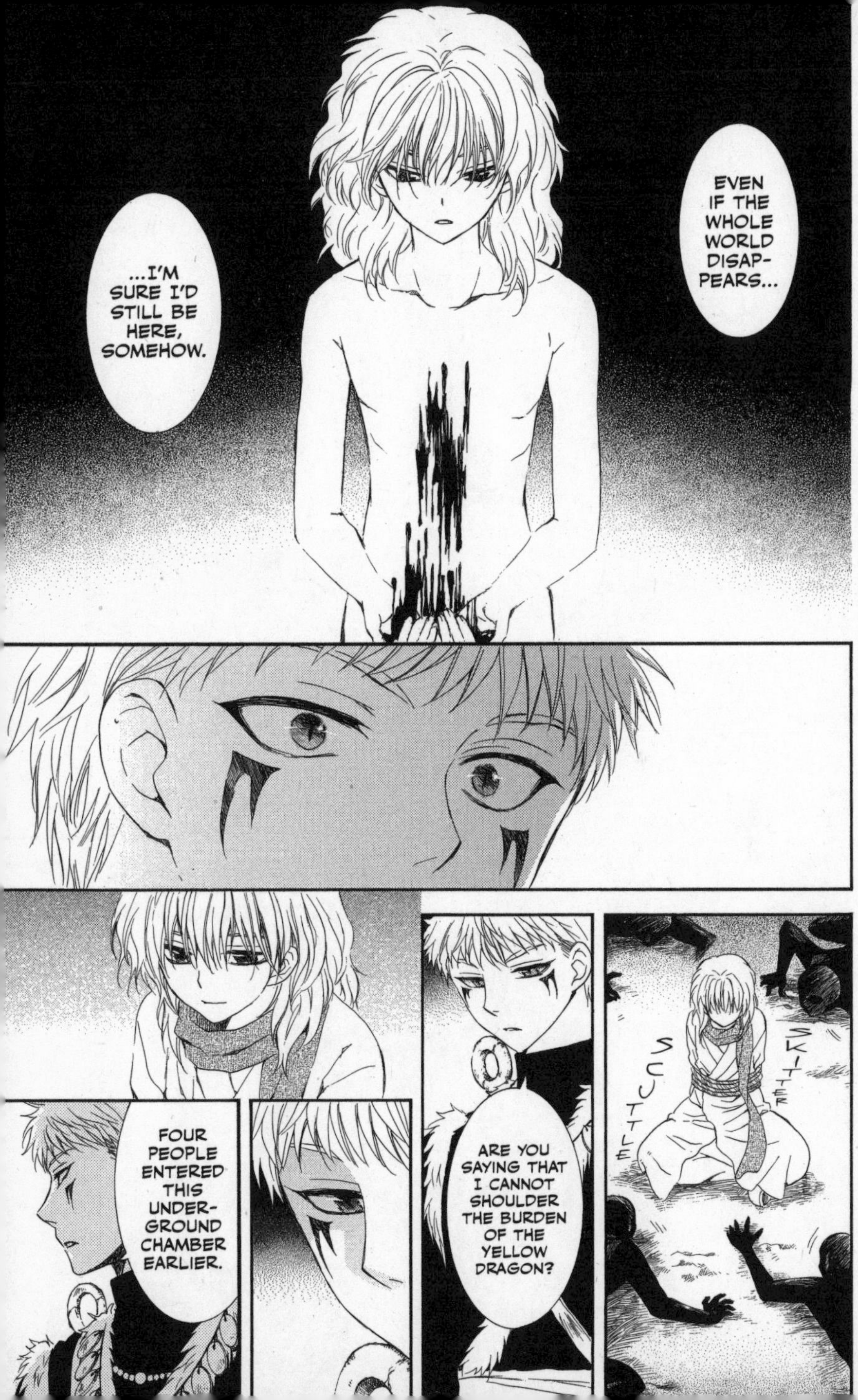
EVEN IF THE WHOLE WORLD DISAPPEARS...
...I'M SURE I'D STILL BE HERE, SOMEHOW.
SKITTER
SCUTTLE
ARE YOU SAYING THAT I CANNOT SHOULDER THE BURDEN OF THE YELLOW DRAGON?
FOUR PEOPLE ENTERED THIS UNDERGROUND CHAMBER EARLIER.

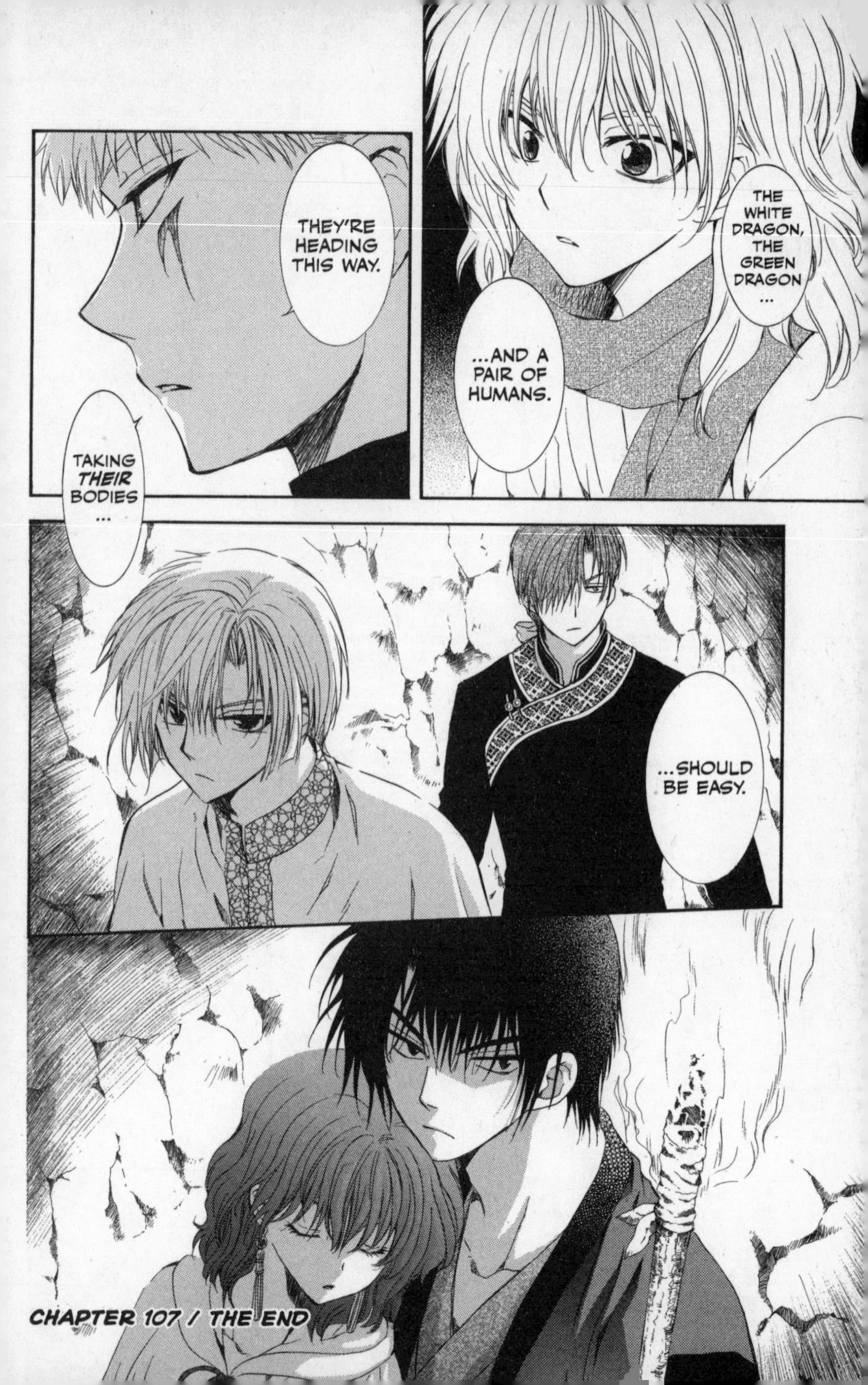
THE WHITE DRAGON, THE GREEN DRAGON ...
...AND A PAIR OF HUMANS.
THEY'RE HEADING THIS WAY.
TAKING *THEIR* BODIES ...
...SHOULD BE EASY.
CHAPTER 107 / THE END

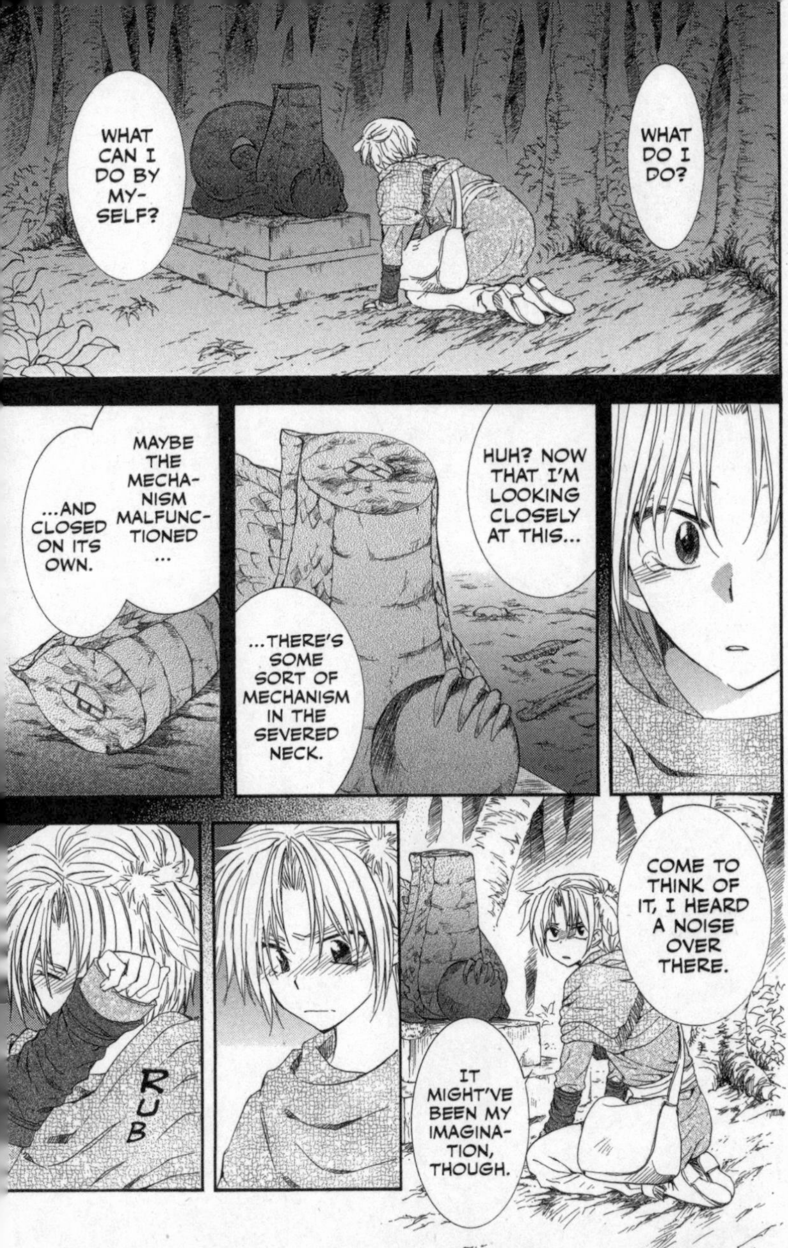
WHAT DO I DO?
WHAT CAN I DO BY MYSELF?
HUH? NOW THAT I'M LOOKING CLOSELY AT THIS...
...THERE'S SOME SORT OF MECHANISM IN THE SEVERED NECK.
MAYBE THE MECHANISM MALFUNCTIONED...
...AND CLOSED ON ITS OWN.
COME TO THINK OF IT, I HEARD A NOISE OVER THERE.
IT MIGHT'VE BEEN MY IMAGINATION, THOUGH.
RUB

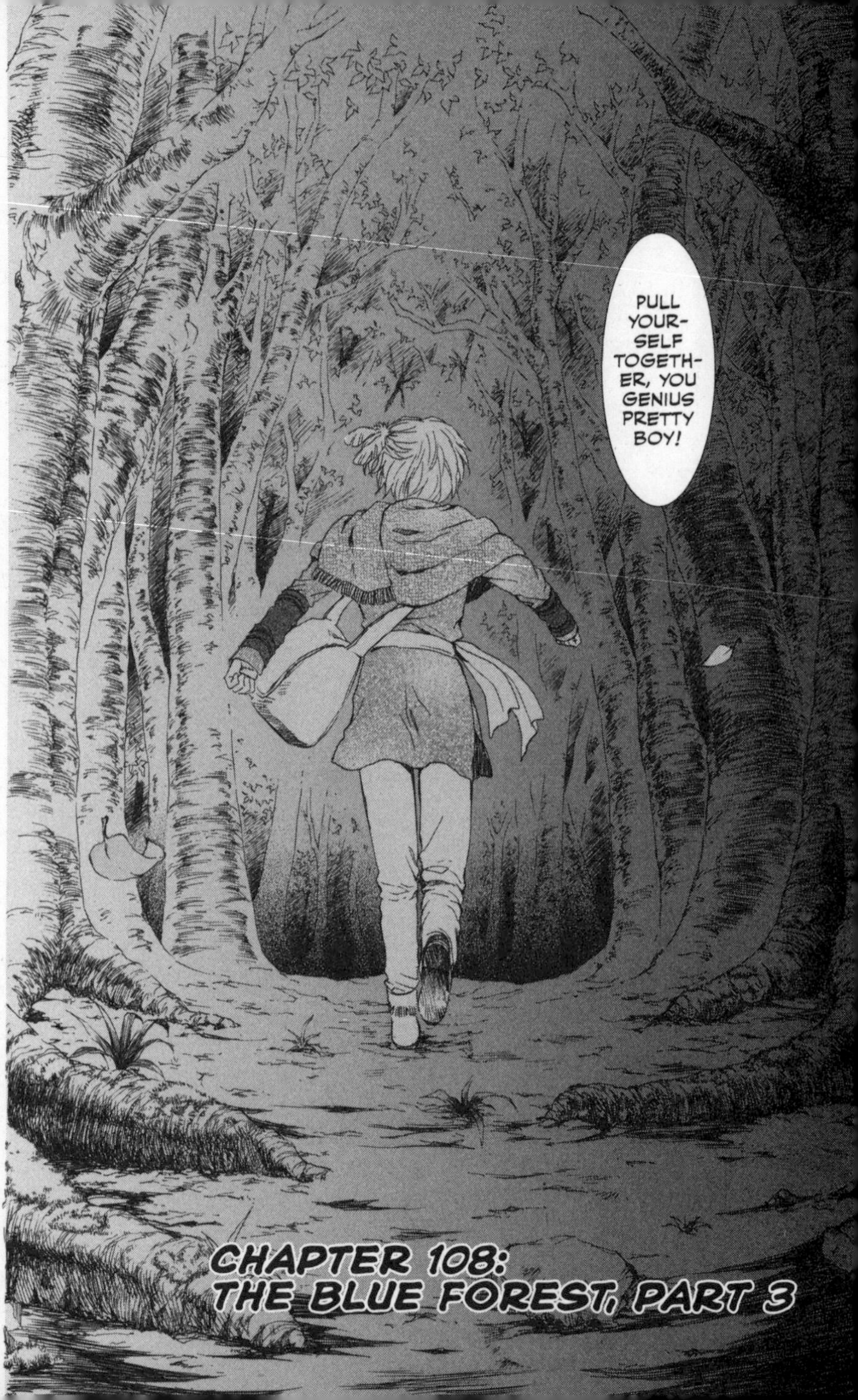
PULL YOURSELF TOGETHER, YOU GENIUS PRETTY BOY!
CHAPTER 108: THE BLUE FOREST, PART 3

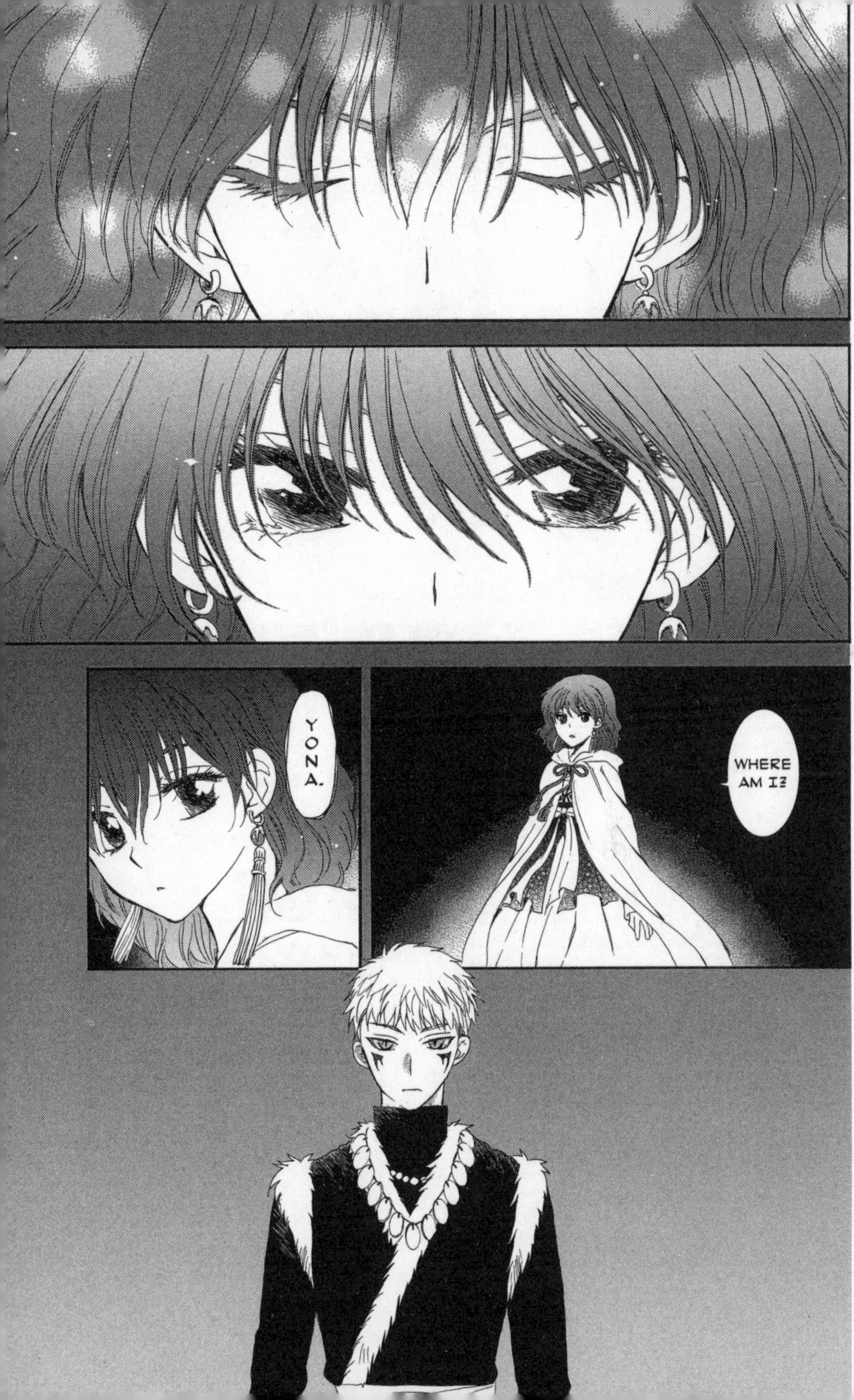
WHERE AM I?
YONA.

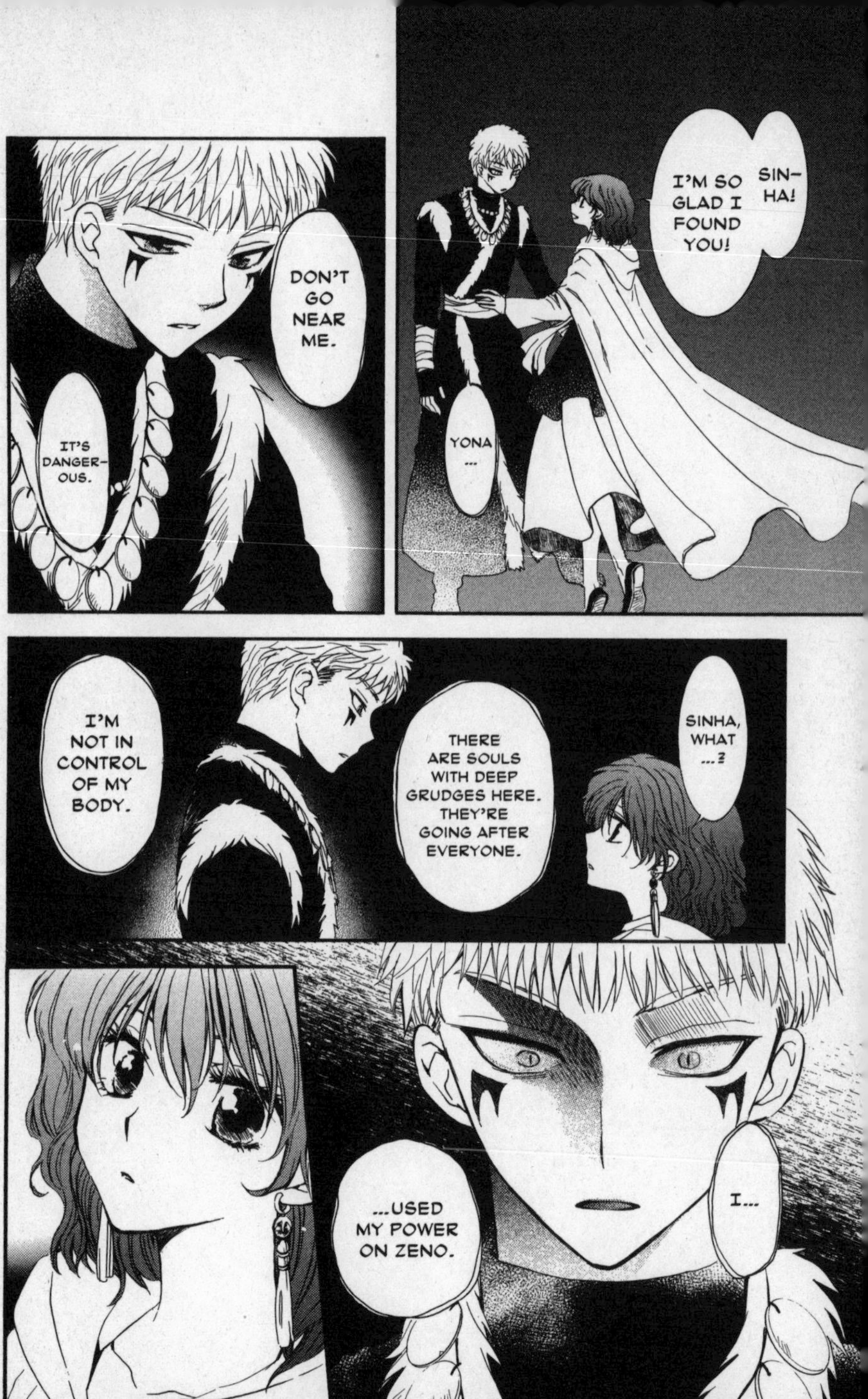
SIN-HA!
I'M SO GLAD I FOUND YOU!
YONA...
DON'T GO NEAR ME.
IT'S DANGER-OUS.
SINHA, WHAT...?
THERE ARE SOULS WITH DEEP GRUDGES HERE. THEY'RE GOING AFTER EVERYONE.
I'M NOT IN CONTROL OF MY BODY.
I...
...USED MY POWER ON ZENO.

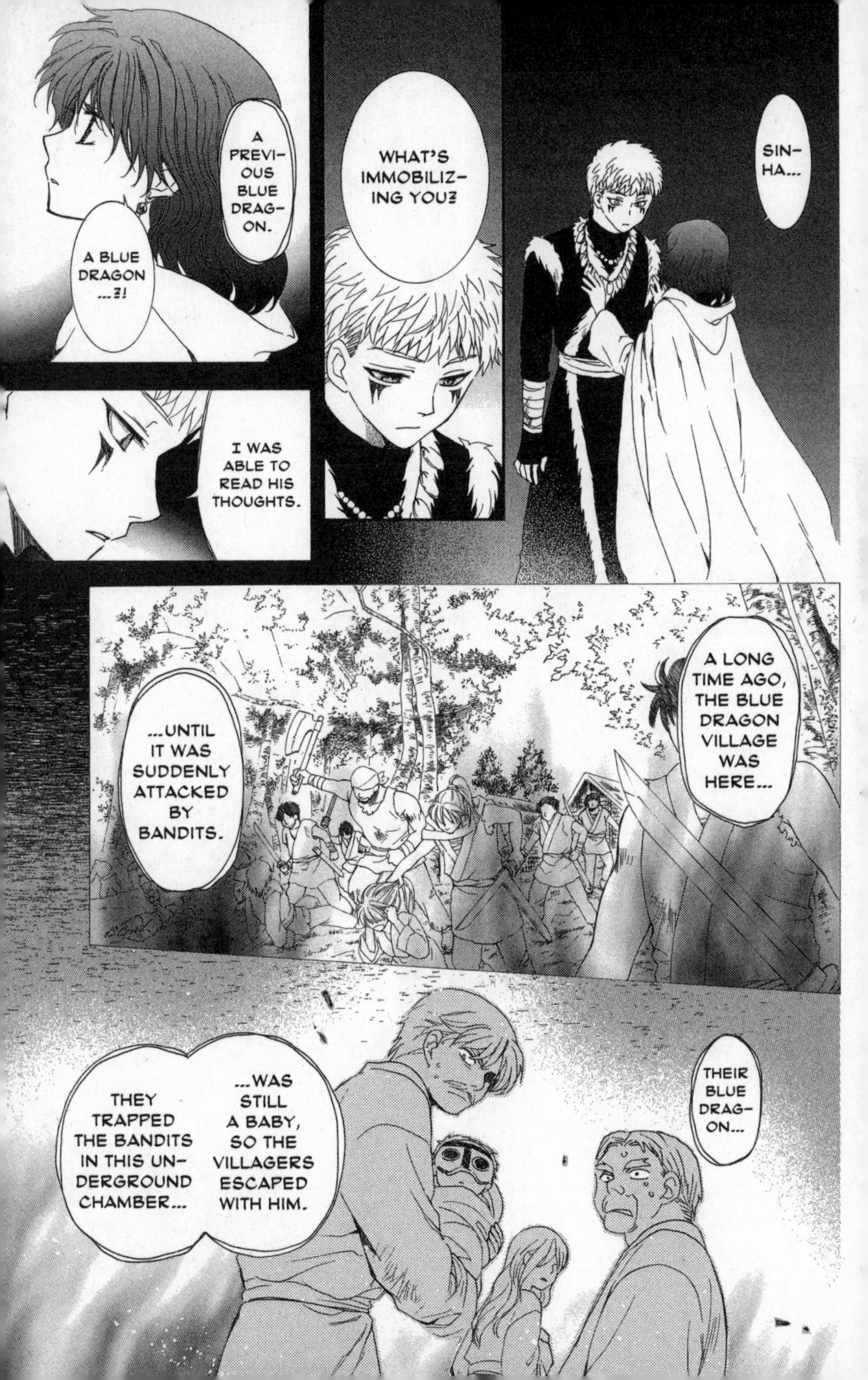
SIN-HA...
WHAT'S IMMOBILIZING YOU?
A PREVIOUS BLUE DRAGON.
A BLUE DRAGON ...?!
I WAS ABLE TO READ HIS THOUGHTS.
A LONG TIME AGO, THE BLUE DRAGON VILLAGE WAS HERE...
...UNTIL IT WAS SUDDENLY ATTACKED BY BANDITS.
THEIR BLUE DRAGON...
...WAS STILL A BABY, SO THE VILLAGERS ESCAPED WITH HIM.
THEY TRAPPED THE BANDITS IN THIS UNDERGROUND CHAMBER...

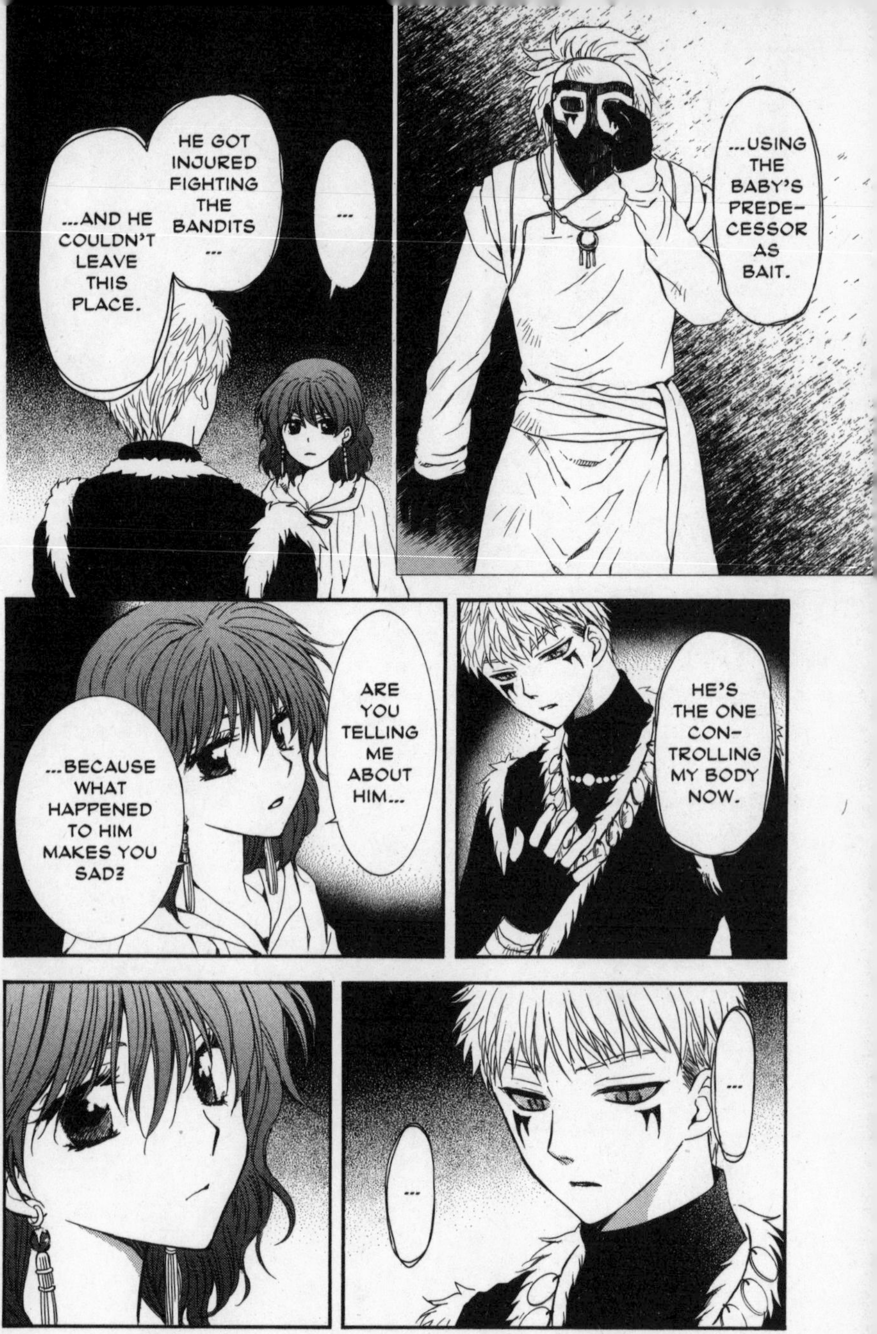
...USING THE BABY'S PREDECESSOR AS BAIT.
...
HE GOT INJURED FIGHTING THE BANDITS ...
...AND HE COULDN'T LEAVE THIS PLACE.
HE'S THE ONE CONTROLLING MY BODY NOW.
ARE YOU TELLING ME ABOUT HIM...
...BECAUSE WHAT HAPPENED TO HIM MAKES YOU SAD?
...
...

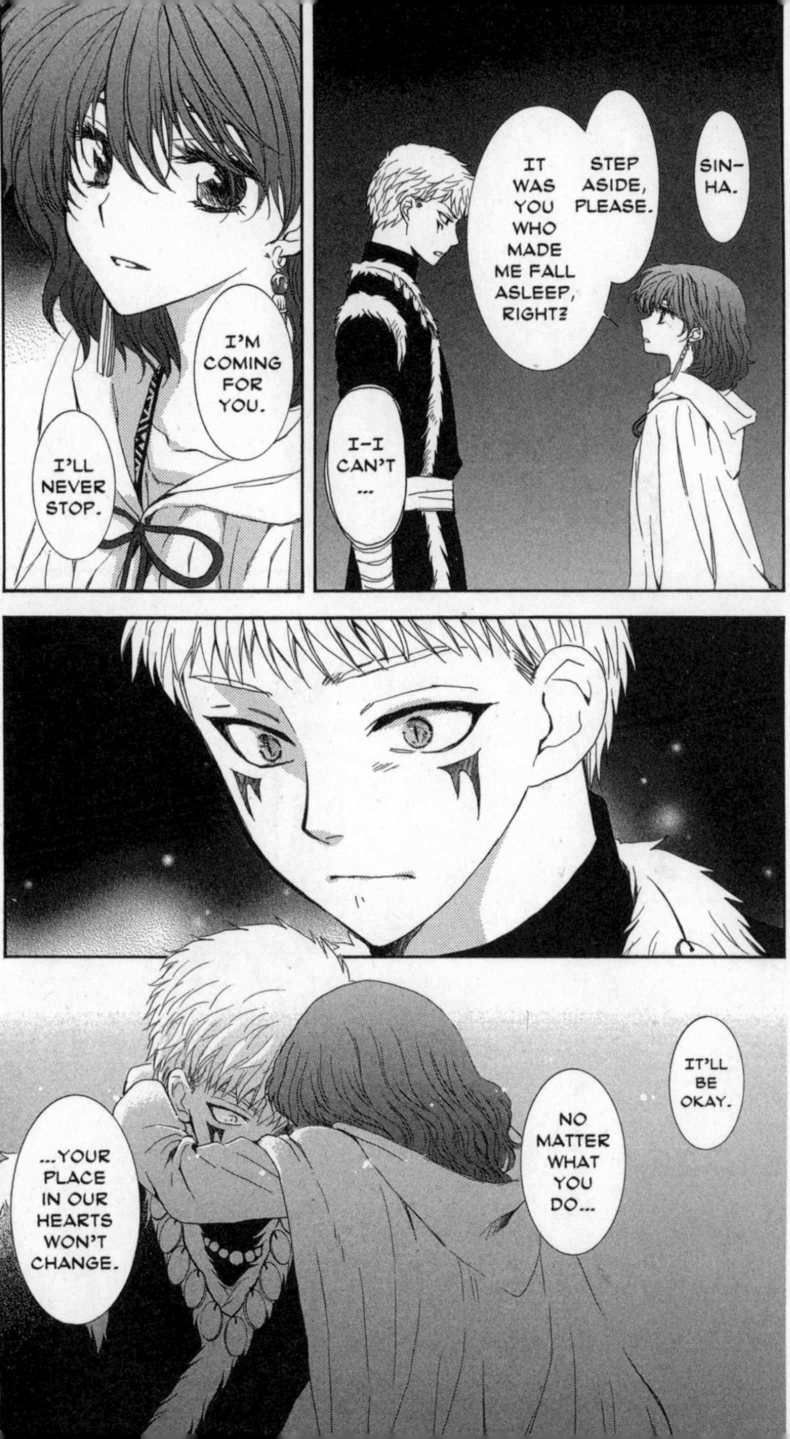
SIN-HA.
STEP ASIDE, PLEASE.
IT WAS YOU WHO MADE ME FALL ASLEEP, RIGHT?
I-I CAN'T...
I'M COMING FOR YOU.
I'LL NEVER STOP.
IT'LL BE OKAY.
NO MATTER WHAT YOU DO...
...YOUR PLACE IN OUR HEARTS WON'T CHANGE.

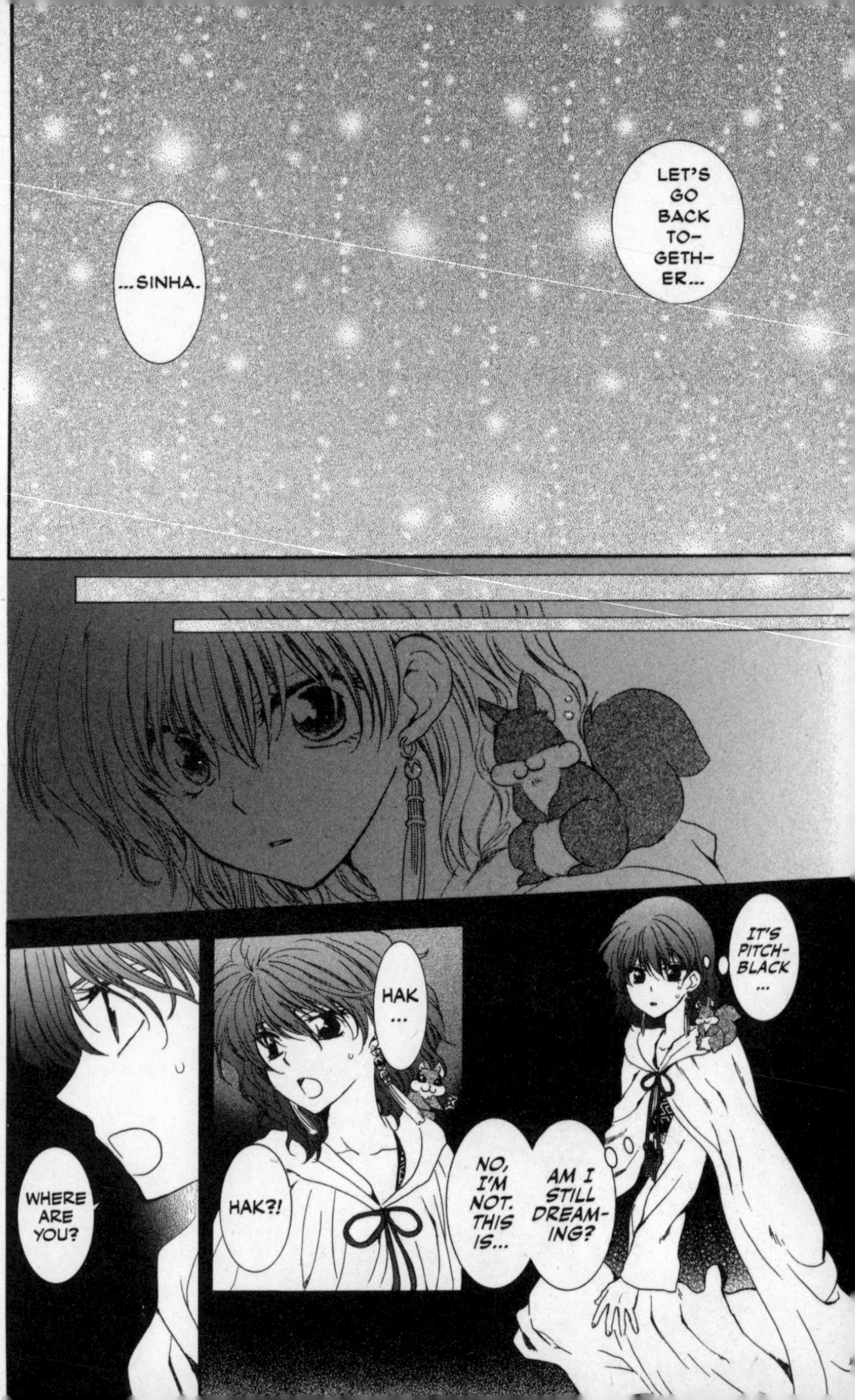
LET'S GO BACK TO-GETH-ER...
...SINHA.
IT'S PITCH-BLACK...
AM I STILL DREAM-ING?
NO, I'M NOT. THIS IS...
HAK...
HAK?!
WHERE ARE YOU?

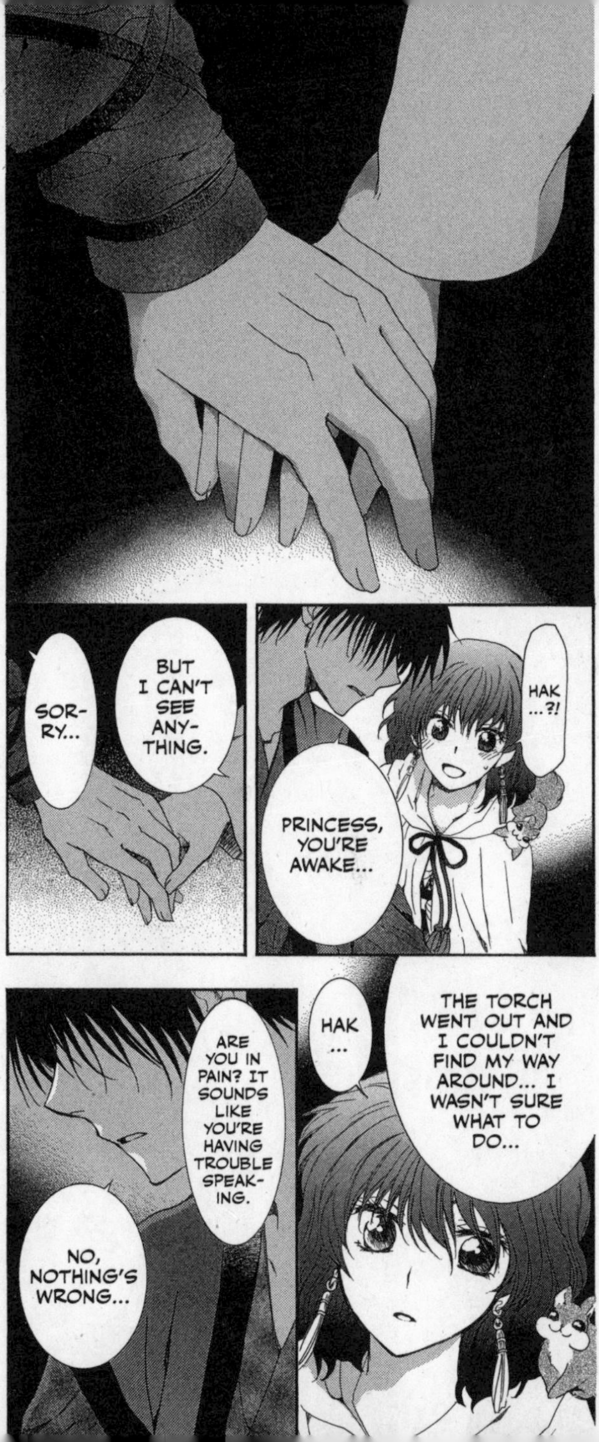
HAK ...?!
PRINCESS, YOU'RE AWAKE...
BUT I CAN'T SEE ANYTHING.
SOR-RY...
THE TORCH WENT OUT AND I COULDN'T FIND MY WAY AROUND... I WASN'T SURE WHAT TO DO...
HAK ...
ARE YOU IN PAIN? IT SOUNDS LIKE YOU'RE HAVING TROUBLE SPEAK-ING.
NO, NOTHING'S WRONG...

When I was offered the chance to create a drama CD for this volume, I didn't have a suitable short story, so I went with a short arc instead and decided on "The Blue Forest." It spanned three chapters, and since it was going to be a CD, I had script deadlines and dubbing sessions... My schedule was so packed that I had to fax the storyboard for part 3 to the writers so they could work on the script. I'm really sorry that things were so chaotic...

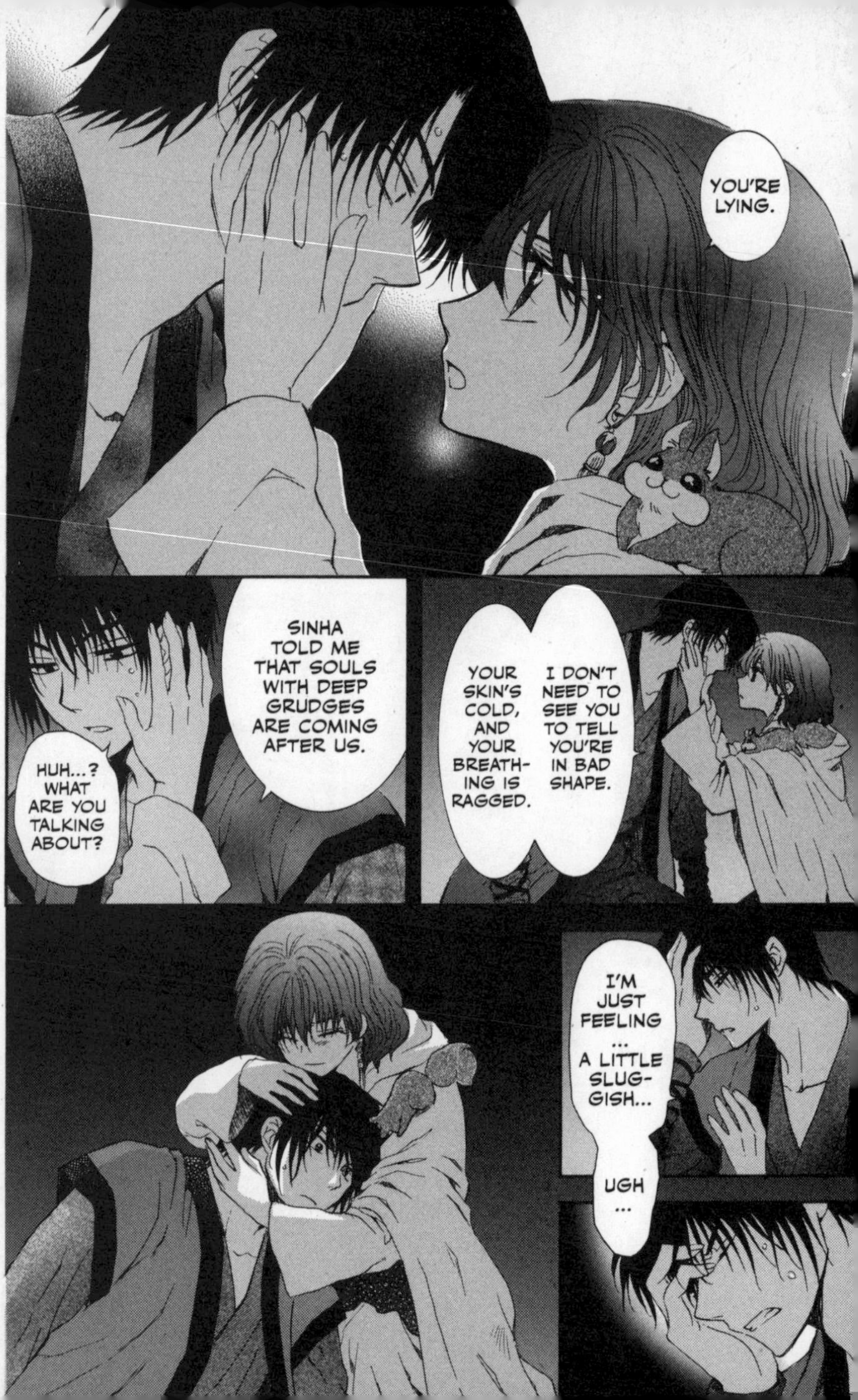
YOU'RE LYING.
I DON'T NEED TO SEE YOU TO TELL YOU'RE IN BAD SHAPE.
YOUR SKIN'S COLD, AND YOUR BREATHING IS RAGGED.
SINHA TOLD ME THAT SOULS WITH DEEP GRUDGES ARE COMING AFTER US.
HUH...? WHAT ARE YOU TALKING ABOUT?
I'M JUST FEELING ... A LITTLE SLUGGISH...
UGH ...

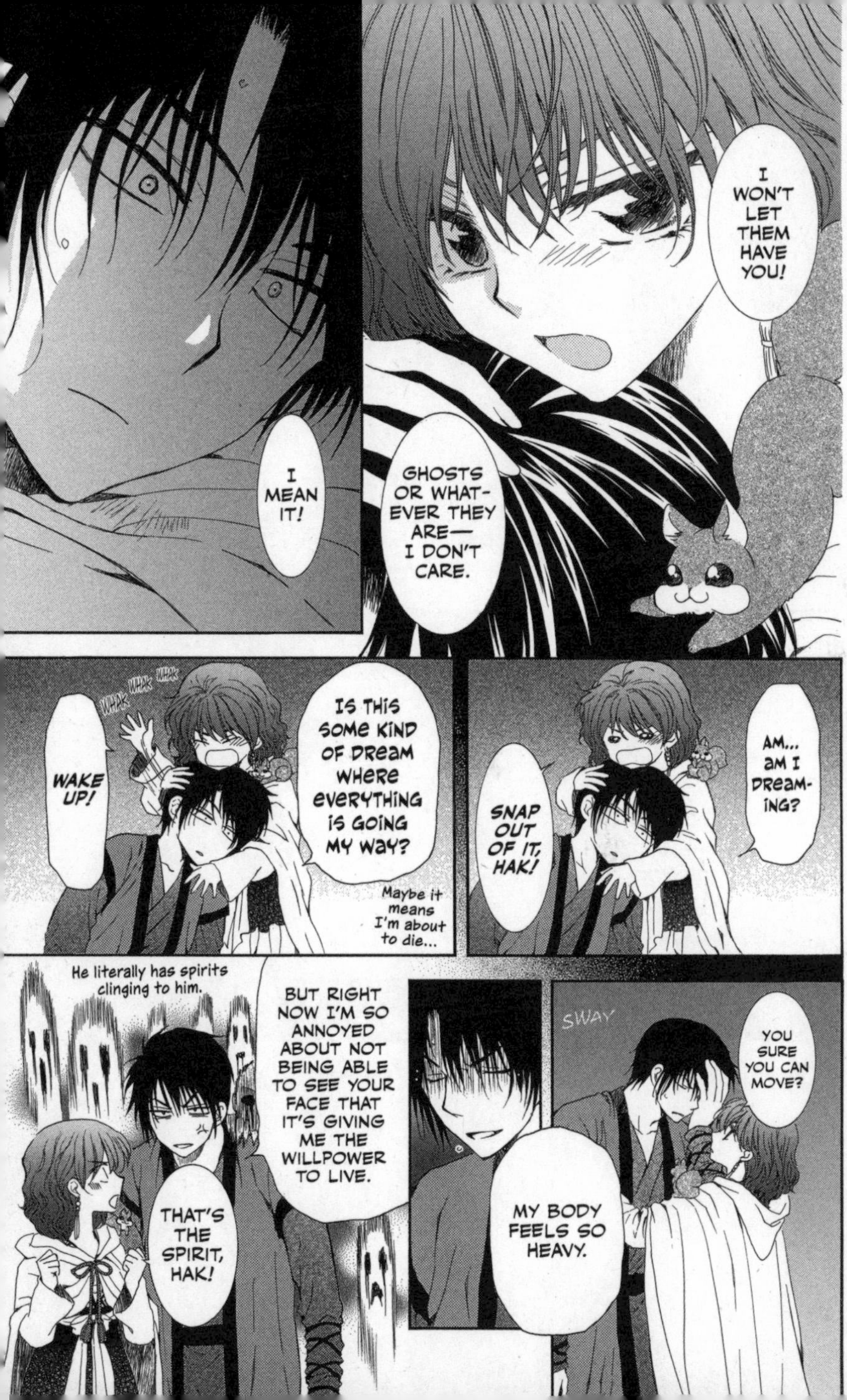
I WON'T LET THEM HAVE YOU!
GHOSTS OR WHAT-EVER THEY ARE— I DON'T CARE.
I MEAN IT!
AM... AM I DREAMING?
SNAP OUT OF IT, HAK!
IS THIS SOME KIND OF DREAM WHERE EVERYTHING IS GOING MY WAY?
WHAK WHAK WHAK
WAKE UP!
Maybe it means I'm about to die...
SWAY
YOU SURE YOU CAN MOVE?
MY BODY FEELS SO HEAVY.
BUT RIGHT NOW I'M SO ANNOYED ABOUT NOT BEING ABLE TO SEE YOUR FACE THAT IT'S GIVING ME THE WILLPOWER TO LIVE.
He literally has spirits clinging to him.
THAT'S THE SPIRIT, HAK!

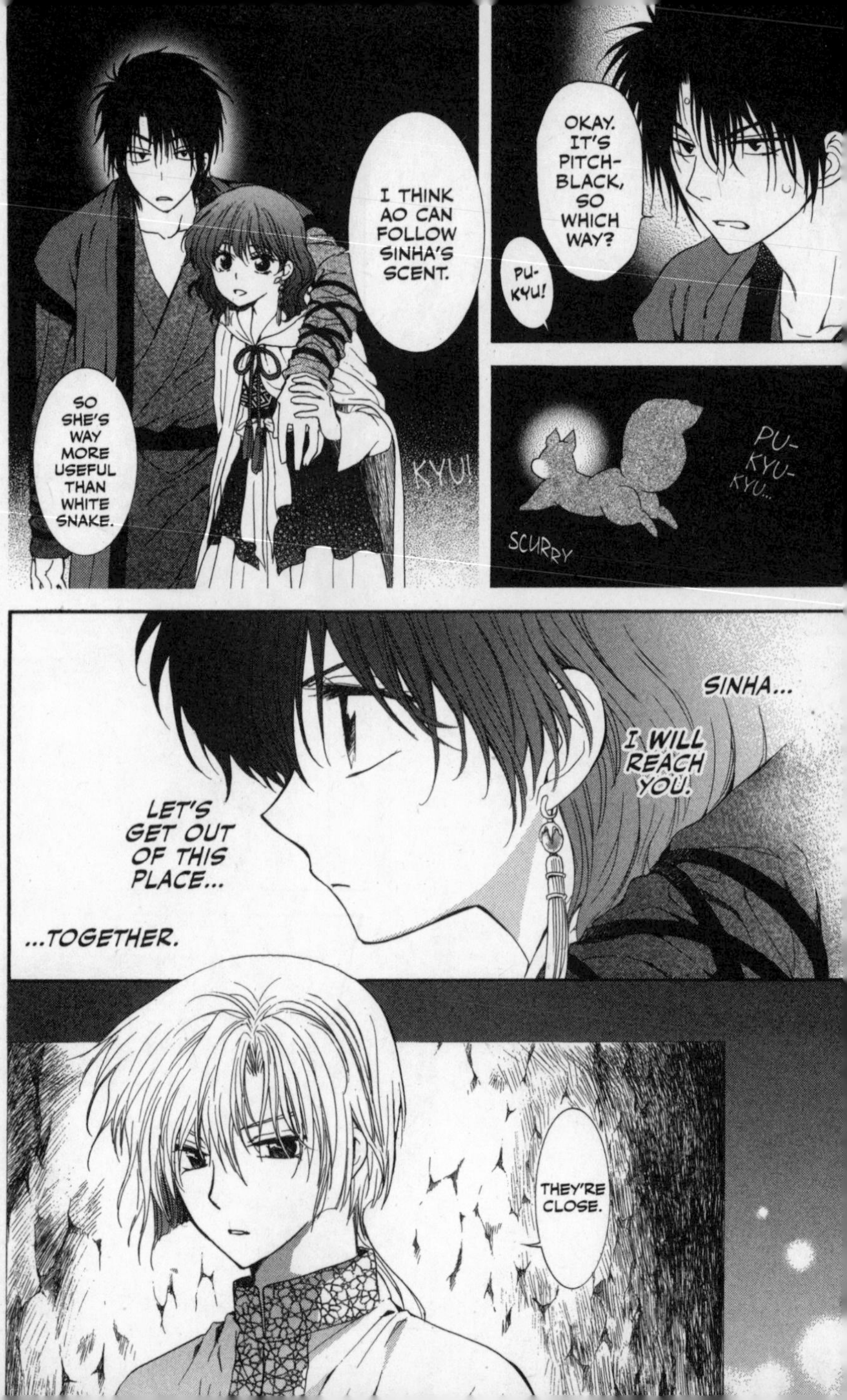
OKAY. IT'S PITCH-BLACK, SO WHICH WAY?
PU-KYU!
PU-KYU-KYU...
SCURRY
I THINK AO CAN FOLLOW SINHA'S SCENT.
SO SHE'S WAY MORE USEFUL THAN WHITE SNAKE.
KYU!
SINHA...
I WILL REACH YOU.
LET'S GET OUT OF THIS PLACE...
...TOGETHER.
THEY'RE CLOSE.

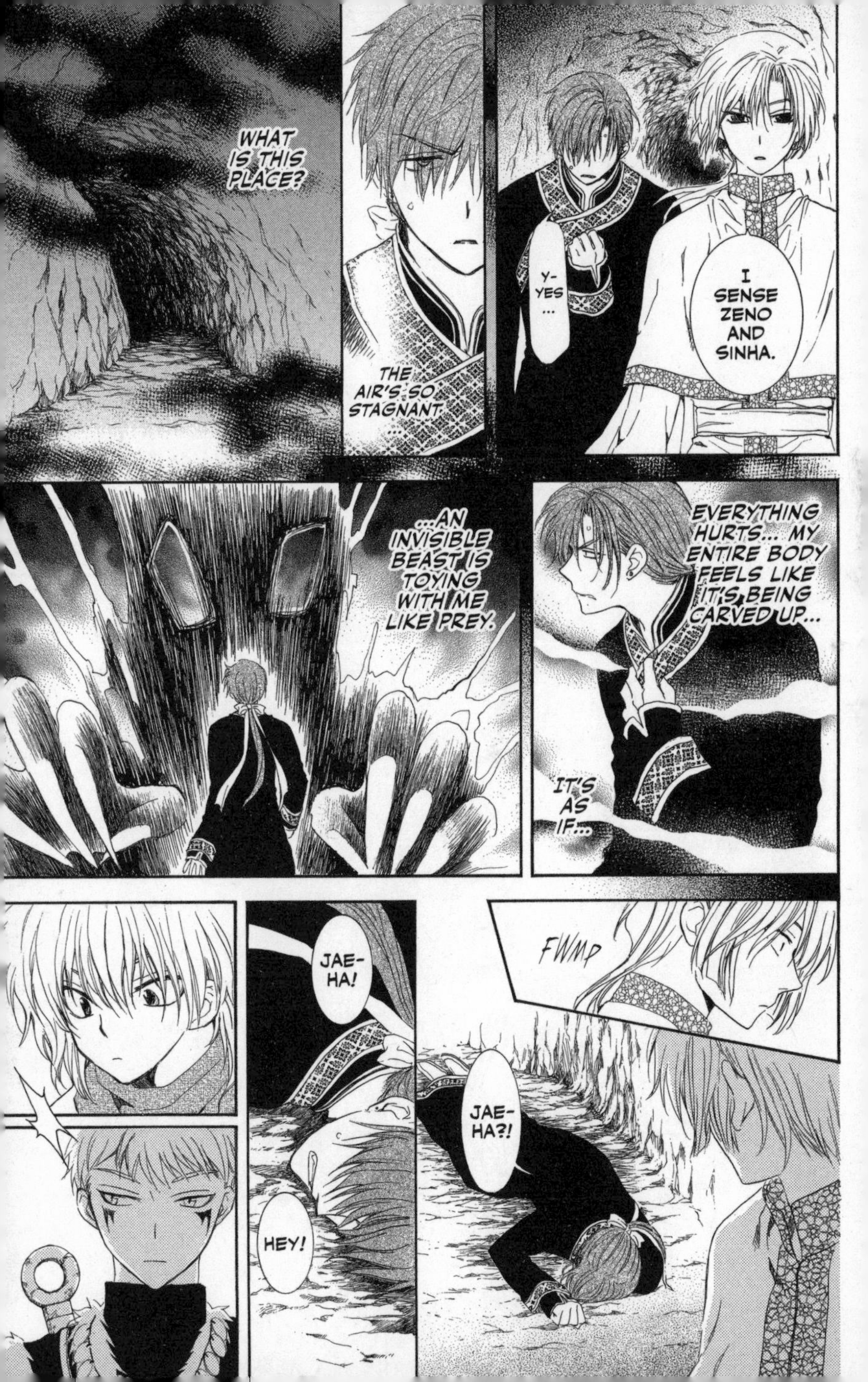
I SENSE ZENO AND SINHA.
Y-YES...
THE AIR'S SO STAGNANT...
WHAT IS THIS PLACE?
EVERYTHING HURTS... MY ENTIRE BODY FEELS LIKE IT'S BEING CARVED UP...
IT'S AS IF...
...AN INVISIBLE BEAST IS TOYING WITH ME LIKE PREY.
FWMP
JAE-HA!
JAE-HA?!
HEY!

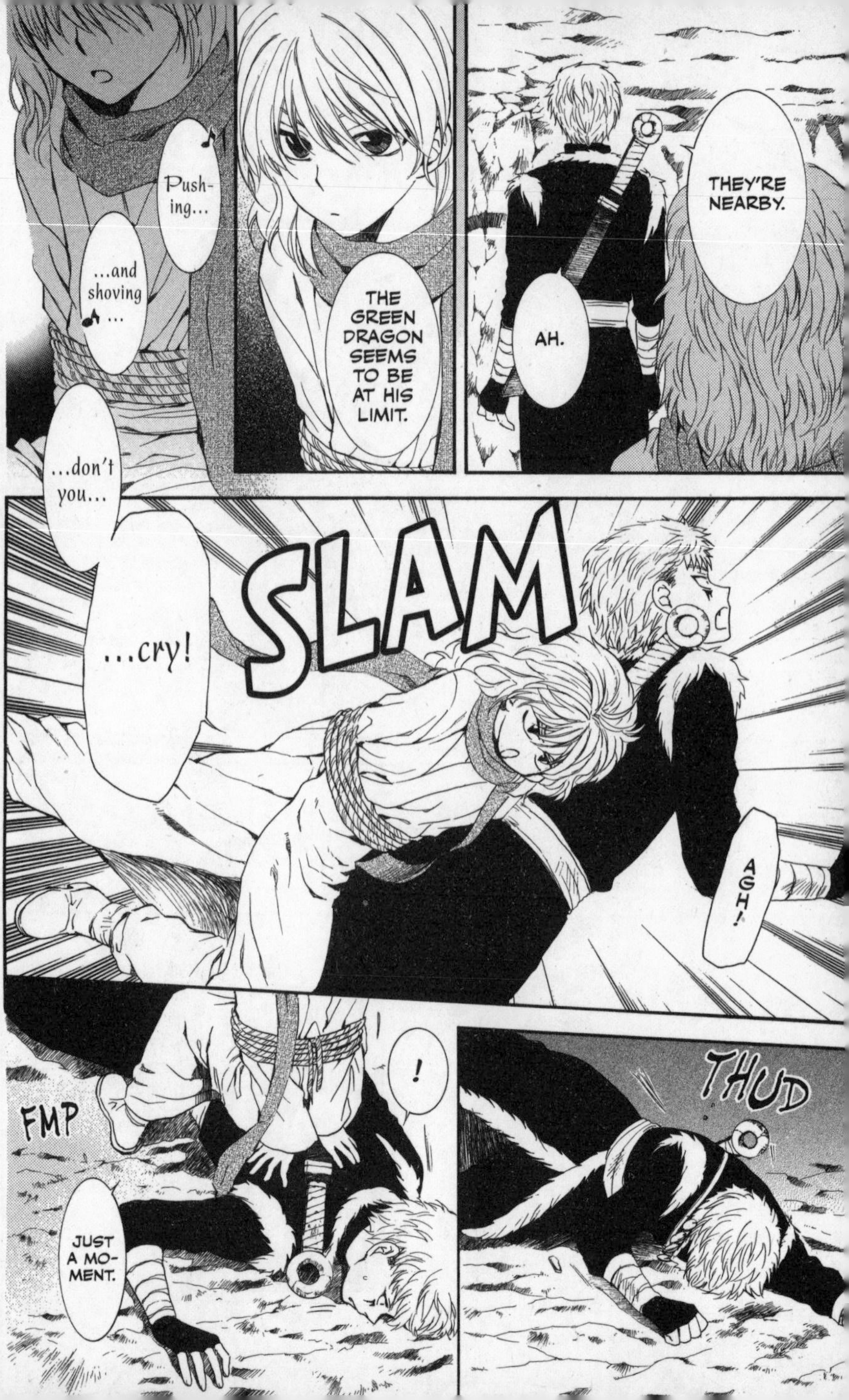
THEY'RE NEARBY.
AH.
THE GREEN DRAGON SEEMS TO BE AT HIS LIMIT.
Push-ing...
...and shoving...
...don't you...
...cry!
SLAM
AGH!
THUD
!
FMP
JUST A MO-MENT.

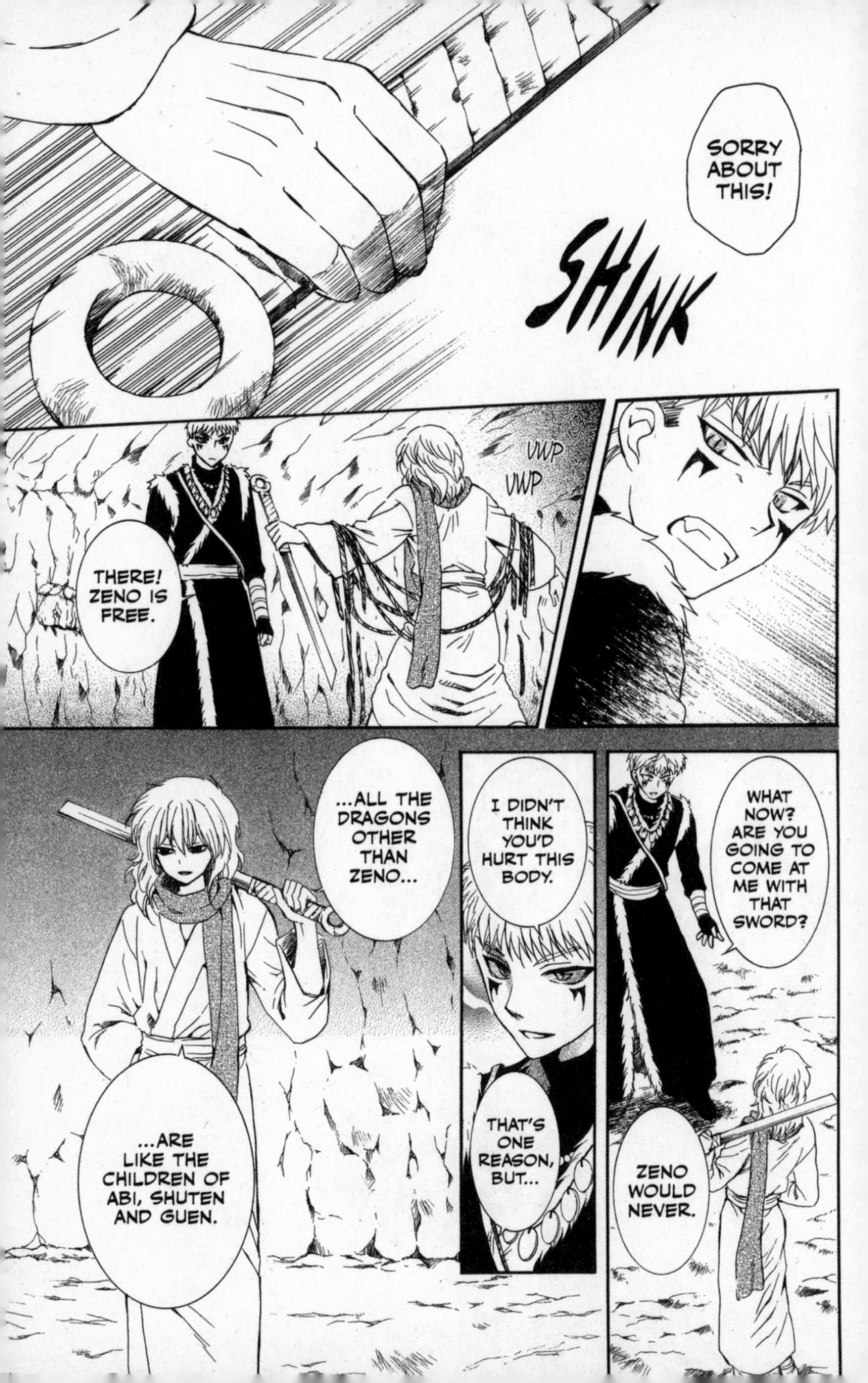
SORRY ABOUT THIS!
SHINK
UWP UWP
THERE! ZENO IS FREE.
WHAT NOW? ARE YOU GOING TO COME AT ME WITH THAT SWORD?
ZENO WOULD NEVER.
I DIDN'T THINK YOU'D HURT THIS BODY.
THAT'S ONE REASON, BUT...
...ALL THE DRAGONS OTHER THAN ZENO...
...ARE LIKE THE CHILDREN OF ABI, SHUTEN AND GUEN.

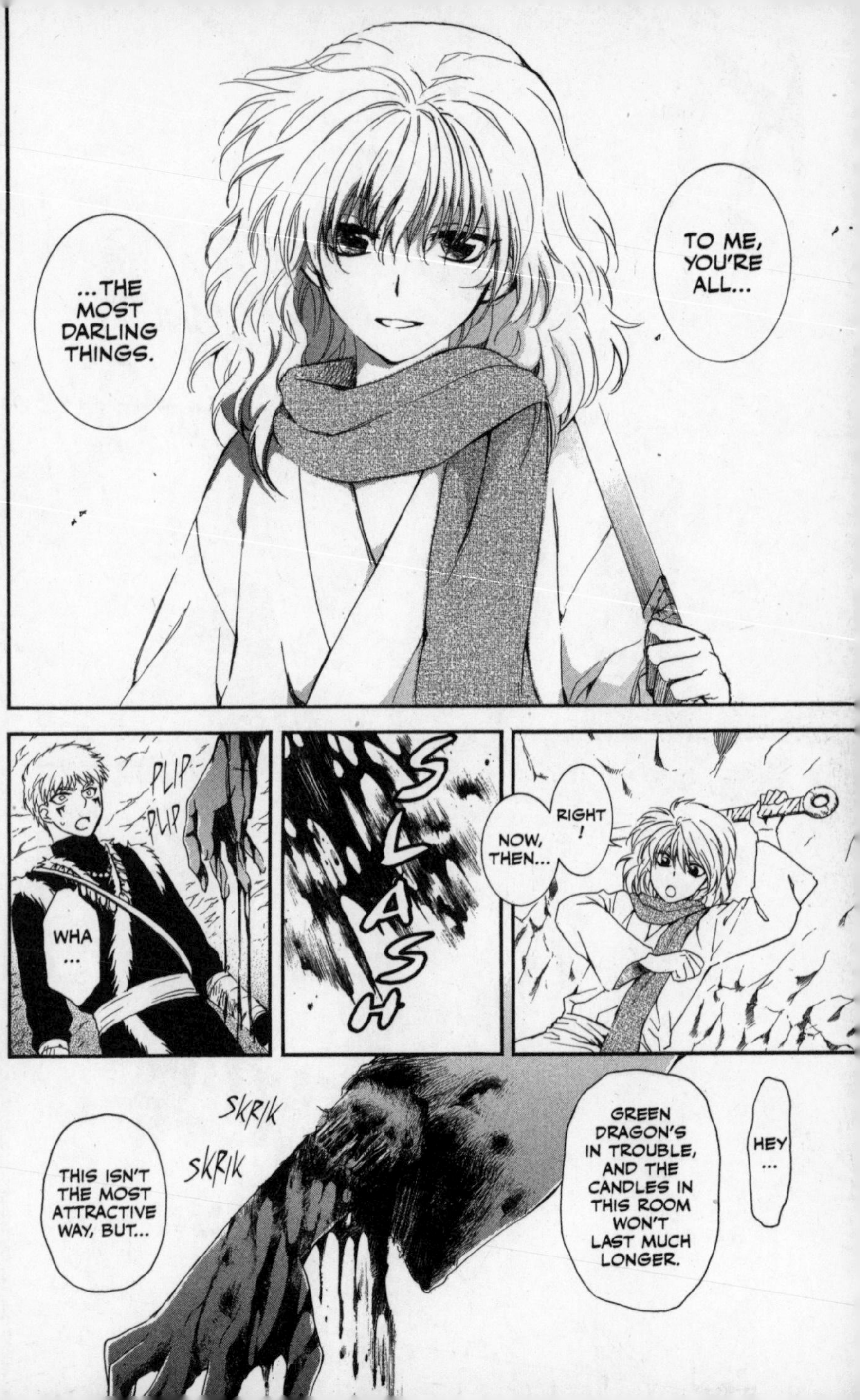
TO ME, YOU'RE ALL...
...THE MOST DARLING THINGS.
RIGHT!
NOW, THEN...
SLASH
PLIP PLIP
WHA...
HEY...
GREEN DRAGON'S IN TROUBLE, AND THE CANDLES IN THIS ROOM WON'T LAST MUCH LONGER.
SKRIK SKRIK
THIS ISN'T THE MOST ATTRACTIVE WAY, BUT...

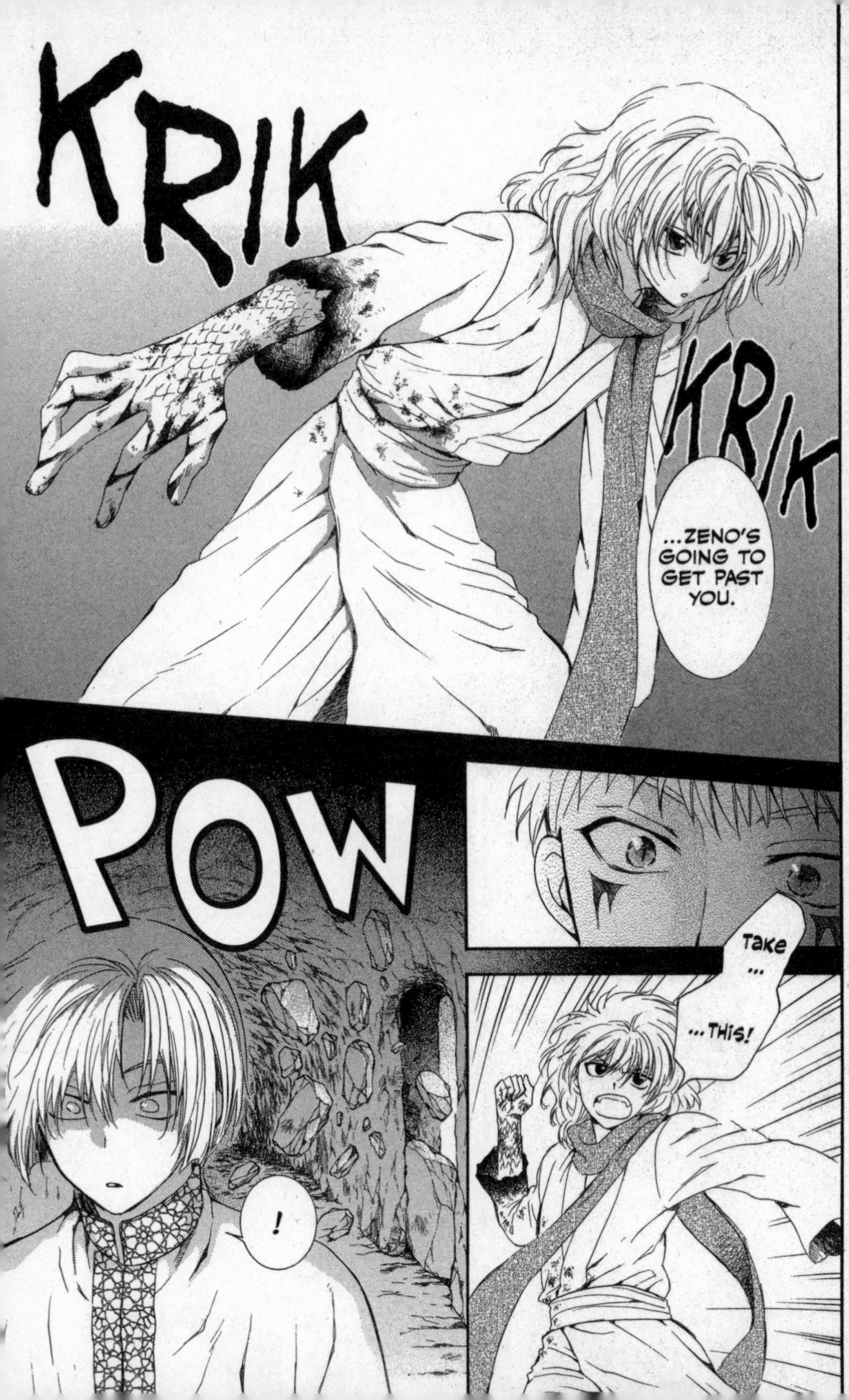
KRIK
KRIK
...ZENO'S GOING TO GET PAST YOU.
Take ...
...THIS!
POW
!

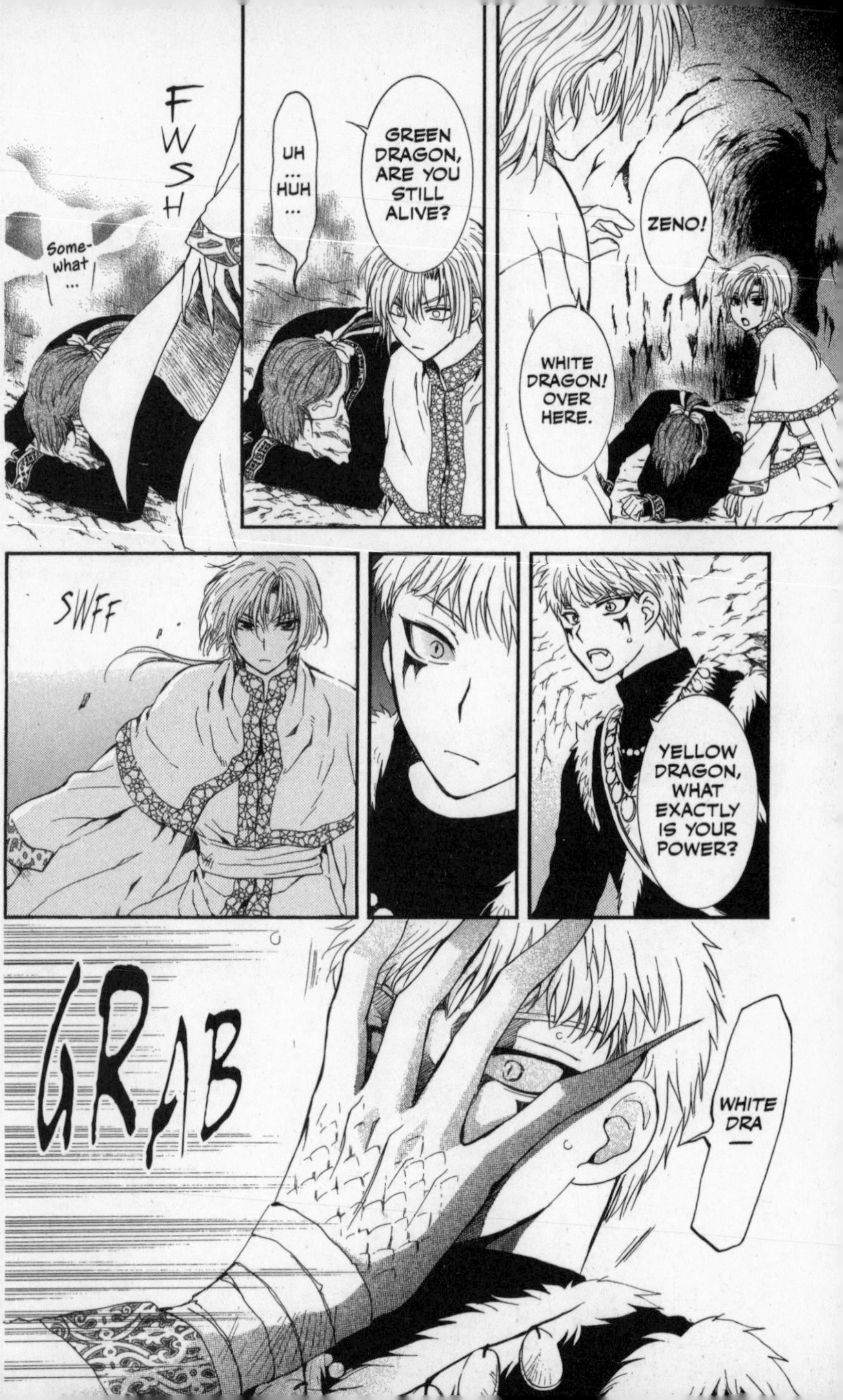
ZENO!
WHITE DRAGON! OVER HERE.
GREEN DRAGON, ARE YOU STILL ALIVE?
UH ... HUH ...
FWSH
Some-what ...
YELLOW DRAGON, WHAT EXACTLY IS YOUR POWER?
SWFF
WHITE DRA—
GRAB

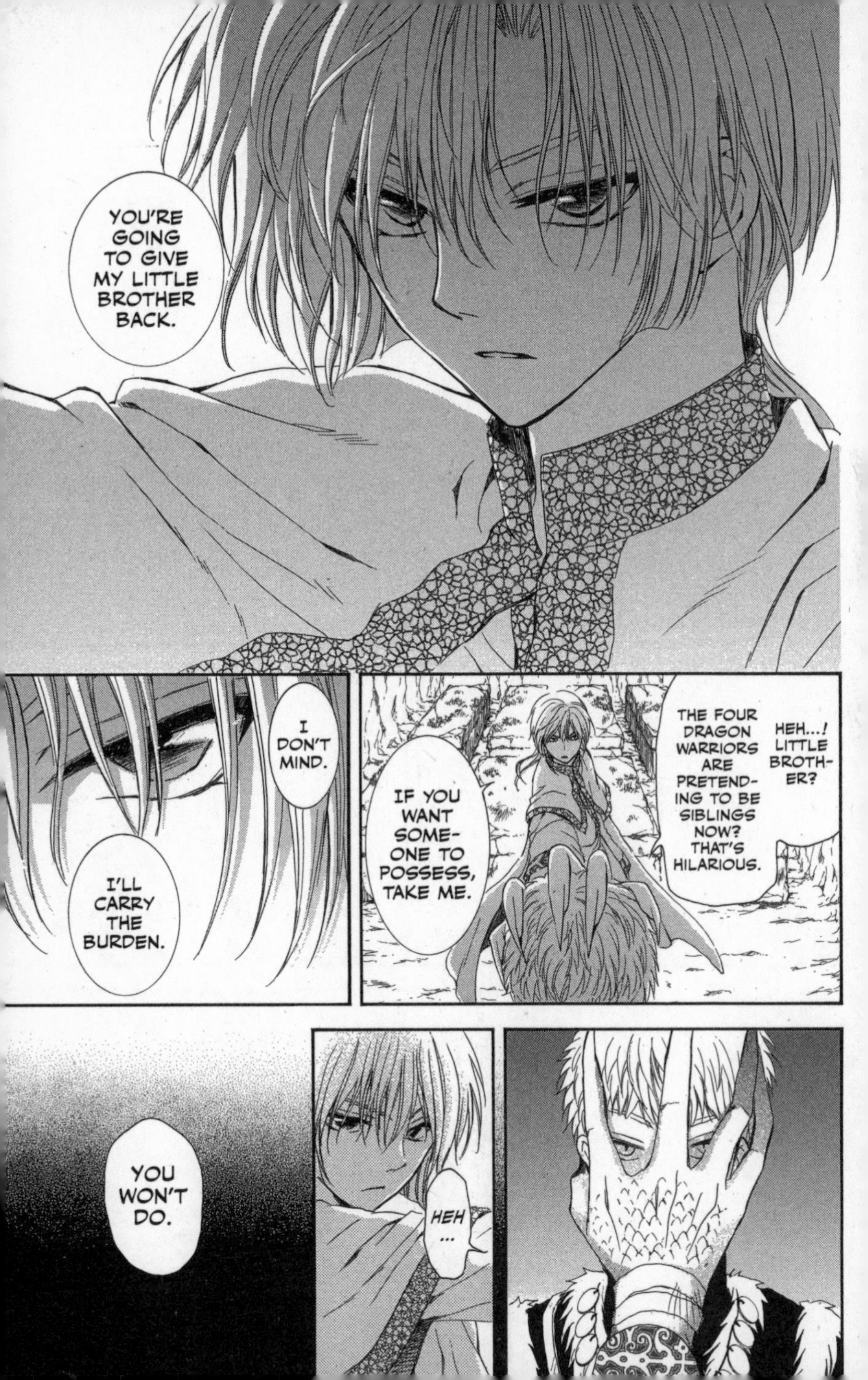
YOU'RE GOING TO GIVE MY LITTLE BROTHER BACK.
HEH...! LITTLE BROTH-ER?
THE FOUR DRAGON WARRIORS ARE PRETEND-ING TO BE SIBLINGS NOW? THAT'S HILARIOUS.
IF YOU WANT SOME-ONE TO POSSESS, TAKE ME.
I DON'T MIND.
I'LL CARRY THE BURDEN.
HEH ...
YOU WON'T DO.

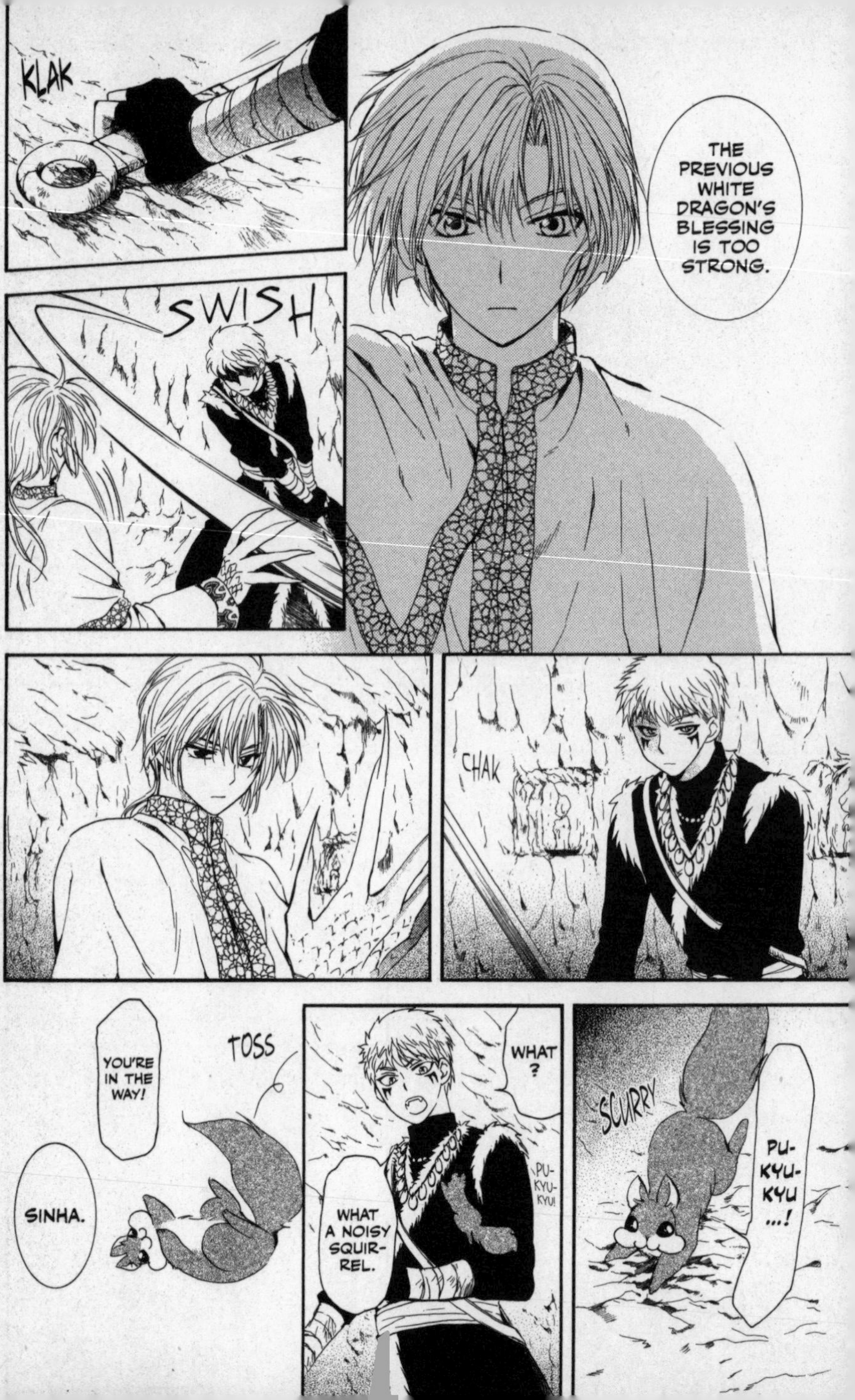
THE PREVIOUS WHITE DRAGON'S BLESSING IS TOO STRONG.
KLAK
SWISH
CHAK
SCURRY
PU-KYU-KYU...!
WHAT?
PU-KYU-KYU!
WHAT A NOISY SQUIR-REL.
TOSS
YOU'RE IN THE WAY!
SINHA.

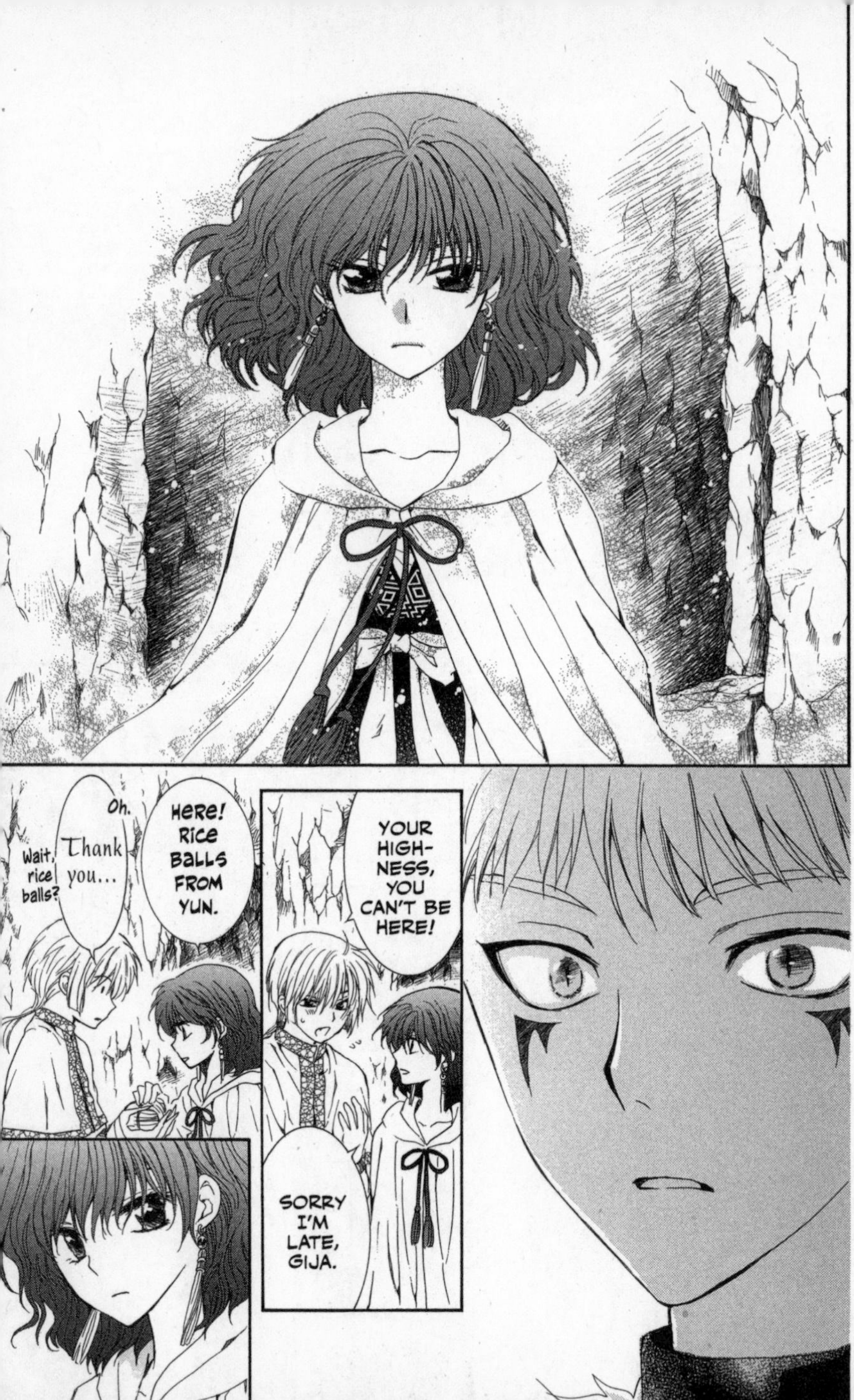
YOUR HIGHNESS, YOU CAN'T BE HERE!
SORRY I'M LATE, GIJA.
HERE! RICE BALLS FROM YUN.
Oh. Thank you...
Wait, rice balls?

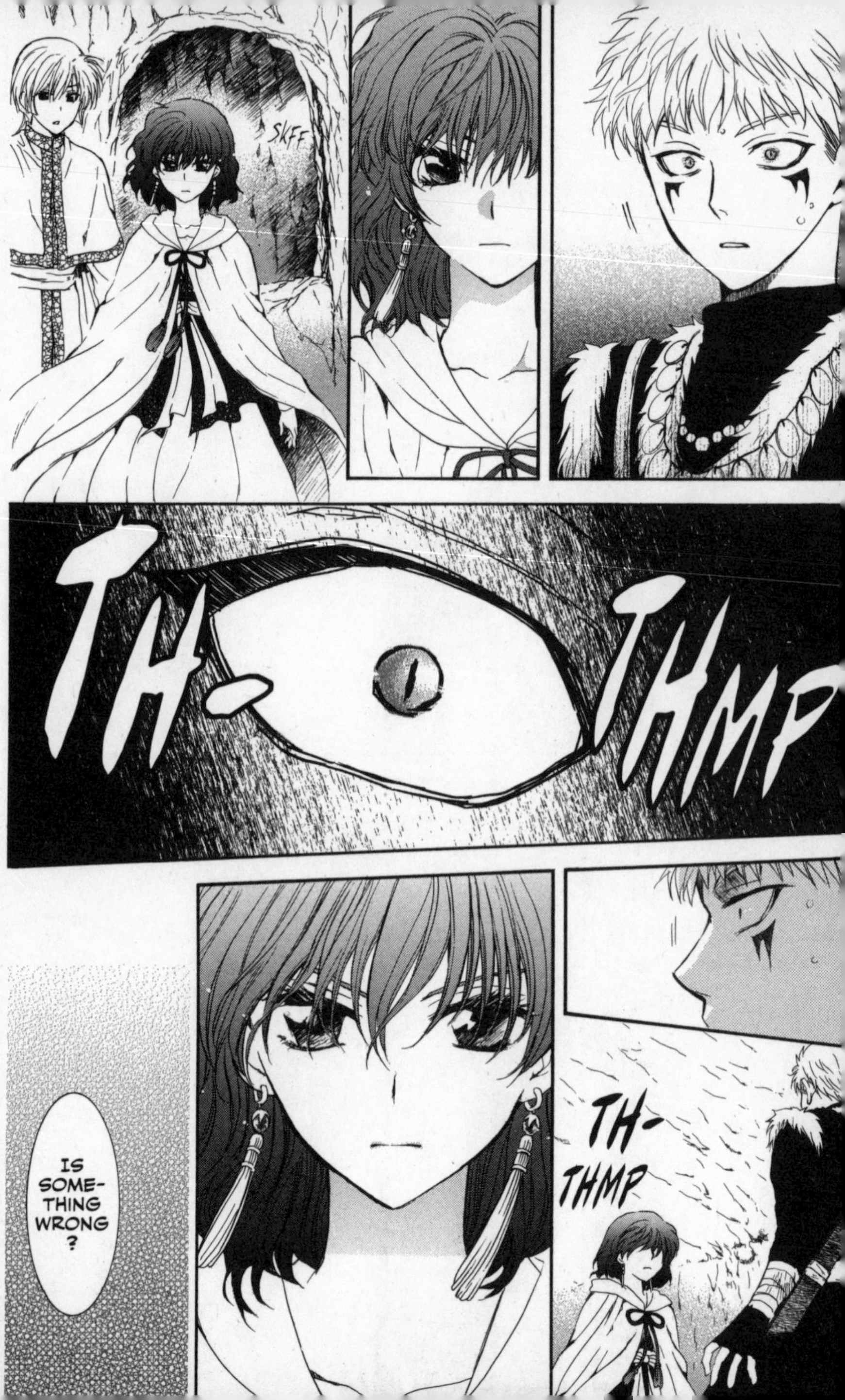
SKFF
TH-THMP
TH-THMP
IS SOMETHING WRONG?

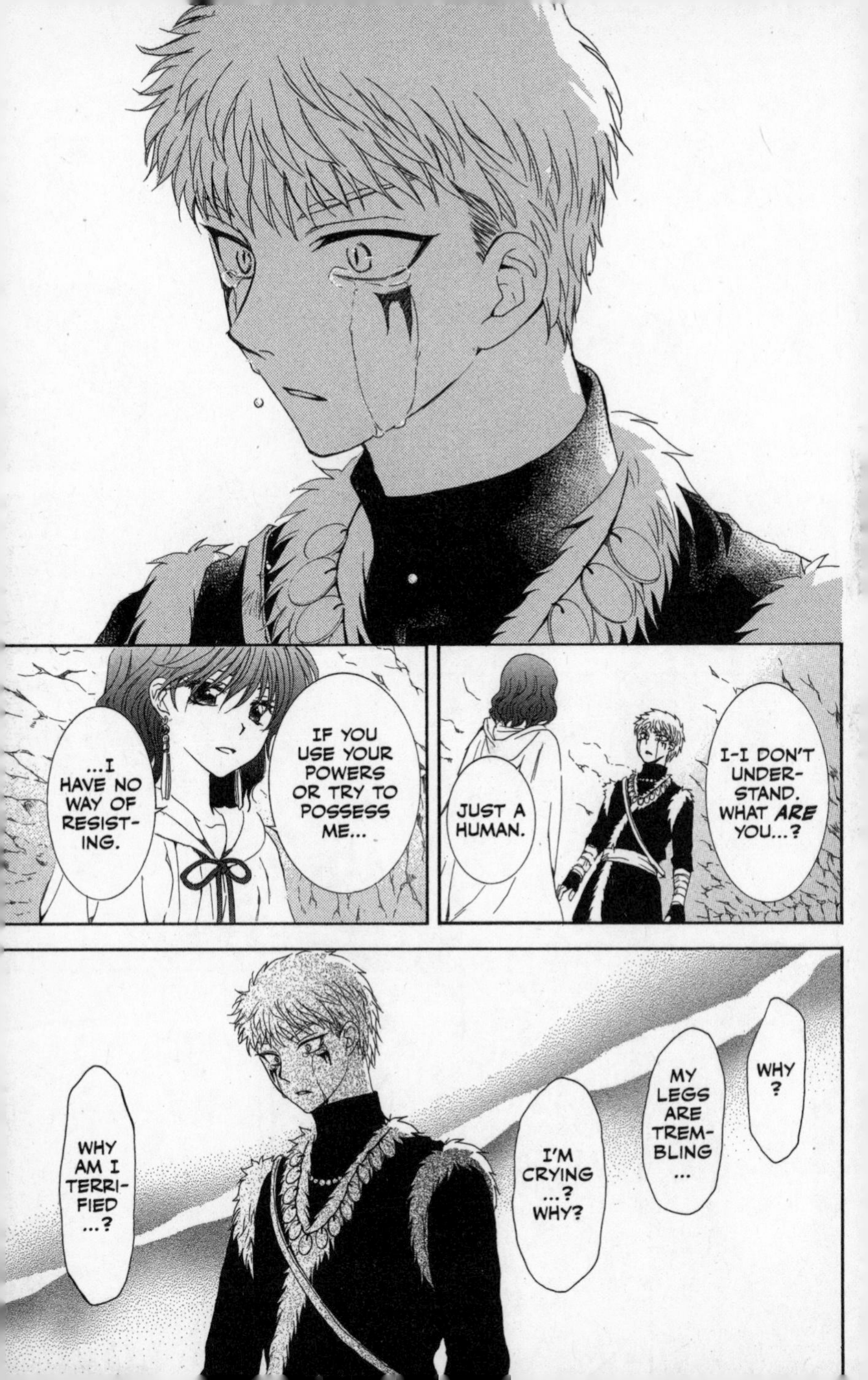
I-I DON'T UNDER-STAND. WHAT *ARE* YOU...?
JUST A HUMAN.
IF YOU USE YOUR POWERS OR TRY TO POSSESS ME...
...I HAVE NO WAY OF RESIST-ING.
WHY?
MY LEGS ARE TREM-BLING...
I'M CRYING...? WHY?
WHY AM I TERRI-FIED...?

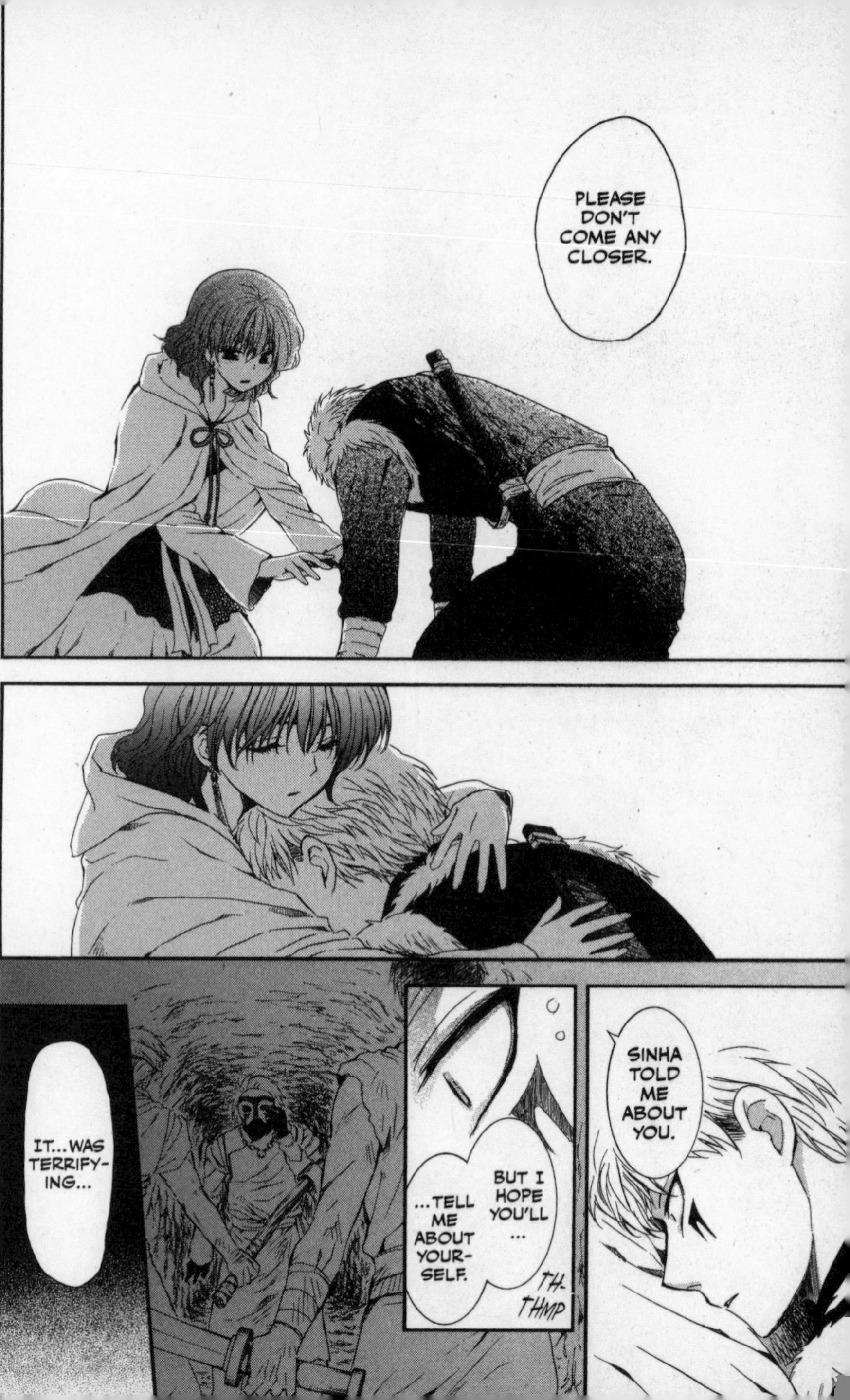
PLEASE DON'T COME ANY CLOSER.
SINHA TOLD ME ABOUT YOU.
BUT I HOPE YOU'LL ...
...TELL ME ABOUT YOUR-SELF.
TH-THMP
IT...WAS TERRIFY-ING...

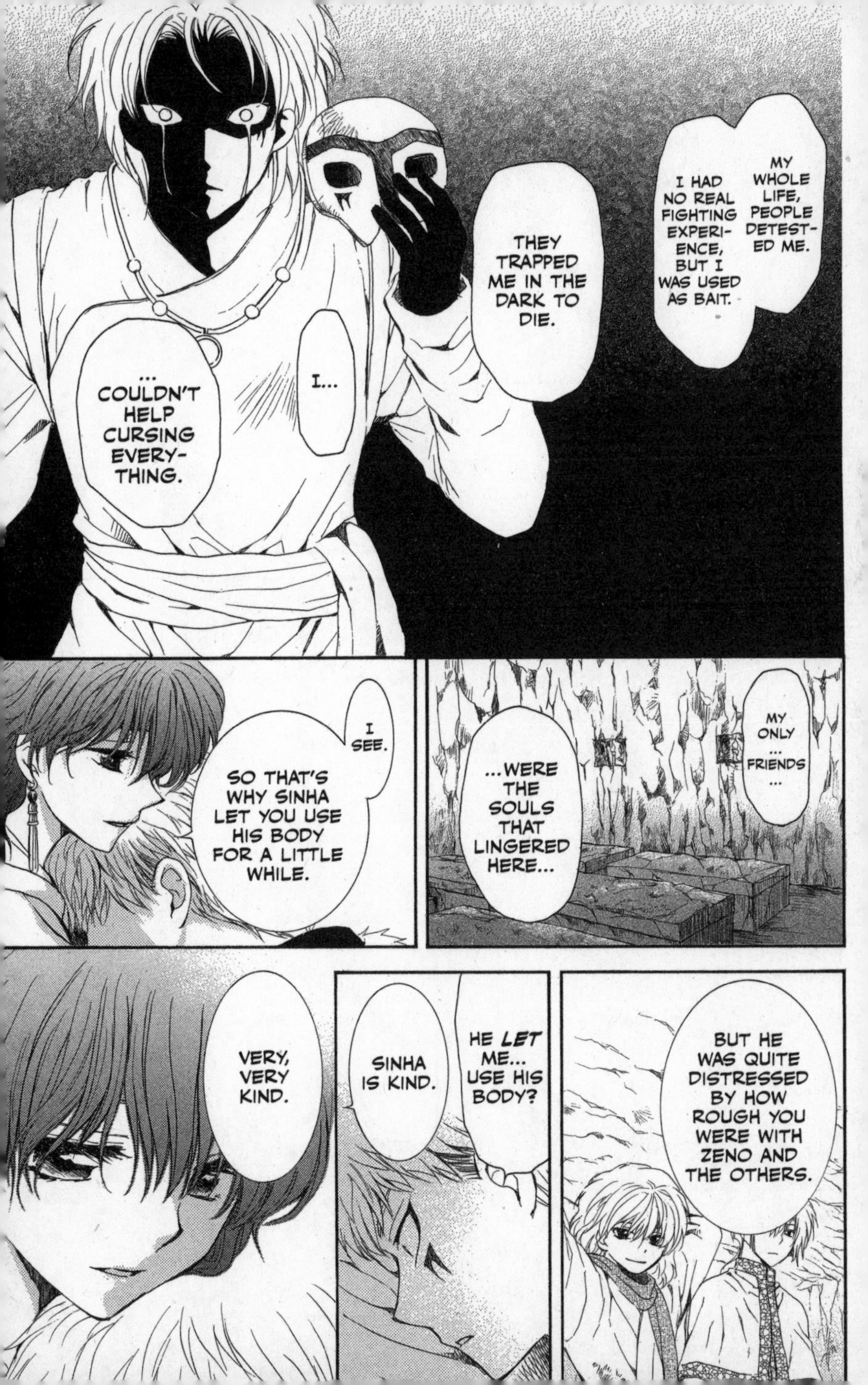
MY WHOLE LIFE, PEOPLE DETESTED ME.
I HAD NO REAL FIGHTING EXPERIENCE, BUT I WAS USED AS BAIT.
THEY TRAPPED ME IN THE DARK TO DIE.
I...
...COULDN'T HELP CURSING EVERYTHING.
MY ONLY ... FRIENDS ...
...WERE THE SOULS THAT LINGERED HERE...
I SEE.
SO THAT'S WHY SINHA LET YOU USE HIS BODY FOR A LITTLE WHILE.
BUT HE WAS QUITE DISTRESSED BY HOW ROUGH YOU WERE WITH ZENO AND THE OTHERS.
HE *LET* ME... USE HIS BODY?
SINHA IS KIND.
VERY, VERY KIND.

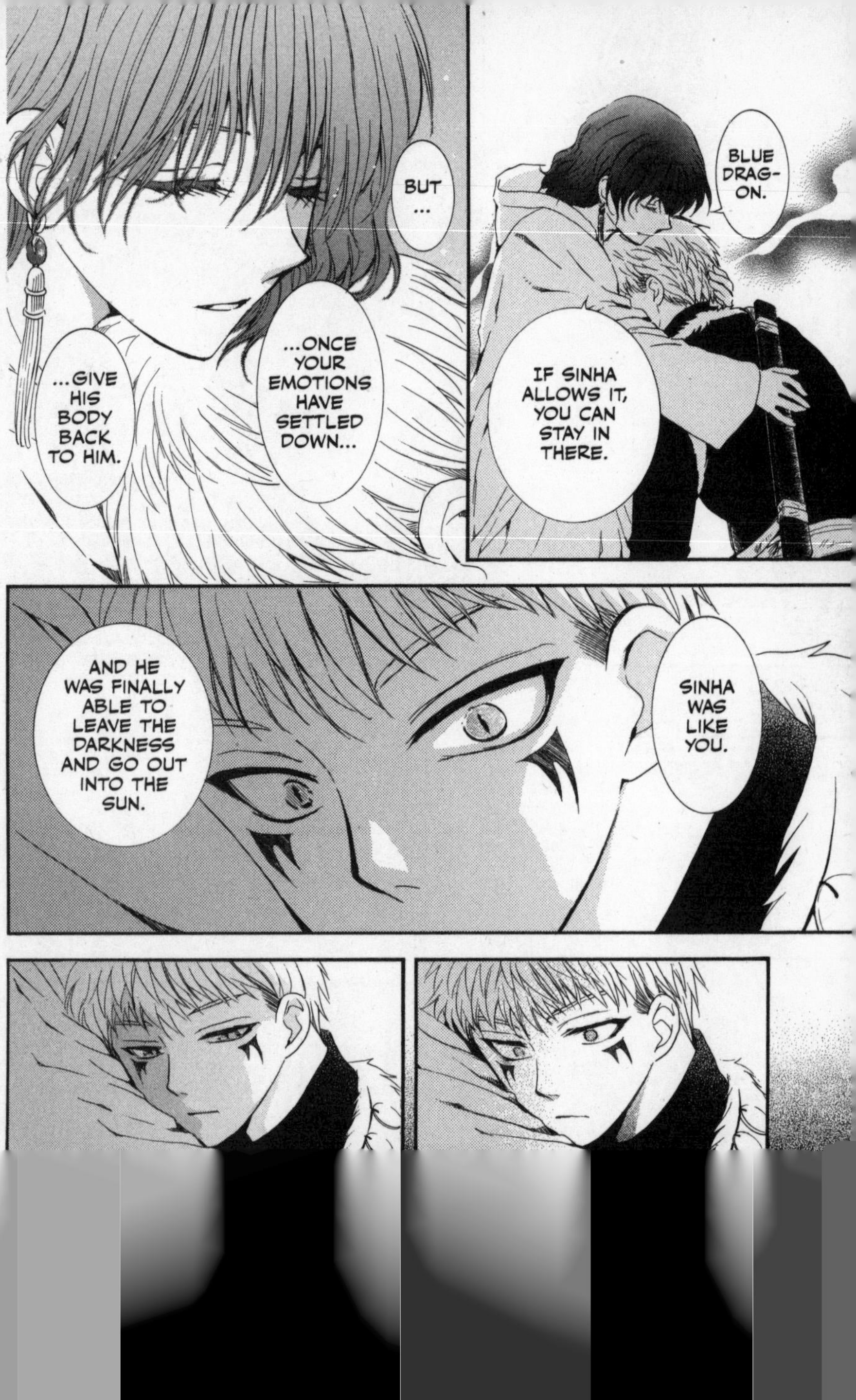
BLUE DRAGON.
IF SINHA ALLOWS IT, YOU CAN STAY IN THERE.
BUT...
...ONCE YOUR EMOTIONS HAVE SETTLED DOWN...
...GIVE HIS BODY BACK TO HIM.
SINHA WAS LIKE YOU.
AND HE WAS FINALLY ABLE TO LEAVE THE DARKNESS AND GO OUT INTO THE SUN.

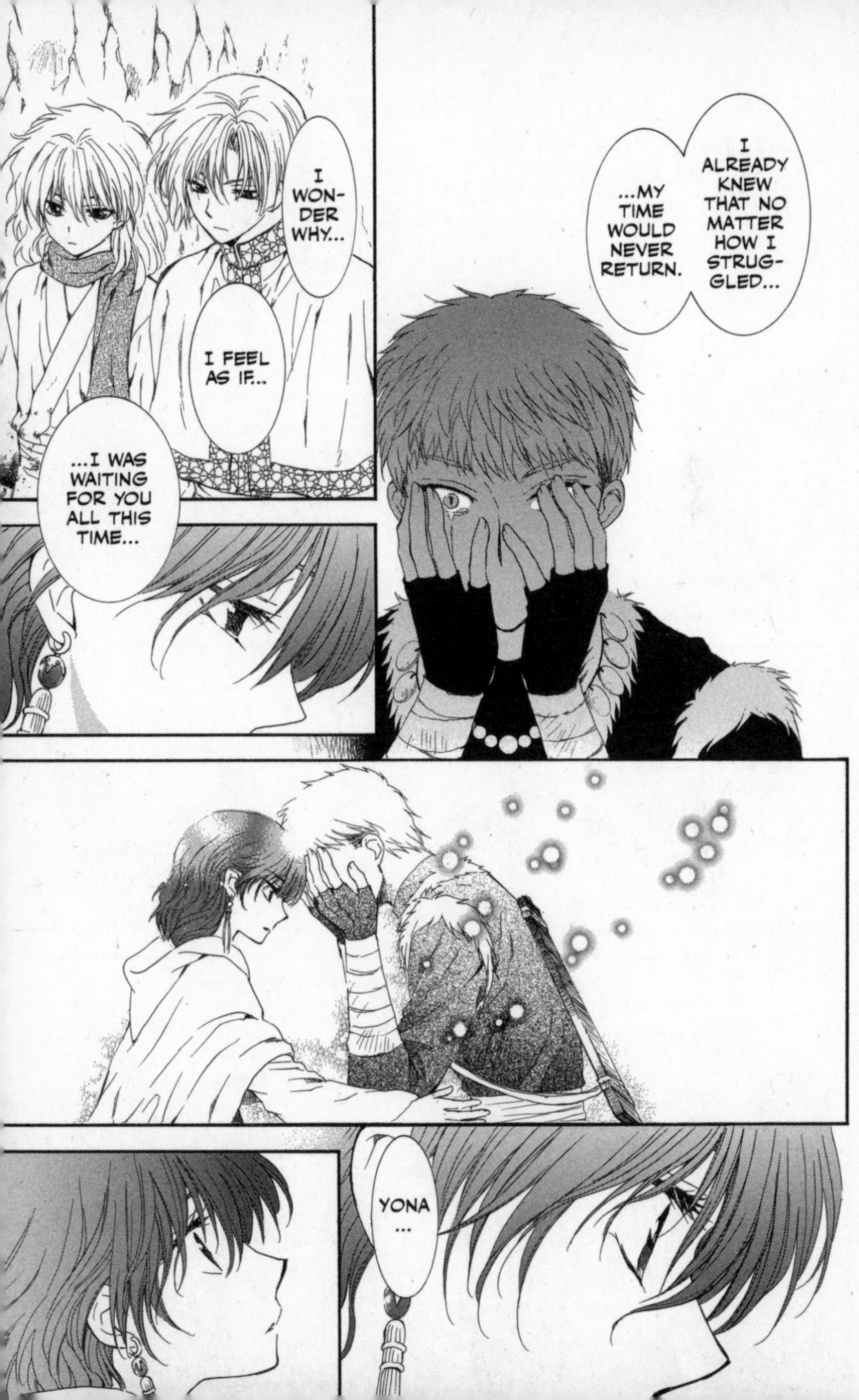
I ALREADY KNEW THAT NO MATTER HOW I STRUG-GLED...
...MY TIME WOULD NEVER RETURN.
I WON-DER WHY...
I FEEL AS IF...
...I WAS WAITING FOR YOU ALL THIS TIME...
YONA ...

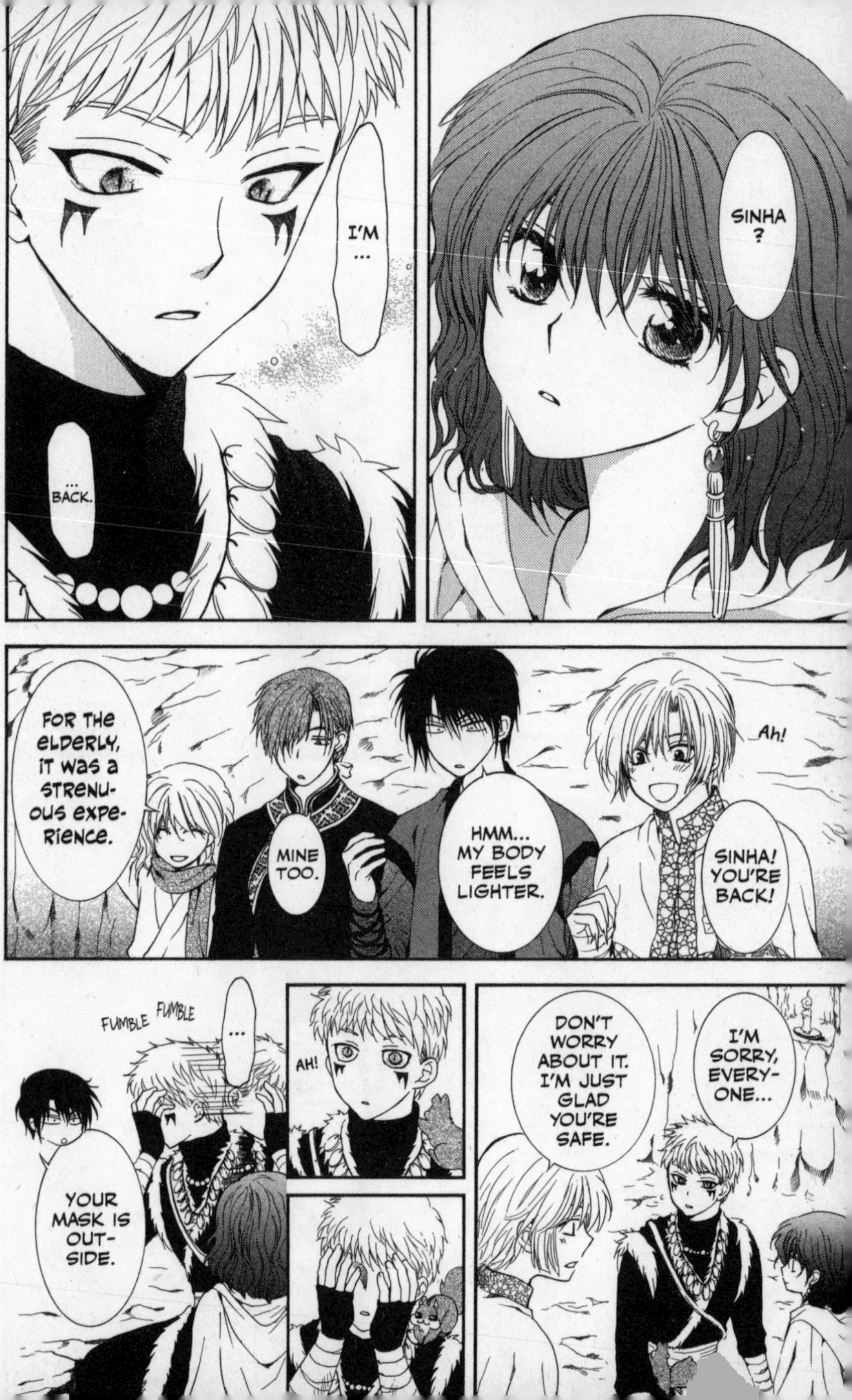
SINHA ?
I'M ...
... BACK.
Ah!
SINHA! YOU'RE BACK!
HMM... MY BODY FEELS LIGHTER.
MINE TOO.
FOR THE ELDERLY, IT WAS A STRENUOUS EXPERIENCE.
I'M SORRY, EVERYONE...
DON'T WORRY ABOUT IT. I'M JUST GLAD YOU'RE SAFE.
AH!
...
FUMBLE FUMBLE
YOUR MASK IS OUTSIDE.

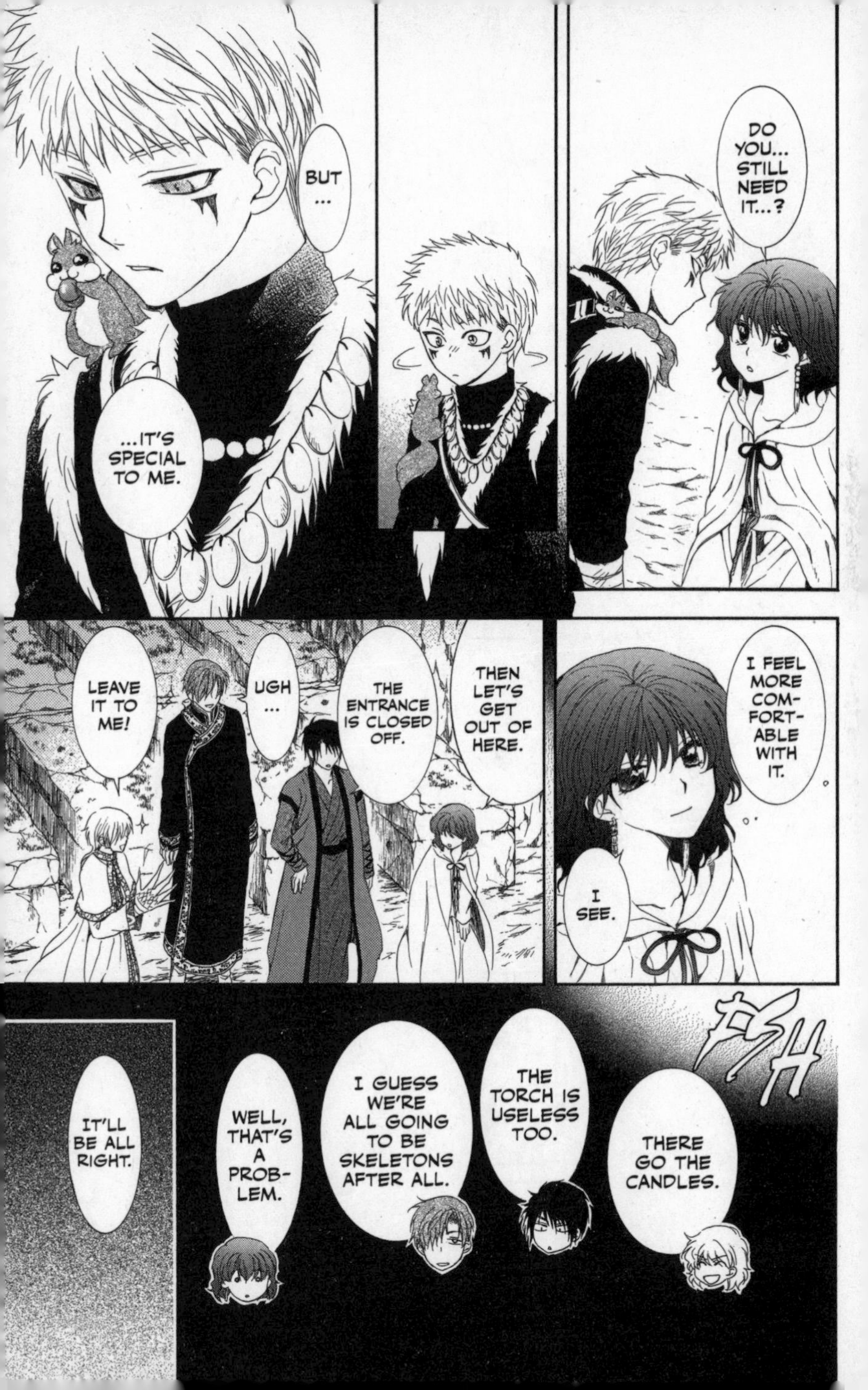
DO YOU... STILL NEED IT...?
BUT ...
...IT'S SPECIAL TO ME.
I FEEL MORE COM-FORT-ABLE WITH IT.
I SEE.
THEN LET'S GET OUT OF HERE.
THE ENTRANCE IS CLOSED OFF.
UGH ...
LEAVE IT TO ME!
FSH
THERE GO THE CANDLES.
THE TORCH IS USELESS TOO.
I GUESS WE'RE ALL GOING TO BE SKELETONS AFTER ALL.
WELL, THAT'S A PROB-LEM.
IT'LL BE ALL RIGHT.

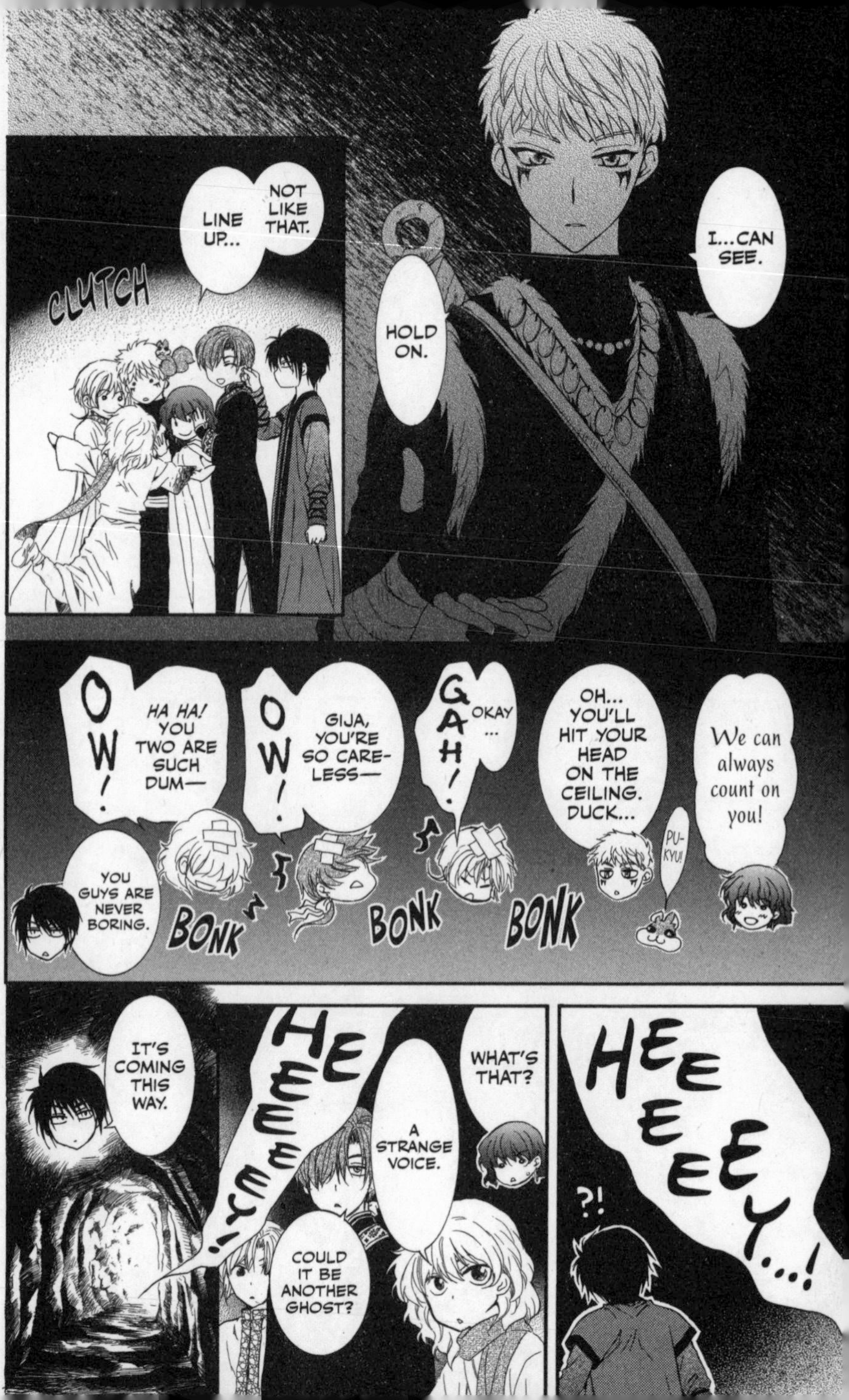
I...CAN SEE.
HOLD ON.
NOT LIKE THAT.
LINE UP...
CLUTCH
We can always count on you!
PU-KYU!
OH... YOU'LL HIT YOUR HEAD ON THE CEILING. DUCK...
OKAY ...
GAH!
BONK
GIJA, YOU'RE SO CARE-LESS—
OW!
BONK
HA HA! YOU TWO ARE SUCH DUM—
OW!
BONK
YOU GUYS ARE NEVER BORING.
HEEEEEY...!
?!
WHAT'S THAT?
A STRANGE VOICE.
COULD IT BE ANOTHER GHOST?
HEEEEEY!
IT'S COMING THIS WAY.

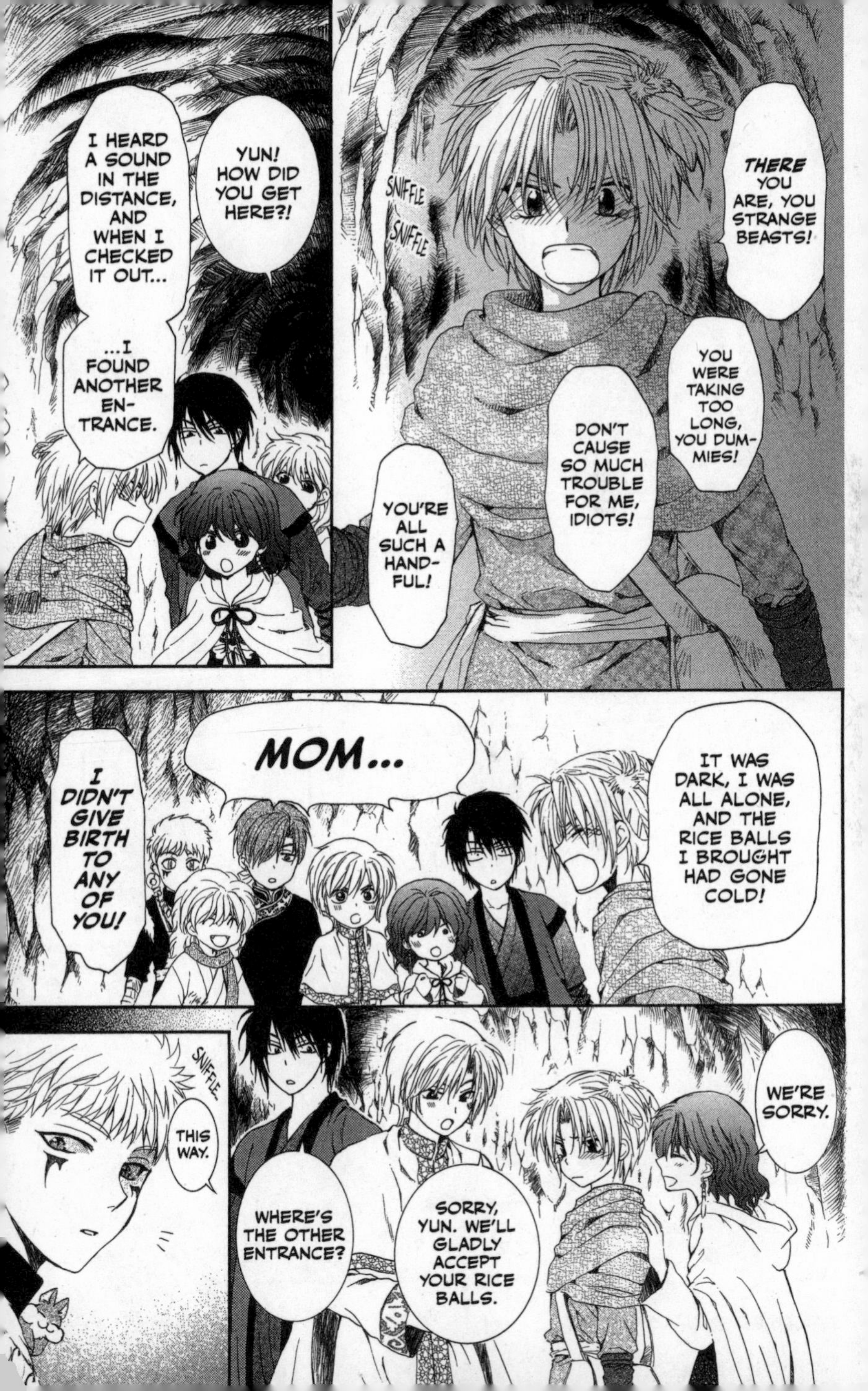
SNIFFLE
SNIFFLE
THERE YOU ARE, YOU STRANGE BEASTS!
YOU WERE TAKING TOO LONG, YOU DUM-MIES!
DON'T CAUSE SO MUCH TROUBLE FOR ME, IDIOTS!
YOU'RE ALL SUCH A HAND-FUL!
YUN! HOW DID YOU GET HERE?!
I HEARD A SOUND IN THE DISTANCE, AND WHEN I CHECKED IT OUT...
...I FOUND ANOTHER EN-TRANCE.
IT WAS DARK, I WAS ALL ALONE, AND THE RICE BALLS I BROUGHT HAD GONE COLD!
MOM...
I DIDN'T GIVE BIRTH TO ANY OF YOU!
WE'RE SORRY.
SORRY, YUN. WE'LL GLADLY ACCEPT YOUR RICE BALLS.
WHERE'S THE OTHER ENTRANCE?
SNIFFLE
THIS WAY.

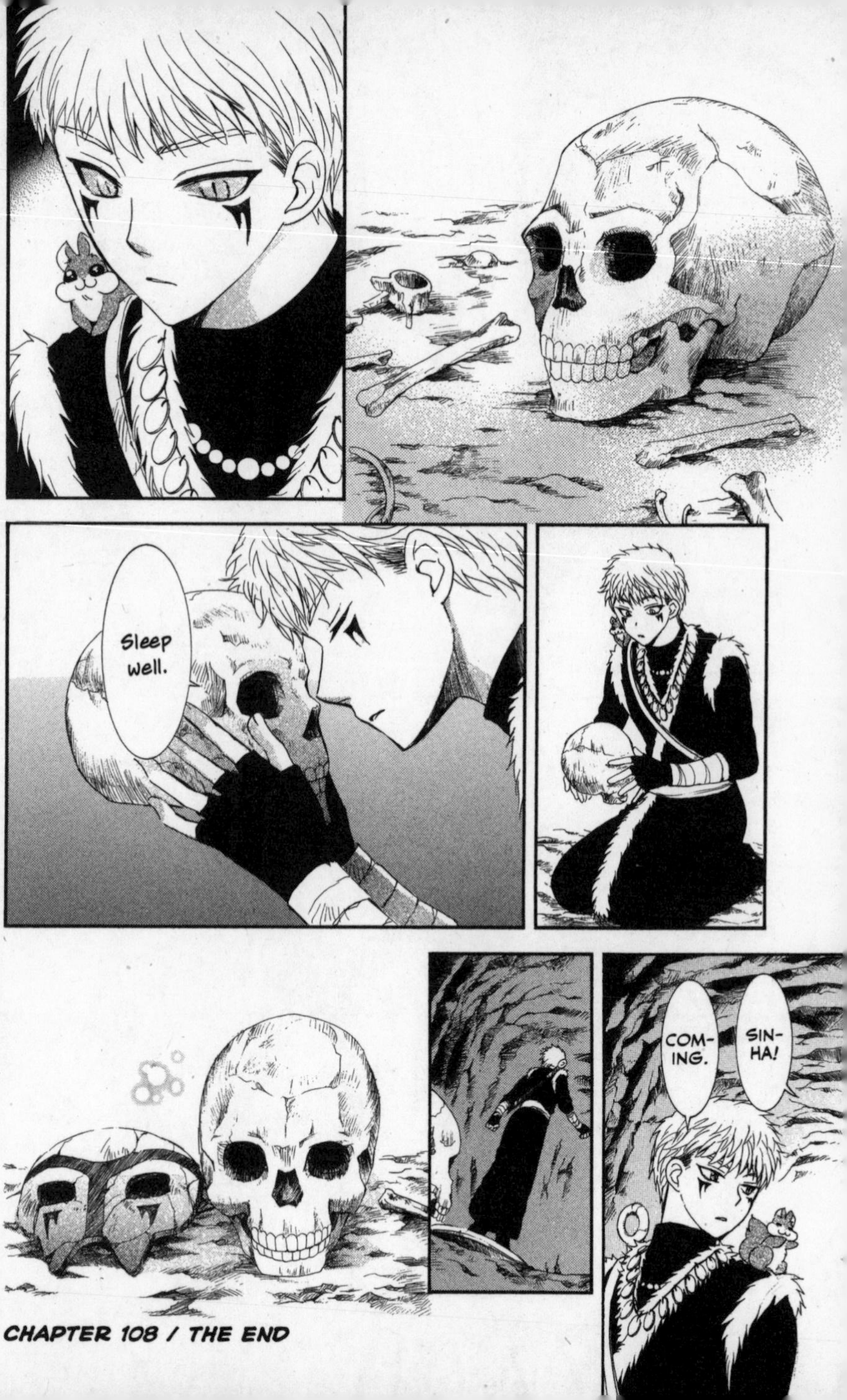
Sleep well.
SIN-HA!
COM-ING.

CHAPTER 108 / THE END

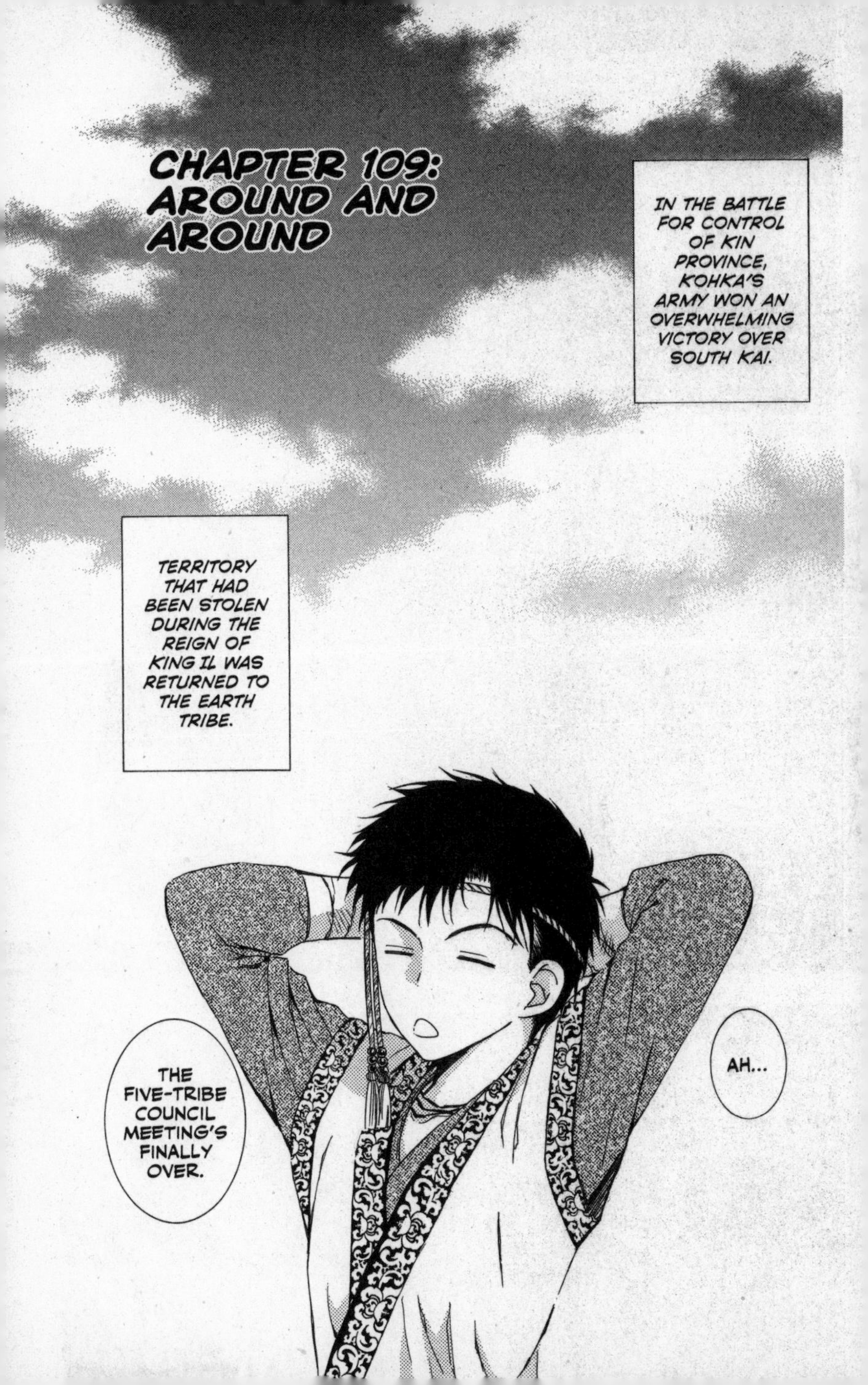
CHAPTER 109: AROUND AND AROUND
IN THE BATTLE FOR CONTROL OF KIN PROVINCE, KOHKA'S ARMY WON AN OVERWHELMING VICTORY OVER SOUTH KAI.
TERRITORY THAT HAD BEEN STOLEN DURING THE REIGN OF KING IL WAS RETURNED TO THE EARTH TRIBE.
AH...
THE FIVE-TRIBE COUNCIL MEETING'S FINALLY OVER.

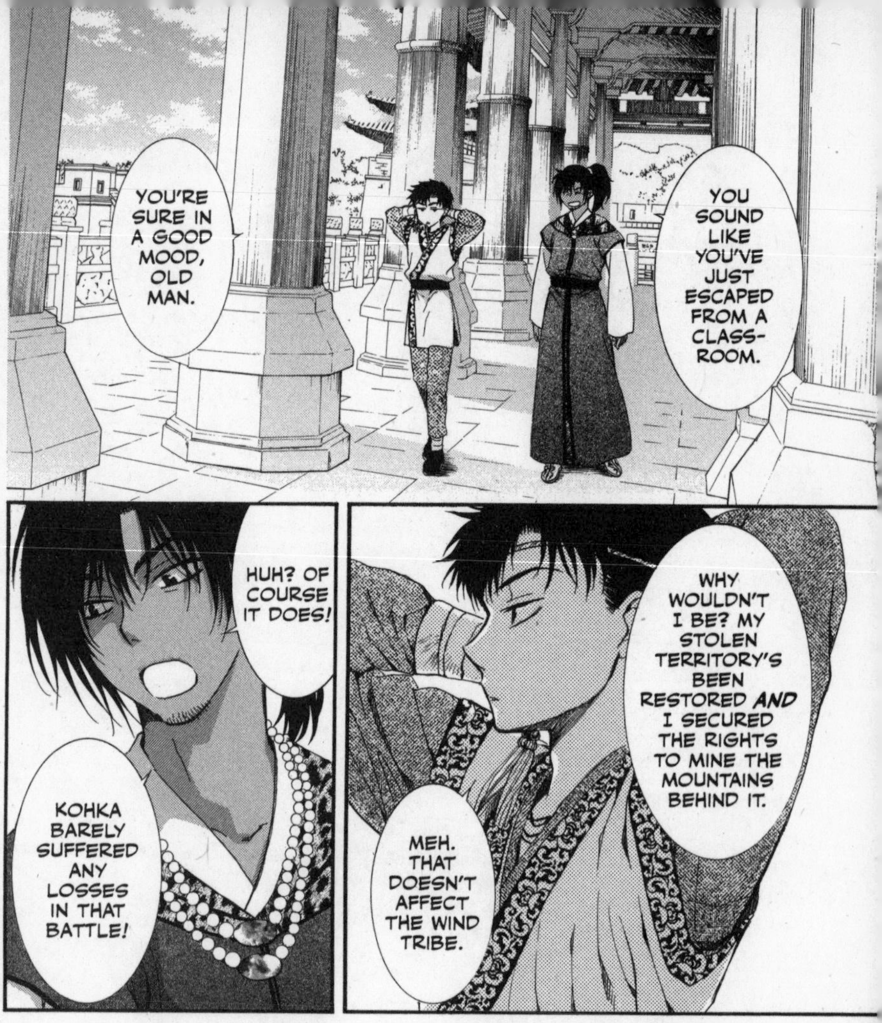
YOU SOUND LIKE YOU'VE JUST ESCAPED FROM A CLASS-ROOM.
YOU'RE SURE IN A GOOD MOOD, OLD MAN.
WHY WOULDN'T I BE? MY STOLEN TERRITORY'S BEEN RESTORED *AND* I SECURED THE RIGHTS TO MINE THE MOUNTAINS BEHIND IT.
MEH. THAT DOESN'T AFFECT THE WIND TRIBE.
HUH? OF COURSE IT DOES!
KOHKA BARELY SUFFERED ANY LOSSES IN THAT BATTLE!

Yona of the Dawn

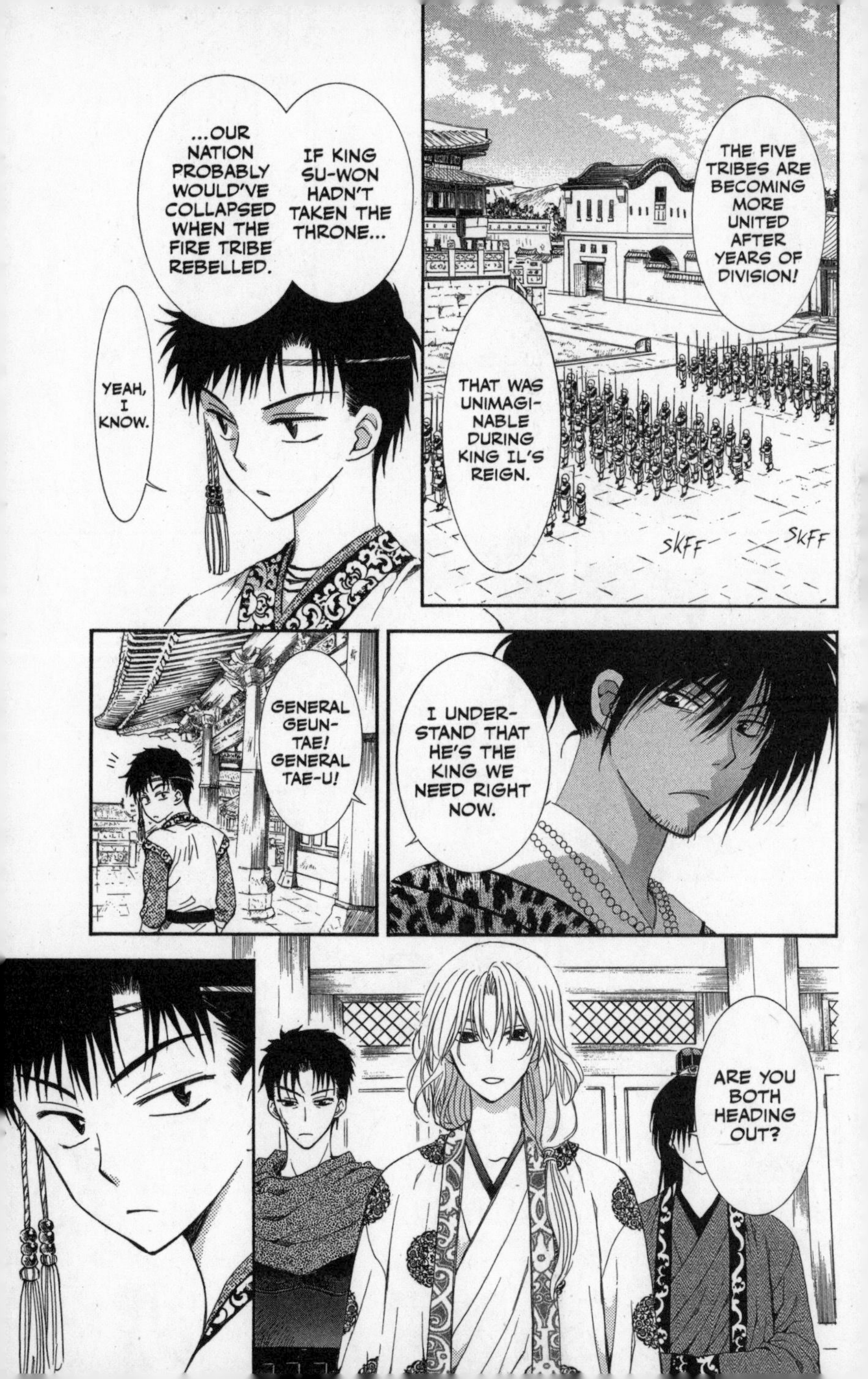
THE FIVE TRIBES ARE BECOMING MORE UNITED AFTER YEARS OF DIVISION!
THAT WAS UNIMAGINABLE DURING KING IL'S REIGN.
SKFF
SKFF
IF KING SU-WON HADN'T TAKEN THE THRONE...
...OUR NATION PROBABLY WOULD'VE COLLAPSED WHEN THE FIRE TRIBE REBELLED.
YEAH, I KNOW.
I UNDERSTAND THAT HE'S THE KING WE NEED RIGHT NOW.
GENERAL GEUN-TAE! GENERAL TAE-U!
ARE YOU BOTH HEADING OUT?

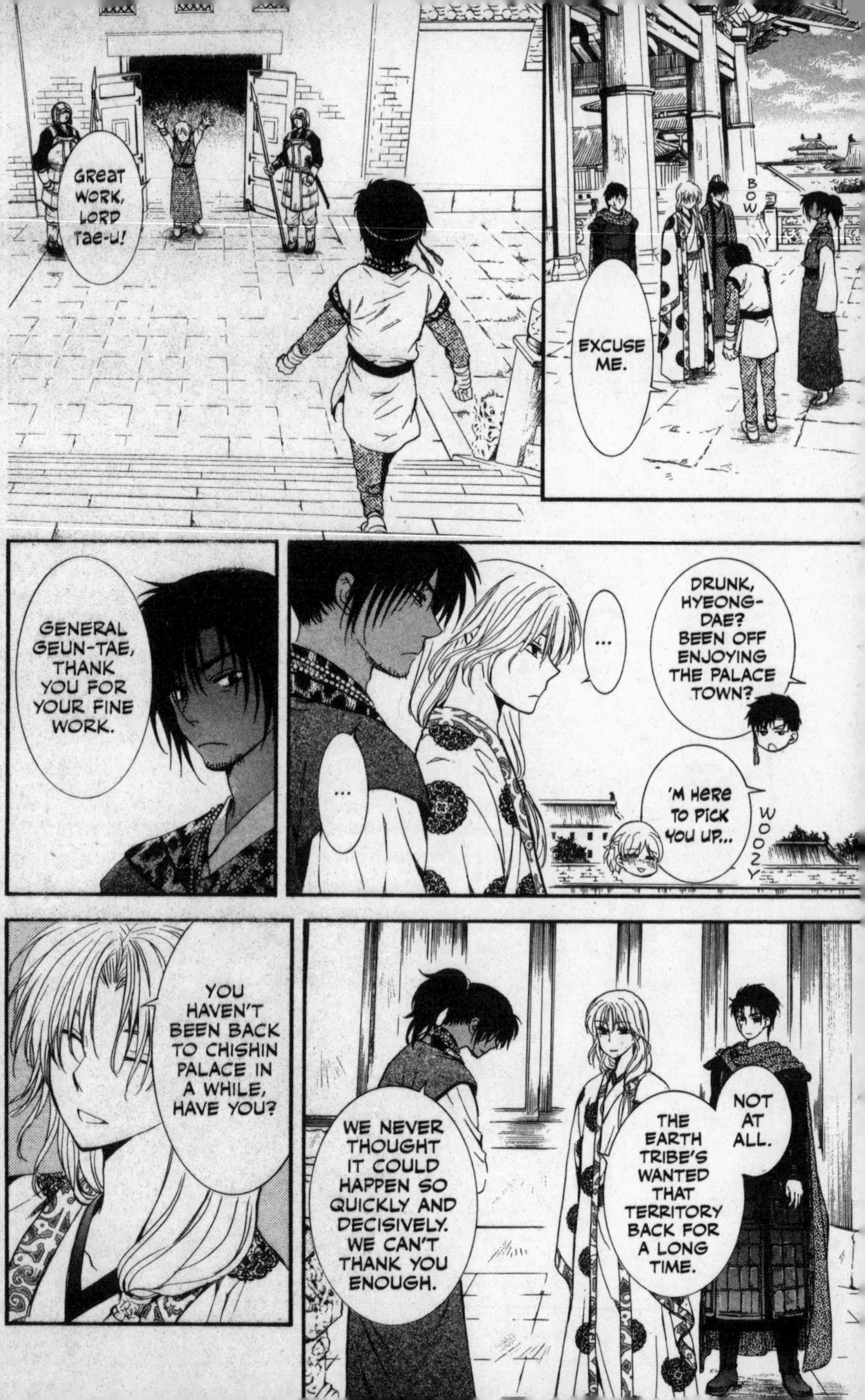
BOW
EXCUSE ME.
GREAT WORK, LORD TAE-U!
DRUNK, HYEONG-DAE? BEEN OFF ENJOYING THE PALACE TOWN?
...
'M HERE TO PICK YOU UP...
WOOZY
...
GENERAL GEUN-TAE, THANK YOU FOR YOUR FINE WORK.
NOT AT ALL.
THE EARTH TRIBE'S WANTED THAT TERRITORY BACK FOR A LONG TIME.
WE NEVER THOUGHT IT COULD HAPPEN SO QUICKLY AND DECISIVELY. WE CAN'T THANK YOU ENOUGH.
YOU HAVEN'T BEEN BACK TO CHISHIN PALACE IN A WHILE, HAVE YOU?

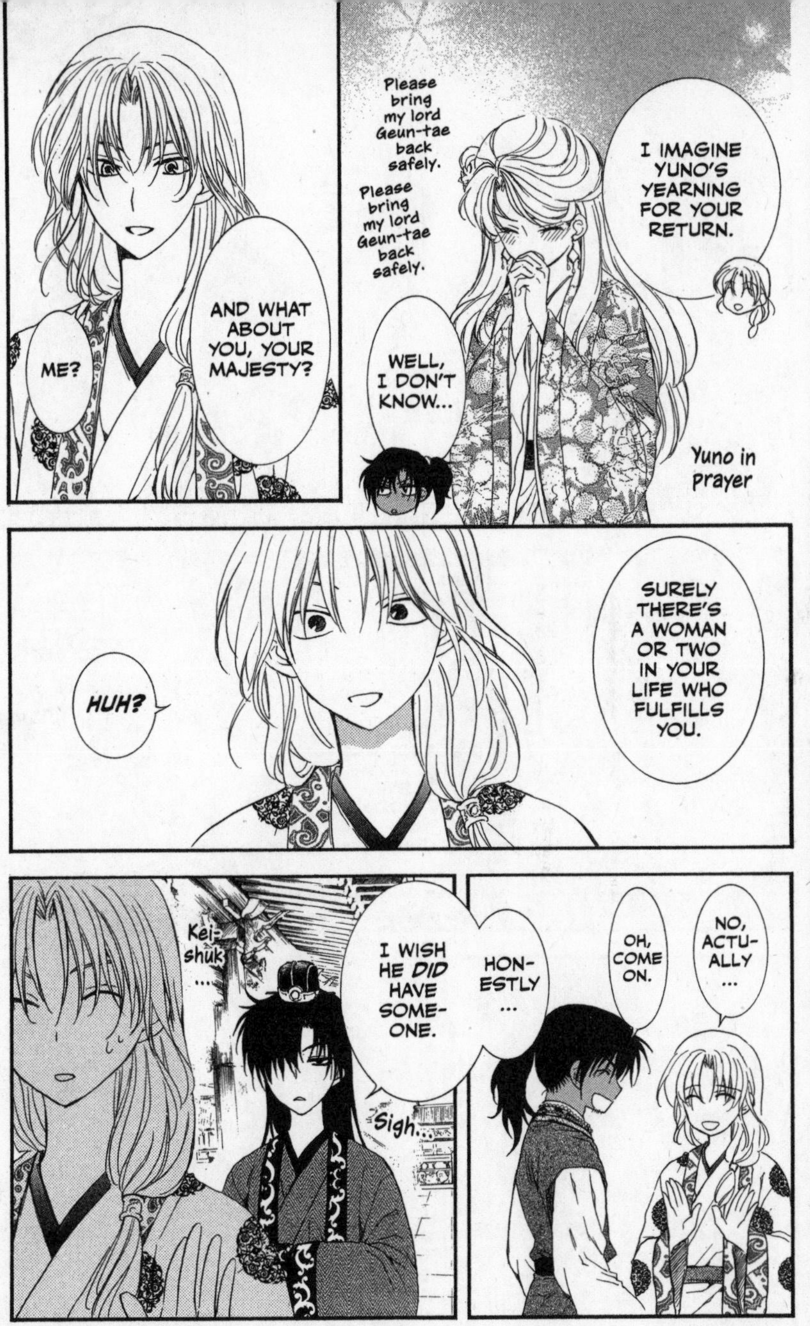
I IMAGINE YUNO'S YEARNING FOR YOUR RETURN.
Please bring my lord Geun-tae back safely.
Please bring my lord Geun-tae back safely.
Yuno in prayer
WELL, I DON'T KNOW...
AND WHAT ABOUT YOU, YOUR MAJESTY?
ME?
SURELY THERE'S A WOMAN OR TWO IN YOUR LIFE WHO FULFILLS YOU.
HUH?
NO, ACTU-ALLY...
OH, COME ON.
HON-ESTLY...
I WISH HE *DID* HAVE SOME-ONE.
Sigh...
Kei-shuk...

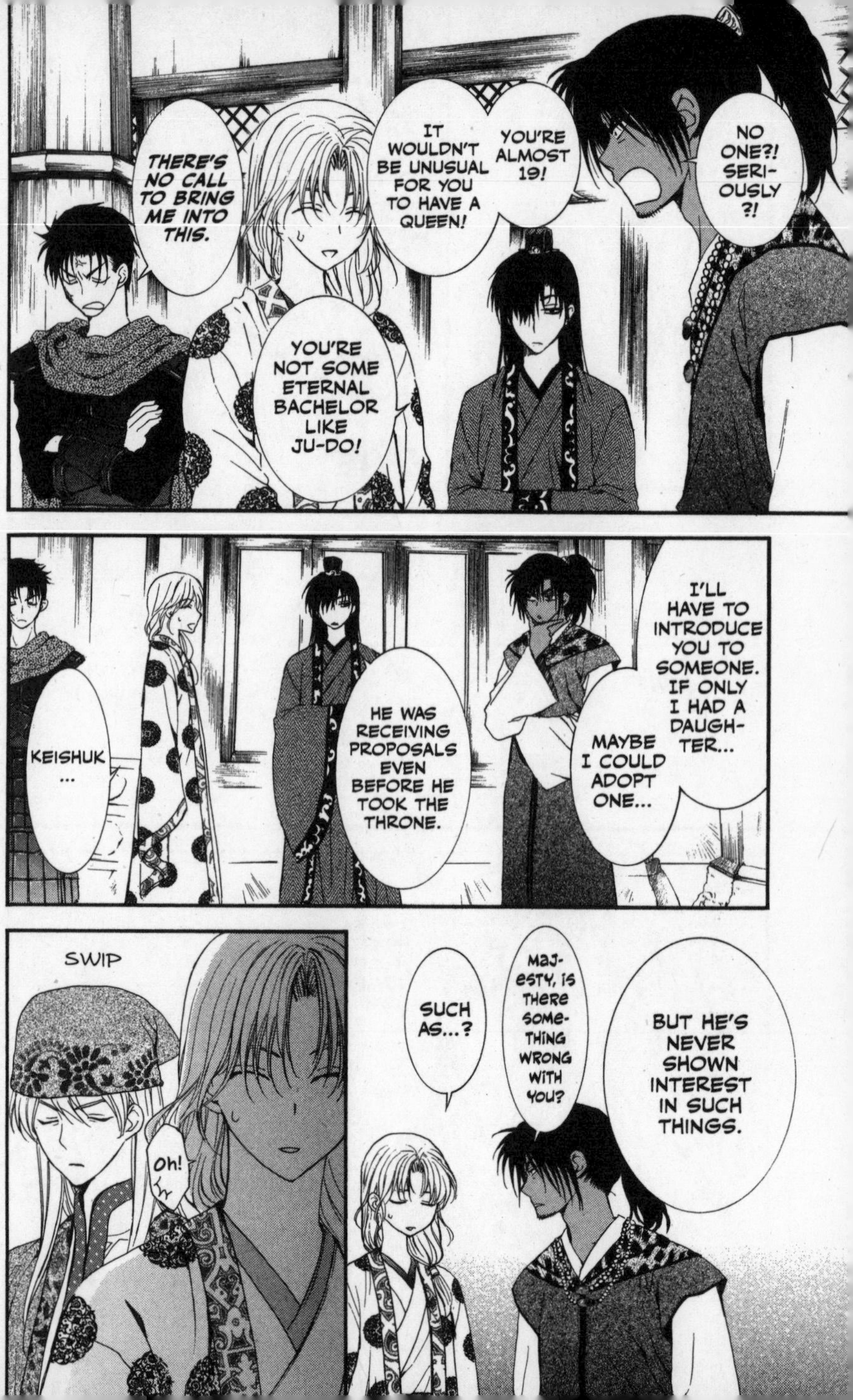
NO ONE?! SERIOUSLY?!
YOU'RE ALMOST 19!
IT WOULDN'T BE UNUSUAL FOR YOU TO HAVE A QUEEN!
YOU'RE NOT SOME ETERNAL BACHELOR LIKE JU-DO!
THERE'S NO CALL TO BRING ME INTO THIS.
I'LL HAVE TO INTRODUCE YOU TO SOMEONE. IF ONLY I HAD A DAUGHTER...
MAYBE I COULD ADOPT ONE...
HE WAS RECEIVING PROPOSALS EVEN BEFORE HE TOOK THE THRONE.
KEISHUK...
BUT HE'S NEVER SHOWN INTEREST IN SUCH THINGS.
Majesty, is there something wrong with you?
SUCH AS...?
SWIP
Oh!

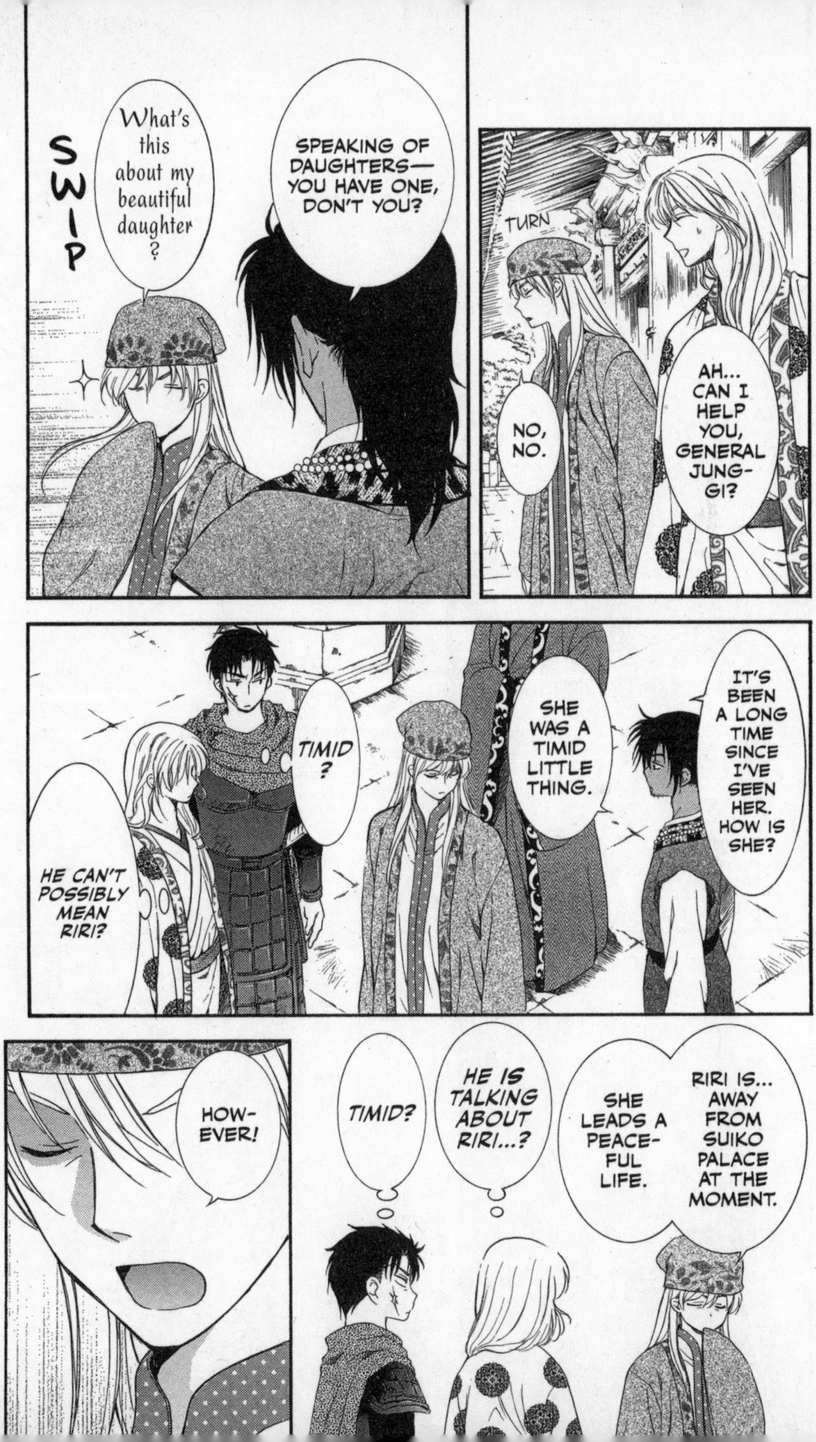
TURN
AH... CAN I HELP YOU, GENERAL JUNG-GI?
NO, NO.
SPEAKING OF DAUGHTERS—YOU HAVE ONE, DON'T YOU?
What's this about my beautiful daughter?
SWIP
IT'S BEEN A LONG TIME SINCE I'VE SEEN HER. HOW IS SHE?
SHE WAS A TIMID LITTLE THING.
TIMID?
HE CAN'T POSSIBLY MEAN RIRI?
RIRI IS... AWAY FROM SUIKO PALACE AT THE MOMENT.
SHE LEADS A PEACE-FUL LIFE.
HE IS TALKING ABOUT RIRI...?
TIMID?
HOW-EVER!

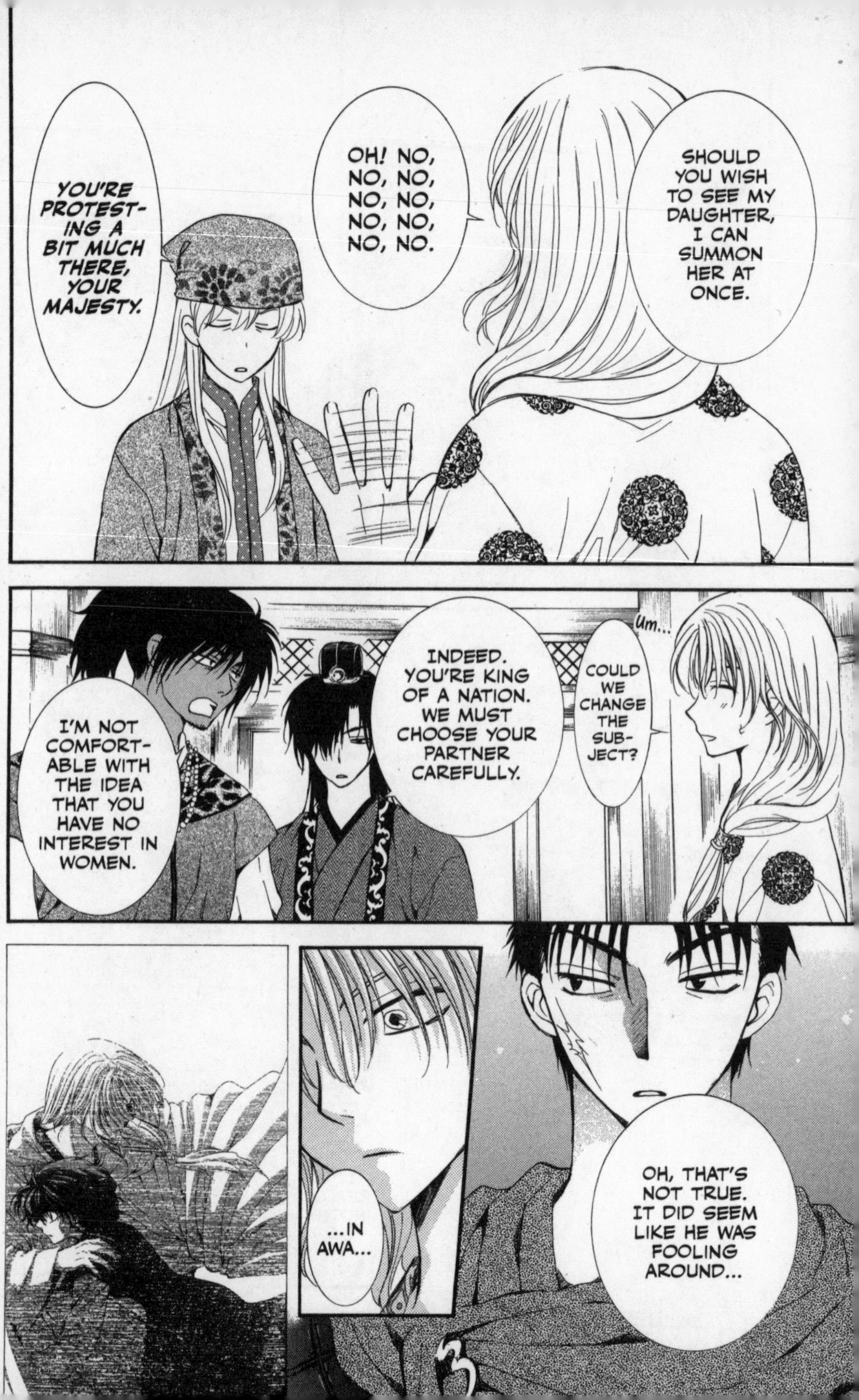
SHOULD YOU WISH TO SEE MY DAUGHTER, I CAN SUMMON HER AT ONCE.
OH! NO, NO, NO, NO, NO, NO, NO, NO, NO.
YOU'RE PROTESTING A BIT MUCH THERE, YOUR MAJESTY.
Um...
COULD WE CHANGE THE SUBJECT?
INDEED. YOU'RE KING OF A NATION. WE MUST CHOOSE YOUR PARTNER CAREFULLY.
I'M NOT COMFORTABLE WITH THE IDEA THAT YOU HAVE NO INTEREST IN WOMEN.
OH, THAT'S NOT TRUE. IT DID SEEM LIKE HE WAS FOOLING AROUND...
...IN AWA...

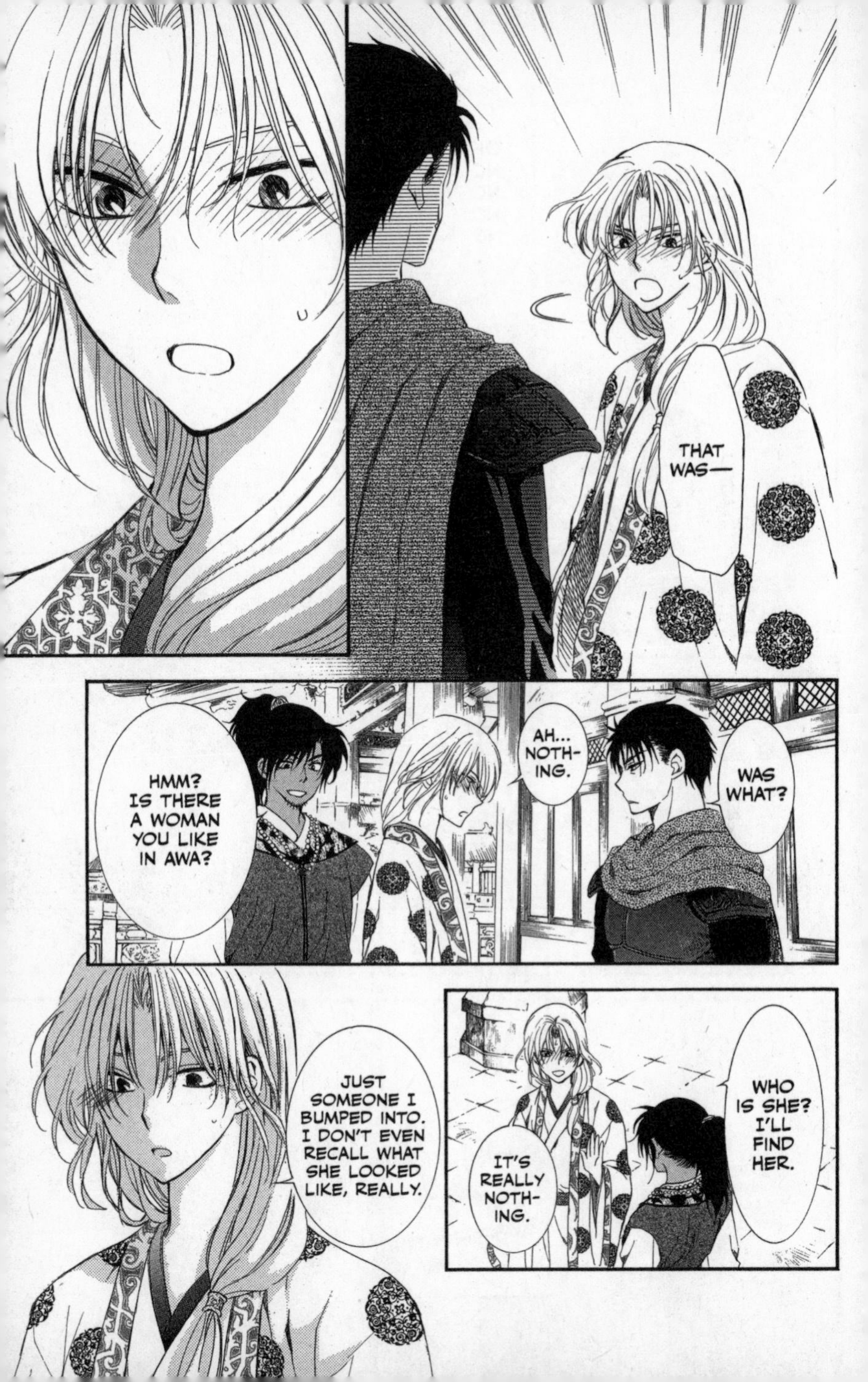
THAT WAS—
WAS WHAT?
AH... NOTHING.
HMM? IS THERE A WOMAN YOU LIKE IN AWA?
WHO IS SHE? I'LL FIND HER.
IT'S REALLY NOTHING.
JUST SOMEONE I BUMPED INTO. I DON'T EVEN RECALL WHAT SHE LOOKED LIKE, REALLY.

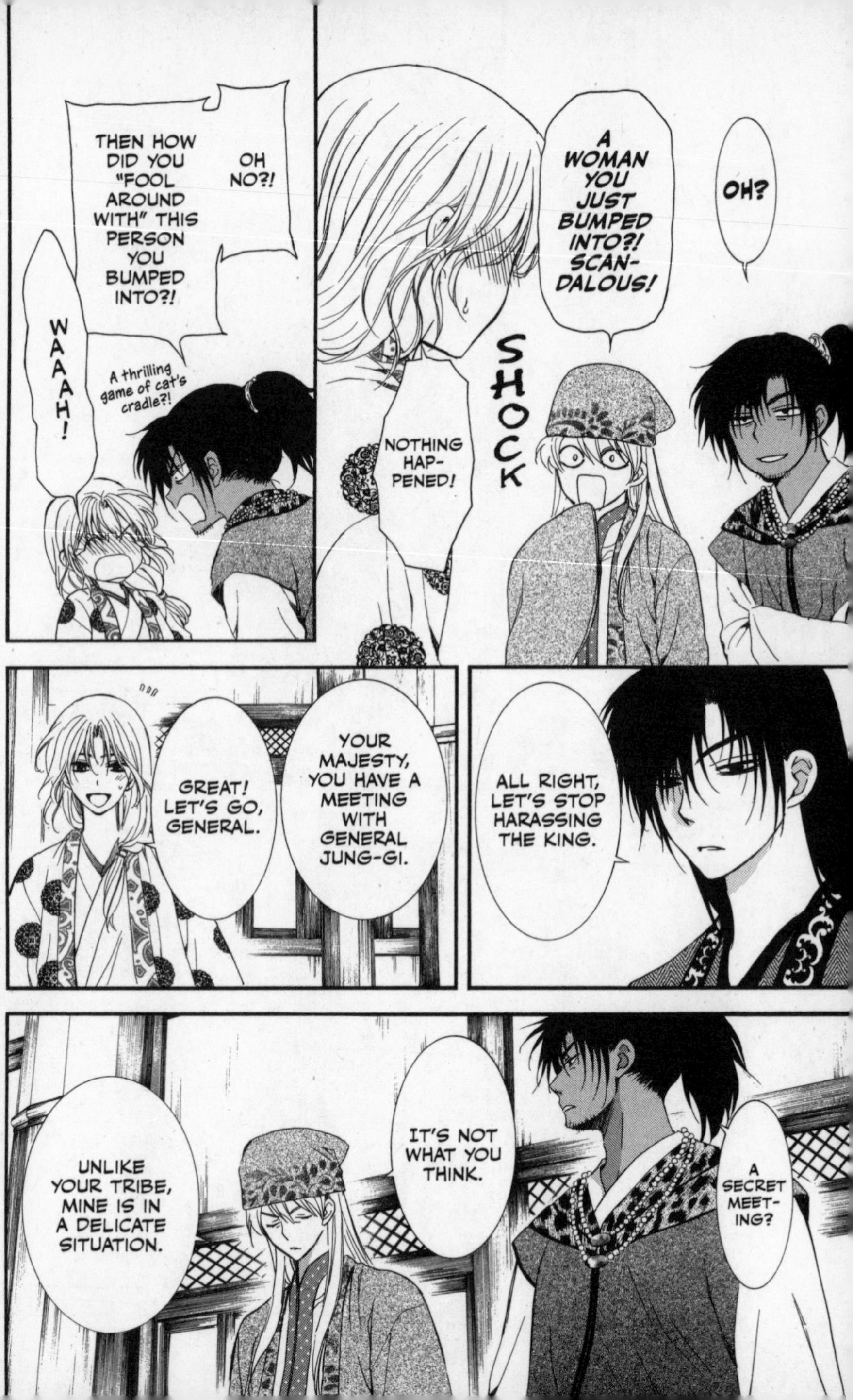
OH?
A WOMAN YOU JUST BUMPED INTO?! SCAN-DALOUS!
SHOCK
NOTHING HAP-PENED!
THEN HOW DID YOU "FOOL AROUND WITH" THIS PERSON YOU BUMPED INTO?!
OH NO?!
WAAAH!
A thrilling game of cat's cradle?!
ALL RIGHT, LET'S STOP HARASSING THE KING.
YOUR MAJESTY, YOU HAVE A MEETING WITH GENERAL JUNG-GI.
GREAT! LET'S GO, GENERAL.
A SECRET MEET-ING?
IT'S NOT WHAT YOU THINK.
UNLIKE YOUR TRIBE, MINE IS IN A DELICATE SITUATION.

My biggest worry regarding the drama CD was **getting Sinha to talk.** Unlike Gija, Jaeha and Yun, who would just talk anyway (Ha ha), Sinha doesn't speak unless the story is about him. That's why I chose this story.

Zeno didn't have much screen time in the anime, but I'm glad he had lots of opportunities to speak.

Also, I'm deeply touched that the cast for the current Dragons also voiced the first Dragons. Thank you very much! I like that it feels as if the Four Dragon Warriors have reunited after many years.

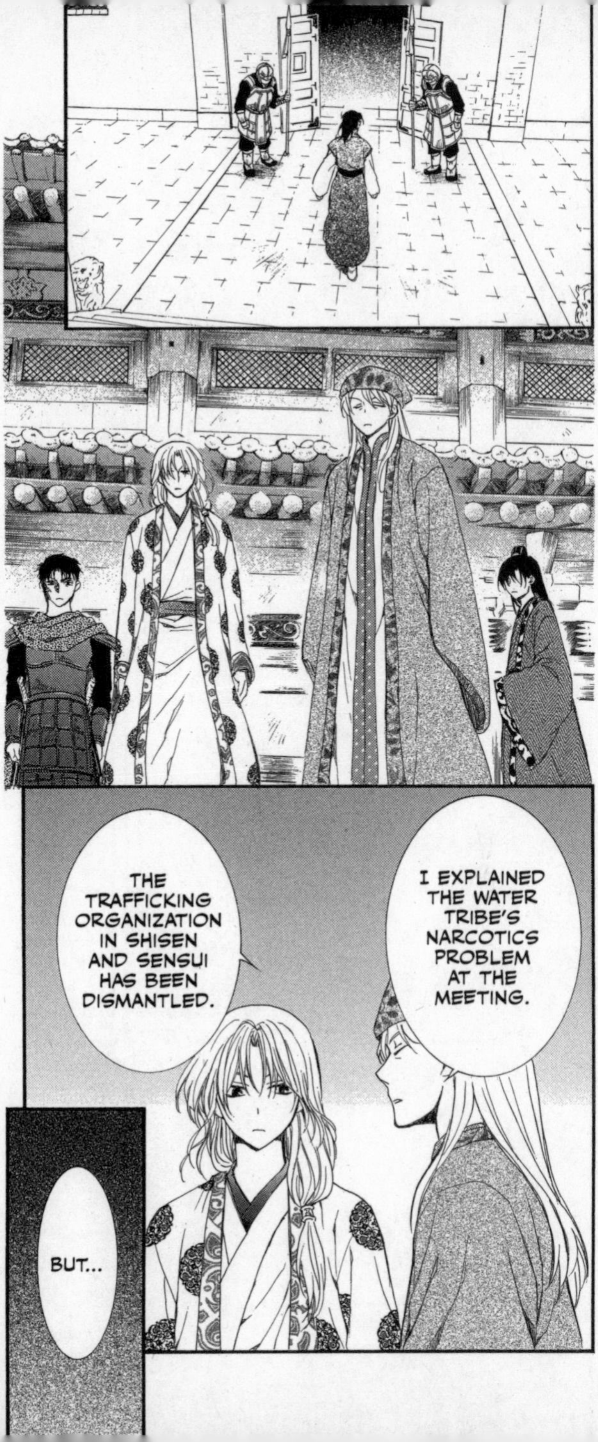
I EXPLAINED THE WATER TRIBE'S NARCOTICS PROBLEM AT THE MEETING.
THE TRAFFICKING ORGANIZATION IN SHISEN AND SENSUI HAS BEEN DISMANTLED.
BUT...

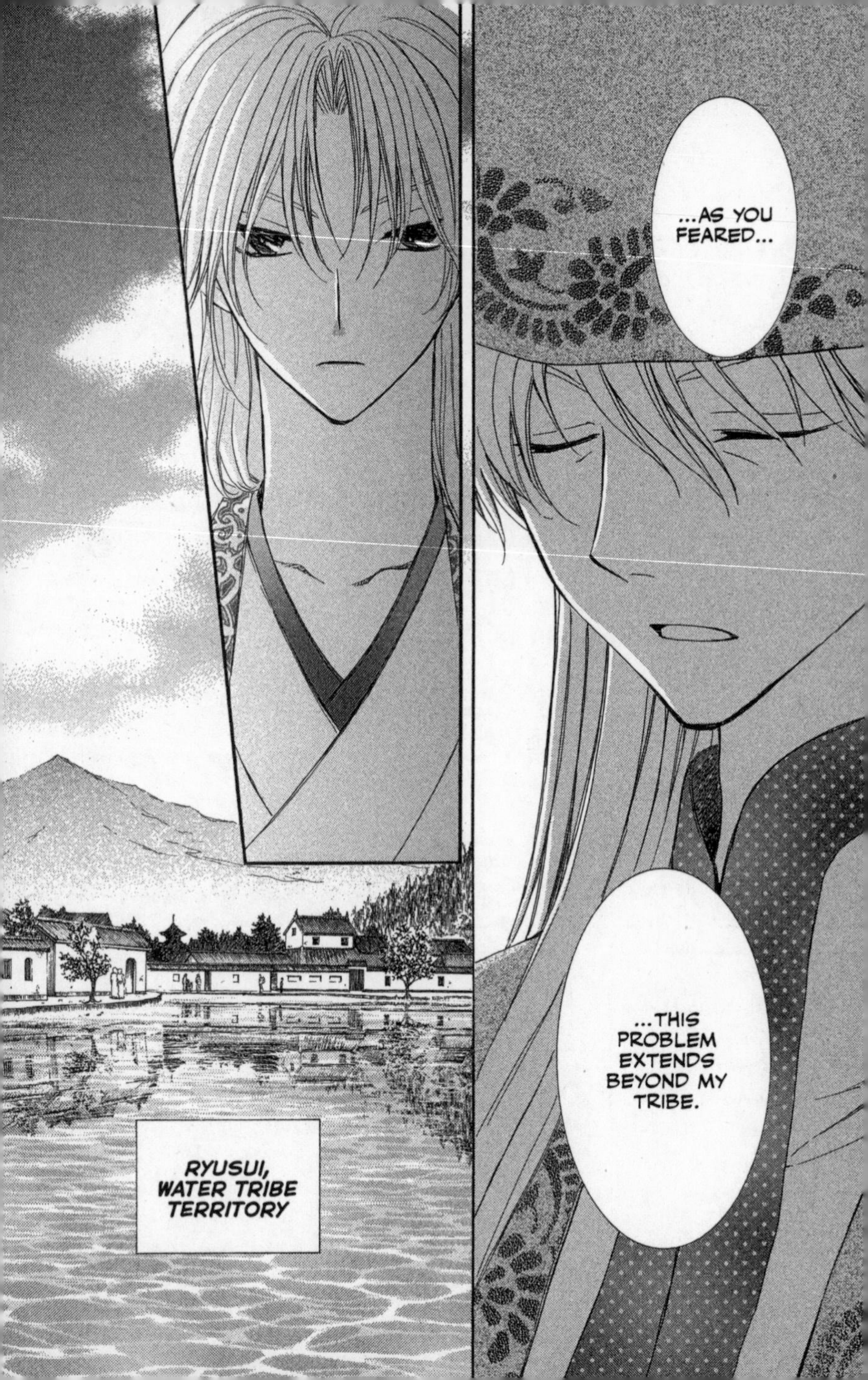
...AS YOU FEARED...
...THIS PROBLEM EXTENDS BEYOND MY TRIBE.
RYUSUI, WATER TRIBE TERRITORY

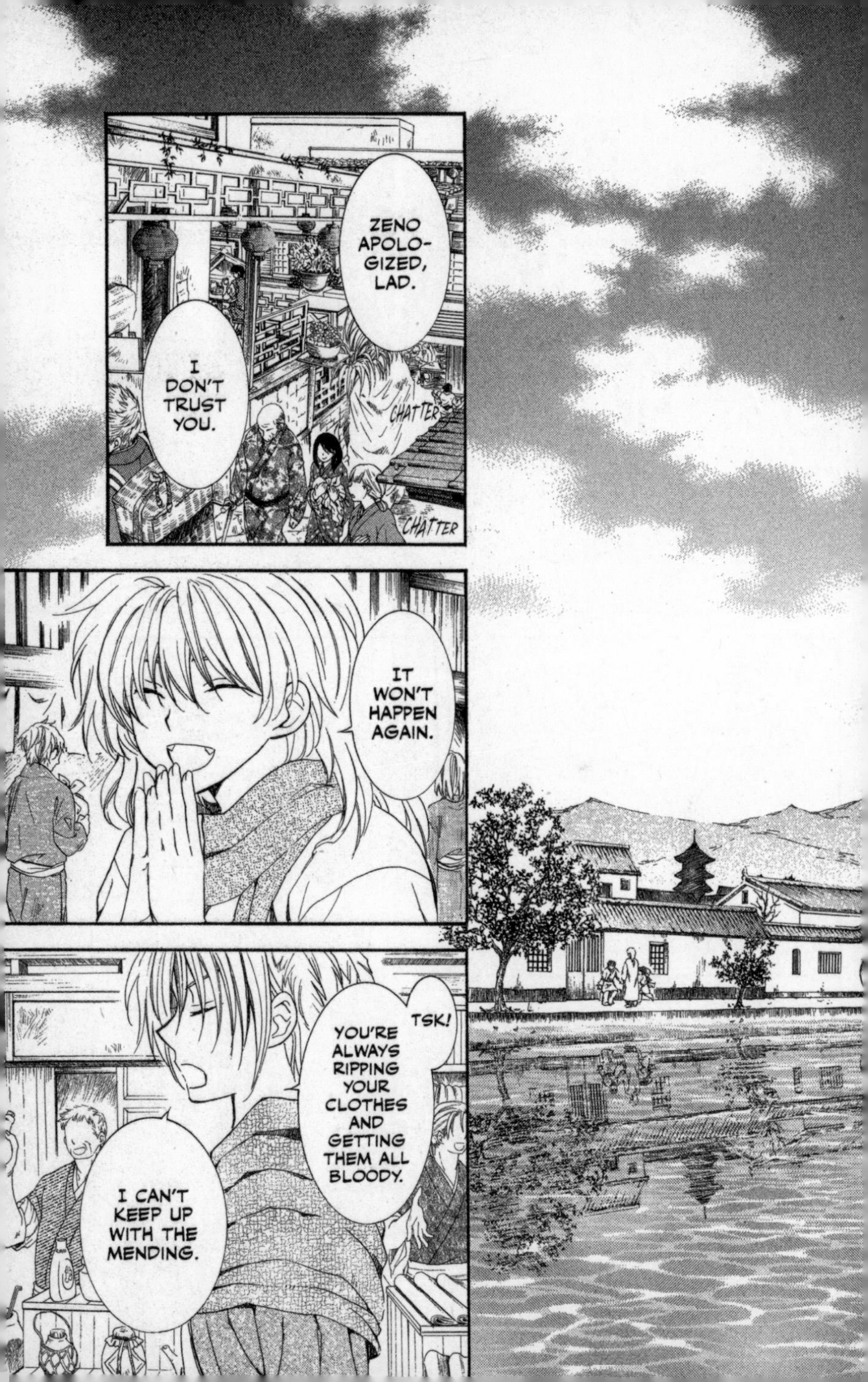
ZENO APOLOGIZED, LAD.
I DON'T TRUST YOU.
CHATTER
CHATTER
IT WON'T HAPPEN AGAIN.
TSK!
YOU'RE ALWAYS RIPPING YOUR CLOTHES AND GETTING THEM ALL BLOODY.
I CAN'T KEEP UP WITH THE MENDING.

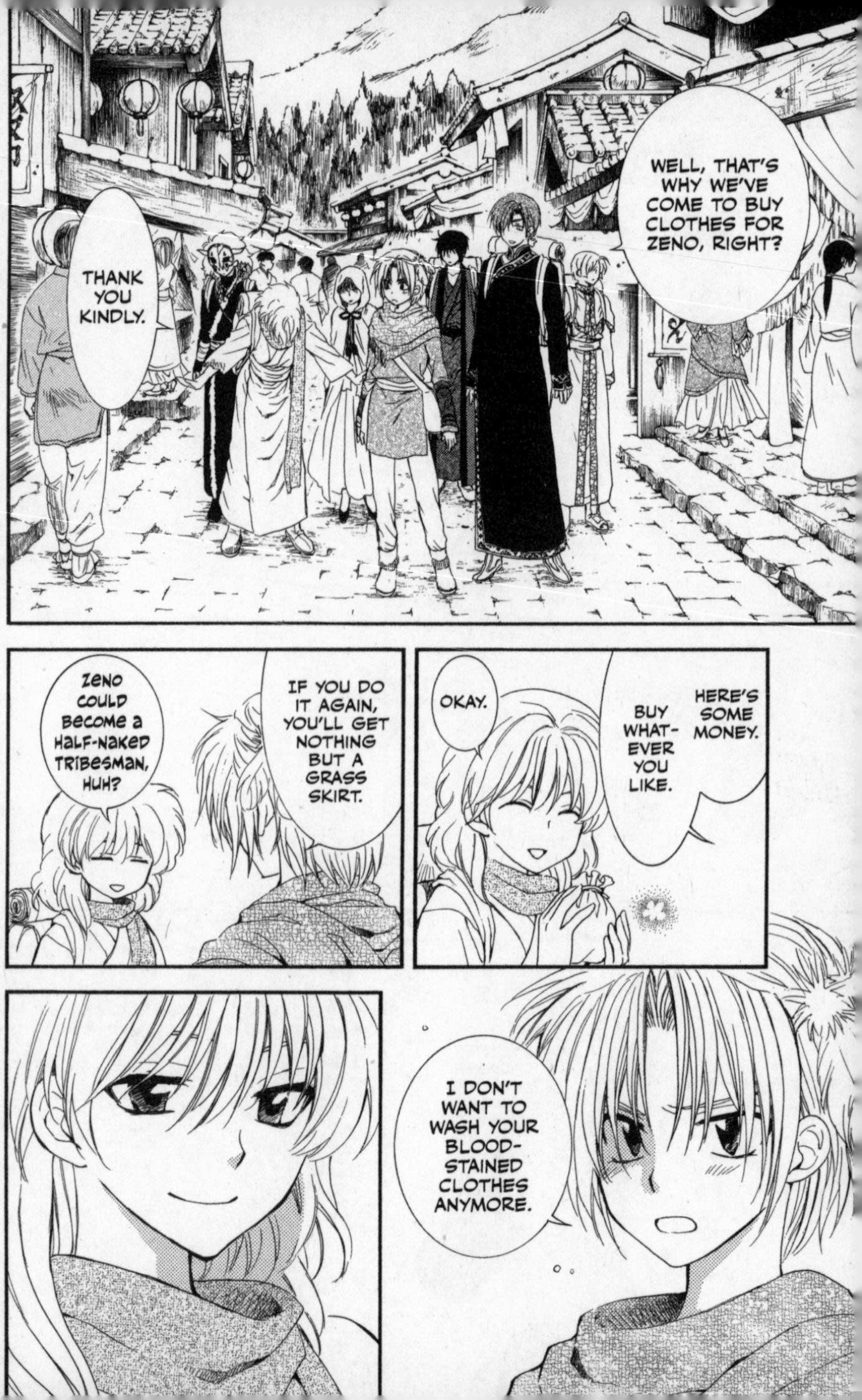
WELL, THAT'S WHY WE'VE COME TO BUY CLOTHES FOR ZENO, RIGHT?
THANK YOU KINDLY.
HERE'S SOME MONEY.
BUY WHATEVER YOU LIKE.
OKAY.
IF YOU DO IT AGAIN, YOU'LL GET NOTHING BUT A GRASS SKIRT.
Zeno could become a Half-naked Tribesman, huh?
I DON'T WANT TO WASH YOUR BLOOD-STAINED CLOTHES ANYMORE.

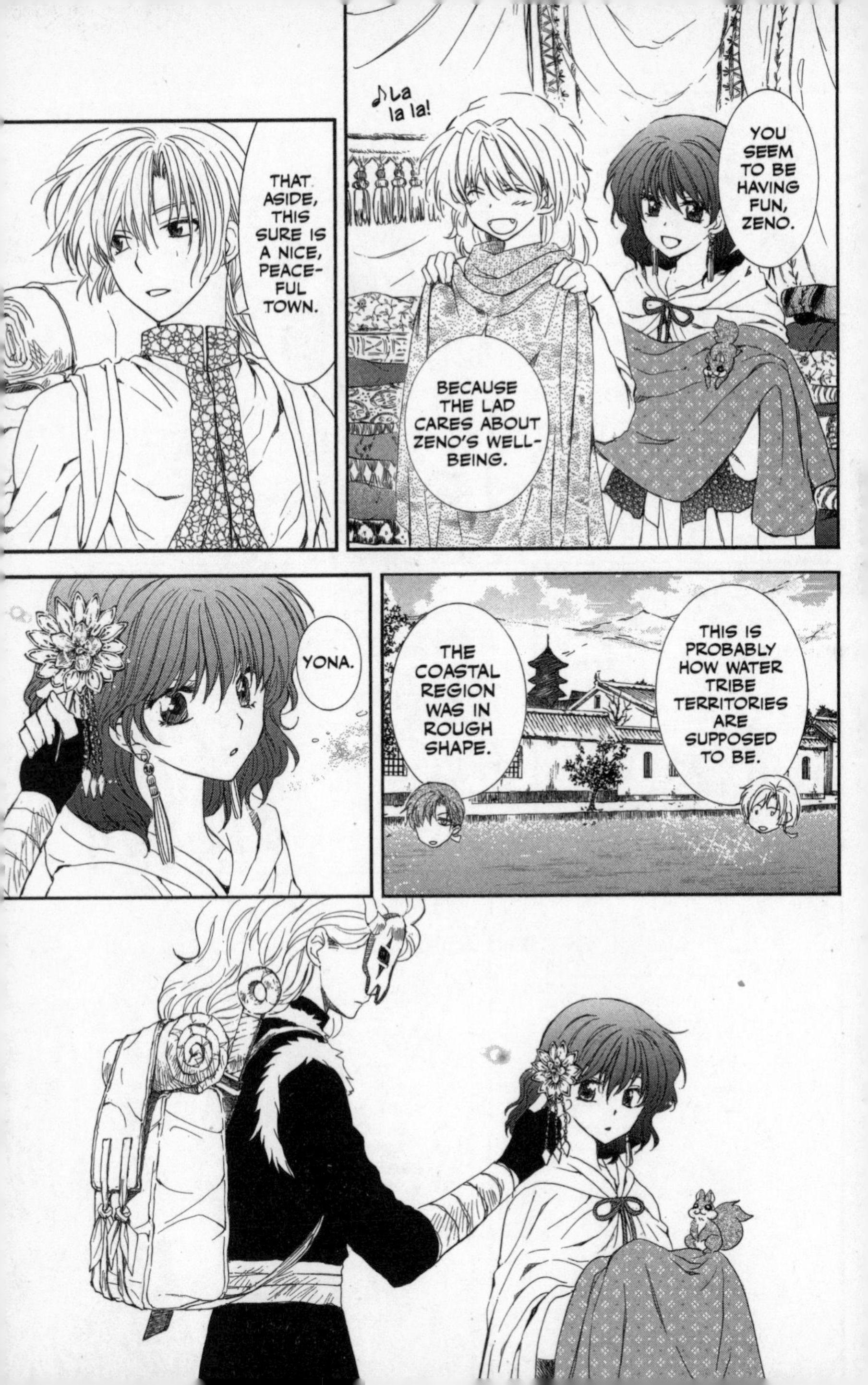
YOU SEEM TO BE HAVING FUN, ZENO.
♪La la la!
BECAUSE THE LAD CARES ABOUT ZENO'S WELL-BEING.
THAT ASIDE, THIS SURE IS A NICE, PEACEFUL TOWN.
THIS IS PROBABLY HOW WATER TRIBE TERRITORIES ARE SUPPOSED TO BE.
THE COASTAL REGION WAS IN ROUGH SHAPE.
YONA.

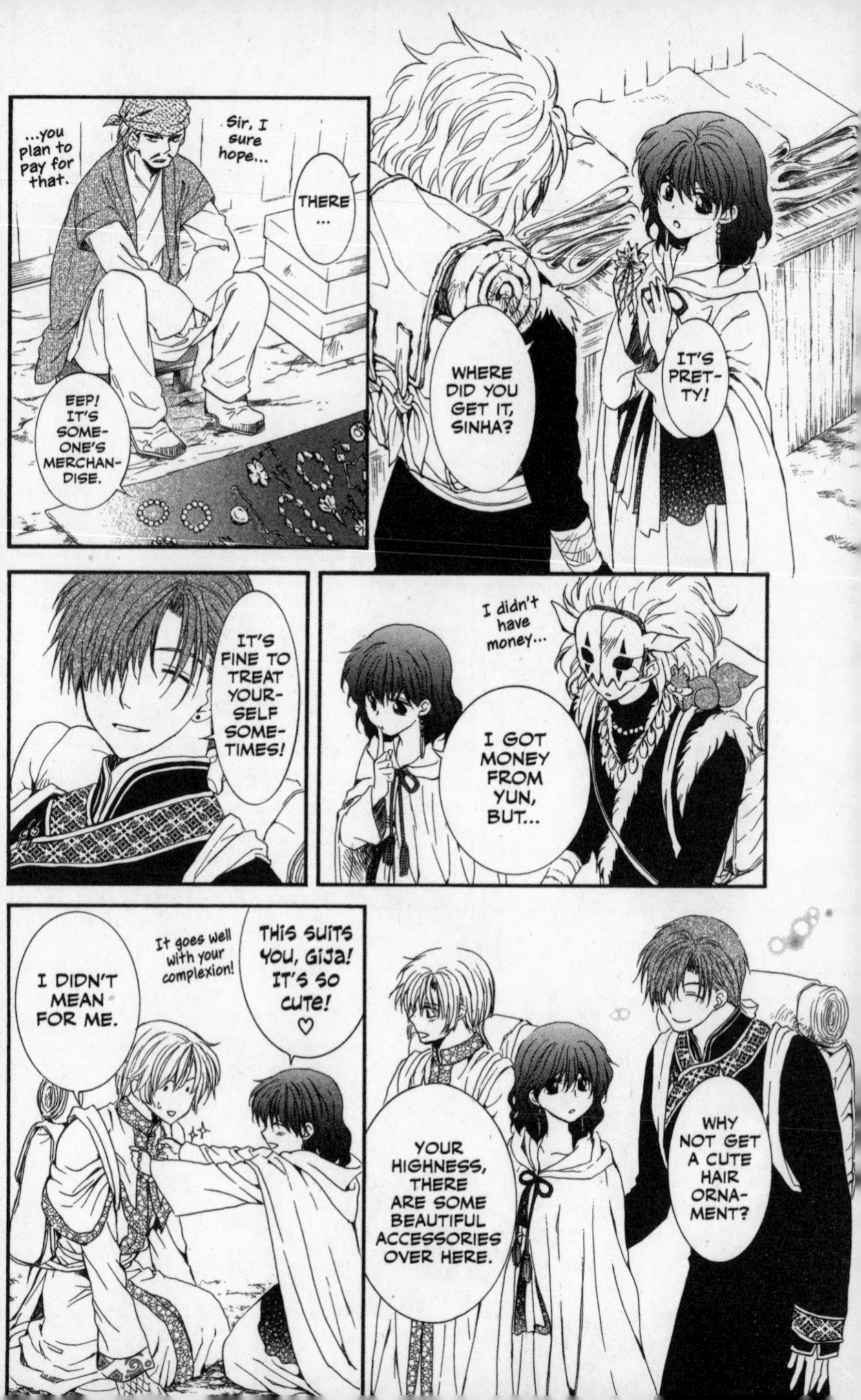
IT'S PRETTY!
WHERE DID YOU GET IT, SINHA?
THERE...
Sir, I sure hope...
...you plan to pay for that.
EEP! IT'S SOMEONE'S MERCHANDISE.
I didn't have money...
I GOT MONEY FROM YUN, BUT...
IT'S FINE TO TREAT YOURSELF SOMETIMES!
WHY NOT GET A CUTE HAIR ORNAMENT?
YOUR HIGHNESS, THERE ARE SOME BEAUTIFUL ACCESSORIES OVER HERE.
THIS SUITS YOU, GIJA! IT'S SO CUTE! ♡
It goes well with your complexion!
I DIDN'T MEAN FOR ME.

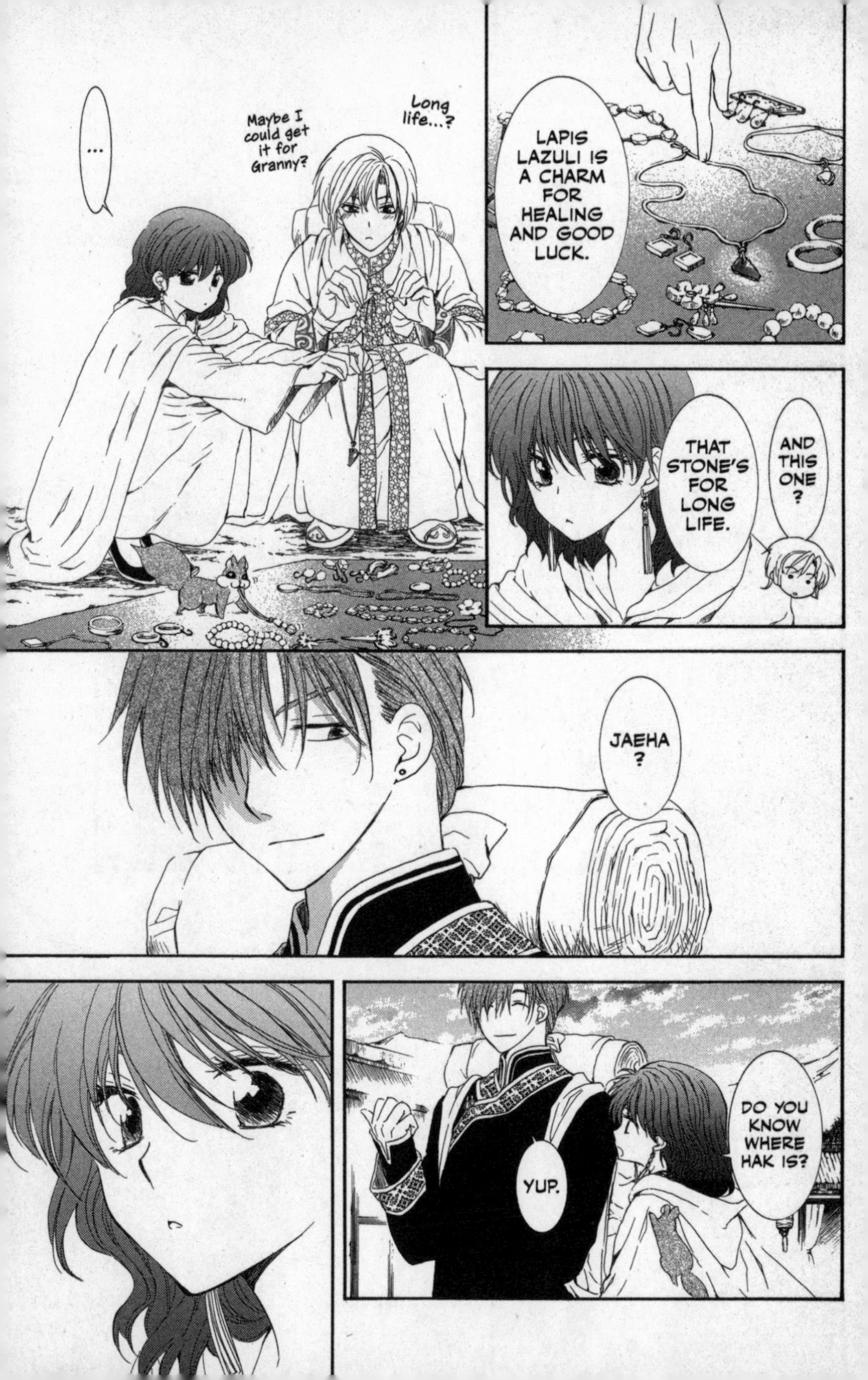
LAPIS LAZULI IS A CHARM FOR HEALING AND GOOD LUCK.
AND THIS ONE?
THAT STONE'S FOR LONG LIFE.
Long life...?
Maybe I could get it for Granny?
...
JAEHA?
DO YOU KNOW WHERE HAK IS?
YUP.

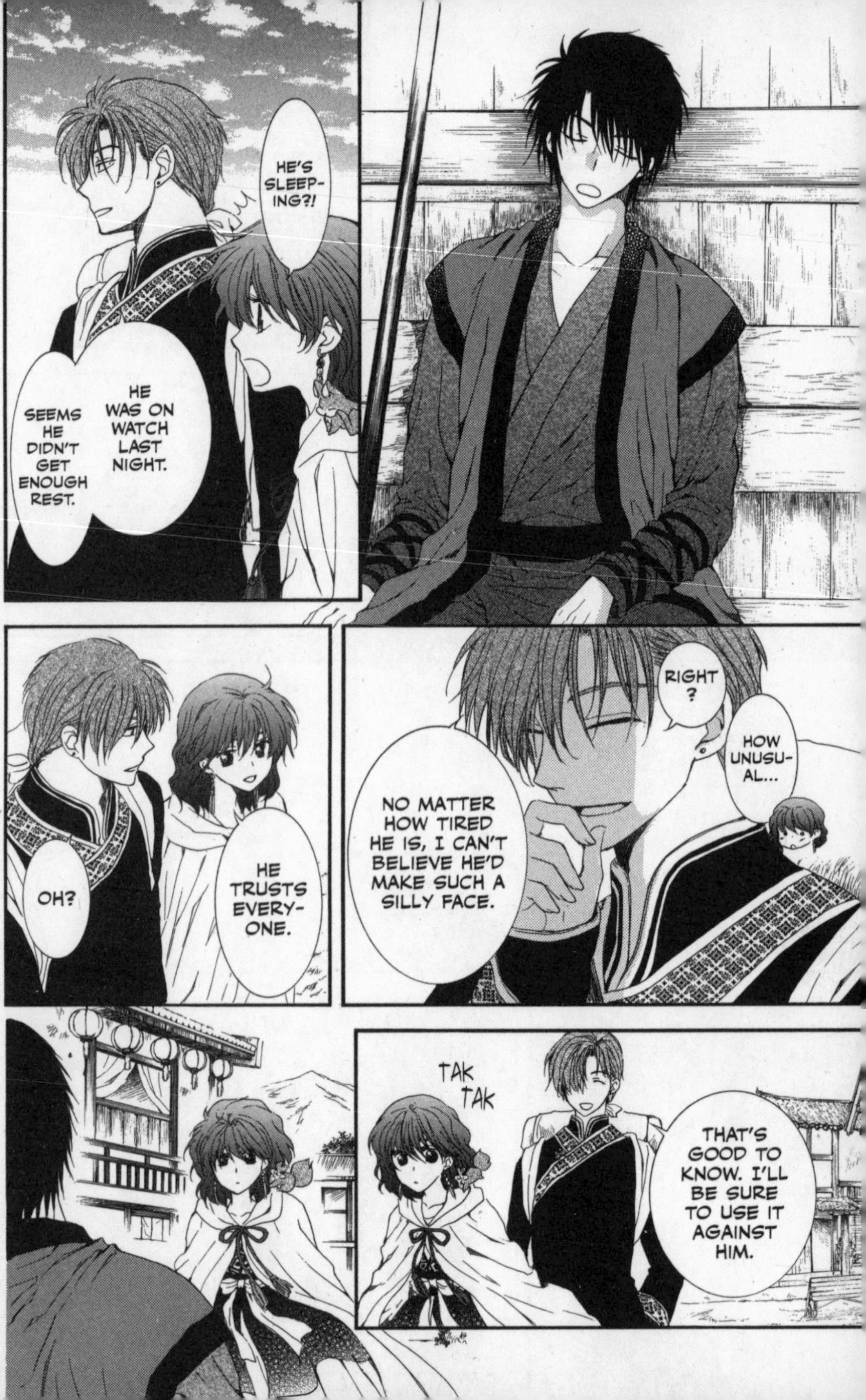
HE'S SLEEPING?!
HE WAS ON WATCH LAST NIGHT.
SEEMS HE DIDN'T GET ENOUGH REST.
RIGHT?
HOW UNUSUAL...
NO MATTER HOW TIRED HE IS, I CAN'T BELIEVE HE'D MAKE SUCH A SILLY FACE.
HE TRUSTS EVERYONE.
OH?
TAK TAK
THAT'S GOOD TO KNOW. I'LL BE SURE TO USE IT AGAINST HIM.

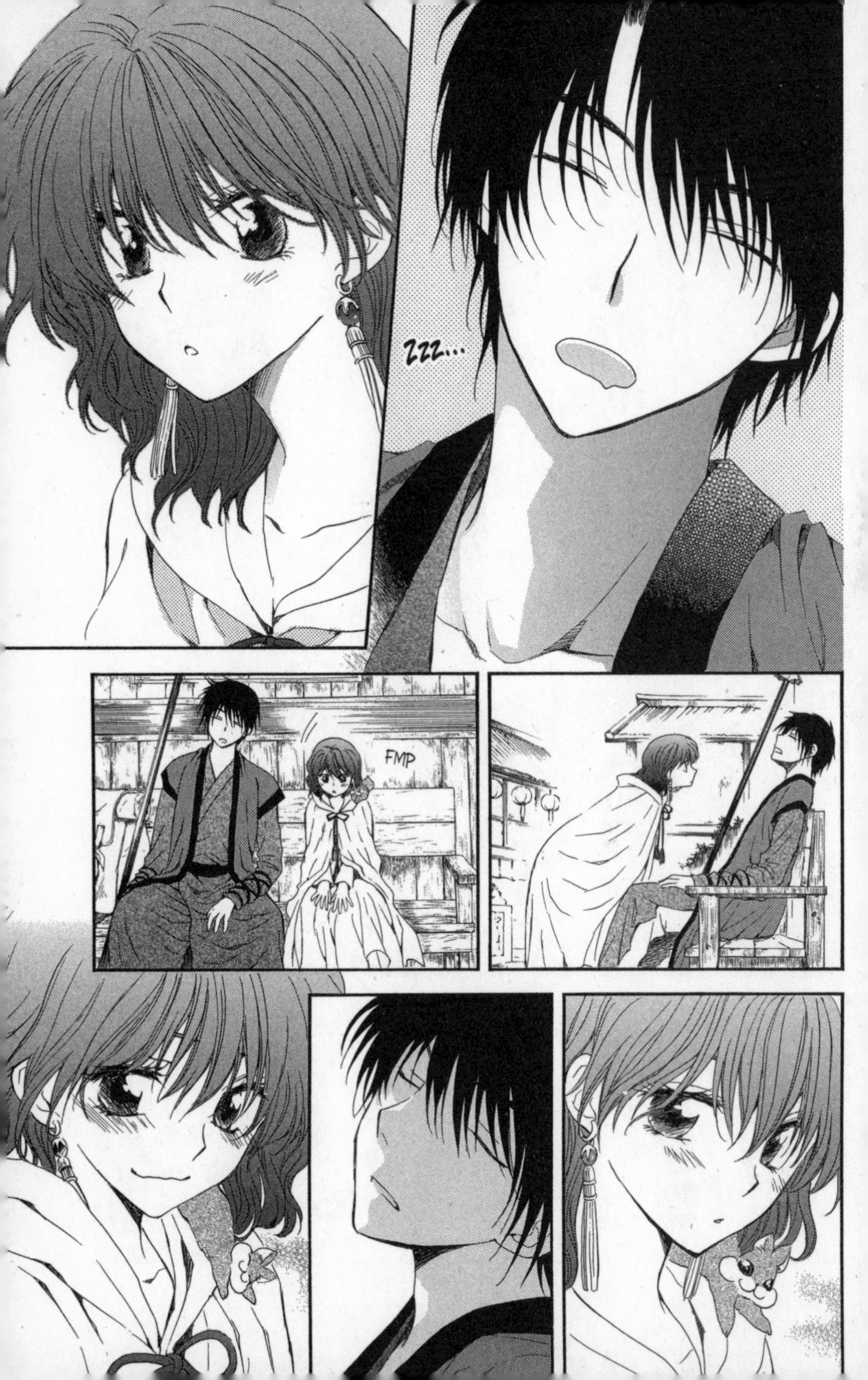
ZZZ...
FMP

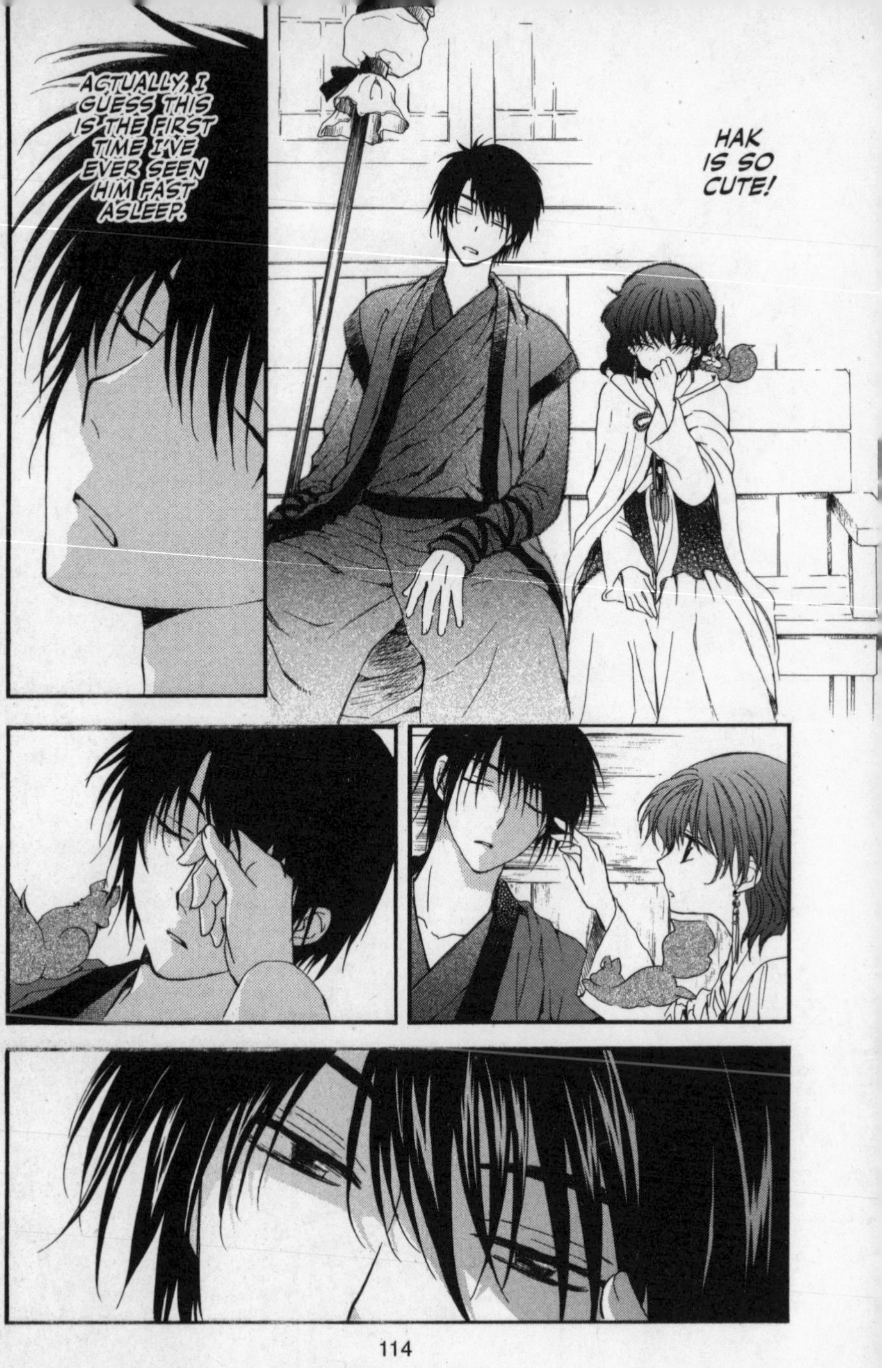
HAK IS SO CUTE!
ACTUALLY, I GUESS THIS IS THE FIRST TIME I'VE EVER SEEN HIM FAST ASLEEP.

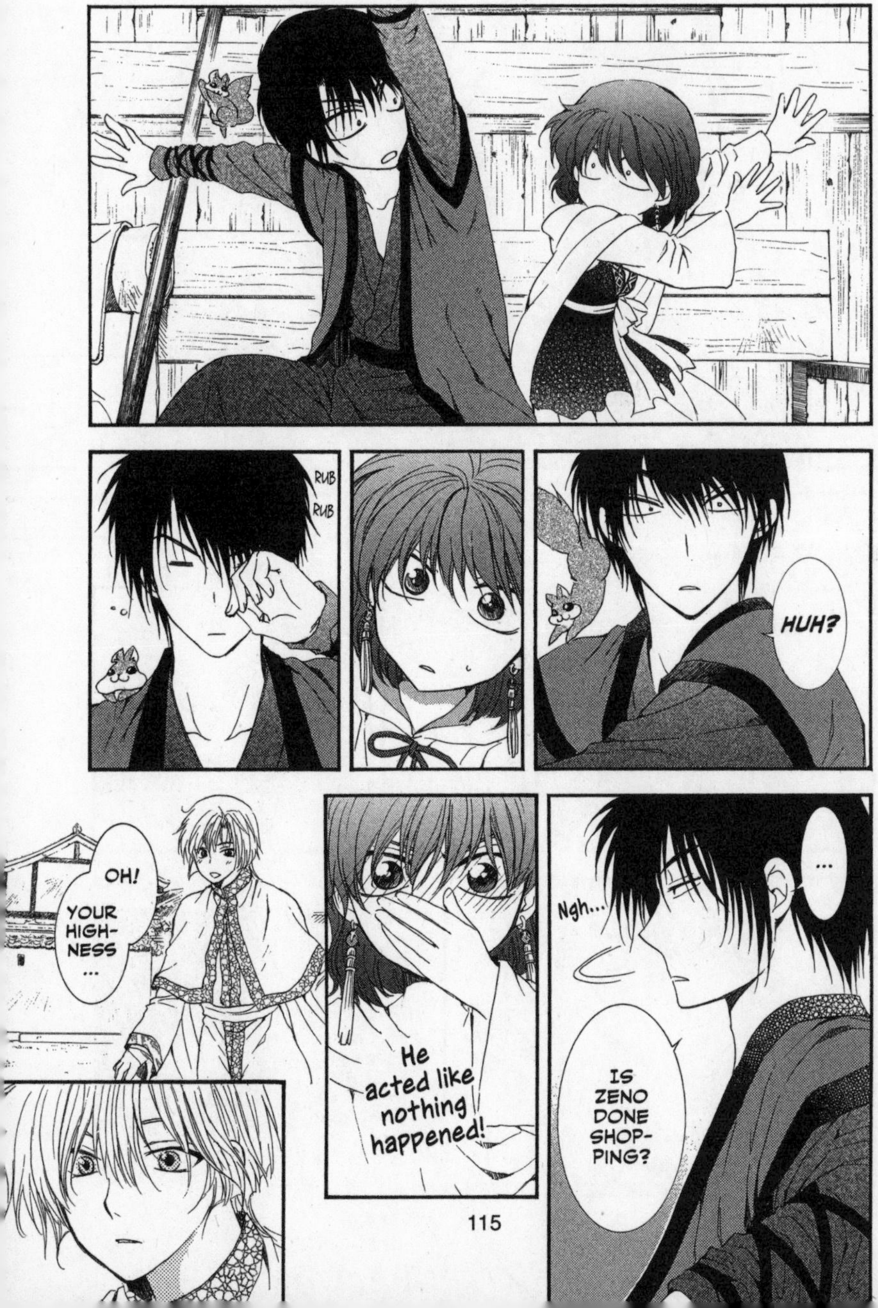
HUH?
RUB RUB
...
Ngh...
IS ZENO DONE SHOPPING?
He acted like nothing happened!
OH!
YOUR HIGHNESS...

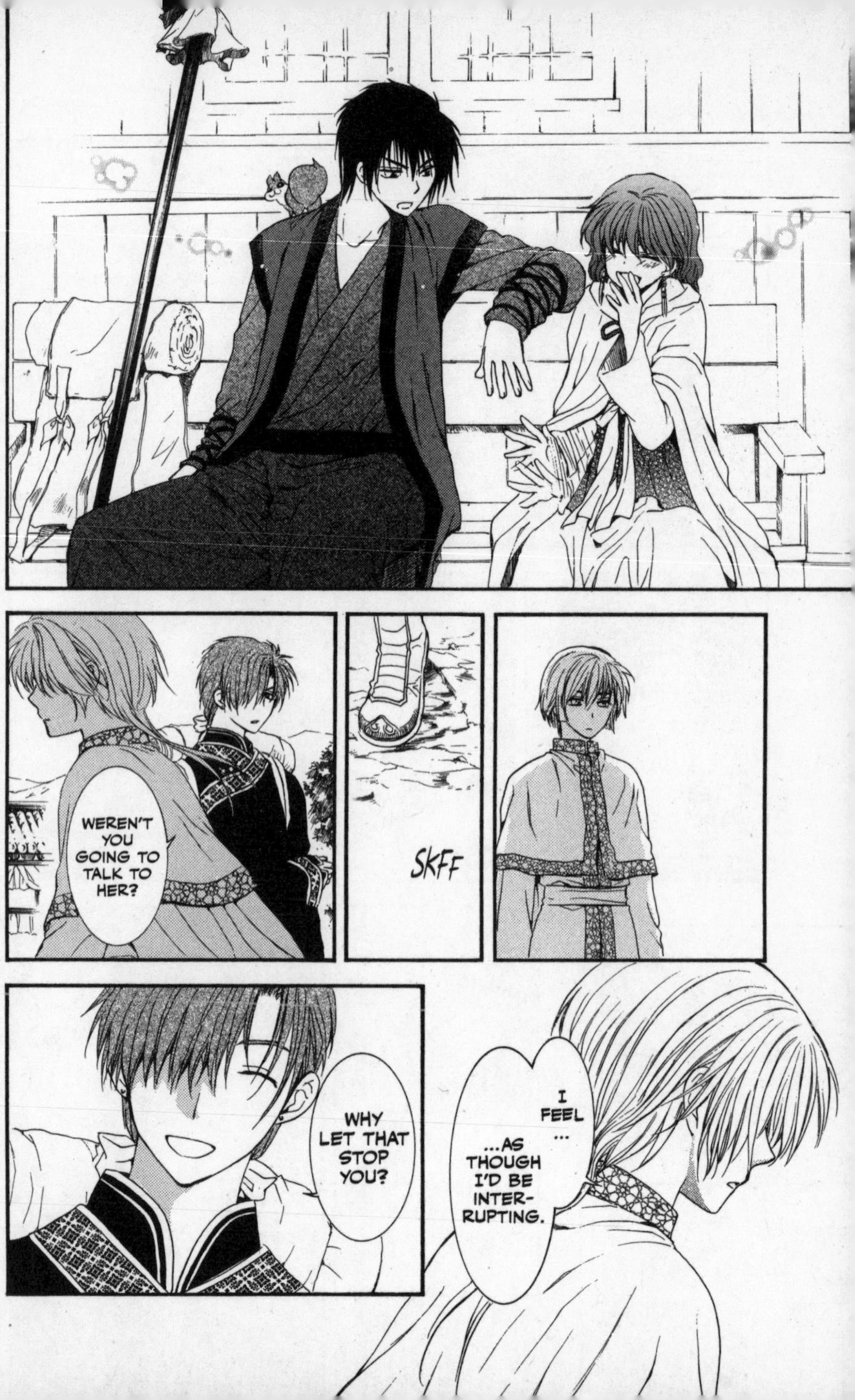
SKFF
WEREN'T YOU GOING TO TALK TO HER?
I FEEL ...
...AS THOUGH I'D BE INTER-RUPTING.
WHY LET THAT STOP YOU?

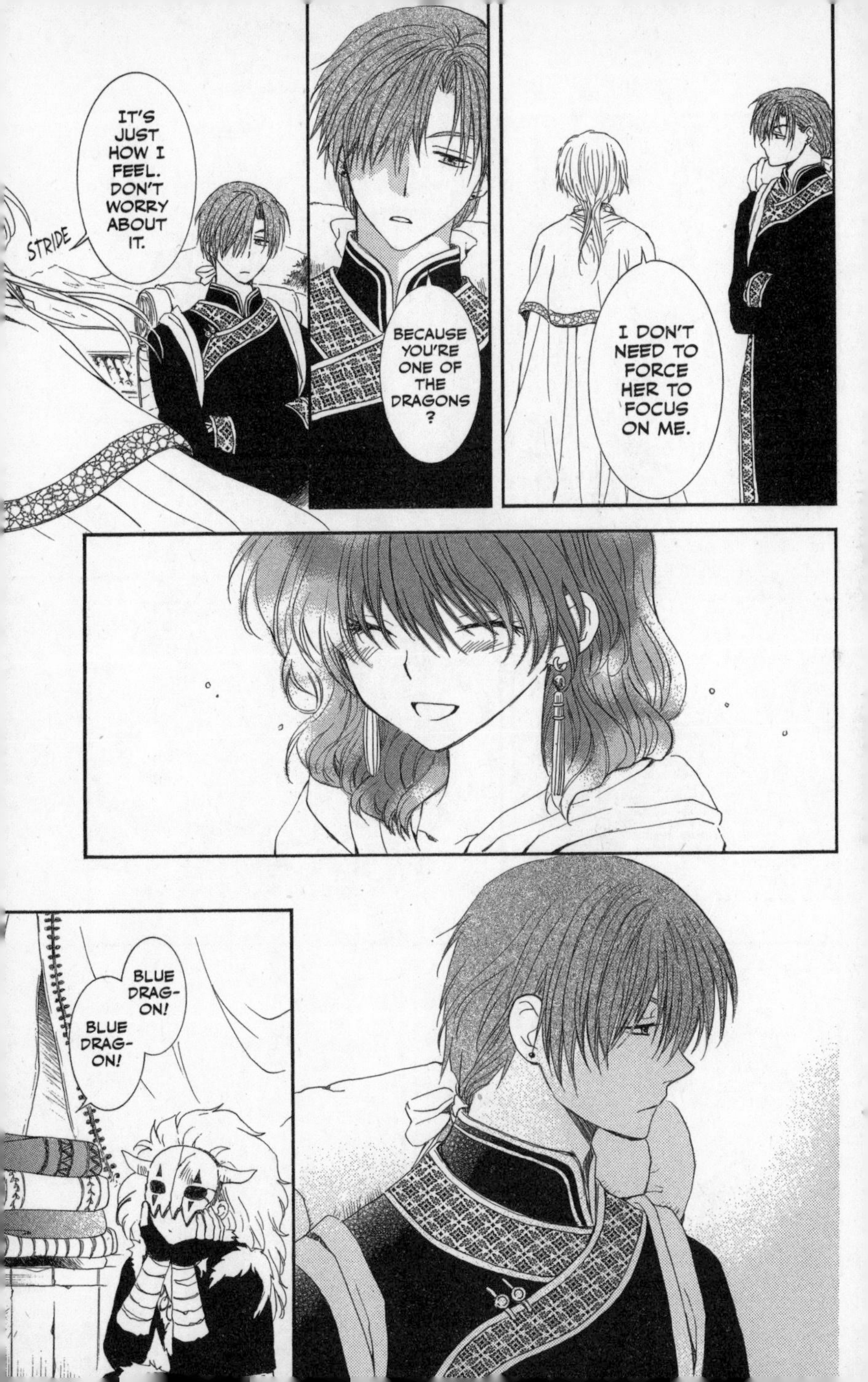
I DON'T NEED TO FORCE HER TO FOCUS ON ME.
BECAUSE YOU'RE ONE OF THE DRAGONS?
IT'S JUST HOW I FEEL. DON'T WORRY ABOUT IT.
STRIDE
BLUE DRAG-ON!
BLUE DRAG-ON!

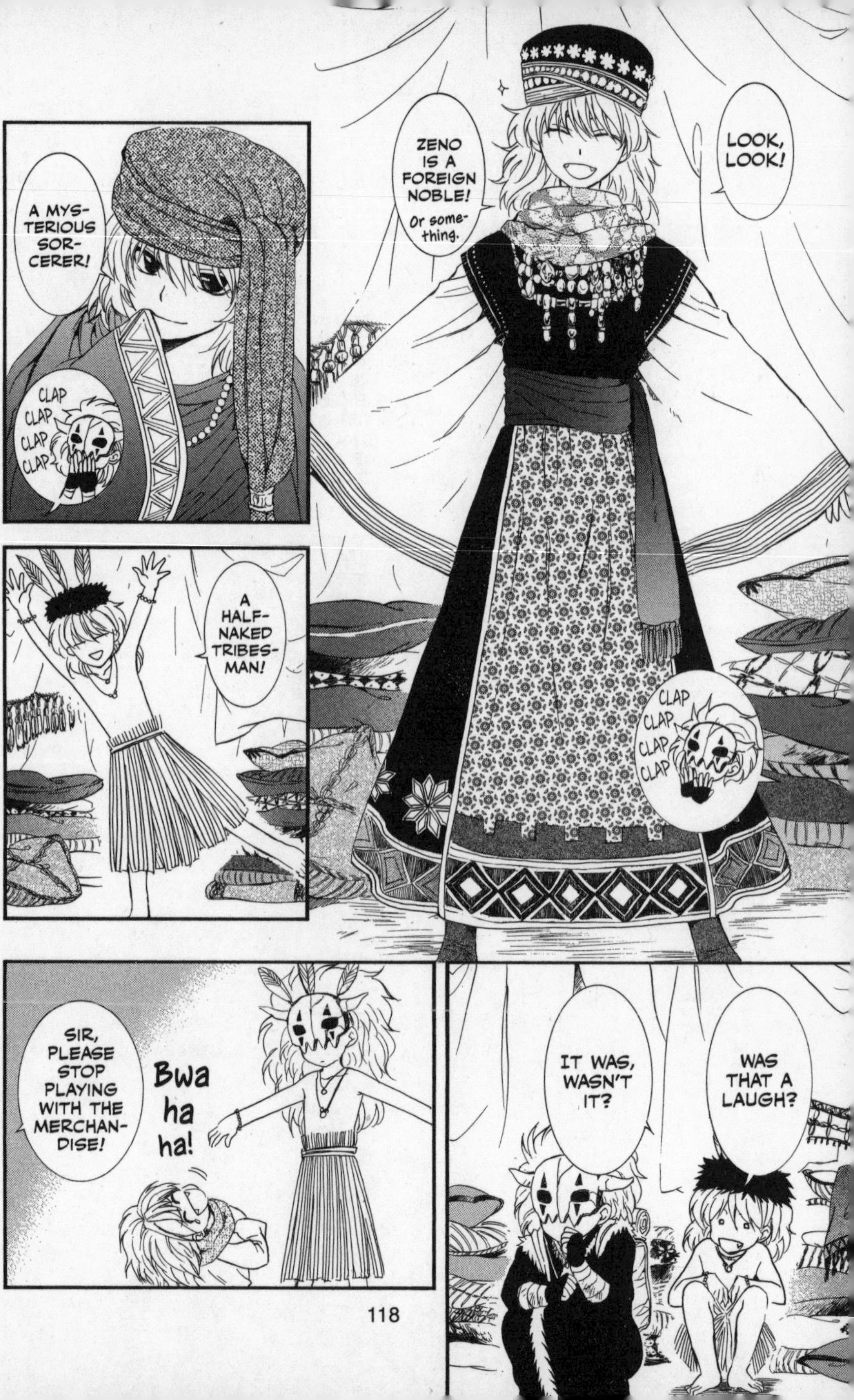
LOOK, LOOK!
ZENO IS A FOREIGN NOBLE!
Or something.
CLAP CLAP CLAP CLAP
A MYSTERIOUS SORCERER!
CLAP CLAP CLAP CLAP
A HALF-NAKED TRIBESMAN!
WAS THAT A LAUGH?
IT WAS, WASN'T IT?
Bwa ha ha!
SIR, PLEASE STOP PLAYING WITH THE MERCHANDISE!

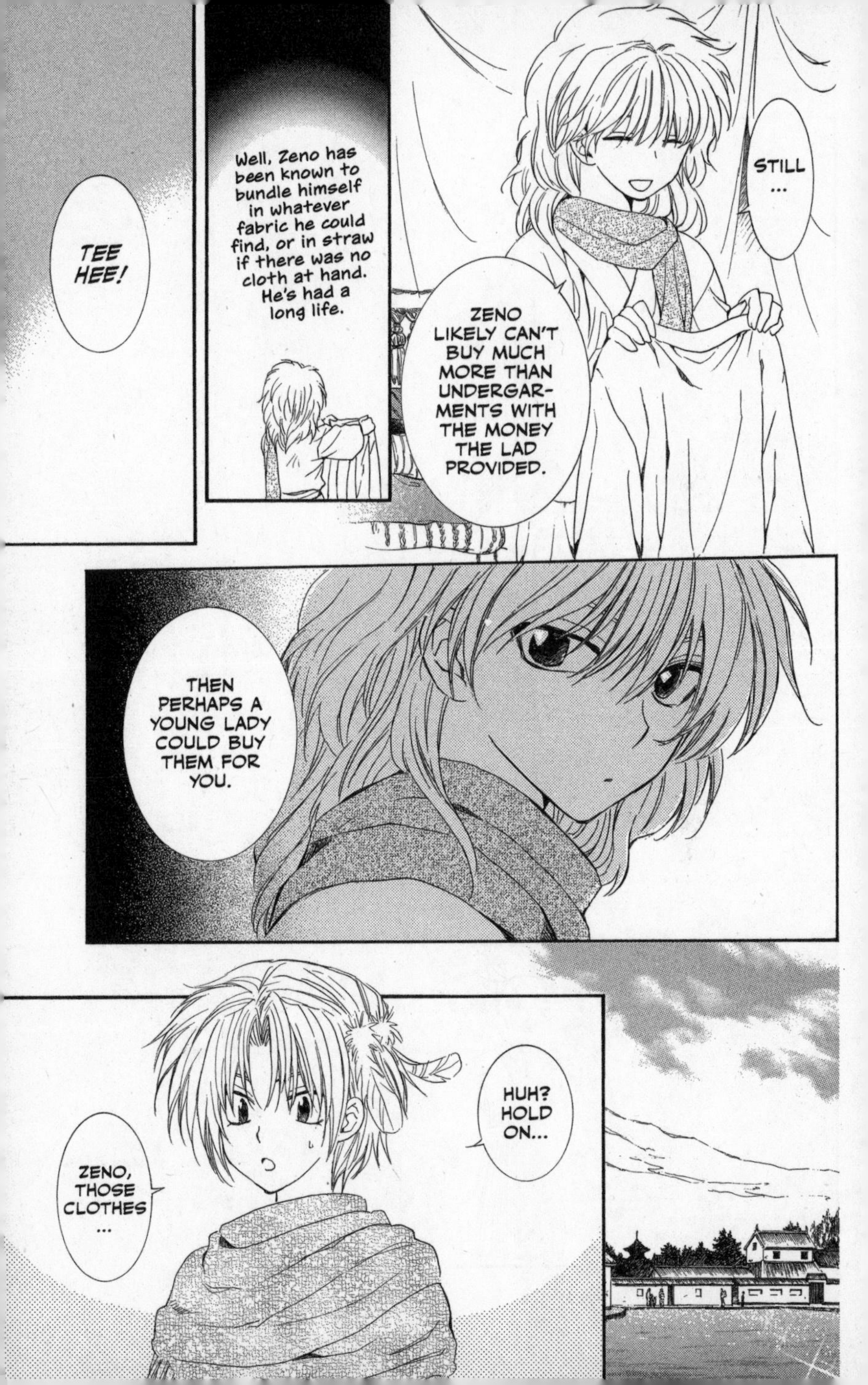
STILL ...
ZENO LIKELY CAN'T BUY MUCH MORE THAN UNDERGAR-MENTS WITH THE MONEY THE LAD PROVIDED.
Well, Zeno has been known to bundle himself in whatever fabric he could find, or in straw if there was no cloth at hand. He's had a long life.
TEE HEE!
THEN PERHAPS A YOUNG LADY COULD BUY THEM FOR YOU.
HUH? HOLD ON...
ZENO, THOSE CLOTHES ...

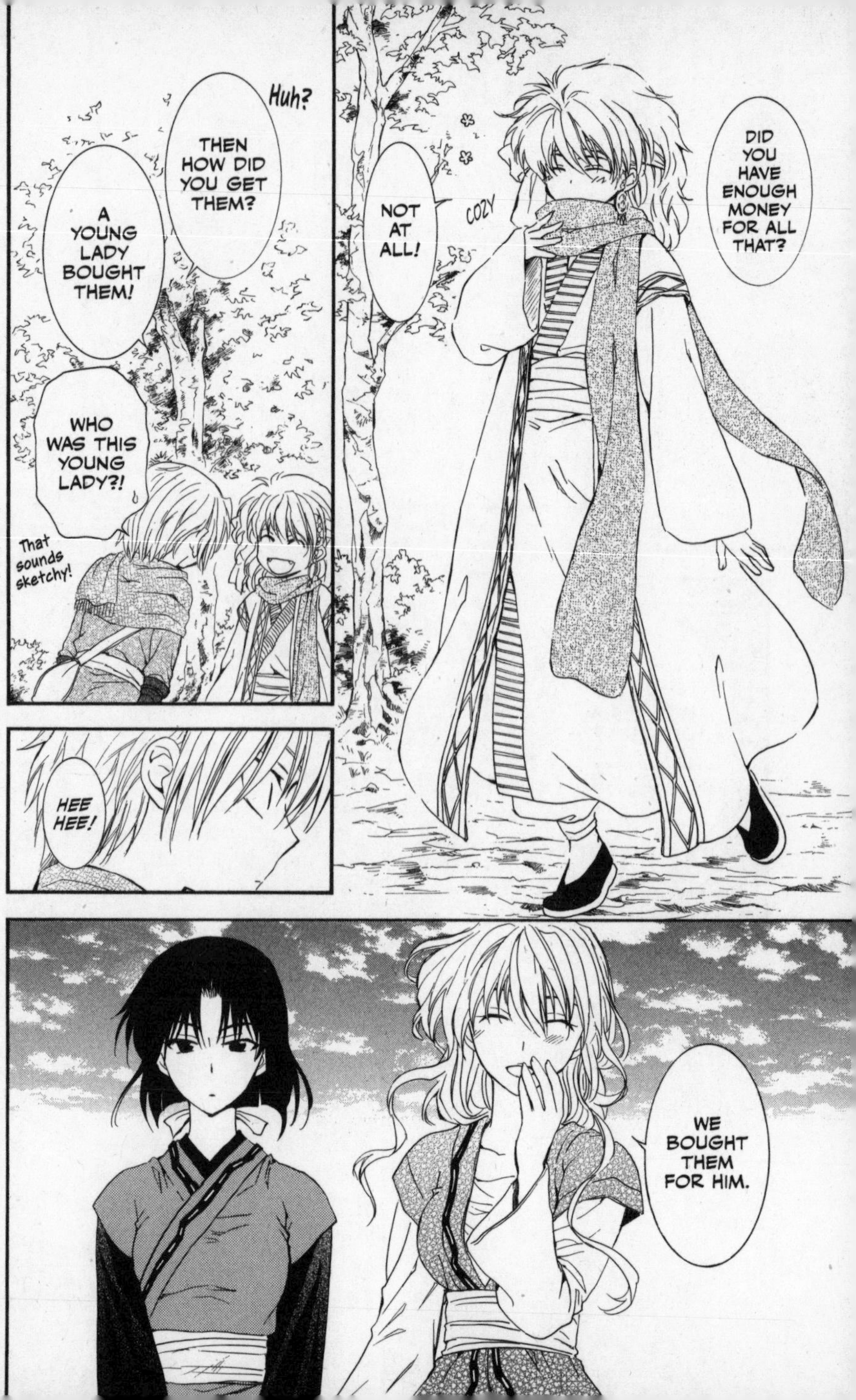
DID YOU HAVE ENOUGH MONEY FOR ALL THAT?
COZY
NOT AT ALL!
Huh?
THEN HOW DID YOU GET THEM?
A YOUNG LADY BOUGHT THEM!
WHO WAS THIS YOUNG LADY?!
That sounds sketchy!
HEE HEE!
WE BOUGHT THEM FOR HIM.

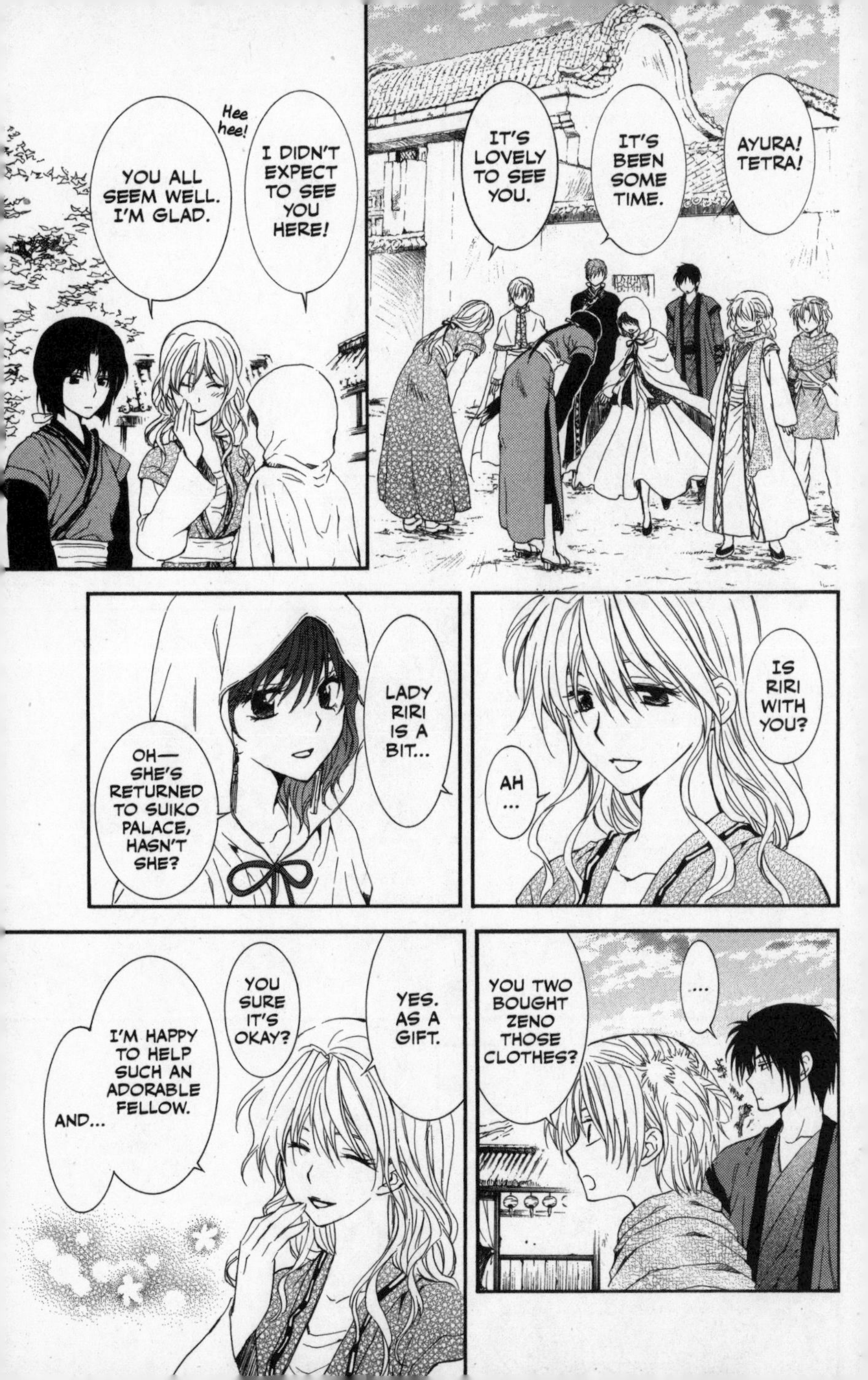
AYURA! TETRA!
IT'S BEEN SOME TIME.
IT'S LOVELY TO SEE YOU.
I DIDN'T EXPECT TO SEE YOU HERE!
Hee hee!
YOU ALL SEEM WELL. I'M GLAD.
IS RIRI WITH YOU?
AH ...
LADY RIRI IS A BIT...
OH— SHE'S RETURNED TO SUIKO PALACE, HASN'T SHE?
....
YOU TWO BOUGHT ZENO THOSE CLOTHES?
YES. AS A GIFT.
YOU SURE IT'S OKAY?
I'M HAPPY TO HELP SUCH AN ADORABLE FELLOW.
AND...

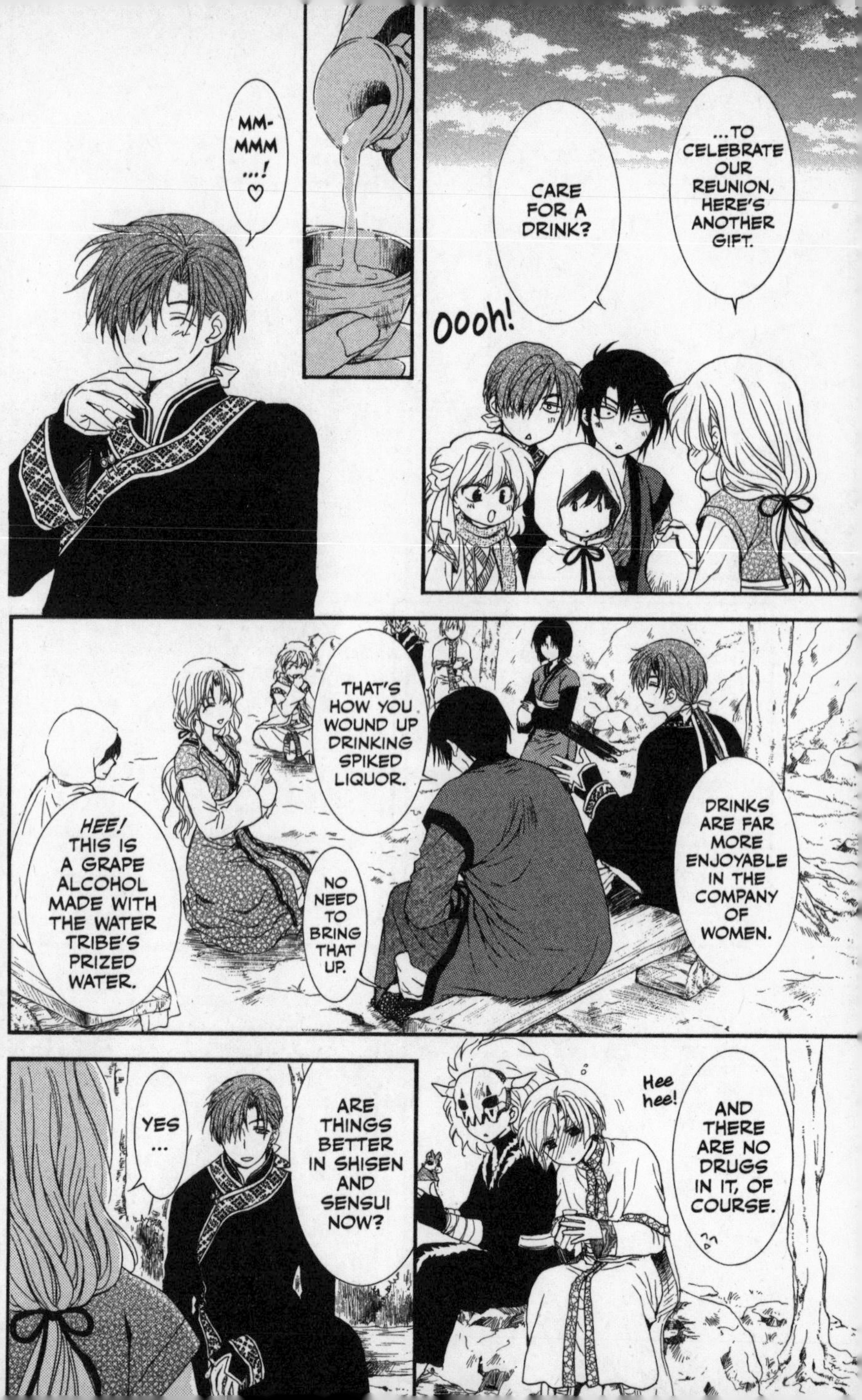
...TO CELEBRATE OUR REUNION, HERE'S ANOTHER GIFT.
CARE FOR A DRINK?
Oooh!
MM-MMM ...! ♡
DRINKS ARE FAR MORE ENJOYABLE IN THE COMPANY OF WOMEN.
THAT'S HOW YOU WOUND UP DRINKING SPIKED LIQUOR.
NO NEED TO BRING THAT UP.
HEE! THIS IS A GRAPE ALCOHOL MADE WITH THE WATER TRIBE'S PRIZED WATER.
AND THERE ARE NO DRUGS IN IT, OF COURSE.
Hee hee!
ARE THINGS BETTER IN SHISEN AND SENSUI NOW?
YES ...

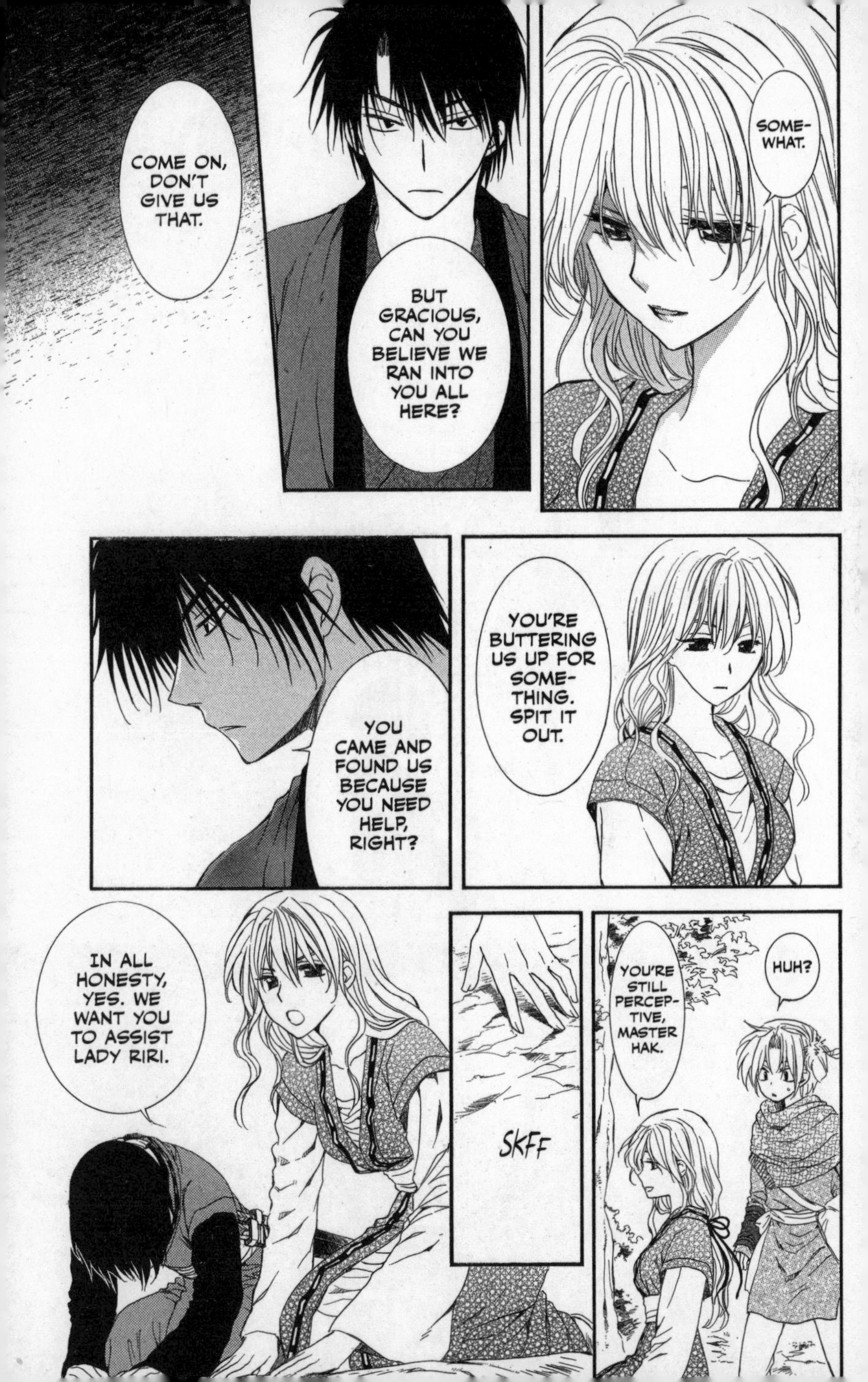
SOME-WHAT.
BUT GRACIOUS, CAN YOU BELIEVE WE RAN INTO YOU ALL HERE?
COME ON, DON'T GIVE US THAT.
YOU'RE BUTTERING US UP FOR SOME-THING. SPIT IT OUT.
YOU CAME AND FOUND US BECAUSE YOU NEED HELP, RIGHT?
YOU'RE STILL PERCEP-TIVE, MASTER HAK.
HUH?
SKFF
IN ALL HONESTY, YES. WE WANT YOU TO ASSIST LADY RIRI.

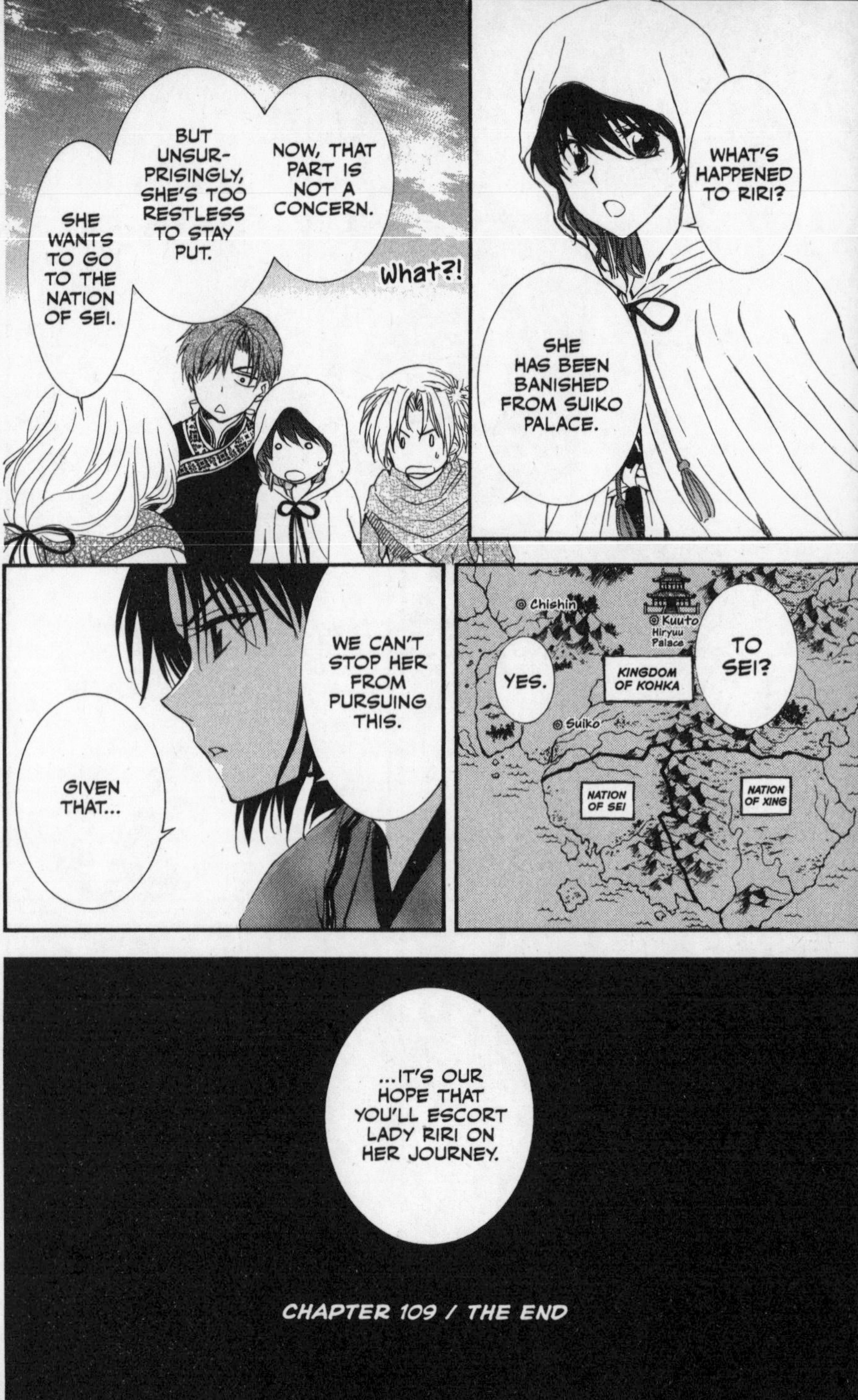
WHAT'S HAPPENED TO RIRI?
SHE HAS BEEN BANISHED FROM SUIKO PALACE.
NOW, THAT PART IS NOT A CONCERN.
BUT UNSURPRISINGLY, SHE'S TOO RESTLESS TO STAY PUT.
SHE WANTS TO GO TO THE NATION OF SEI.
What?!
TO SEI?
YES.
Chishin
Kuuto
Hiryuu Palace
KINGDOM OF KOHKA
Suiko
NATION OF SEI
NATION OF XING
WE CAN'T STOP HER FROM PURSUING THIS.
GIVEN THAT...
...IT'S OUR HOPE THAT YOU'LL ESCORT LADY RIRI ON HER JOURNEY.
CHAPTER 109 / THE END

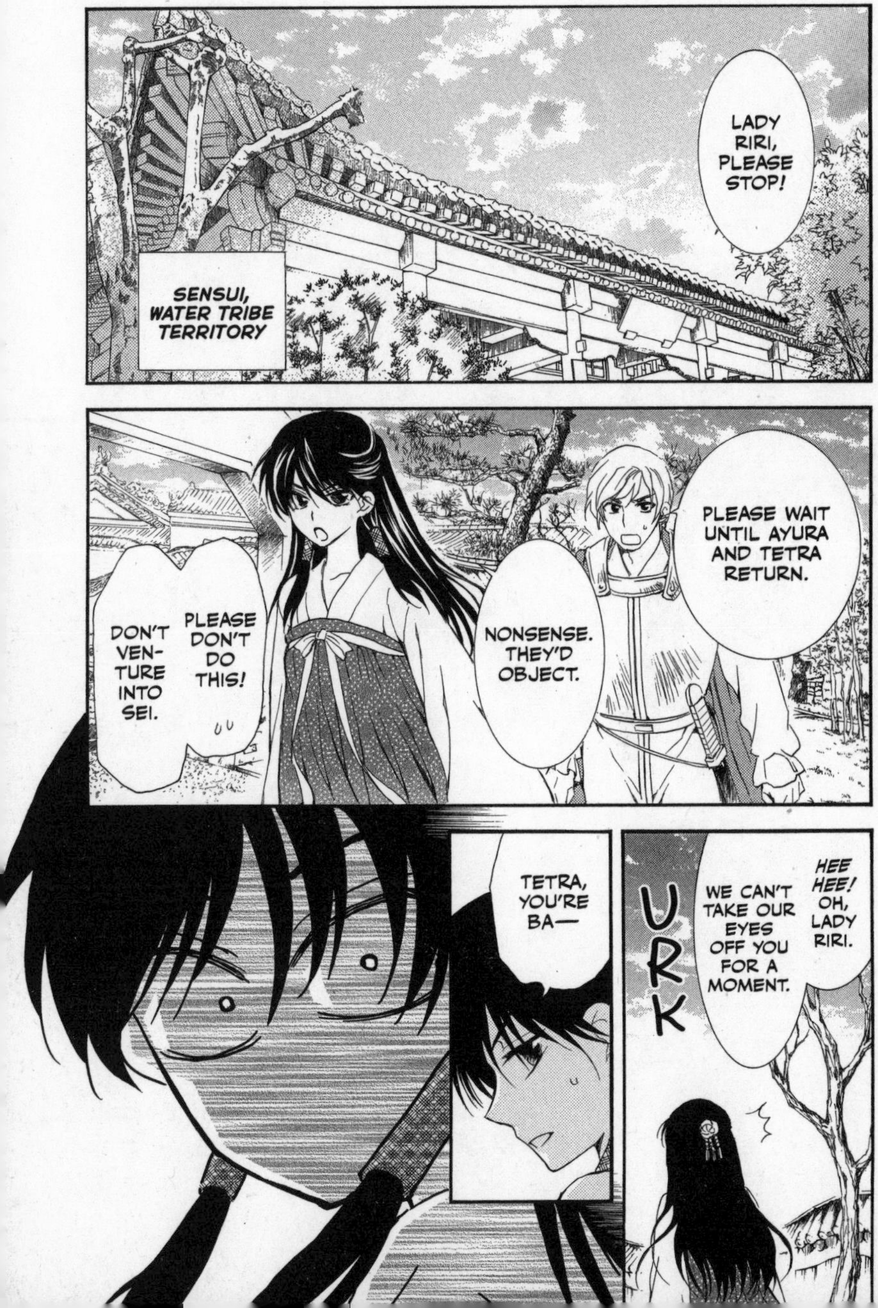
LADY RIRI, PLEASE STOP!
SENSUI, WATER TRIBE TERRITORY
PLEASE WAIT UNTIL AYURA AND TETRA RETURN.
NONSENSE. THEY'D OBJECT.
PLEASE DON'T DO THIS!
DON'T VEN- TURE INTO SEI.
HEE HEE! OH, LADY RIRI.
WE CAN'T TAKE OUR EYES OFF YOU FOR A MOMENT.
URK
TETRA, YOU'RE BA—

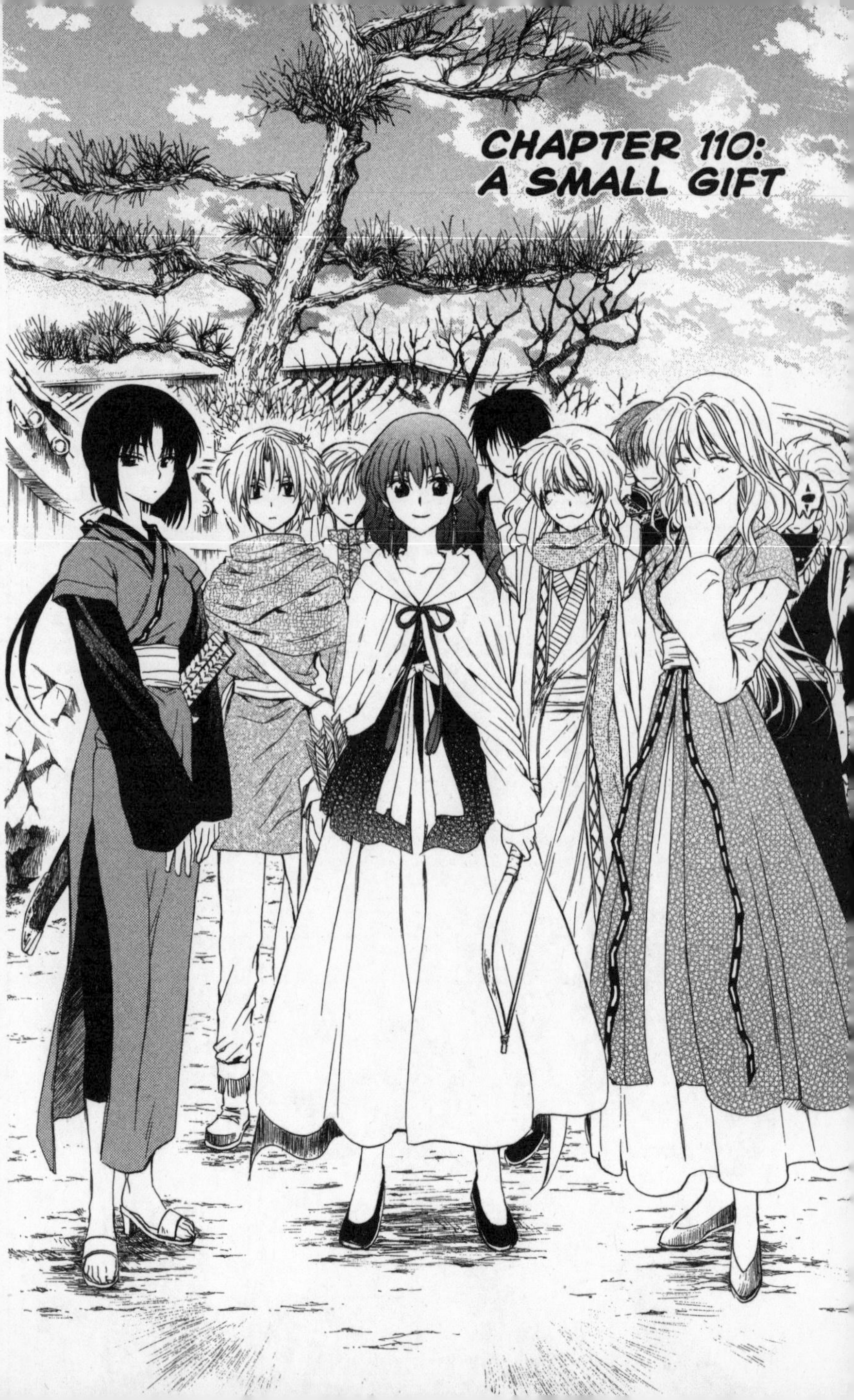
CHAPTER 110:
A SMALL GIFT

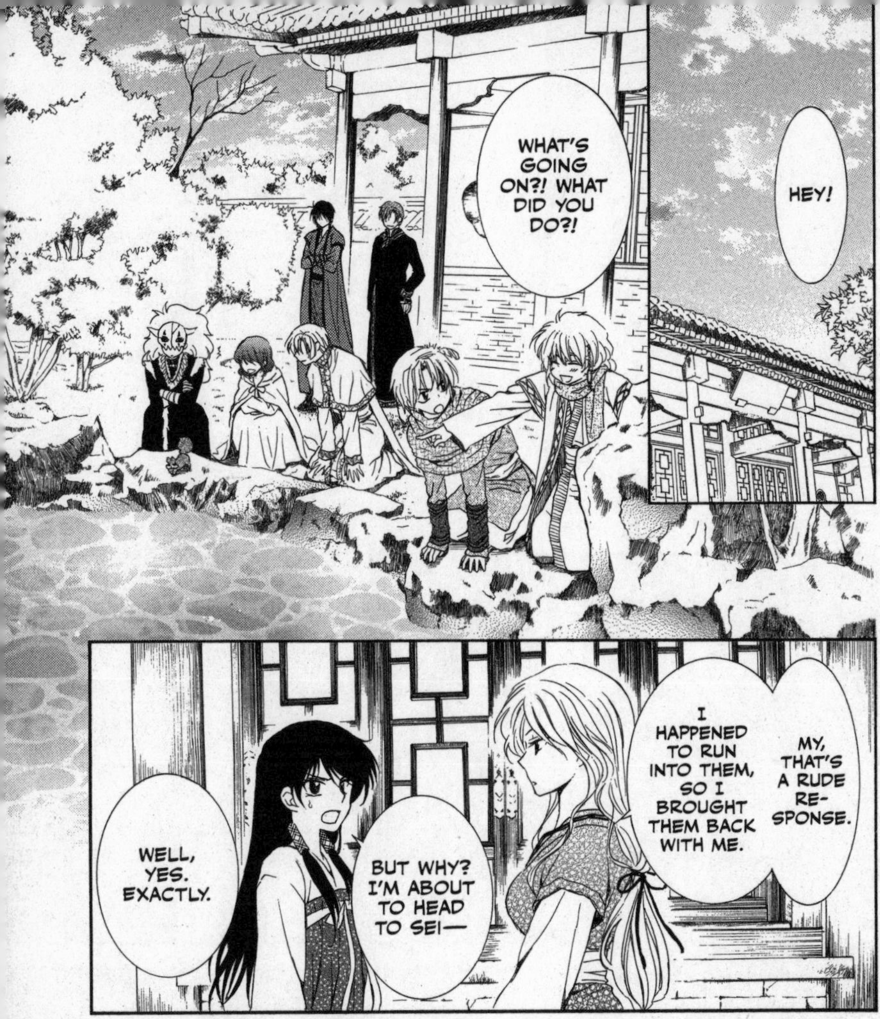
HEY!
WHAT'S GOING ON?! WHAT DID YOU DO?!
MY, THAT'S A RUDE RE-SPONSE.
I HAPPENED TO RUN INTO THEM, SO I BROUGHT THEM BACK WITH ME.
BUT WHY? I'M ABOUT TO HEAD TO SEI—
WELL, YES. EXACTLY.

Yona of the Dawn

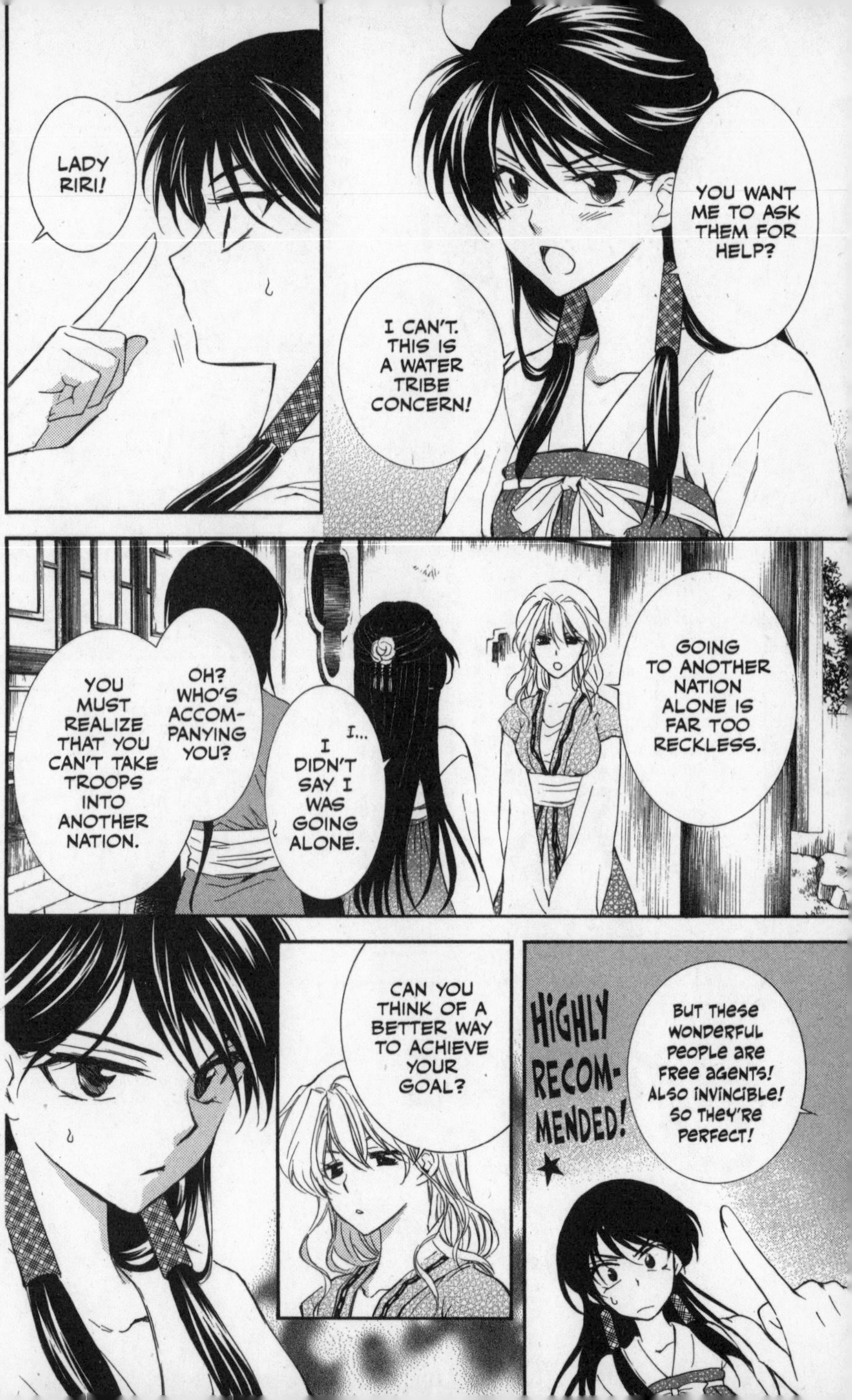
YOU WANT ME TO ASK THEM FOR HELP?
I CAN'T. THIS IS A WATER TRIBE CONCERN!
LADY RIRI!
GOING TO ANOTHER NATION ALONE IS FAR TOO RECKLESS.
I... I DIDN'T SAY I WAS GOING ALONE.
OH? WHO'S ACCOMPANYING YOU?
YOU MUST REALIZE THAT YOU CAN'T TAKE TROOPS INTO ANOTHER NATION.
BUT THESE WONDERFUL PEOPLE ARE FREE AGENTS! ALSO INVINCIBLE! SO THEY'RE PERFECT!
HIGHLY RECOM-MENDED!
CAN YOU THINK OF A BETTER WAY TO ACHIEVE YOUR GOAL?

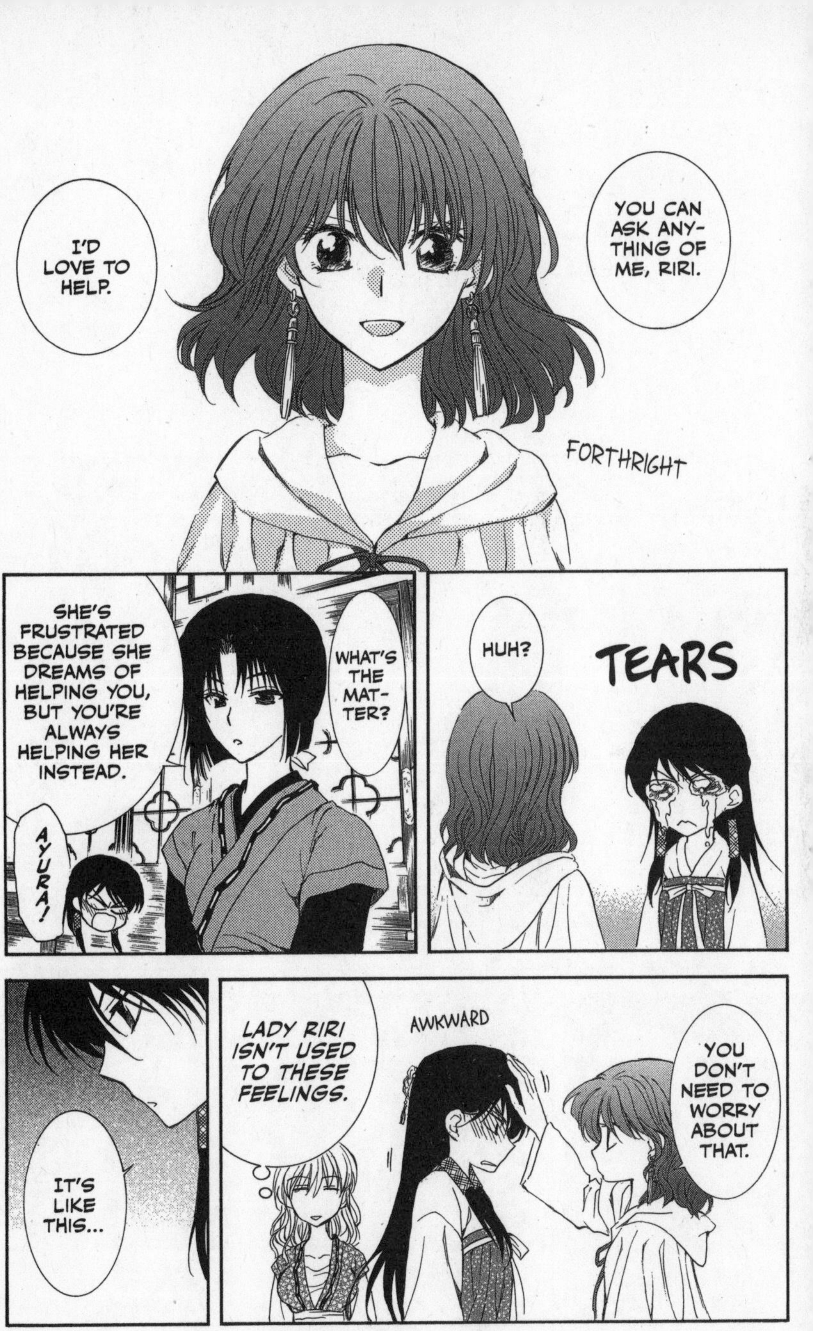
YOU CAN ASK ANYTHING OF ME, RIRI.
I'D LOVE TO HELP.
FORTHRIGHT
TEARS
HUH?
WHAT'S THE MATTER?
SHE'S FRUSTRATED BECAUSE SHE DREAMS OF HELPING YOU, BUT YOU'RE ALWAYS HELPING HER INSTEAD.
AYURA!
YOU DON'T NEED TO WORRY ABOUT THAT.
AWKWARD
LADY RIRI ISN'T USED TO THESE FEELINGS.
IT'S LIKE THIS...

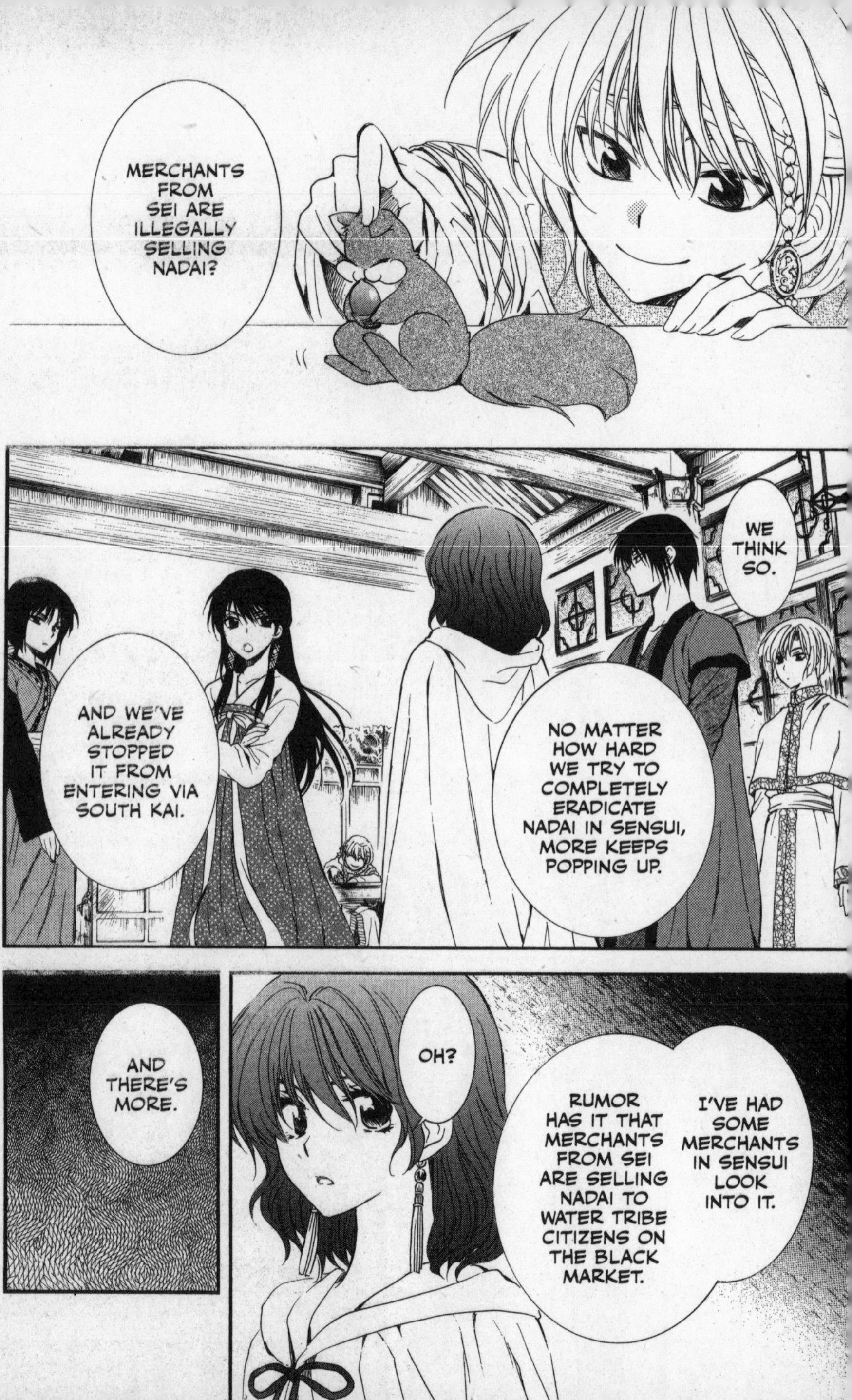
MERCHANTS FROM SEI ARE ILLEGALLY SELLING NADAI?
WE THINK SO.
NO MATTER HOW HARD WE TRY TO COMPLETELY ERADICATE NADAI IN SENSUI, MORE KEEPS POPPING UP.
AND WE'VE ALREADY STOPPED IT FROM ENTERING VIA SOUTH KAI.
OH?
I'VE HAD SOME MERCHANTS IN SENSUI LOOK INTO IT.
RUMOR HAS IT THAT MERCHANTS FROM SEI ARE SELLING NADAI TO WATER TRIBE CITIZENS ON THE BLACK MARKET.
AND THERE'S MORE.

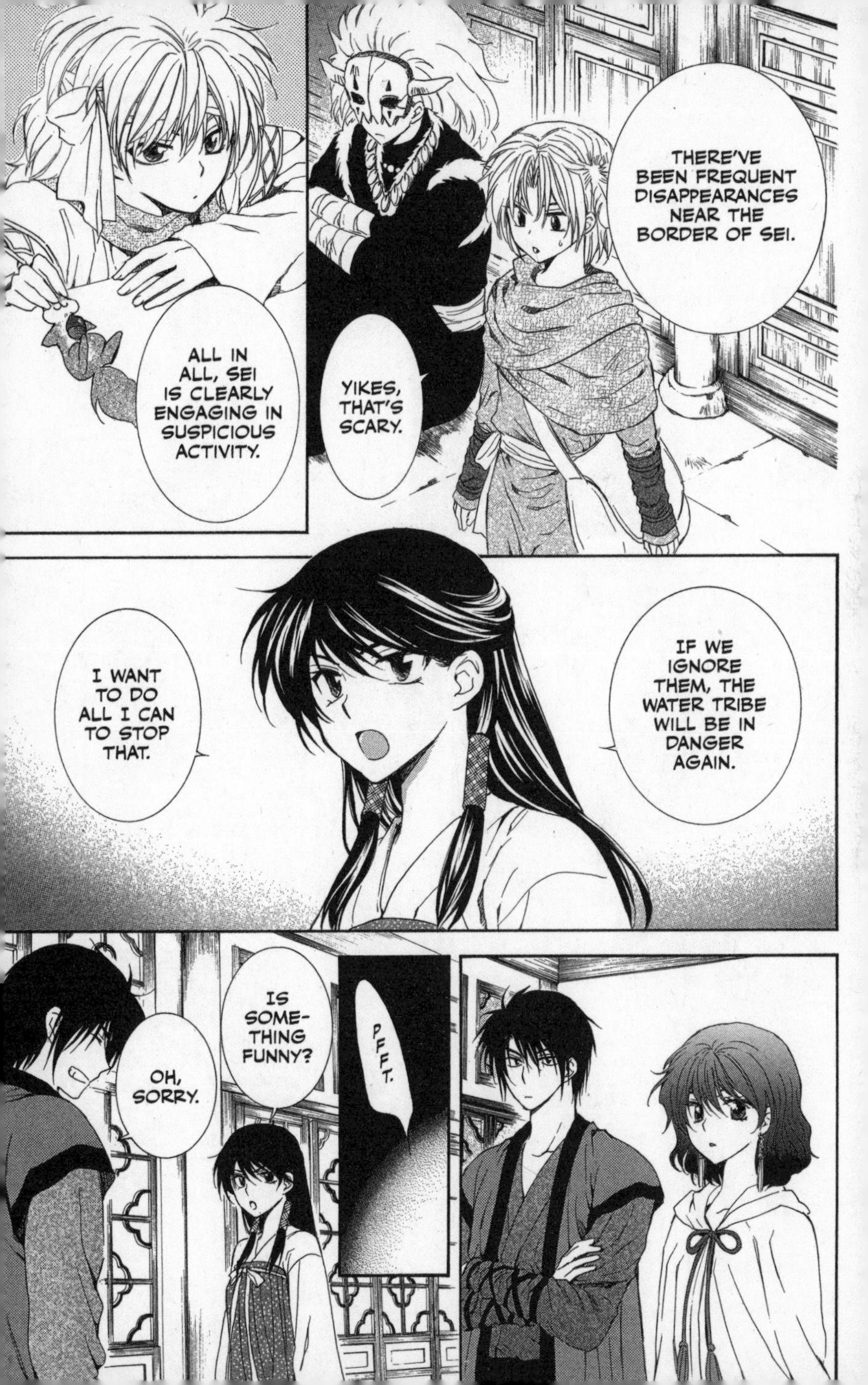
THERE'VE BEEN FREQUENT DISAPPEARANCES NEAR THE BORDER OF SEI.
YIKES, THAT'S SCARY.
ALL IN ALL, SEI IS CLEARLY ENGAGING IN SUSPICIOUS ACTIVITY.
IF WE IGNORE THEM, THE WATER TRIBE WILL BE IN DANGER AGAIN.
I WANT TO DO ALL I CAN TO STOP THAT.
PFFT.
IS SOME-THING FUNNY?
OH, SORRY.

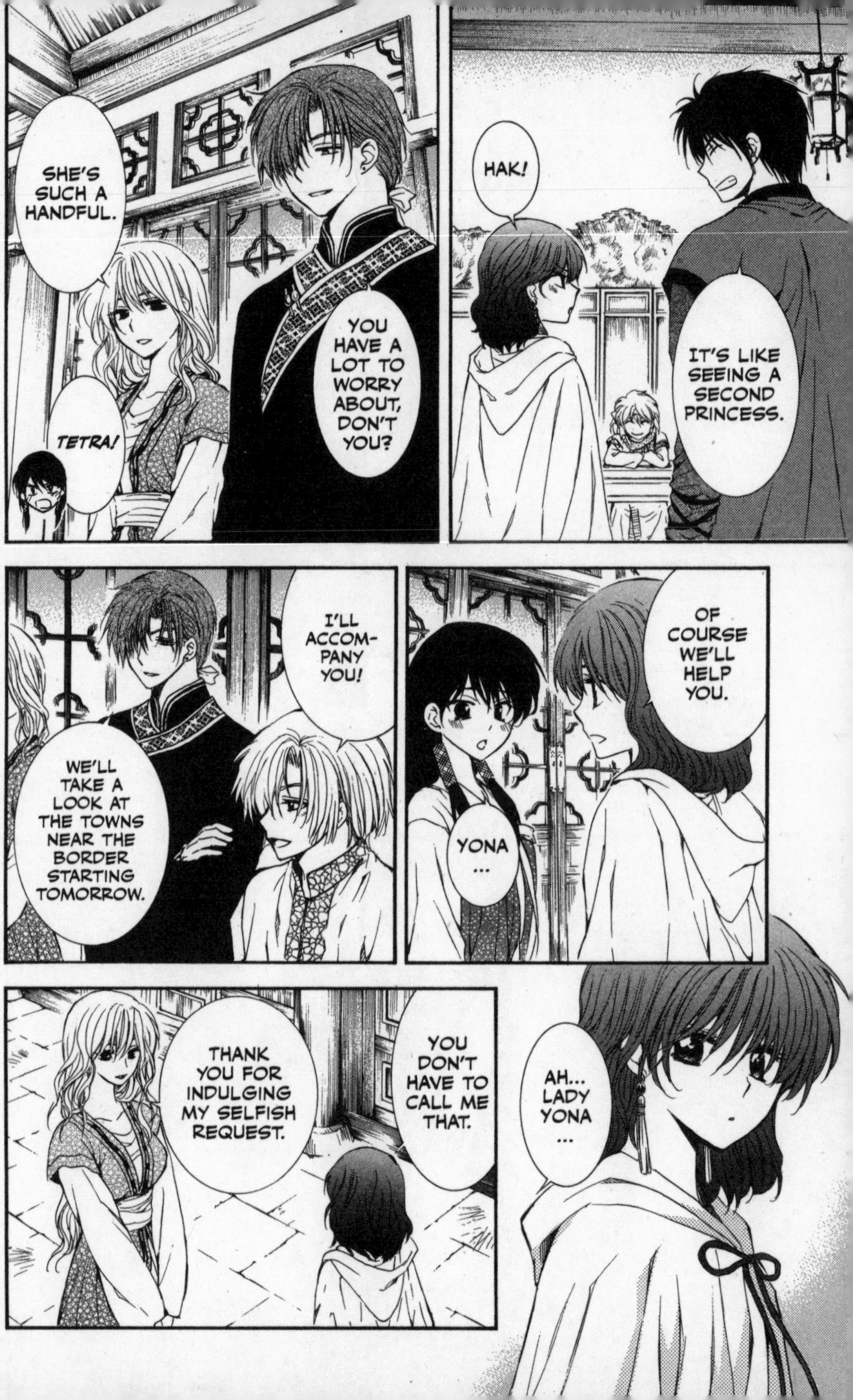
HAK!
IT'S LIKE SEEING A SECOND PRINCESS.
SHE'S SUCH A HANDFUL.
YOU HAVE A LOT TO WORRY ABOUT, DON'T YOU?
TETRA!
OF COURSE WE'LL HELP YOU.
YONA...
I'LL ACCOMPANY YOU!
WE'LL TAKE A LOOK AT THE TOWNS NEAR THE BORDER STARTING TOMORROW.
AH... LADY YONA...
YOU DON'T HAVE TO CALL ME THAT.
THANK YOU FOR INDULGING MY SELFISH REQUEST.

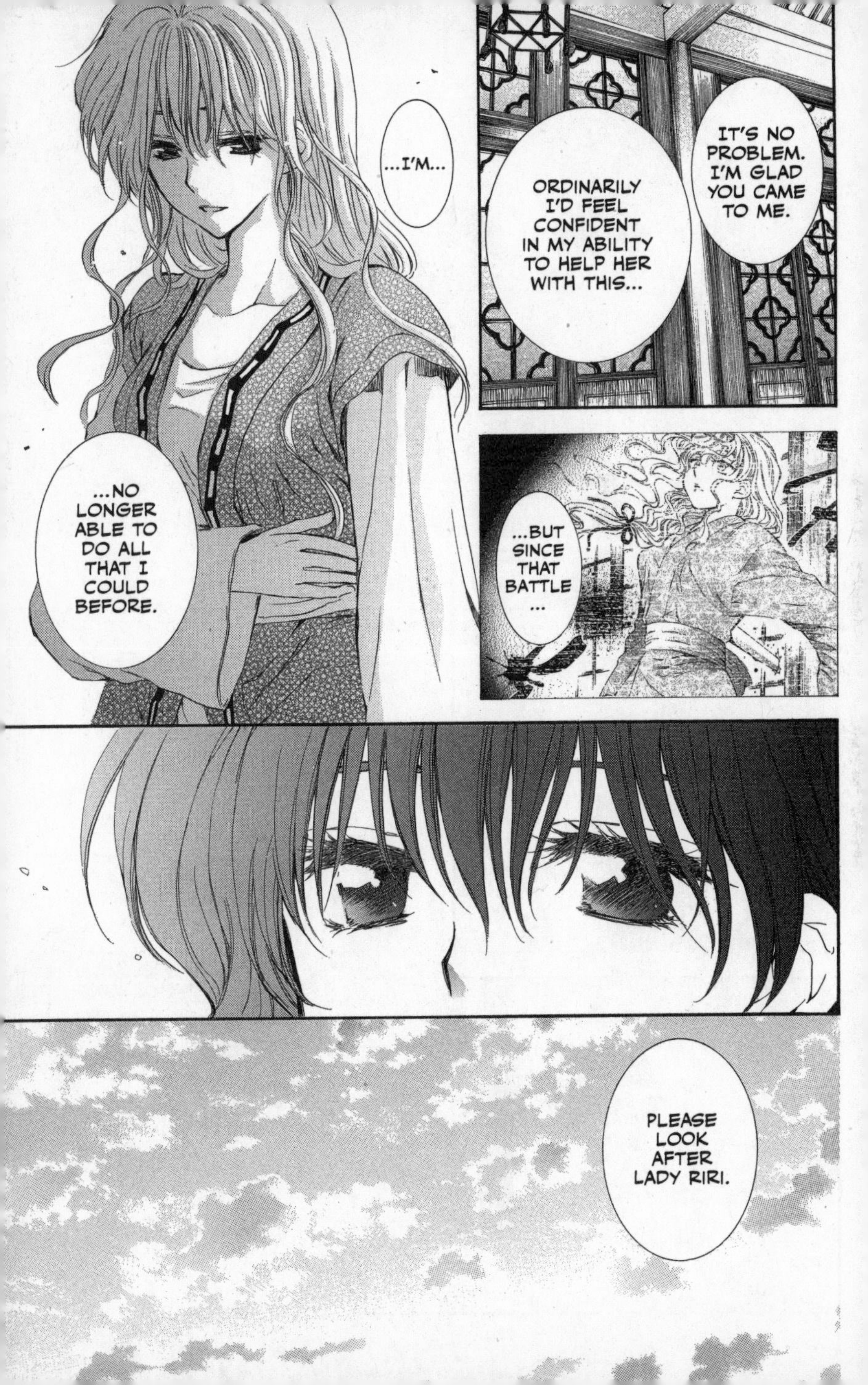
IT'S NO PROBLEM. I'M GLAD YOU CAME TO ME.
ORDINARILY I'D FEEL CONFIDENT IN MY ABILITY TO HELP HER WITH THIS...
...BUT SINCE THAT BATTLE...
...I'M...
...NO LONGER ABLE TO DO ALL THAT I COULD BEFORE.
PLEASE LOOK AFTER LADY RIRI.

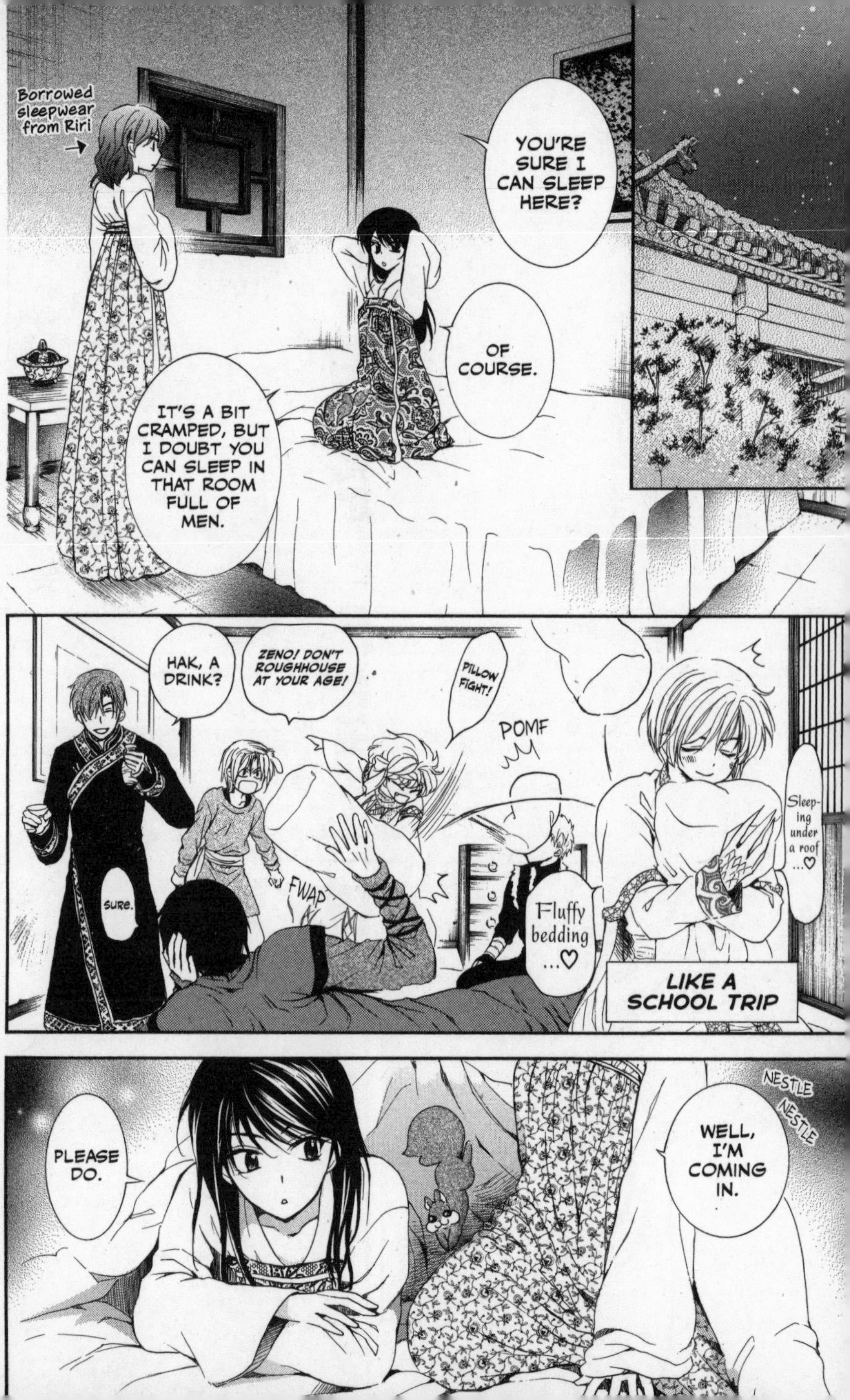
YOU'RE SURE I CAN SLEEP HERE?
OF COURSE.
IT'S A BIT CRAMPED, BUT I DOUBT YOU CAN SLEEP IN THAT ROOM FULL OF MEN.
Borrowed sleepwear from Riri
Sleeping under a roof ...♡
LIKE A SCHOOL TRIP
Fluffy bedding ...♡
POMF
PILLOW FIGHT!
ZENO! DON'T ROUGHHOUSE AT YOUR AGE!
HAK, A DRINK?
FWAP
Sure.
NESTLE NESTLE
WELL, I'M COMING IN.
PLEASE DO.

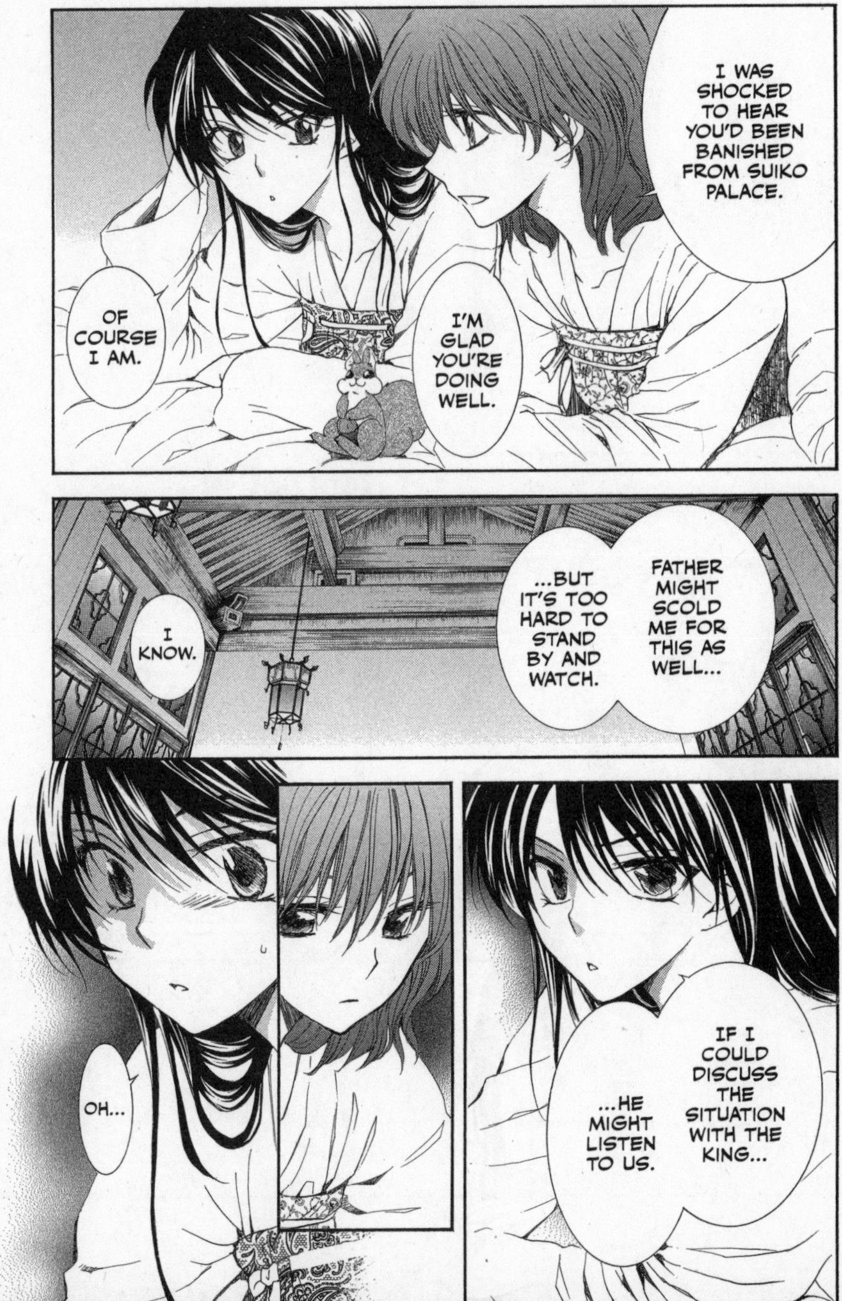
I WAS SHOCKED TO HEAR YOU'D BEEN BANISHED FROM SUIKO PALACE.
I'M GLAD YOU'RE DOING WELL.
OF COURSE I AM.
FATHER MIGHT SCOLD ME FOR THIS AS WELL...
...BUT IT'S TOO HARD TO STAND BY AND WATCH.
I KNOW.
IF I COULD DISCUSS THE SITUATION WITH THE KING...
...HE MIGHT LISTEN TO US.
OH...

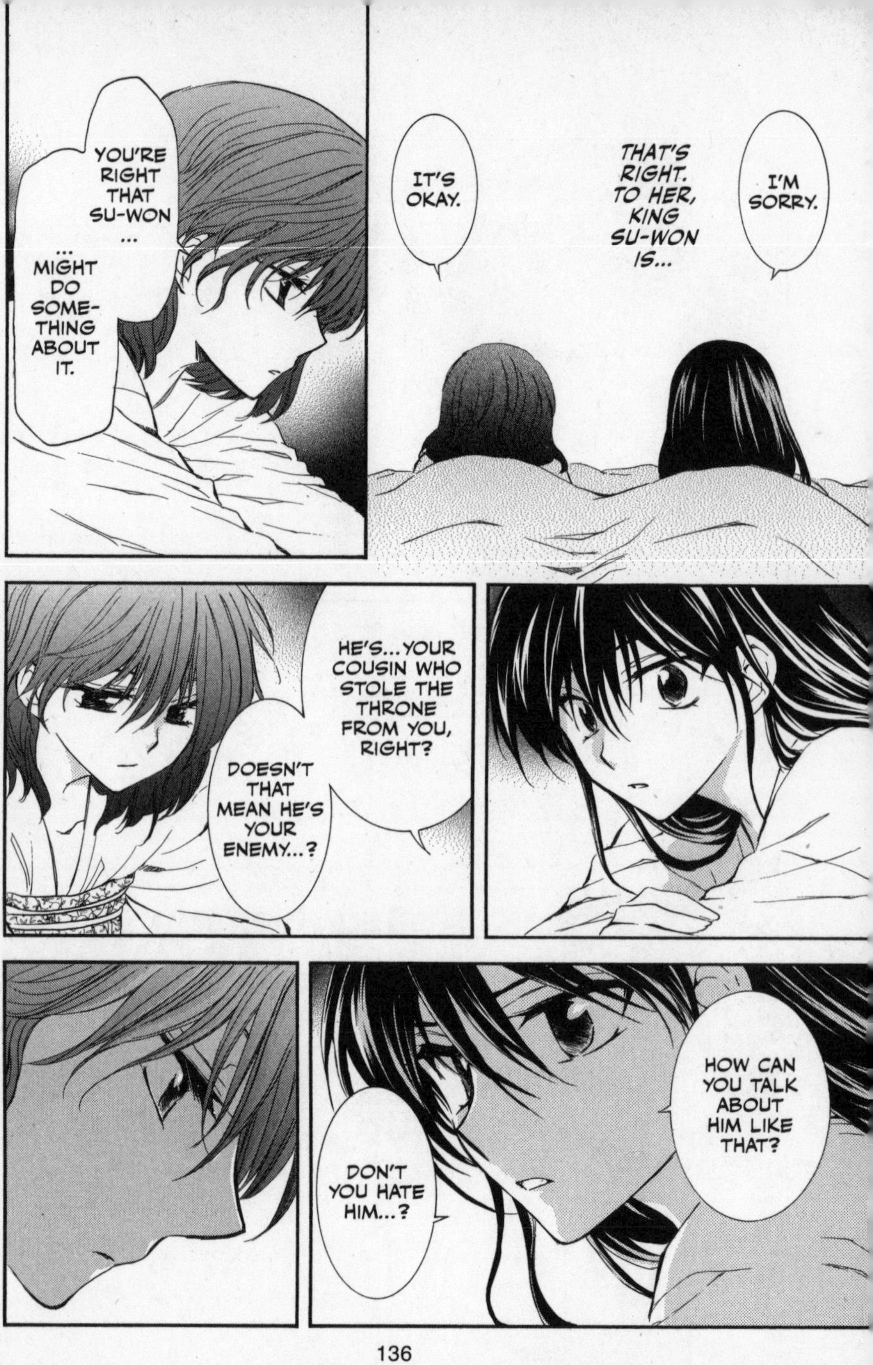
I'M SORRY.
THAT'S RIGHT. TO HER, KING SU-WON IS...
IT'S OKAY.
YOU'RE RIGHT THAT SU-WON ... MIGHT DO SOME-THING ABOUT IT.
HE'S...YOUR COUSIN WHO STOLE THE THRONE FROM YOU, RIGHT?
DOESN'T THAT MEAN HE'S YOUR ENEMY...?
HOW CAN YOU TALK ABOUT HIM LIKE THAT?
DON'T YOU HATE HIM...?

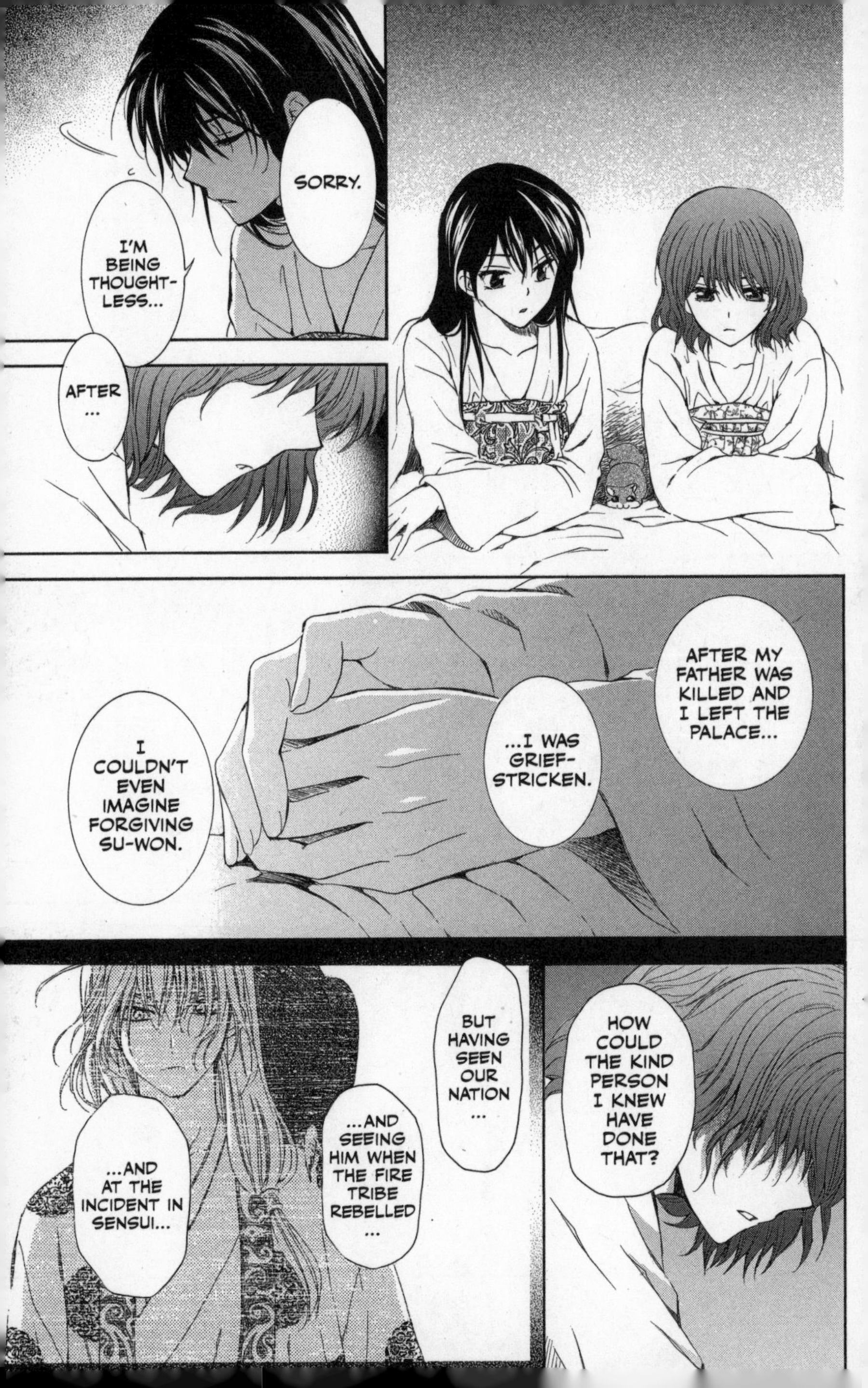
SORRY.
I'M BEING THOUGHTLESS...
AFTER...
AFTER MY FATHER WAS KILLED AND I LEFT THE PALACE...
...I WAS GRIEF-STRICKEN.
I COULDN'T EVEN IMAGINE FORGIVING SU-WON.
HOW COULD THE KIND PERSON I KNEW HAVE DONE THAT?
BUT HAVING SEEN OUR NATION...
...AND SEEING HIM WHEN THE FIRE TRIBE REBELLED...
...AND AT THE INCIDENT IN SENSUI...

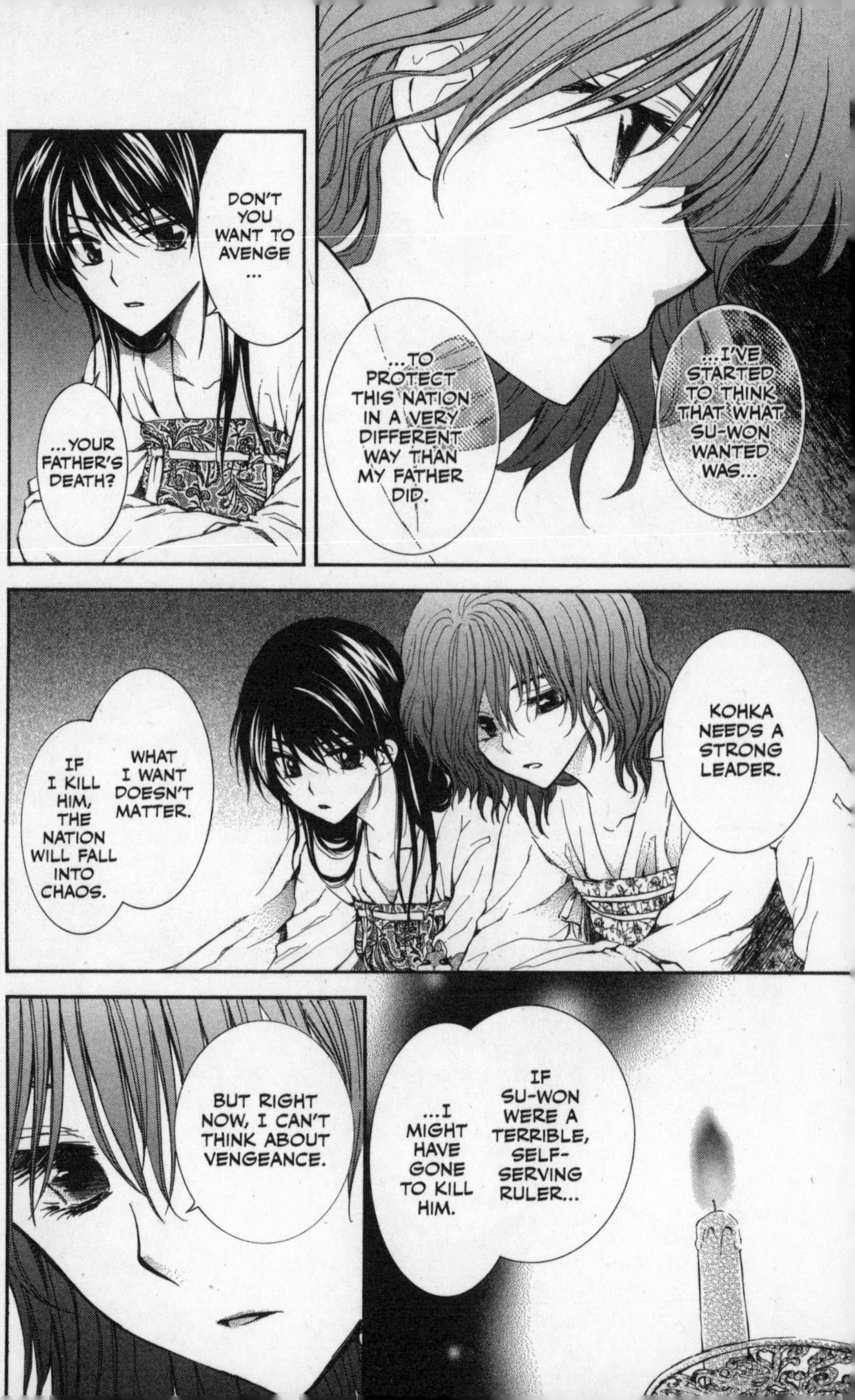
...I'VE STARTED TO THINK THAT WHAT SU-WON WANTED WAS...
...TO PROTECT THIS NATION IN A VERY DIFFERENT WAY THAN MY FATHER DID.
DON'T YOU WANT TO AVENGE ...
...YOUR FATHER'S DEATH?
KOHKA NEEDS A STRONG LEADER.
WHAT I WANT DOESN'T MATTER. IF I KILL HIM, THE NATION WILL FALL INTO CHAOS.
IF SU-WON WERE A TERRIBLE, SELF-SERVING RULER...
...I MIGHT HAVE GONE TO KILL HIM.
BUT RIGHT NOW, I CAN'T THINK ABOUT VENGEANCE.

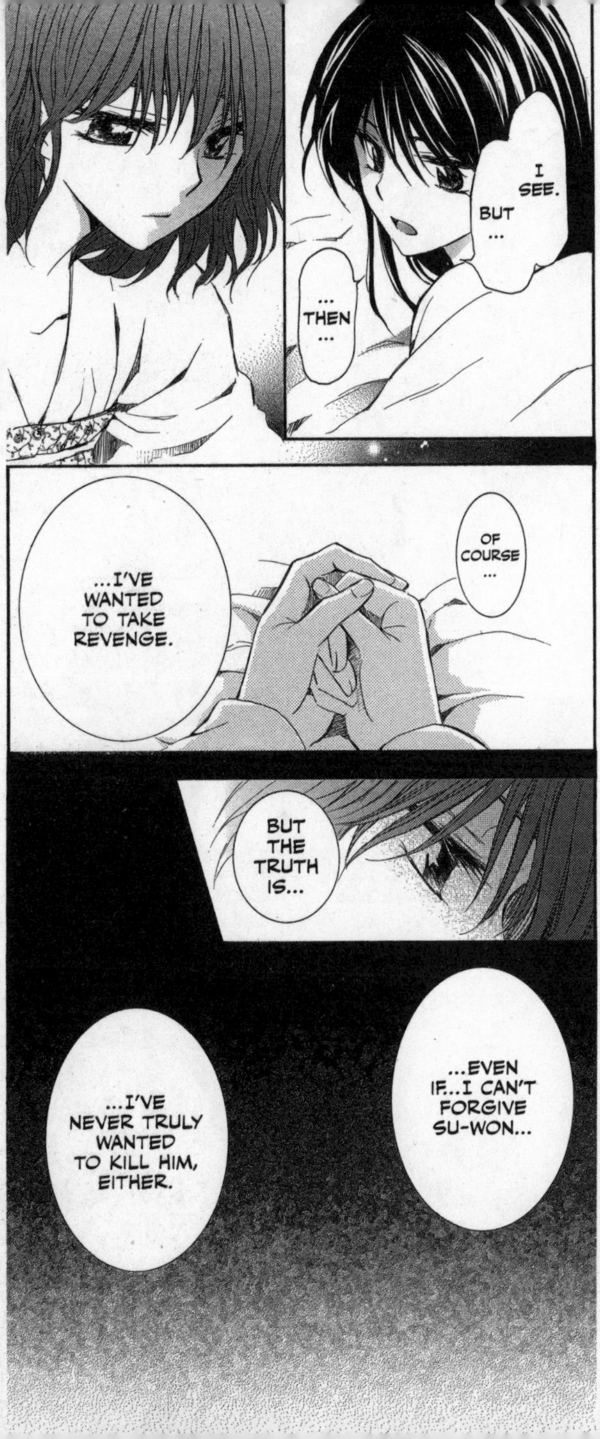
I SEE. BUT ...
... THEN ...
OF COURSE ...
...I'VE WANTED TO TAKE REVENGE.
BUT THE TRUTH IS...
...EVEN IF...I CAN'T FORGIVE SU-WON...
...I'VE NEVER TRULY WANTED TO KILL HIM, EITHER.

Here's a timeline for the spirit of the Blue Dragon that possessed Sinha in "The Blue Forest."

Roughly 2,000 years

- Abi, the first Blue Dragon
- Around here (roughly)
- The Blue Dragon who possessed Sinha in "The Blue Forest"
- Ao, the previous Blue Dragon (Sinha's predecessor)
- Sinha

It's easy to confuse the "first" with the "previous," isn't it? Sorry...

Abi isn't resting with the other Blue Dragons in the tombs we saw in "The Blue Forest." The village moved to different spots over the years.

The White Dragon's group was the only one that passed on knowledge about the Four Dragon Warriors and their powers over the span of those 2,000 years. Guen, the first White Dragon, had amazing leadership skills. The villages' respective peculiarities were each influenced by the first Dragons' personalities.

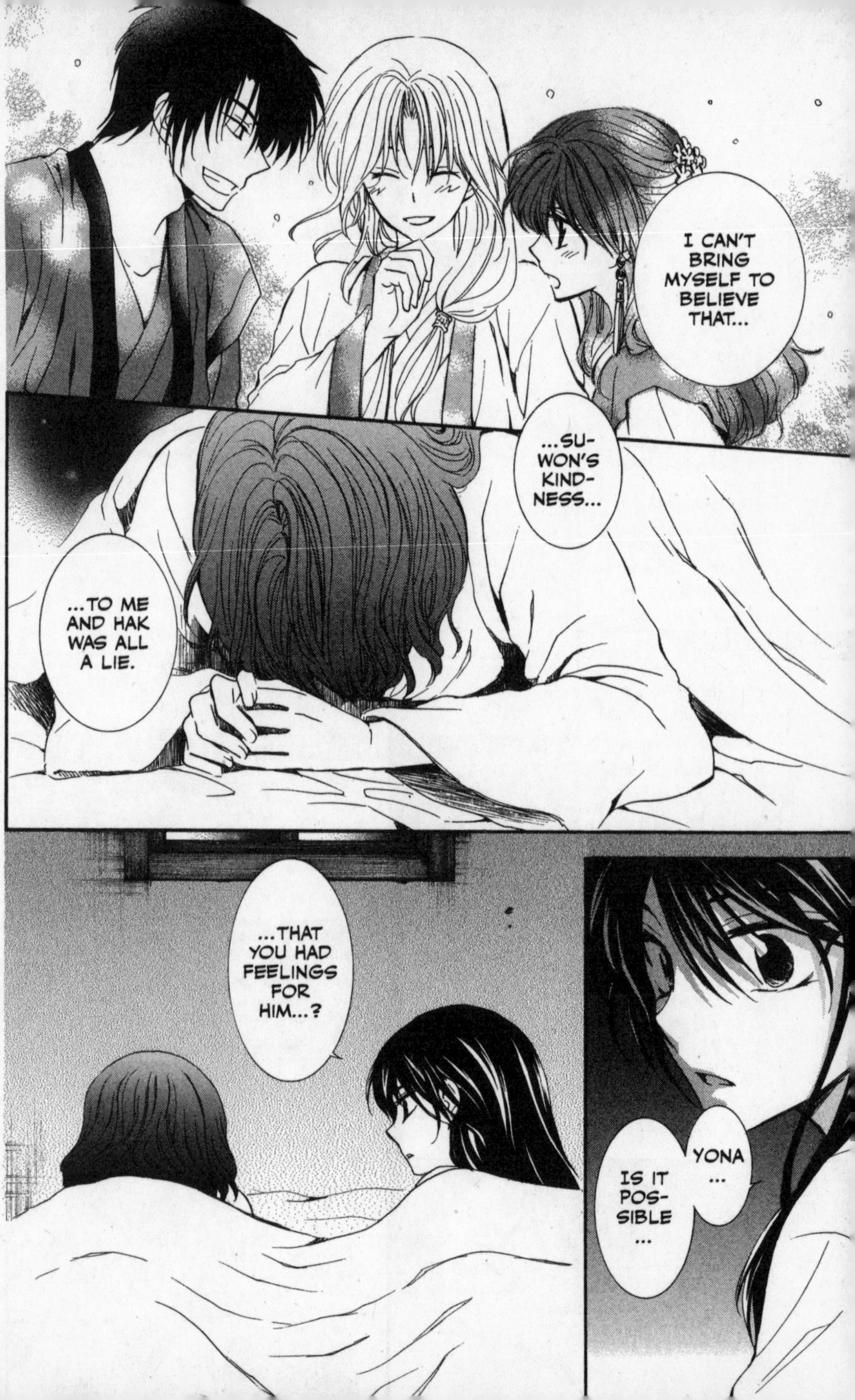
I CAN'T BRING MYSELF TO BELIEVE THAT...
...SU-WON'S KINDNESS...
...TO ME AND HAK WAS ALL A LIE.
YONA ...
IS IT POSSIBLE ...
...THAT YOU HAD FEELINGS FOR HIM...?

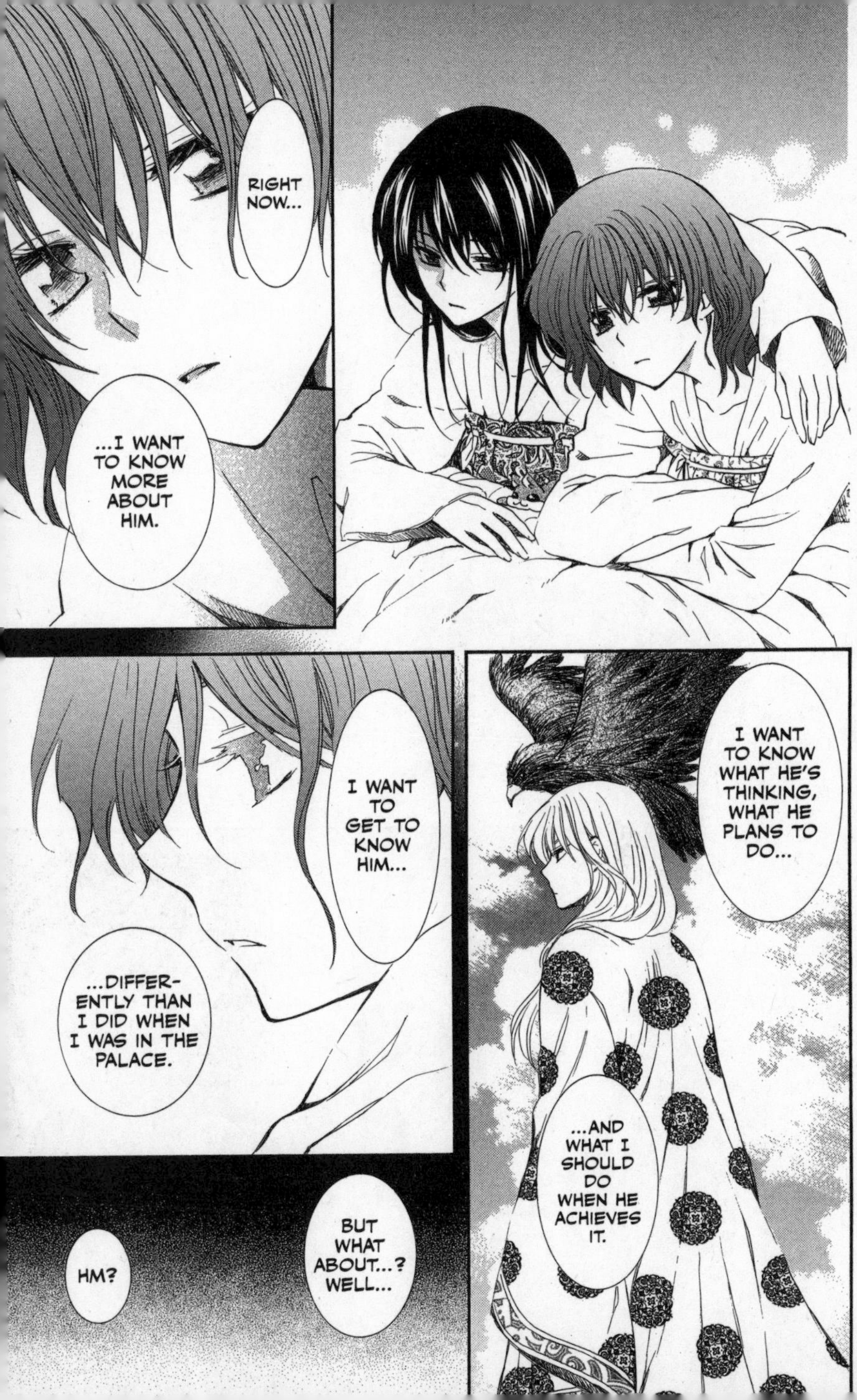
RIGHT NOW...
...I WANT TO KNOW MORE ABOUT HIM.
I WANT TO KNOW WHAT HE'S THINKING, WHAT HE PLANS TO DO...
...AND WHAT I SHOULD DO WHEN HE ACHIEVES IT.
I WANT TO GET TO KNOW HIM...
...DIFFER-ENTLY THAN I DID WHEN I WAS IN THE PALACE.
BUT WHAT ABOUT...? WELL...
HM?

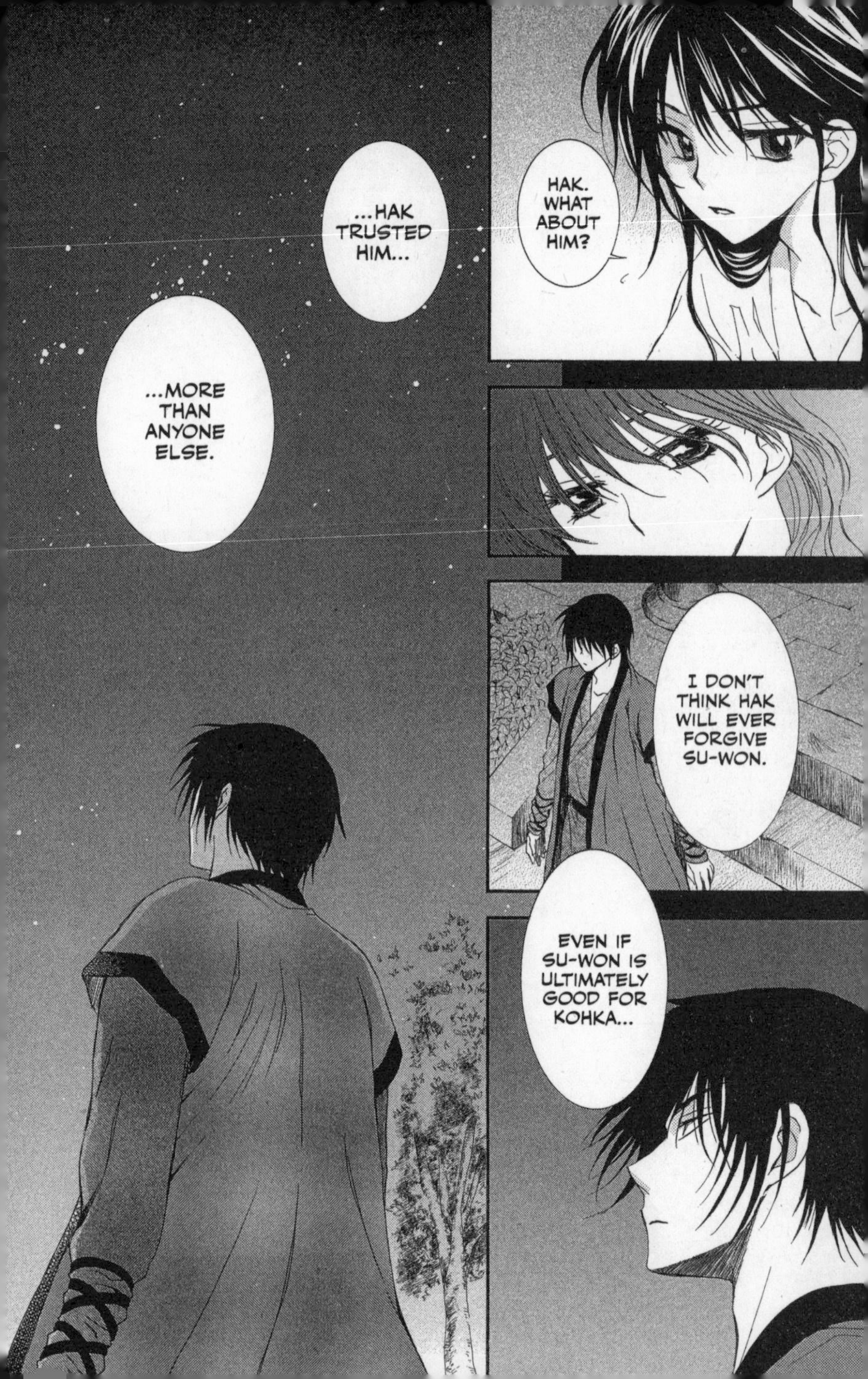
HAK. WHAT ABOUT HIM?
I DON'T THINK HAK WILL EVER FORGIVE SU-WON.
EVEN IF SU-WON IS ULTIMATELY GOOD FOR KOHKA...
...HAK TRUSTED HIM...
...MORE THAN ANYONE ELSE.

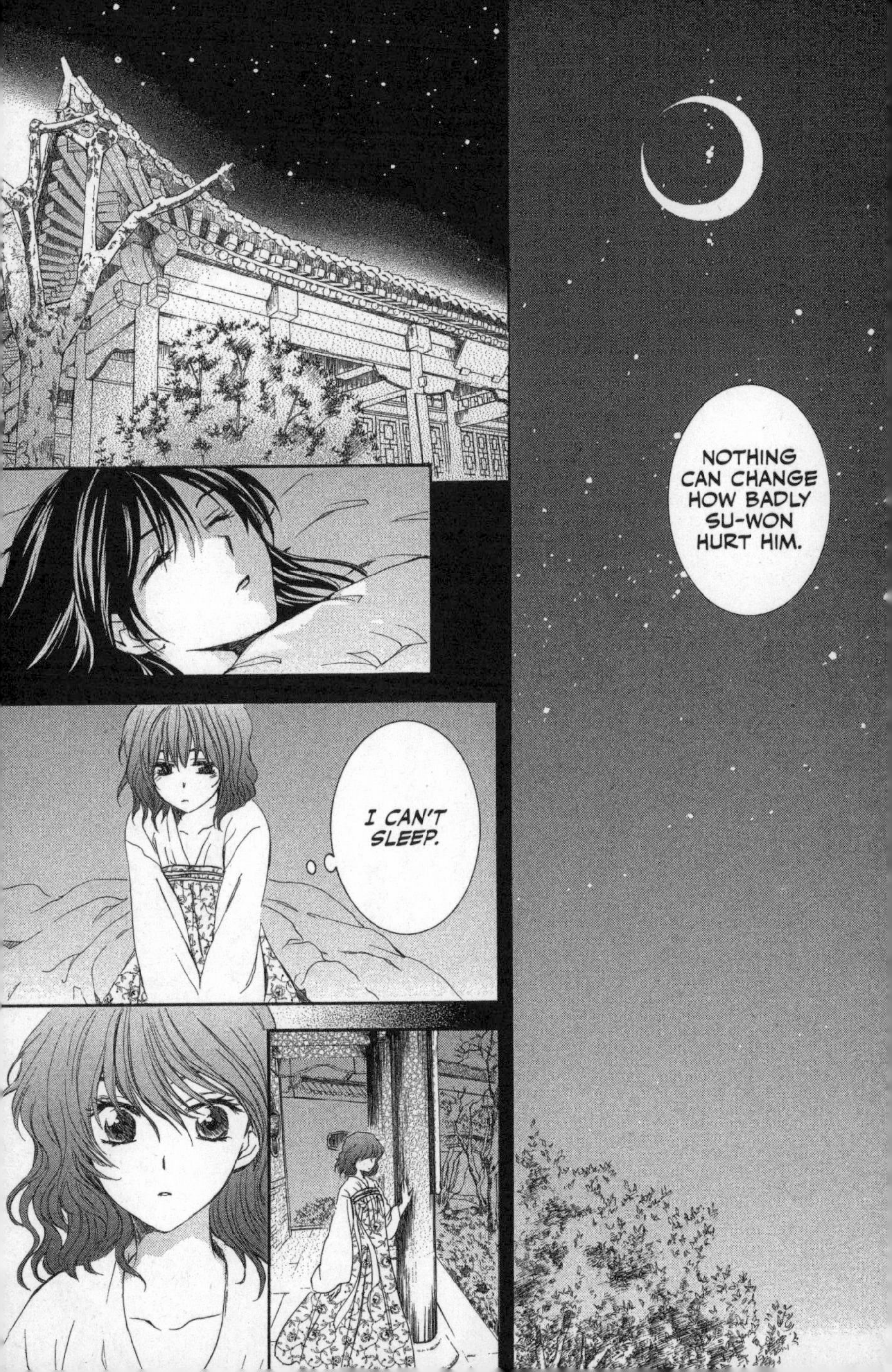
NOTHING CAN CHANGE HOW BADLY SU-WON HURT HIM.
I CAN'T SLEEP.

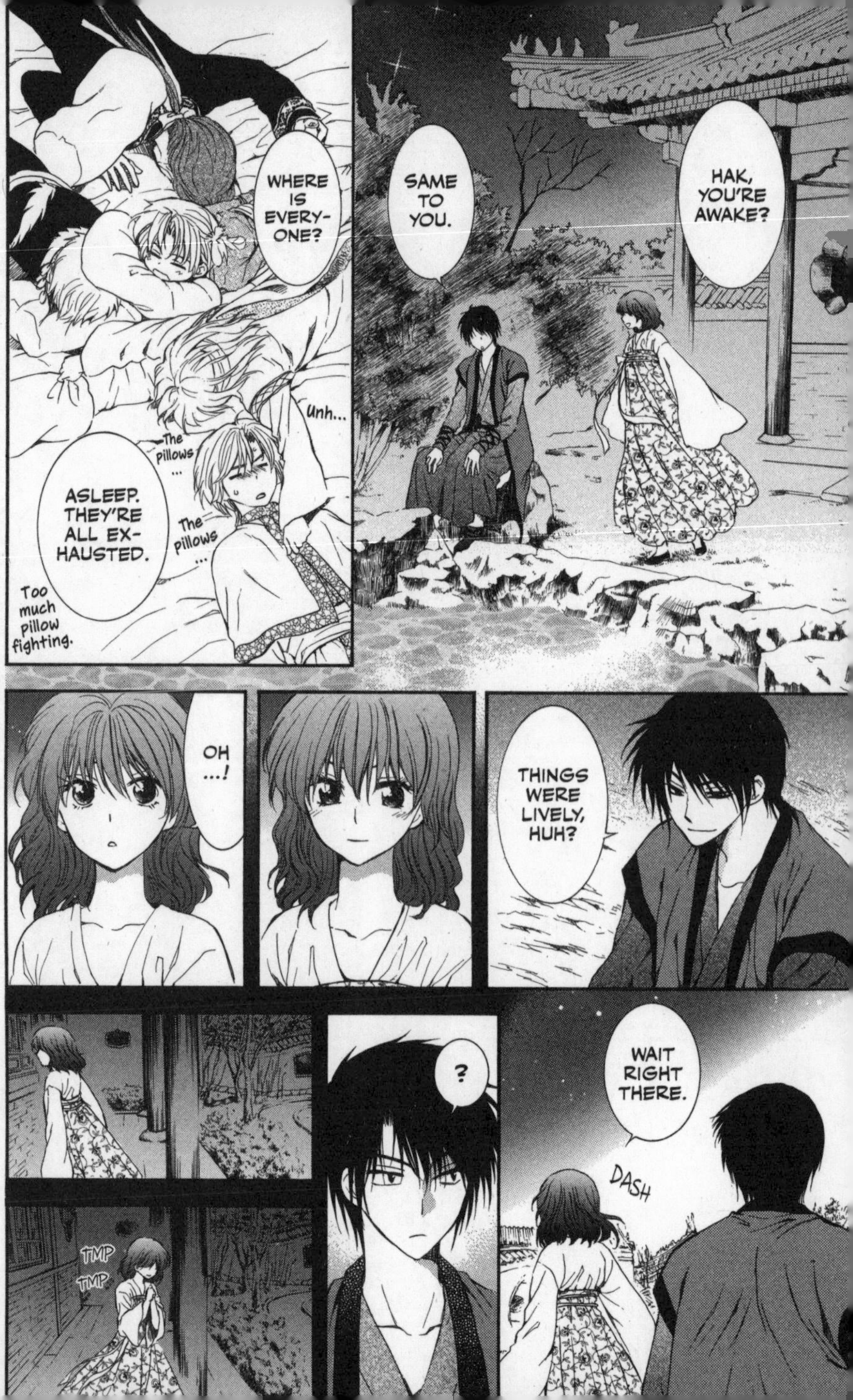
HAK, YOU'RE AWAKE?
SAME TO YOU.
WHERE IS EVERY-ONE?
Unh...
The pillows ...
ASLEEP. THEY'RE ALL EX-HAUSTED.
The pillows ...
Too much pillow fighting.
THINGS WERE LIVELY, HUH?
OH ...!
WAIT RIGHT THERE.
DASH
?
TMP
TMP

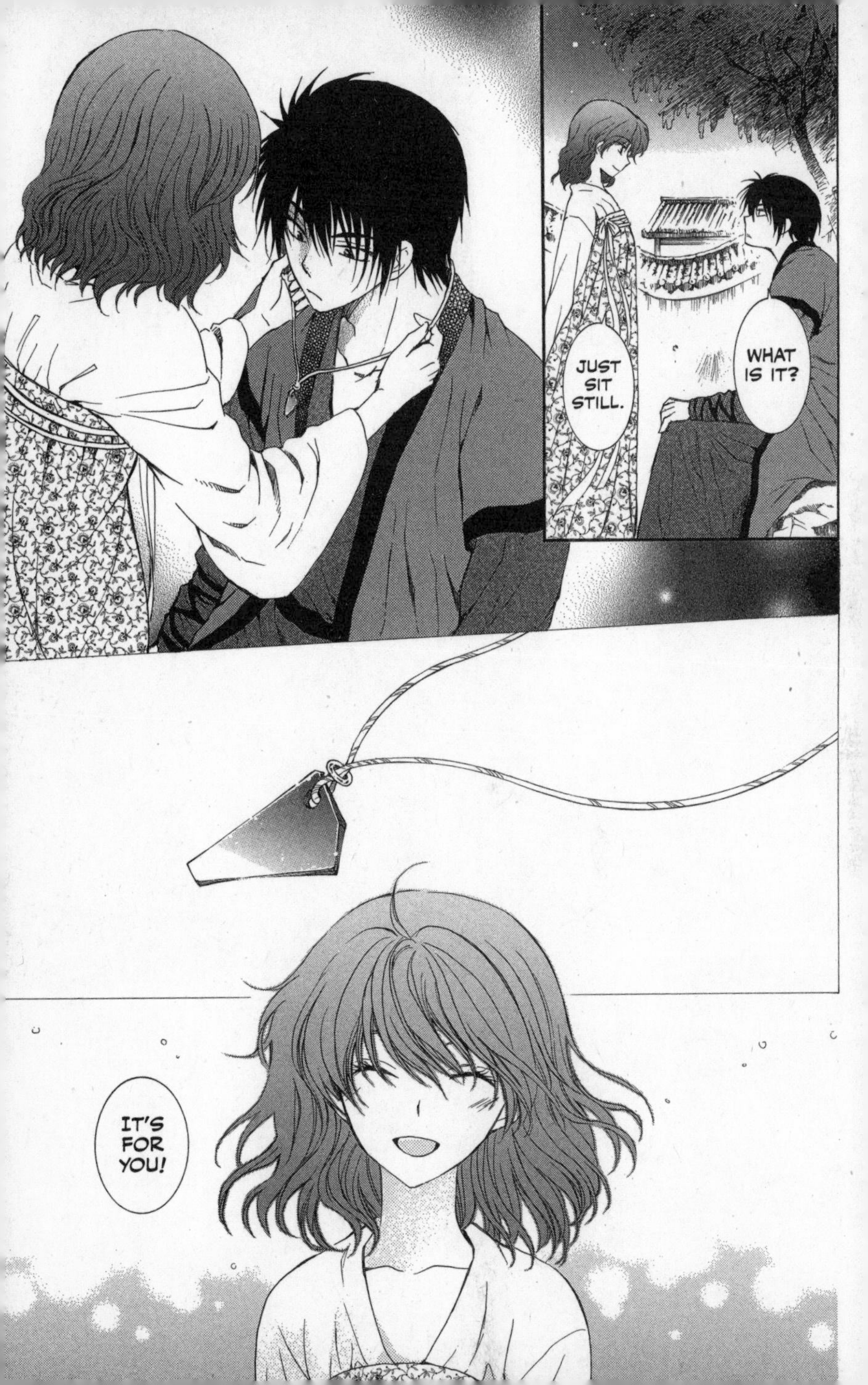
WHAT IS IT?
JUST SIT STILL.
IT'S FOR YOU!

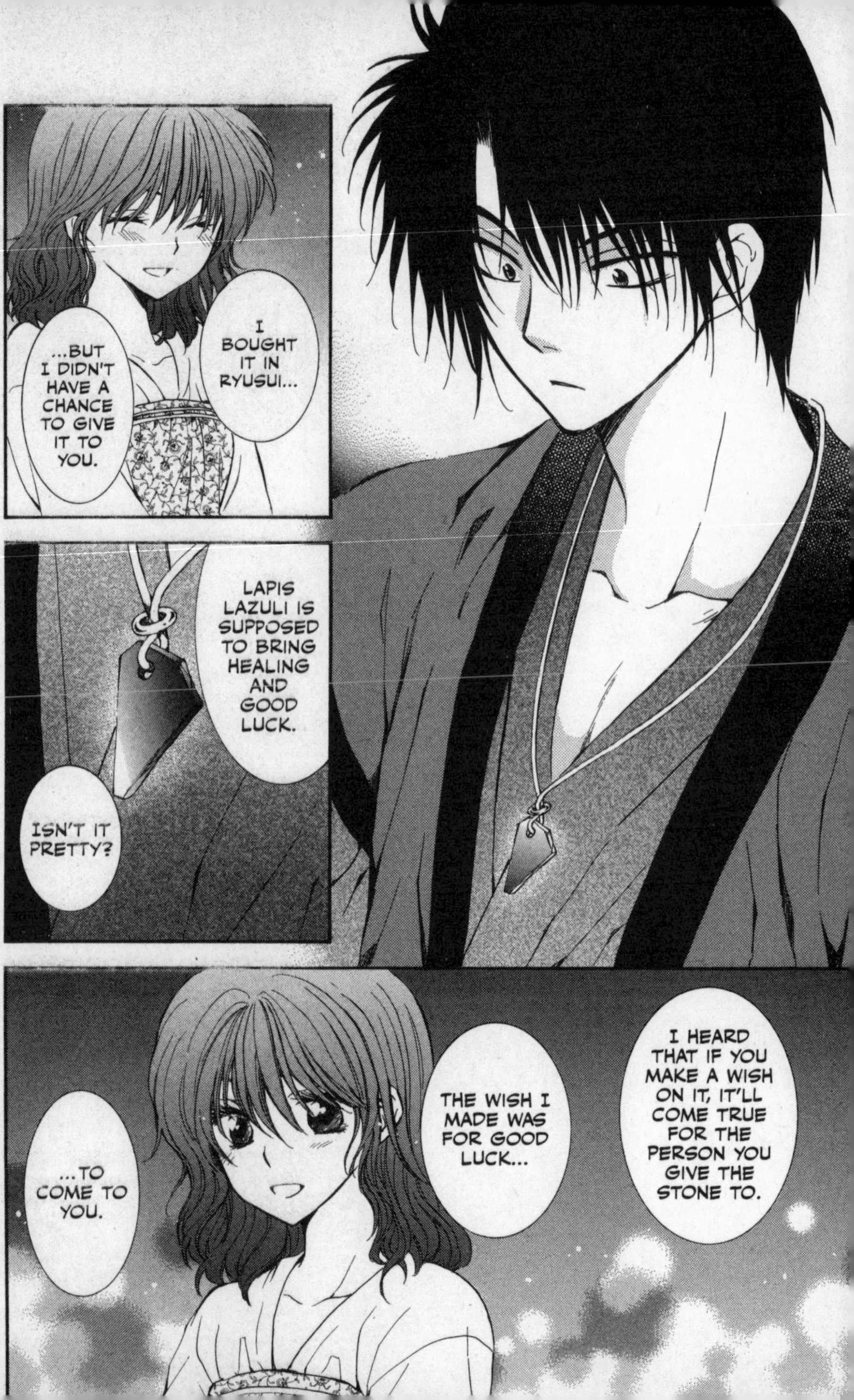
I BOUGHT IT IN RYUSUI...
...BUT I DIDN'T HAVE A CHANCE TO GIVE IT TO YOU.
LAPIS LAZULI IS SUPPOSED TO BRING HEALING AND GOOD LUCK.
ISN'T IT PRETTY?
I HEARD THAT IF YOU MAKE A WISH ON IT, IT'LL COME TRUE FOR THE PERSON YOU GIVE THE STONE TO.
THE WISH I MADE WAS FOR GOOD LUCK...
...TO COME TO YOU.

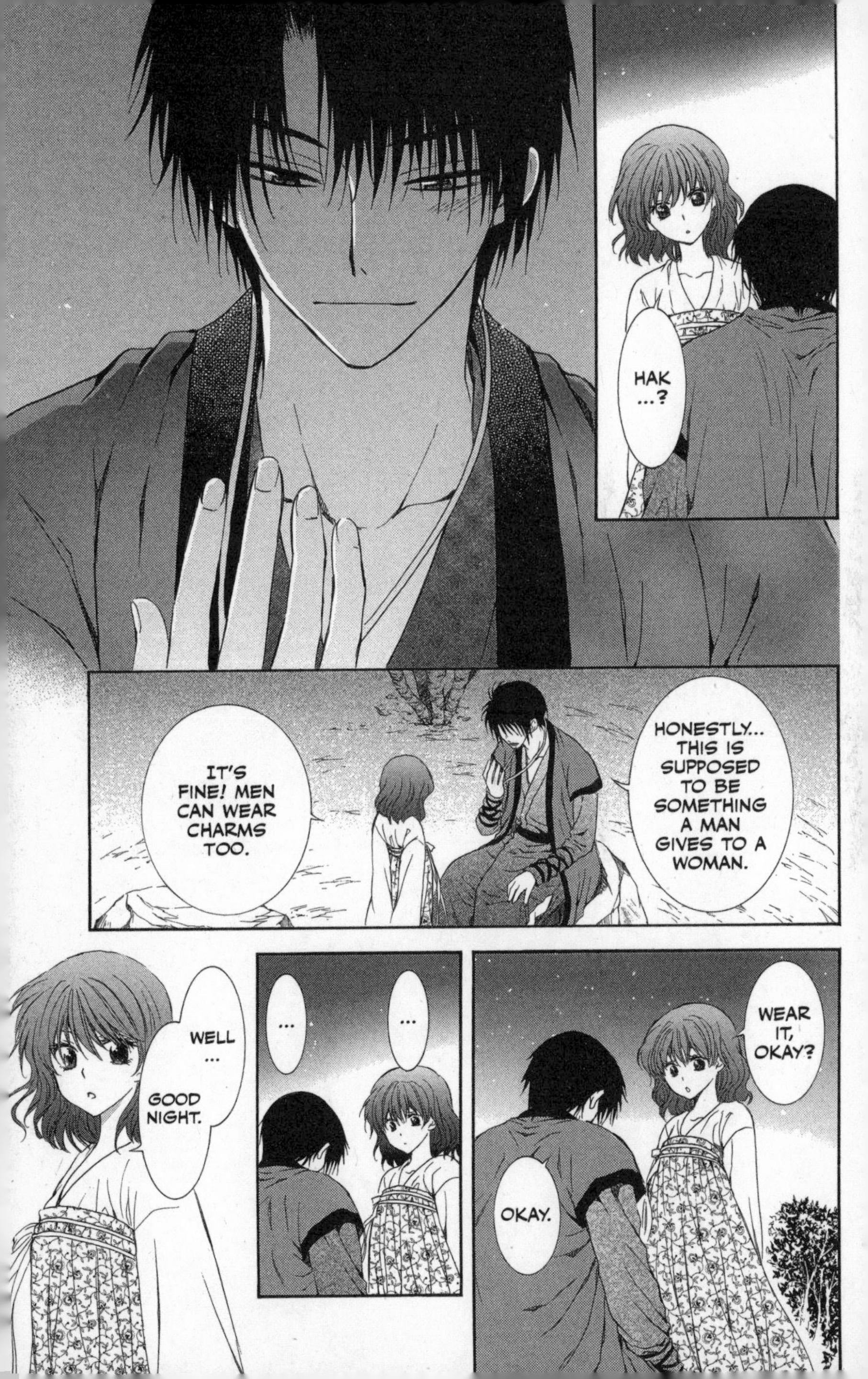
HAK ...?
HONESTLY... THIS IS SUPPOSED TO BE SOMETHING A MAN GIVES TO A WOMAN.
IT'S FINE! MEN CAN WEAR CHARMS TOO.
WEAR IT, OKAY?
OKAY.
...
...
WELL ...
GOOD NIGHT.

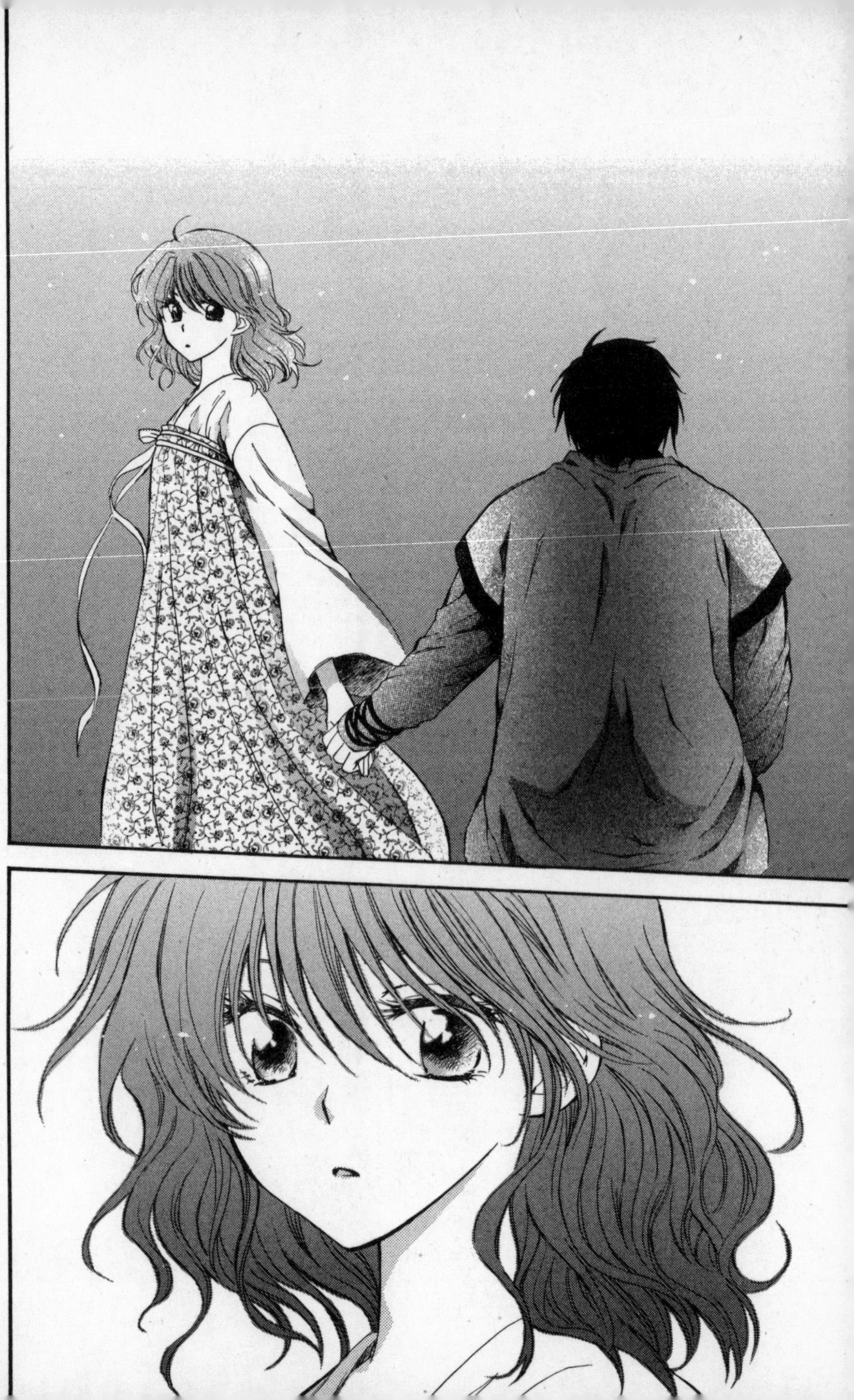

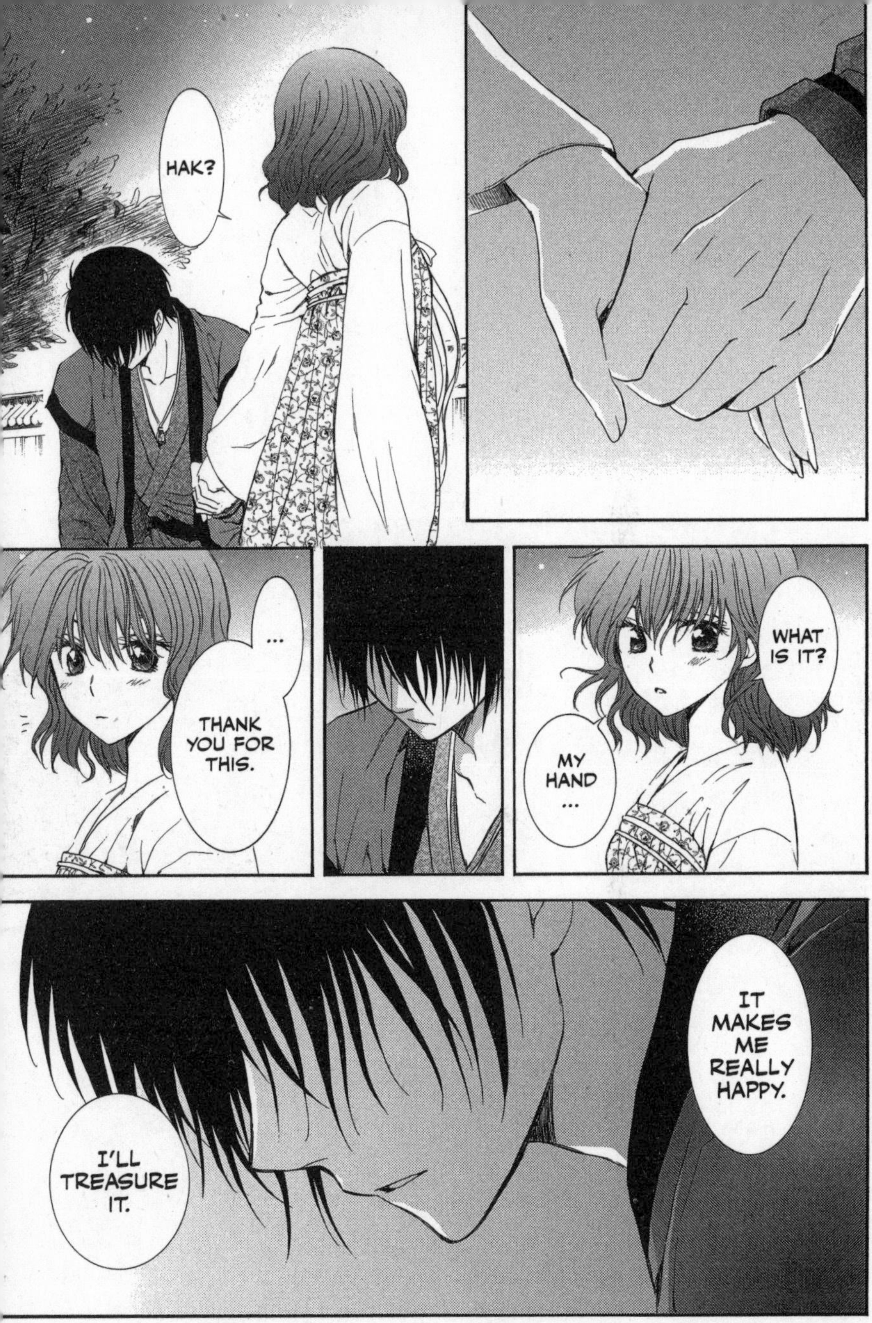
HAK?
WHAT IS IT?
MY HAND ...
...
THANK YOU FOR THIS.
IT MAKES ME REALLY HAPPY.
I'LL TREASURE IT.

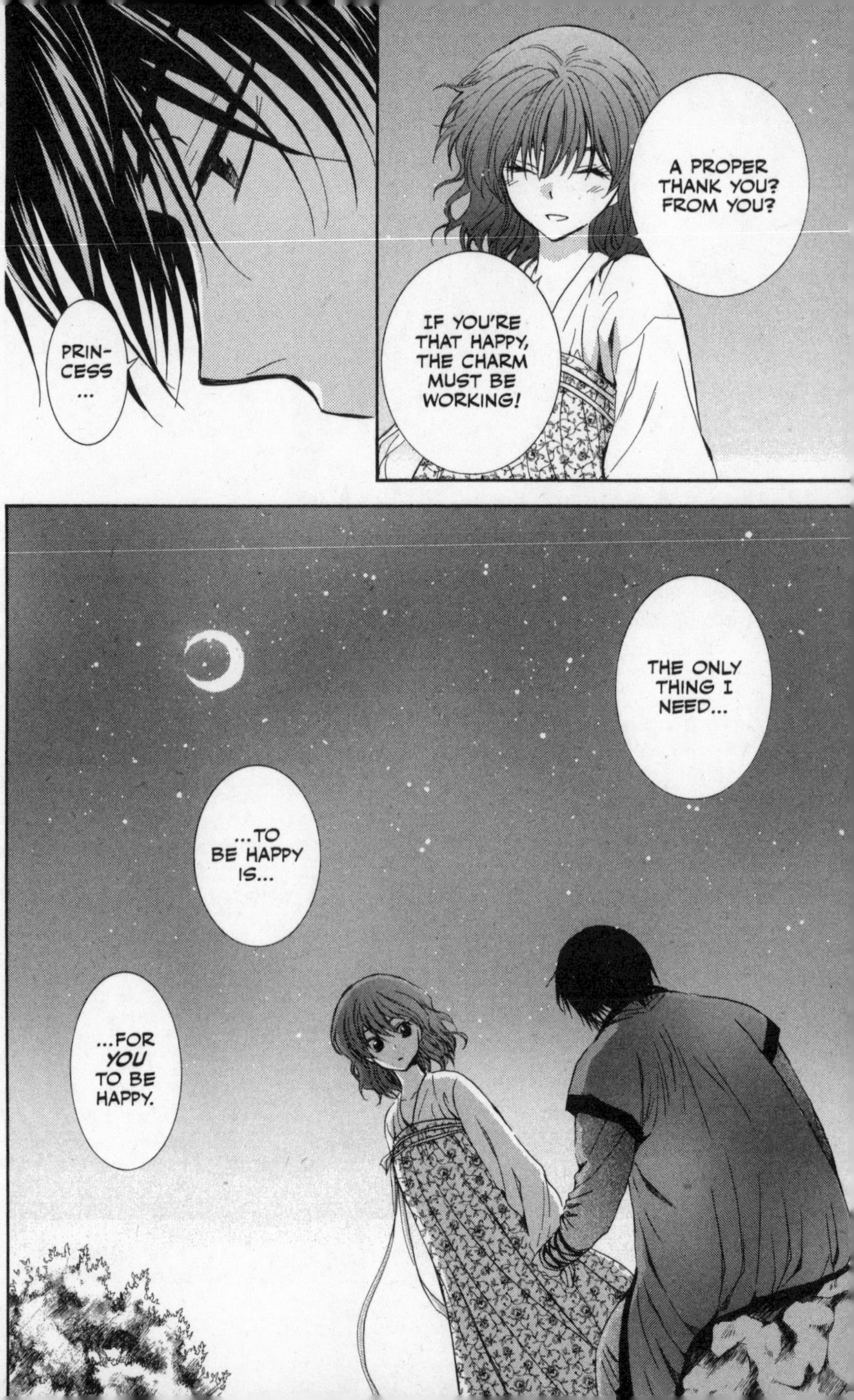
A PROPER THANK YOU? FROM YOU?
IF YOU'RE THAT HAPPY, THE CHARM MUST BE WORKING!
PRIN-CESS...
THE ONLY THING I NEED...
...TO BE HAPPY IS...
...FOR *YOU* TO BE HAPPY.

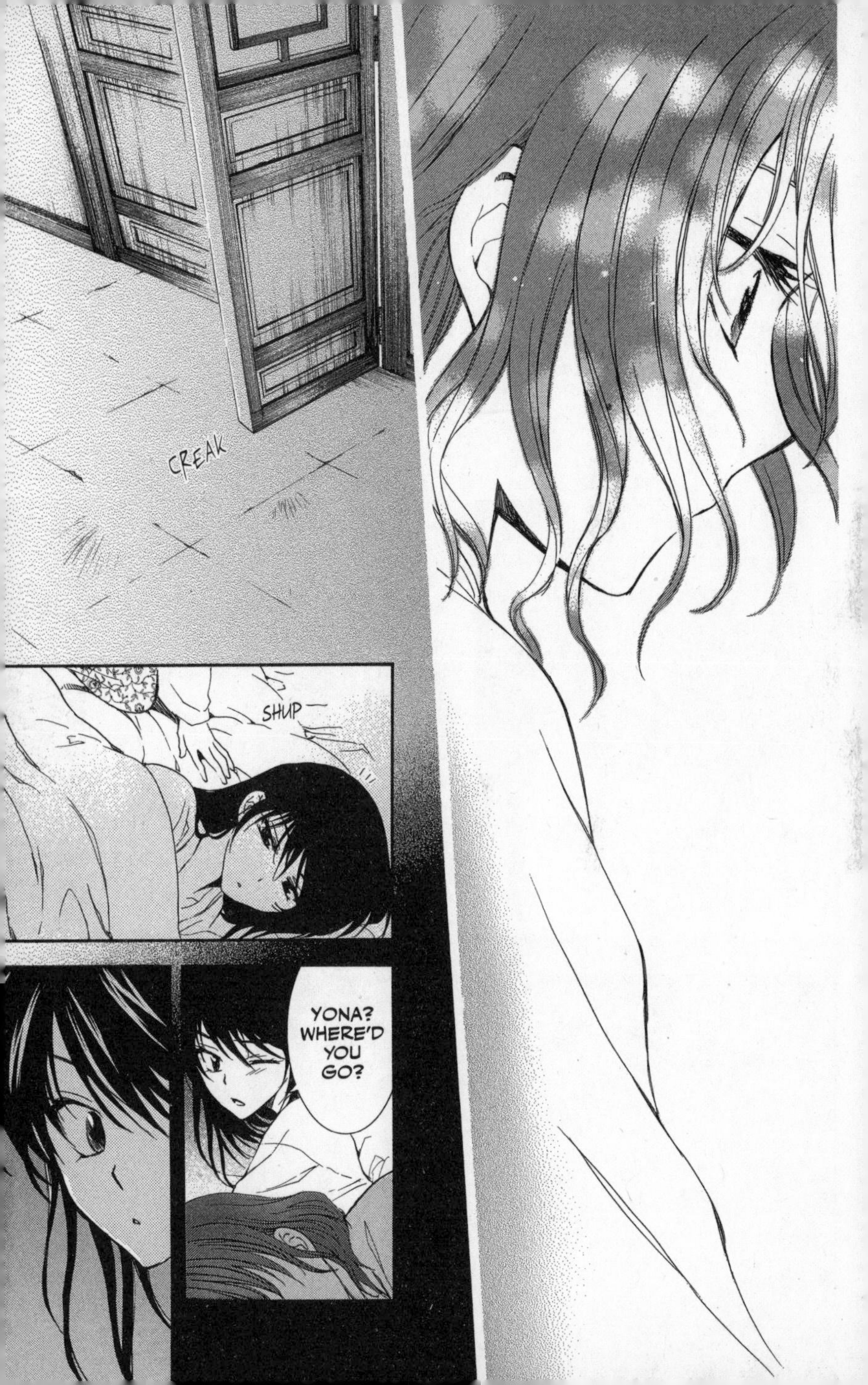
CREAK
SHUP
YONA? WHERE'D YOU GO?

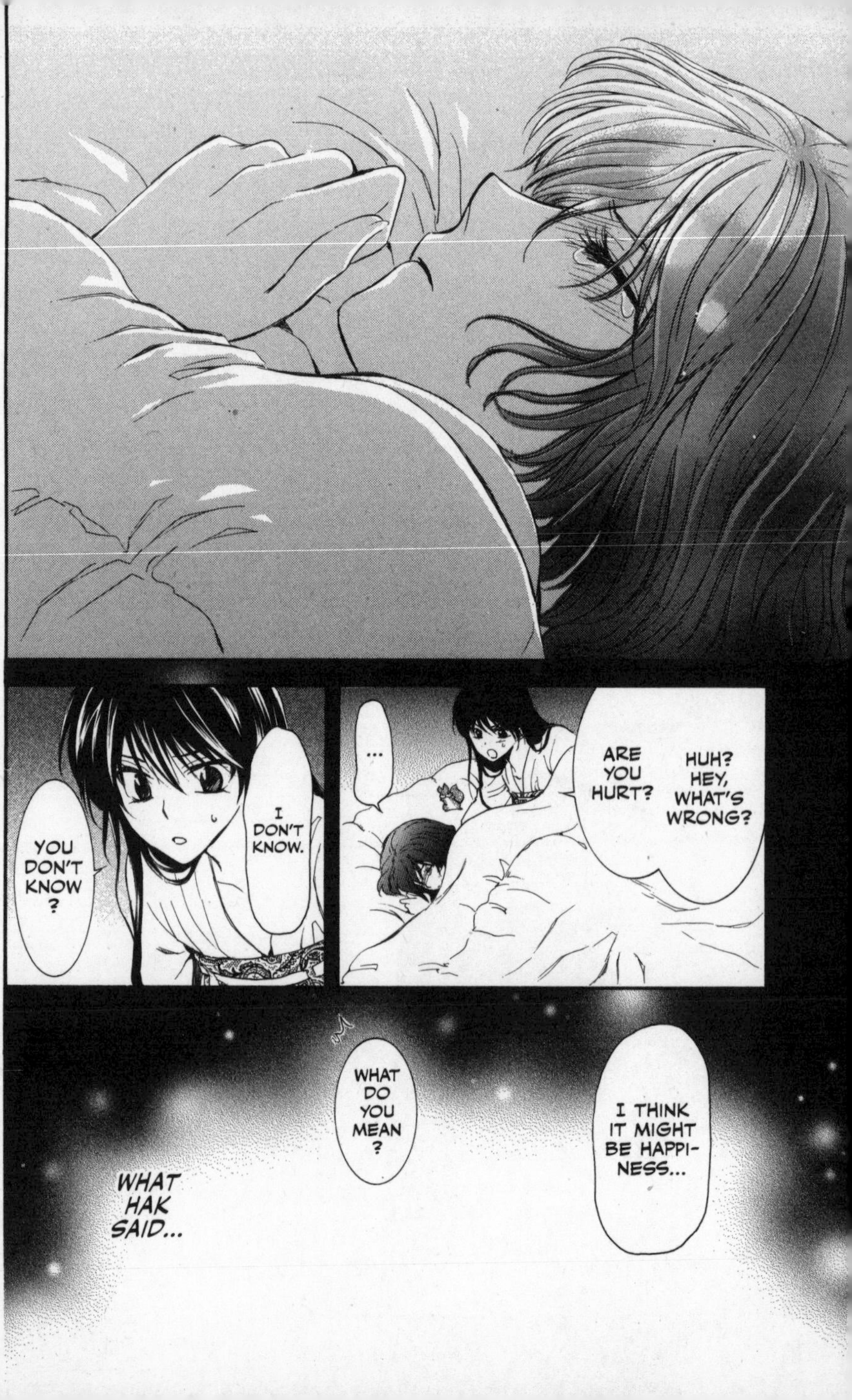
HUH? HEY, WHAT'S WRONG?
ARE YOU HURT?
...
I DON'T KNOW.
YOU DON'T KNOW?
I THINK IT MIGHT BE HAPPINESS...
WHAT DO YOU MEAN?
WHAT HAK SAID...

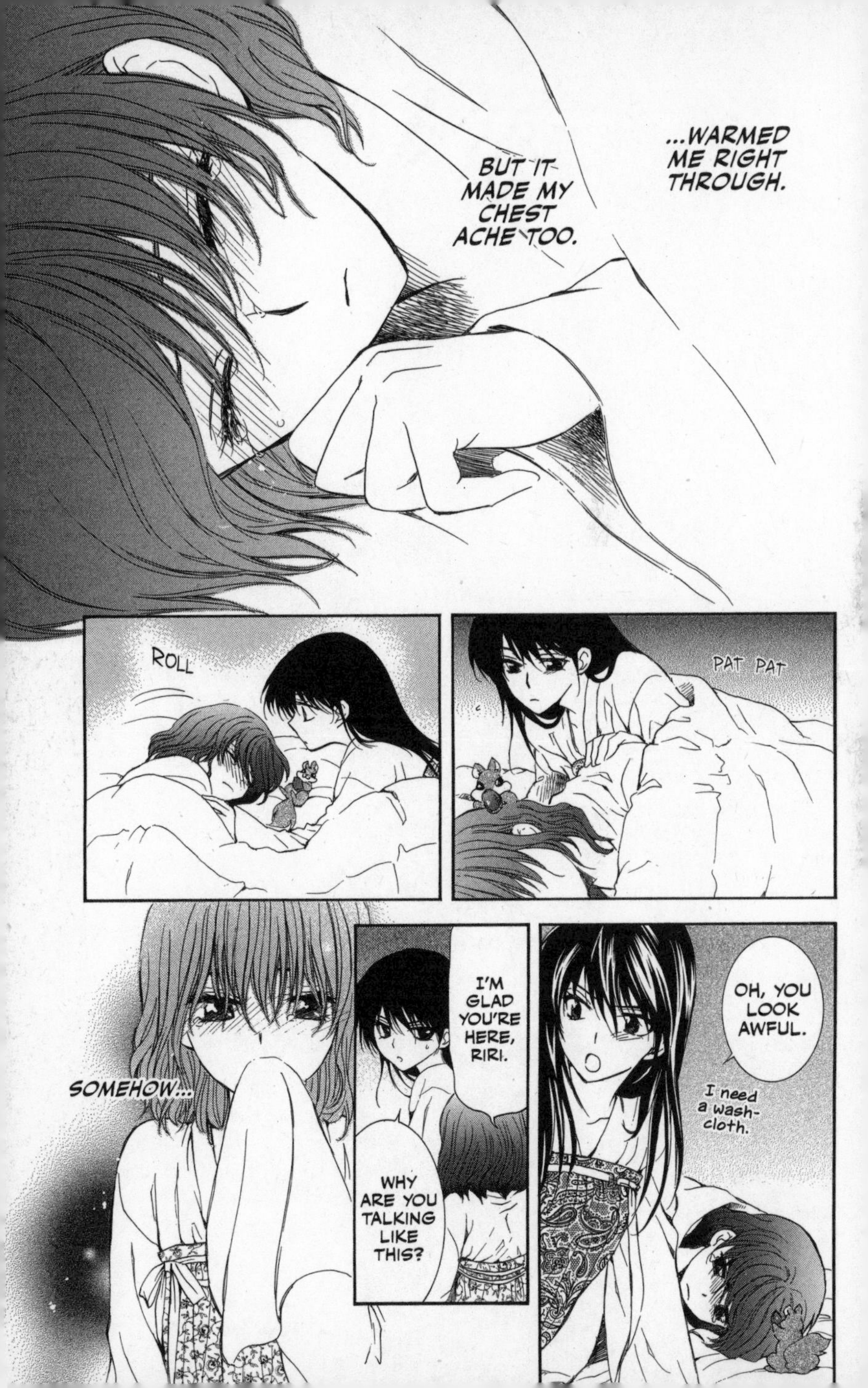
...WARMED ME RIGHT THROUGH.
BUT IT MADE MY CHEST ACHE TOO.
PAT PAT
ROLL
OH, YOU LOOK AWFUL.
I need a wash-cloth.
I'M GLAD YOU'RE HERE, RIRI.
WHY ARE YOU TALKING LIKE THIS?
SOMEHOW...

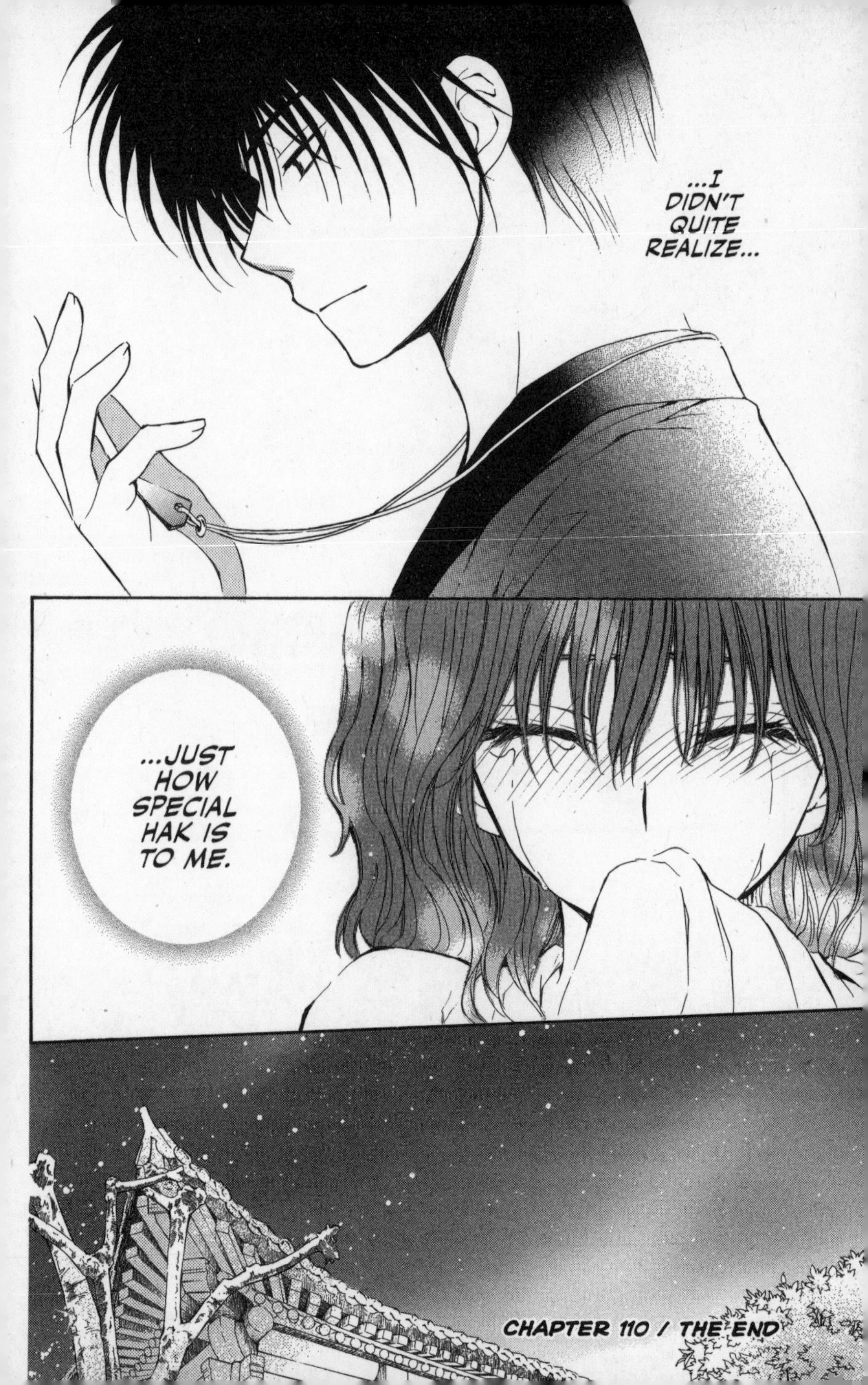
...I DIDN'T QUITE REALIZE...
...JUST HOW SPECIAL HAK IS TO ME.
CHAPTER 110 / THE END

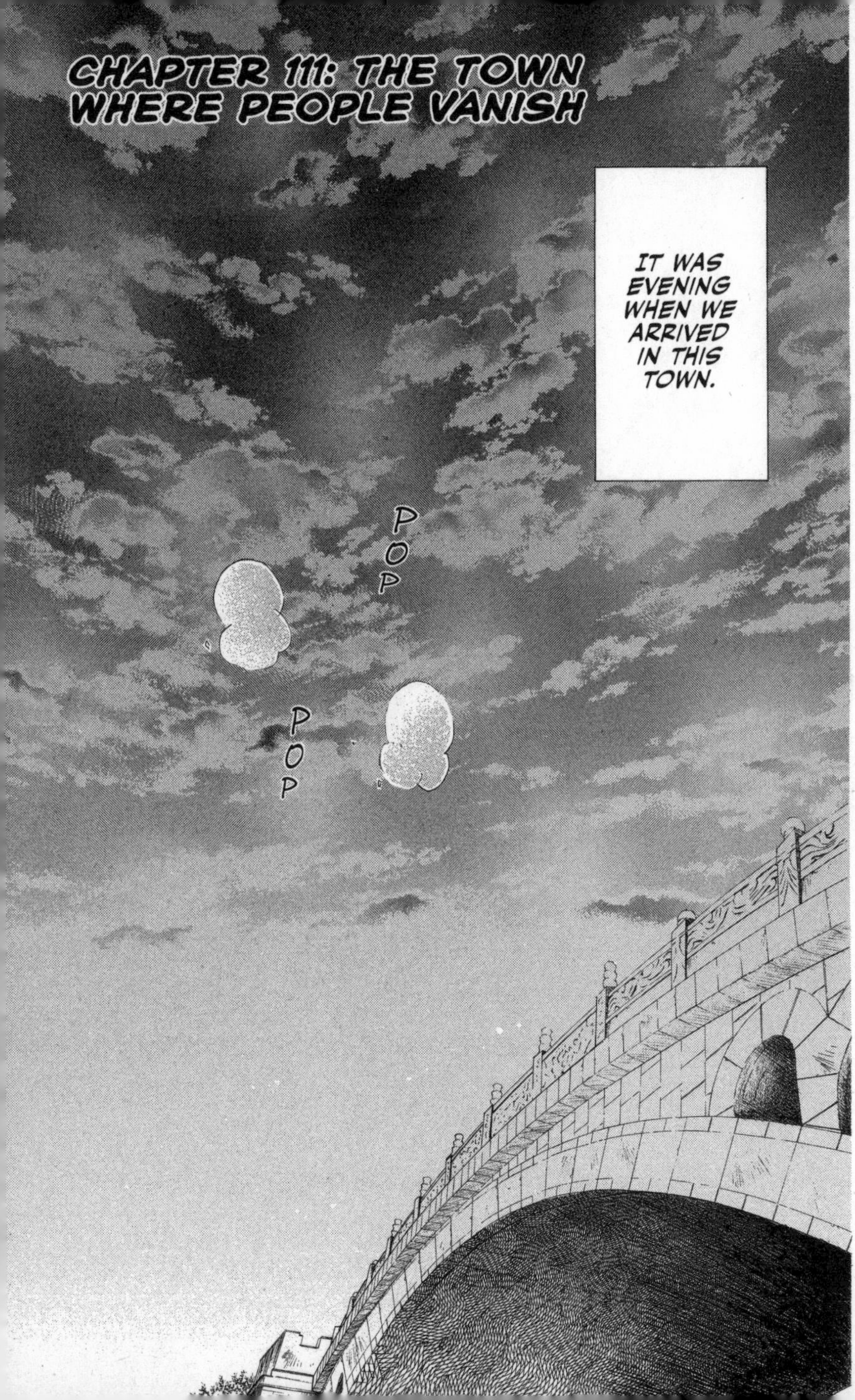
CHAPTER 111: THE TOWN WHERE PEOPLE VANISH
IT WAS EVENING WHEN WE ARRIVED IN THIS TOWN.
POP
POP

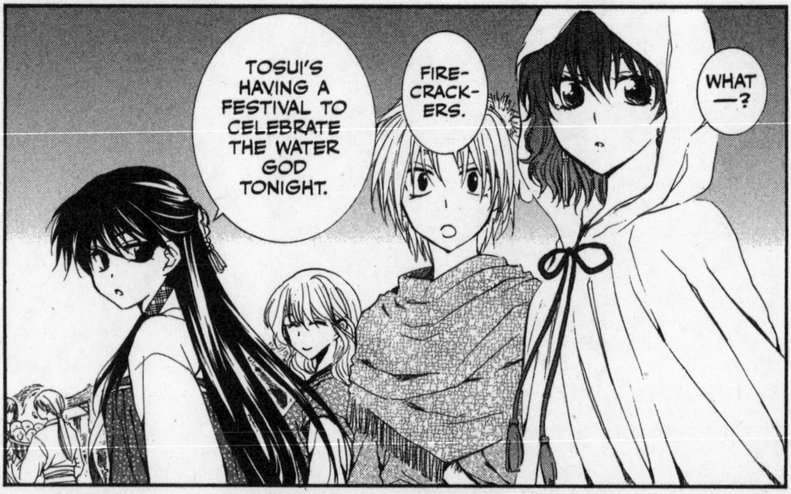
WHAT—?
FIRE-CRACK-ERS.
TOSUI'S HAVING A FESTIVAL TO CELEBRATE THE WATER GOD TONIGHT.

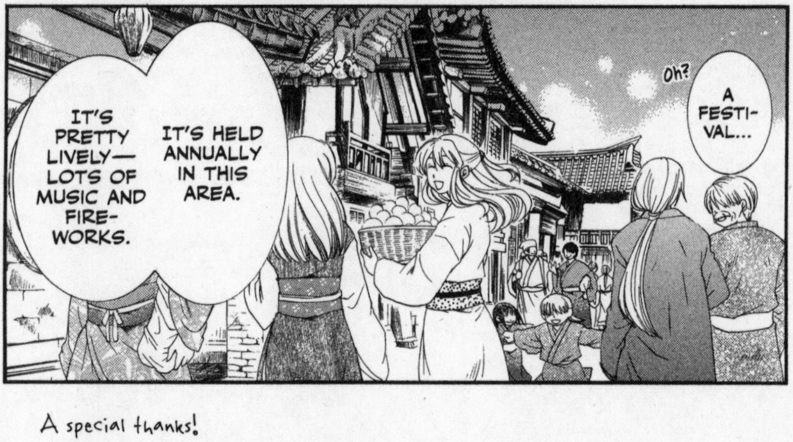
Oh?
A FESTI-VAL...
IT'S HELD ANNUALLY IN THIS AREA.
IT'S PRETTY LIVELY—LOTS OF MUSIC AND FIRE-WORKS.

A special thanks!
My assistants→Mikorun, C.F., Ryo Sakura, Ryo, Oka, Awafuji, Eika and my little sister...
My editor Tokushige, my previous editors and the *Hana to Yume* editorial office...
Everyone who's involved in creating and selling *Yona*-related merchandise...
My beloved family and friends who've always supported me. And you, for reading this!
Thank you so very, very much. You always give me strength. I'll do my best to create a manga that gives you strength too!

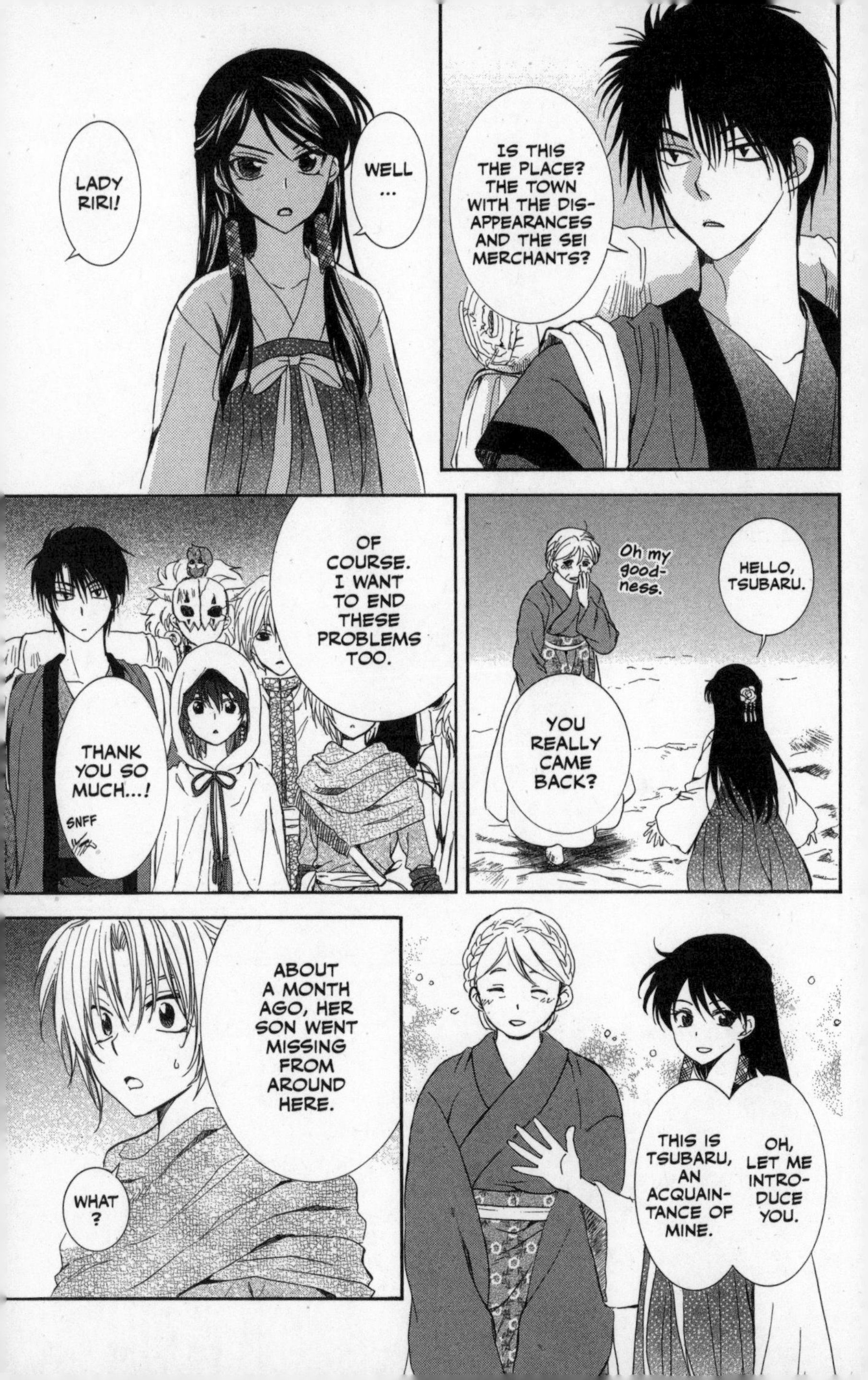
IS THIS THE PLACE? THE TOWN WITH THE DIS-APPEARANCES AND THE SEI MERCHANTS?
WELL ...
LADY RIRI!
HELLO, TSUBARU.
Oh my good-ness.
YOU REALLY CAME BACK?
OF COURSE. I WANT TO END THESE PROBLEMS TOO.
THANK YOU SO MUCH...!
SNFF
OH, LET ME INTRO-DUCE YOU.
THIS IS TSUBARU, AN ACQUAIN-TANCE OF MINE.
ABOUT A MONTH AGO, HER SON WENT MISSING FROM AROUND HERE.
WHAT?

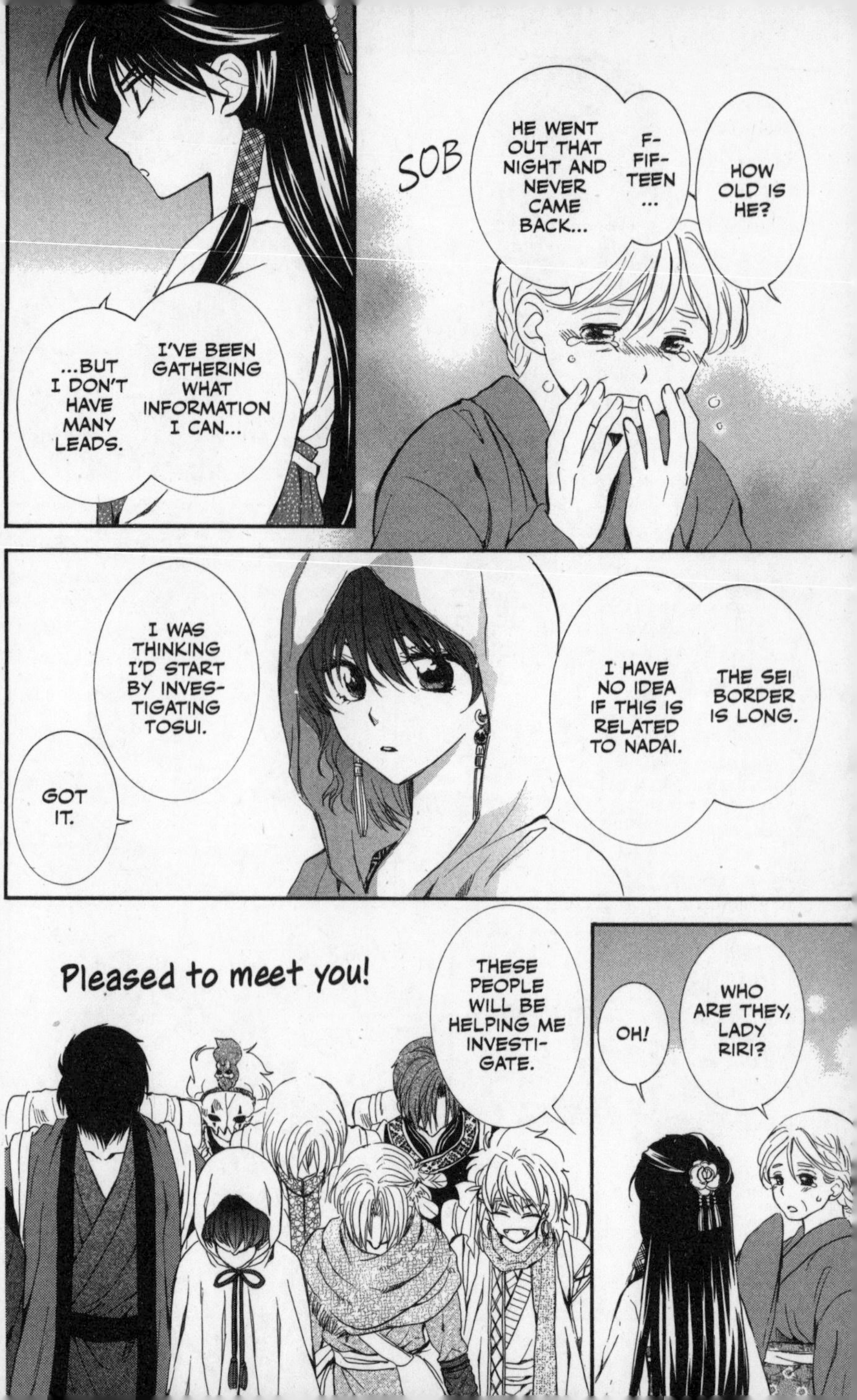
HOW OLD IS HE?
F-FIFTEEN...
HE WENT OUT THAT NIGHT AND NEVER CAME BACK...
SOB
I'VE BEEN GATHERING WHAT INFORMATION I CAN...
...BUT I DON'T HAVE MANY LEADS.
THE SEI BORDER IS LONG.
I HAVE NO IDEA IF THIS IS RELATED TO NADAI.
I WAS THINKING I'D START BY INVESTIGATING TOSUI.
GOT IT.
WHO ARE THEY, LADY RIRI?
OH!
THESE PEOPLE WILL BE HELPING ME INVESTIGATE.
Pleased to meet you!

Here are some things I've been hooked on lately!

Eating mixed caramel and cheese popcorn. It's delicious! Although the caramel attacks my cavities.

Also, dried mango is so yummy. That also really attacks my cavities, but I tolerate the pain.

I've always loved Yoku Moku's Cigare au Chocolat.

The tempura crackers I can buy in Terminal 1 at Haneda Airport.

Hakata Torimon [A white bean cake from Hakata].

I'm waiting on improvements in dentistry!

Let's meet again in Yona volume 20.

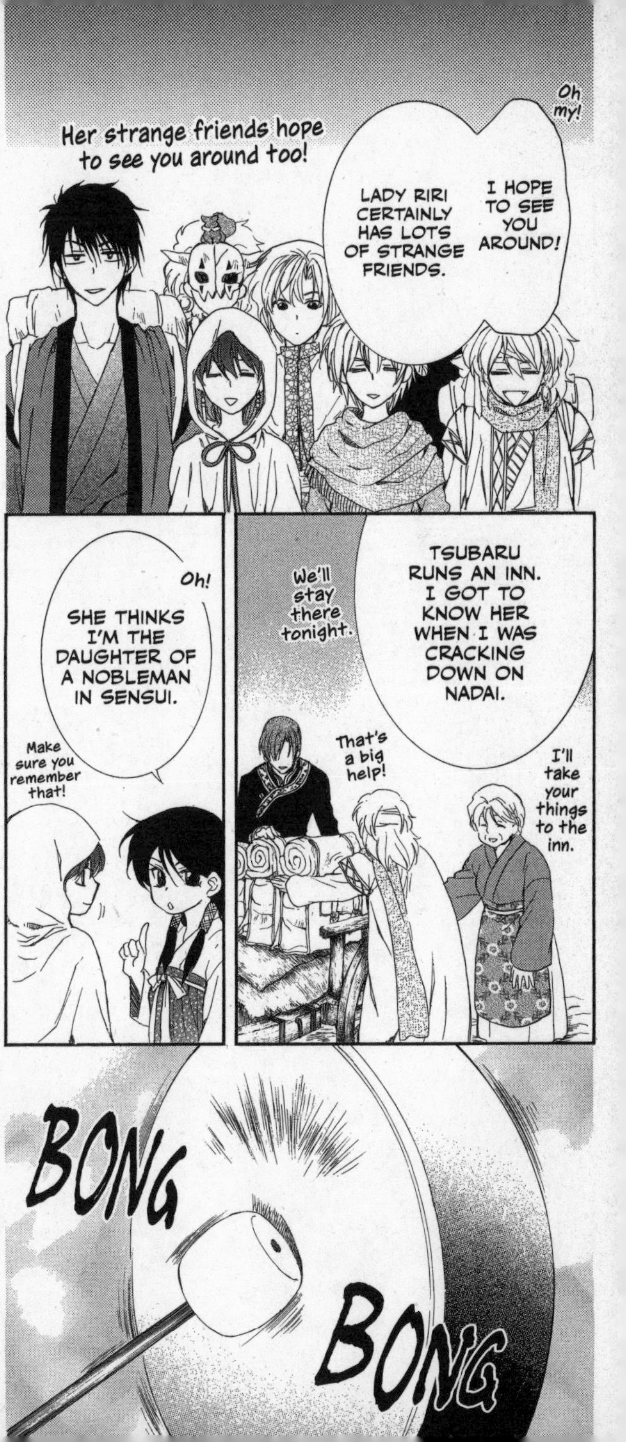
Oh my!
I HOPE TO SEE YOU AROUND!
LADY RIRI CERTAINLY HAS LOTS OF STRANGE FRIENDS.
Her strange friends hope to see you around too!
TSUBARU RUNS AN INN. I GOT TO KNOW HER WHEN I WAS CRACKING DOWN ON NADAI.
We'll stay there tonight.
I'll take your things to the inn.
That's a big help!
Oh!
SHE THINKS I'M THE DAUGHTER OF A NOBLEMAN IN SENSUI.
Make sure you remember that!
BONG
BONG

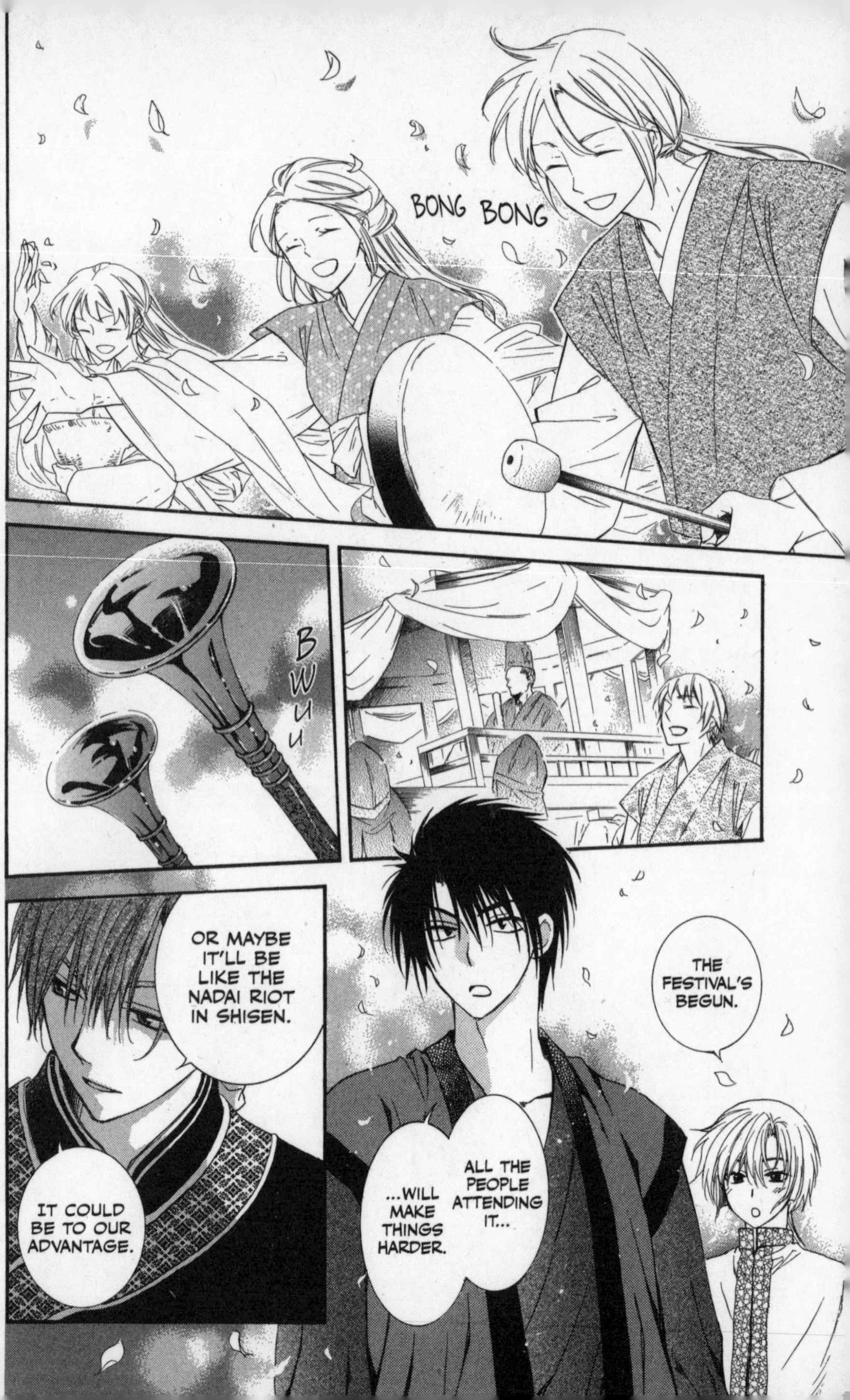
BONG BONG
BWUU
THE FESTIVAL'S BEGUN.
ALL THE PEOPLE ATTENDING IT...
...WILL MAKE THINGS HARDER.
OR MAYBE IT'LL BE LIKE THE NADAI RIOT IN SHISEN.
IT COULD BE TO OUR ADVANTAGE.

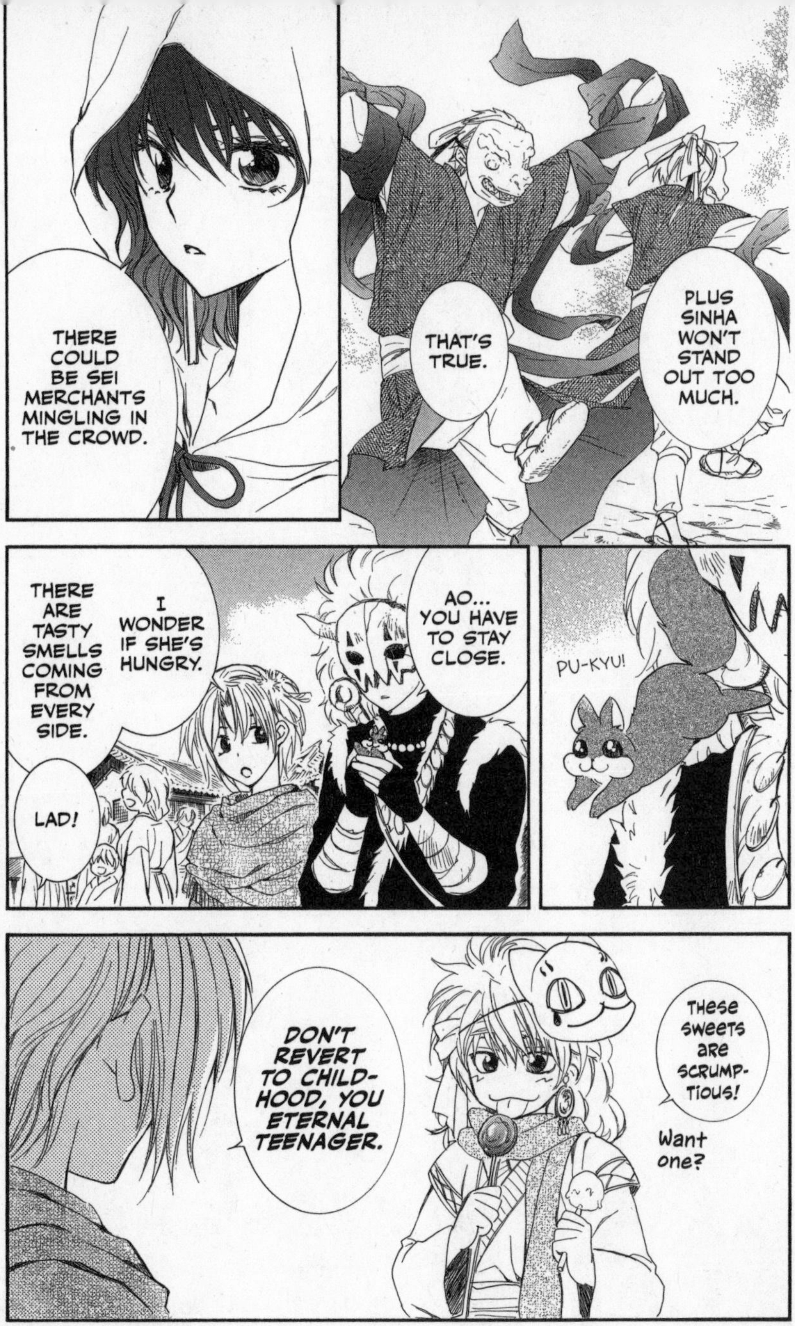
PLUS SINHA WON'T STAND OUT TOO MUCH.
THAT'S TRUE.
THERE COULD BE SEI MERCHANTS MINGLING IN THE CROWD.
PU-KYU!
AO... YOU HAVE TO STAY CLOSE.
I WONDER IF SHE'S HUNGRY.
THERE ARE TASTY SMELLS COMING FROM EVERY SIDE.
LAD!
These sweets are scrump-tious!
Want one?
DON'T REVERT TO CHILD-HOOD, YOU ETERNAL TEENAGER.

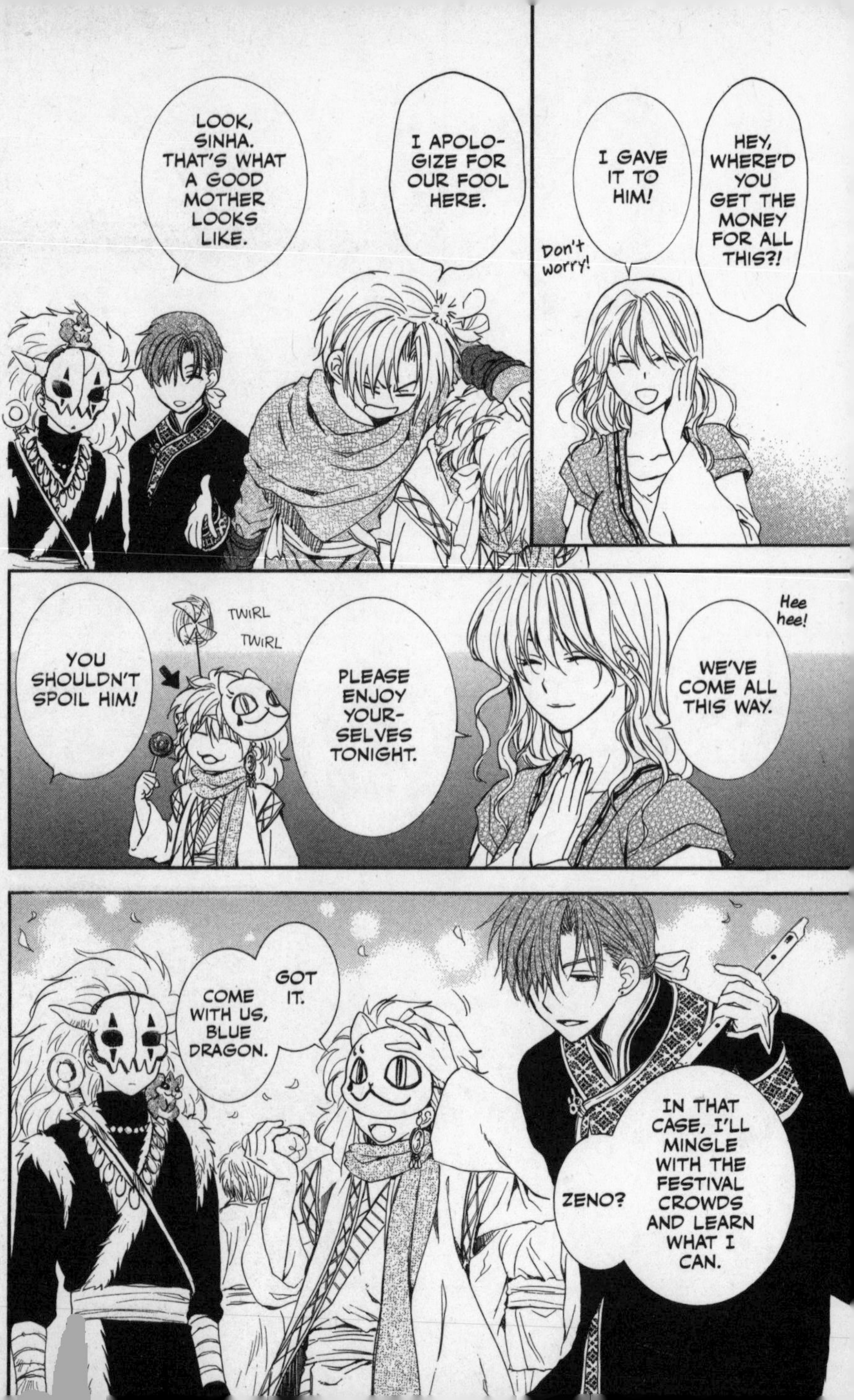
HEY, WHERE'D YOU GET THE MONEY FOR ALL THIS?!
I GAVE IT TO HIM!
Don't worry!
I APOLOGIZE FOR OUR FOOL HERE.
LOOK, SINHA. THAT'S WHAT A GOOD MOTHER LOOKS LIKE.
Hee hee!
WE'VE COME ALL THIS WAY.
PLEASE ENJOY YOURSELVES TONIGHT.
TWIRL
TWIRL
YOU SHOULDN'T SPOIL HIM!
IN THAT CASE, I'LL MINGLE WITH THE FESTIVAL CROWDS AND LEARN WHAT I CAN.
ZENO?
GOT IT.
COME WITH US, BLUE DRAGON.

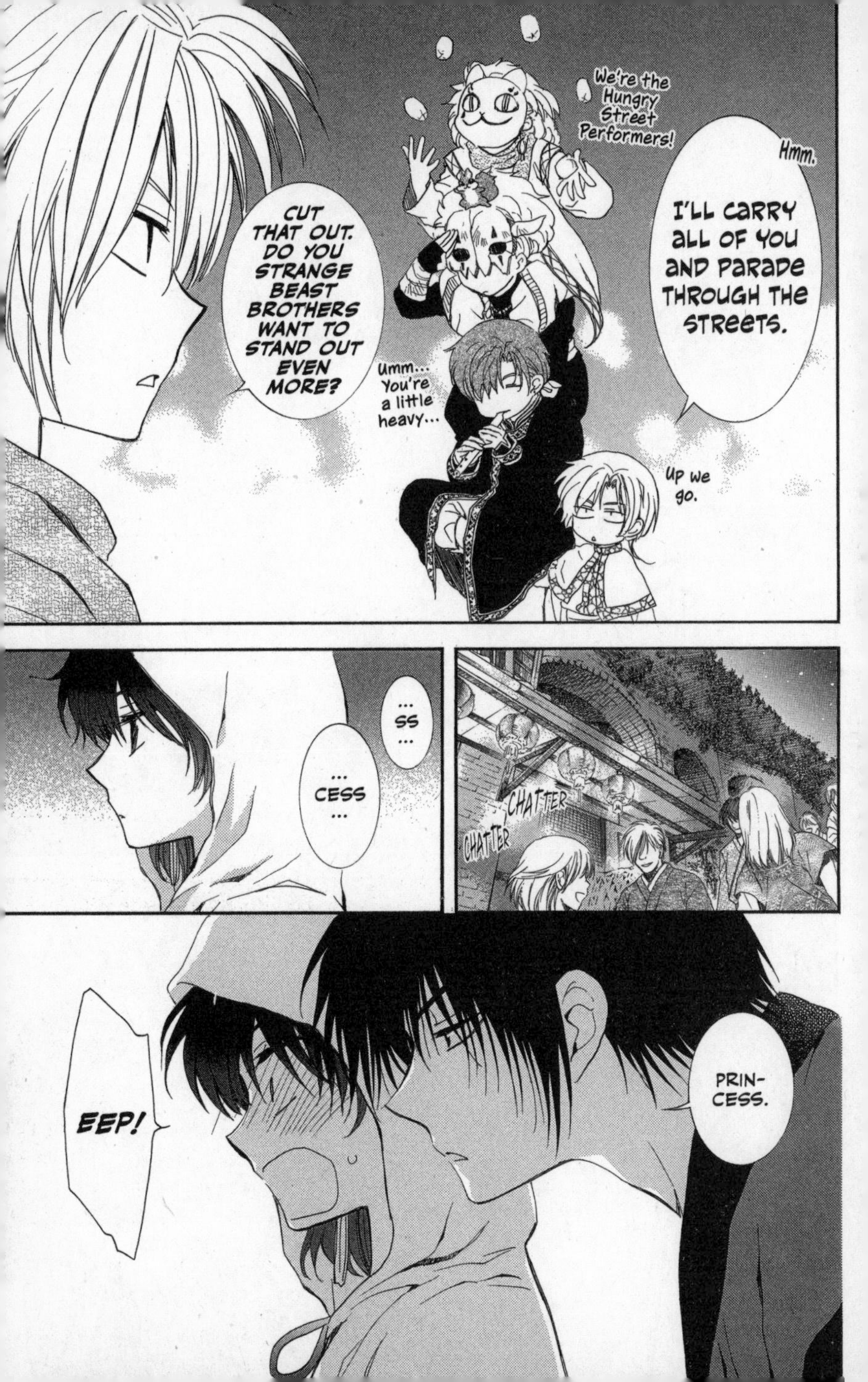
Hmm.
I'LL CARRY ALL OF YOU AND PARADE THROUGH THE STREETS.
Up we go.
We're the Hungry Street Performers!
Umm... You're a little heavy...
CUT THAT OUT. DO YOU STRANGE BEAST BROTHERS WANT TO STAND OUT EVEN MORE?
CHATTER
CHATTER
...SS...
...CESS...
PRIN-CESS.
EEP!

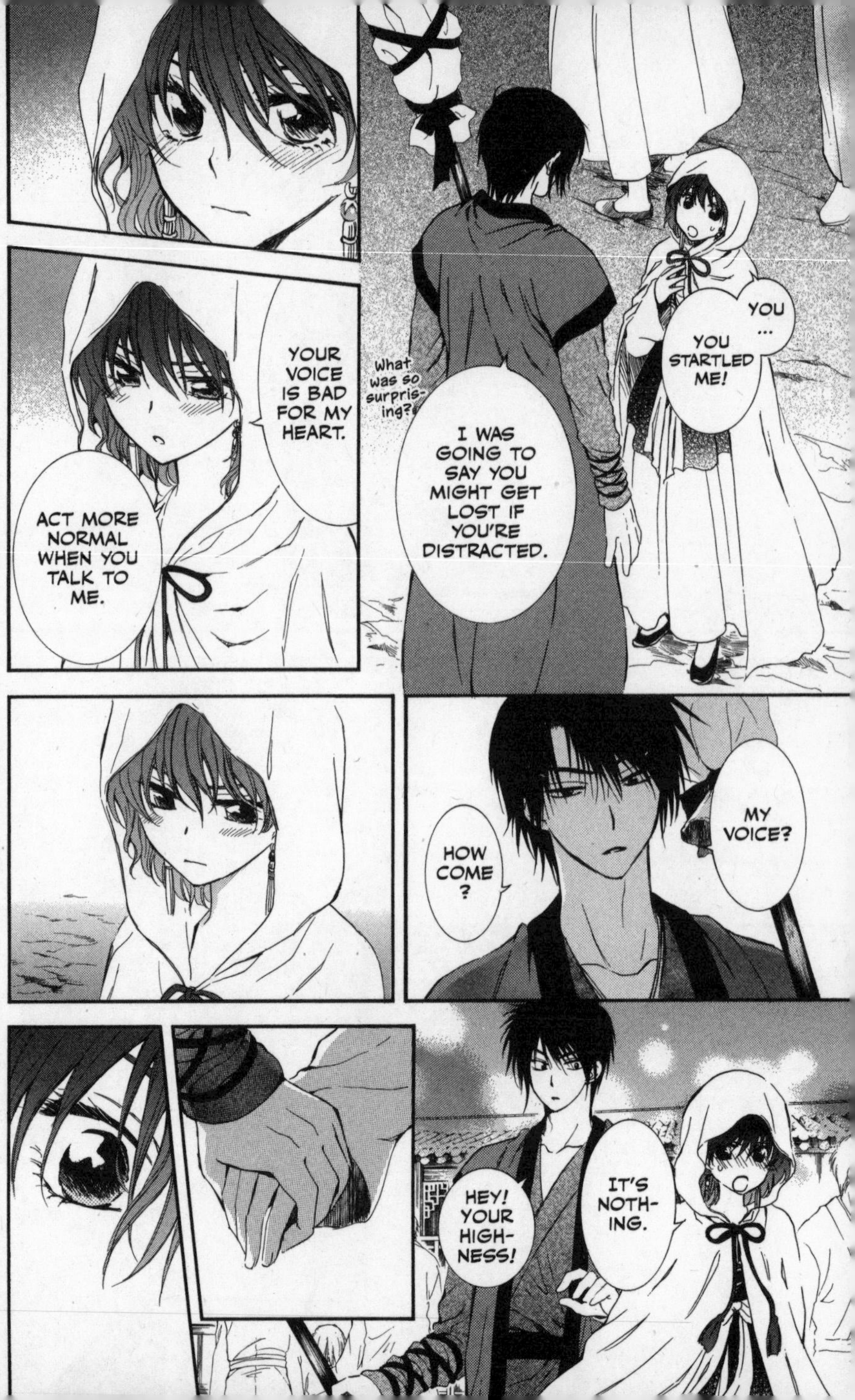
YOU ... YOU STARTLED ME!
What was so surpris-ing?
I WAS GOING TO SAY YOU MIGHT GET LOST IF YOU'RE DISTRACTED.
YOUR VOICE IS BAD FOR MY HEART.
ACT MORE NORMAL WHEN YOU TALK TO ME.
MY VOICE?
HOW COME?
IT'S NOTH-ING.
HEY! YOUR HIGH-NESS!

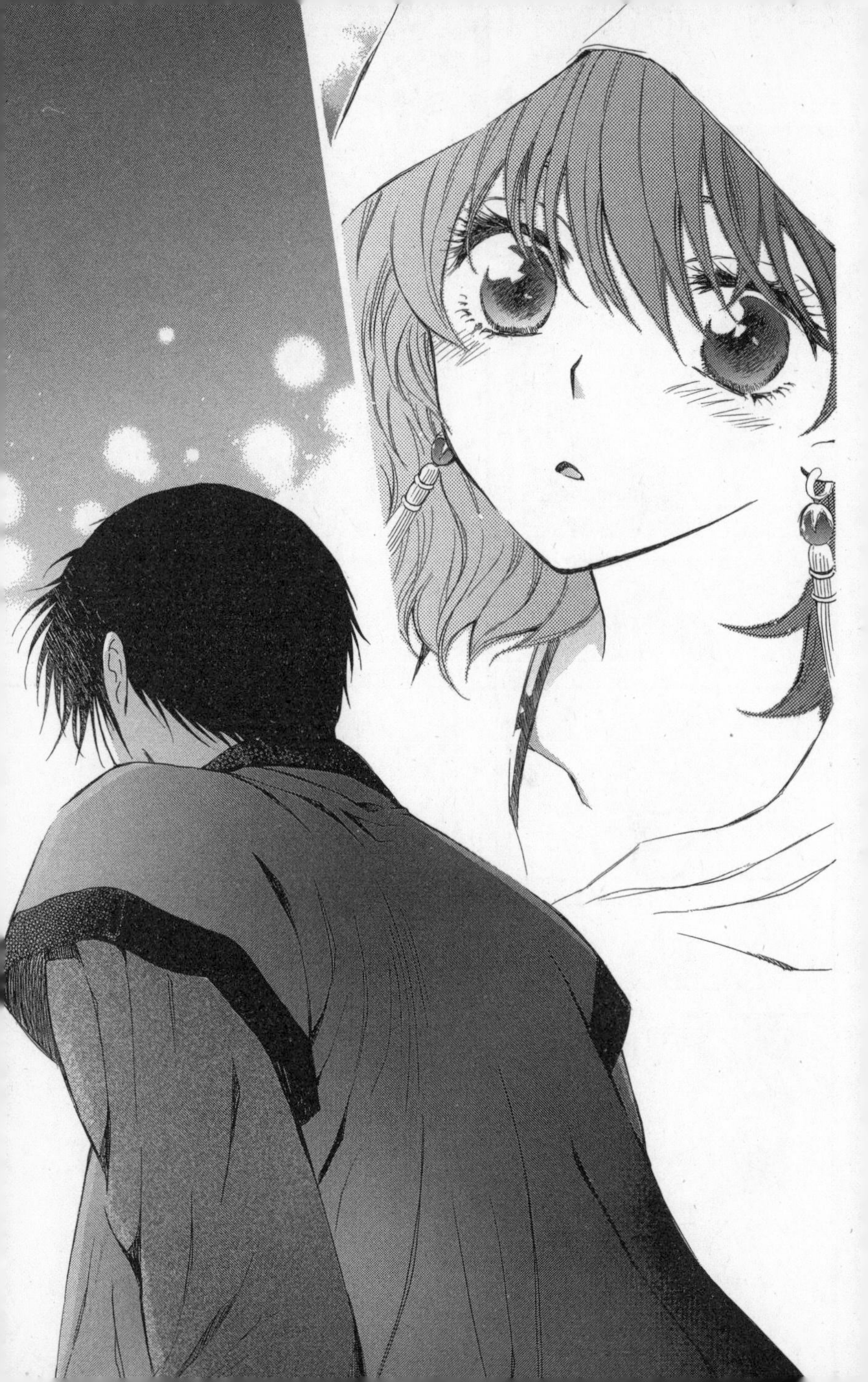

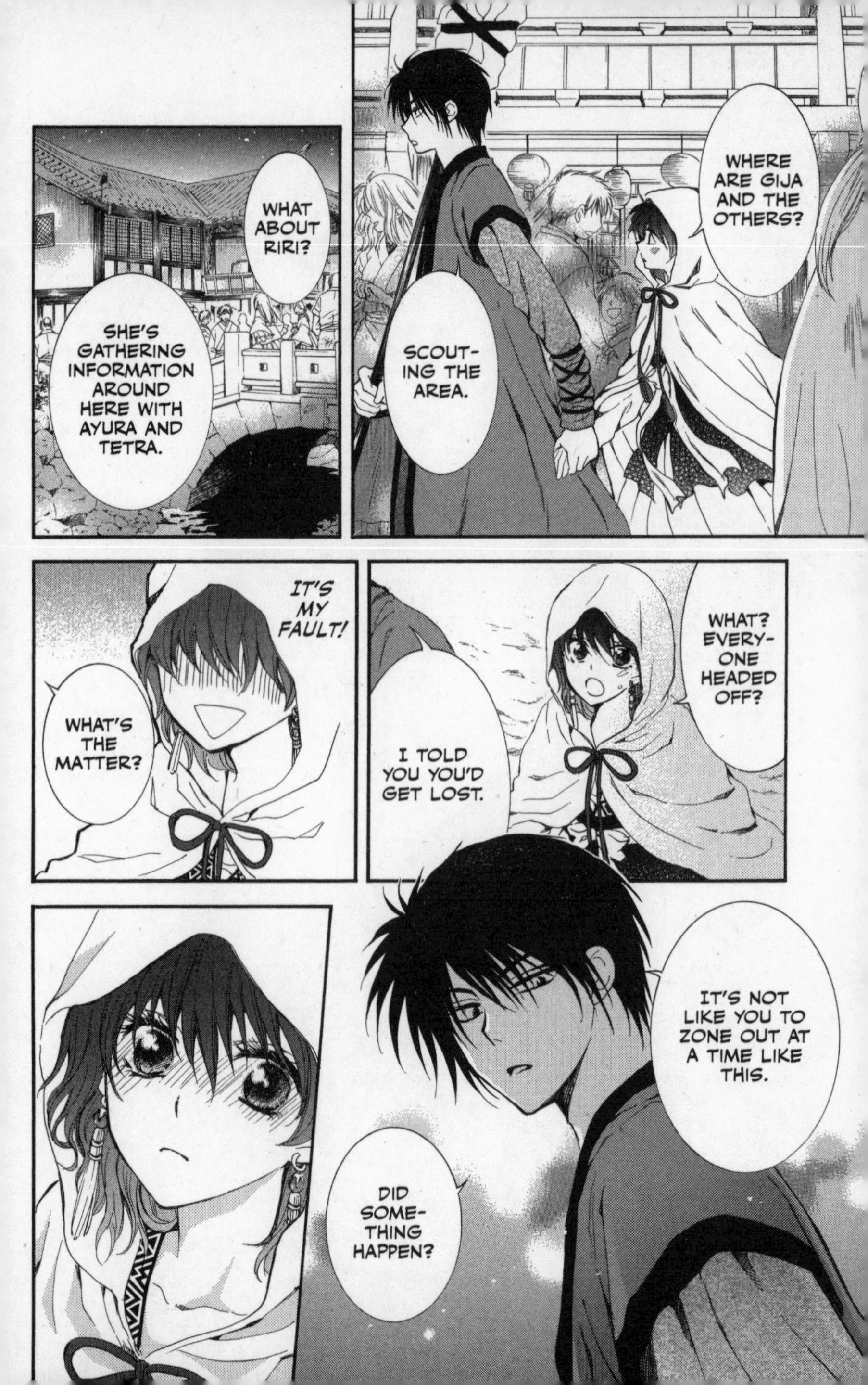
WHERE ARE GIJA AND THE OTHERS?
SCOUTING THE AREA.
WHAT ABOUT RIRI?
SHE'S GATHERING INFORMATION AROUND HERE WITH AYURA AND TETRA.
WHAT? EVERYONE HEADED OFF?
I TOLD YOU YOU'D GET LOST.
IT'S MY FAULT!
WHAT'S THE MATTER?
IT'S NOT LIKE YOU TO ZONE OUT AT A TIME LIKE THIS.
DID SOMETHING HAPPEN?

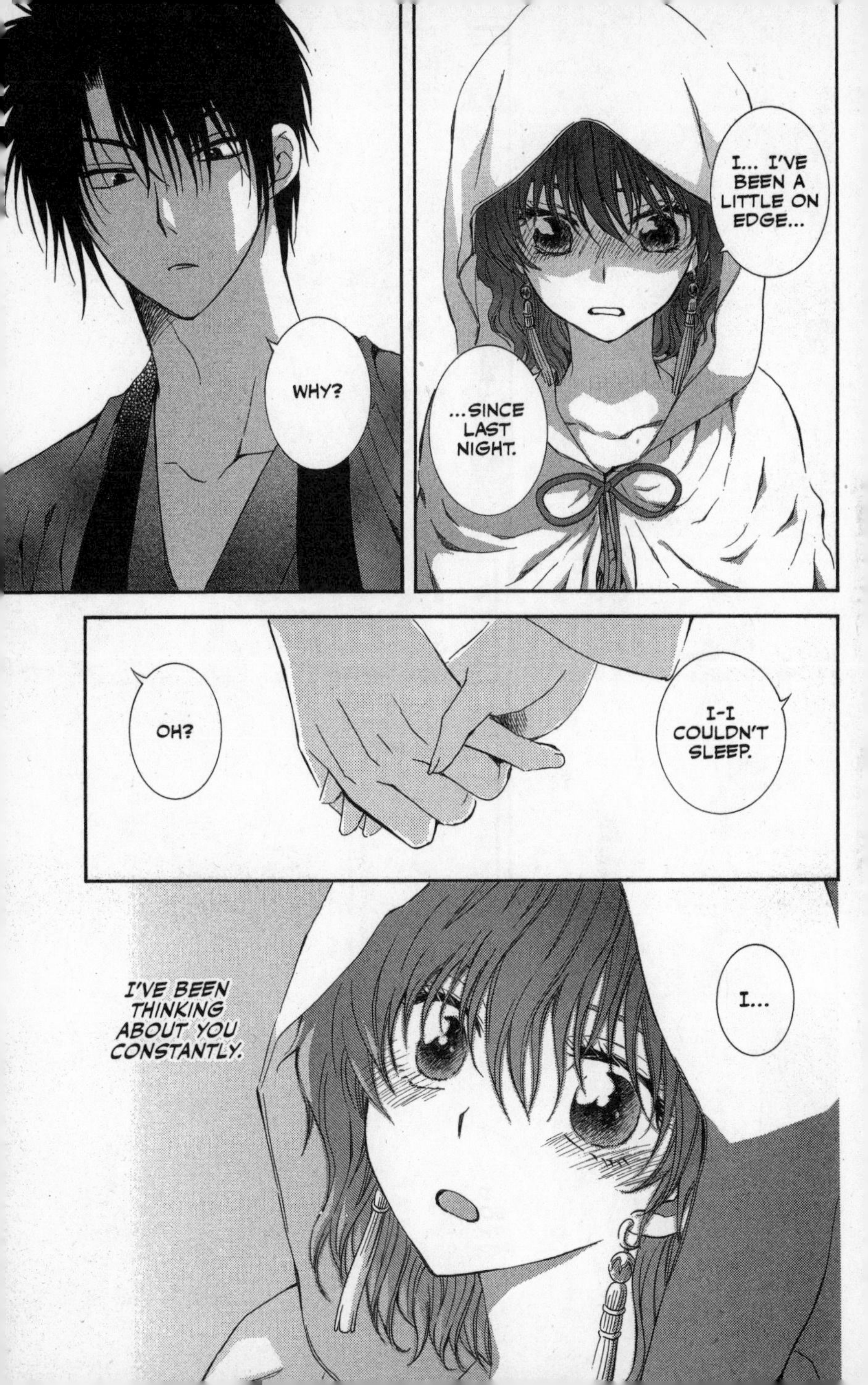
I... I'VE BEEN A LITTLE ON EDGE...
...SINCE LAST NIGHT.
WHY?
I-I COULDN'T SLEEP.
OH?
I...
I'VE BEEN THINKING ABOUT YOU CONSTANTLY.

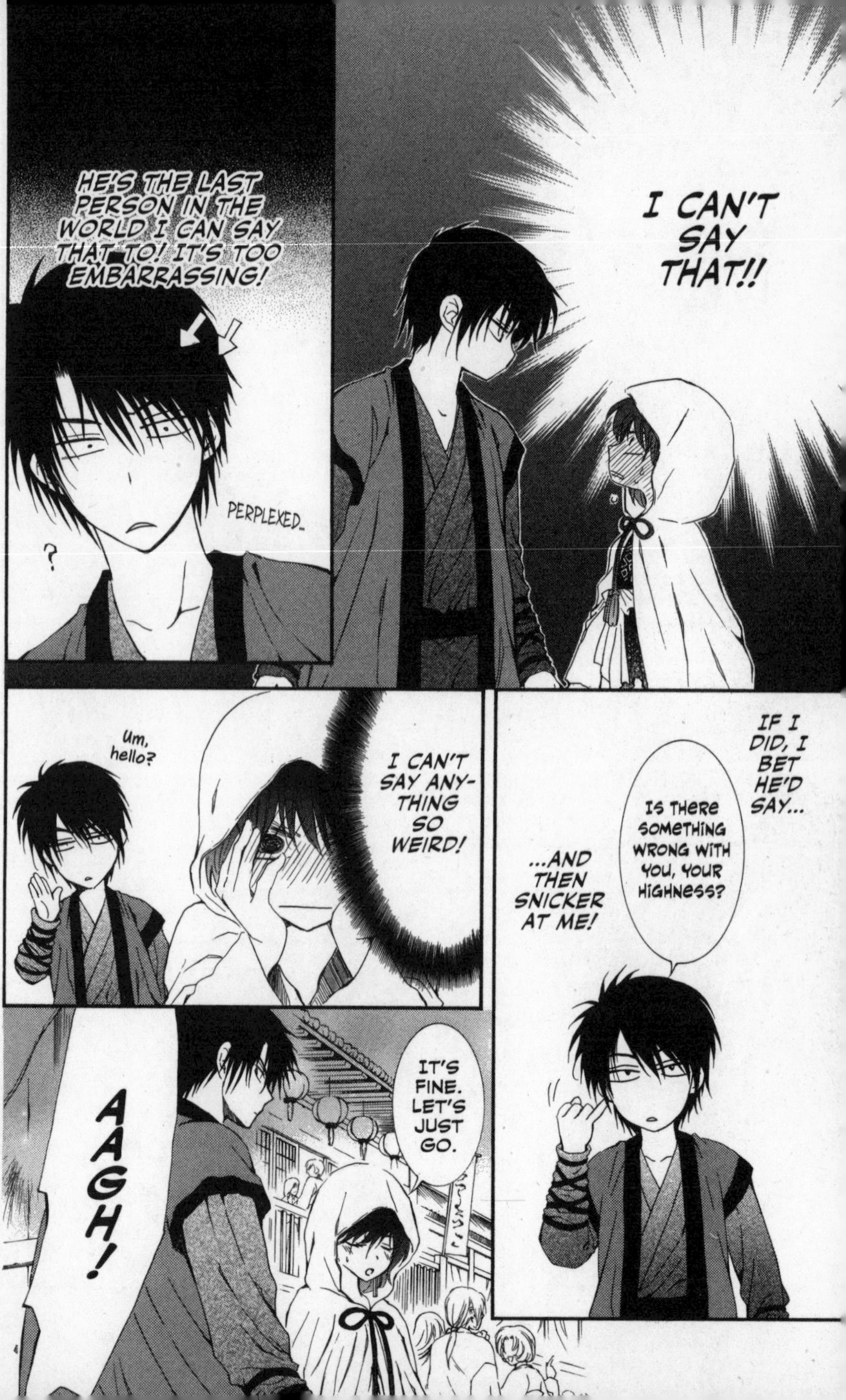
I CAN'T SAY THAT!!
HE'S THE LAST PERSON IN THE WORLD I CAN SAY THAT TO! IT'S TOO EMBARRASSING!
PERPLEXED...
?
IF I DID, I BET HE'D SAY...
IS THERE SOMETHING WRONG WITH YOU, YOUR HIGHNESS?
...AND THEN SNICKER AT ME!
I CAN'T SAY ANY-THING SO WEIRD!
Um, hello?
IT'S FINE. LET'S JUST GO.
AAGH!

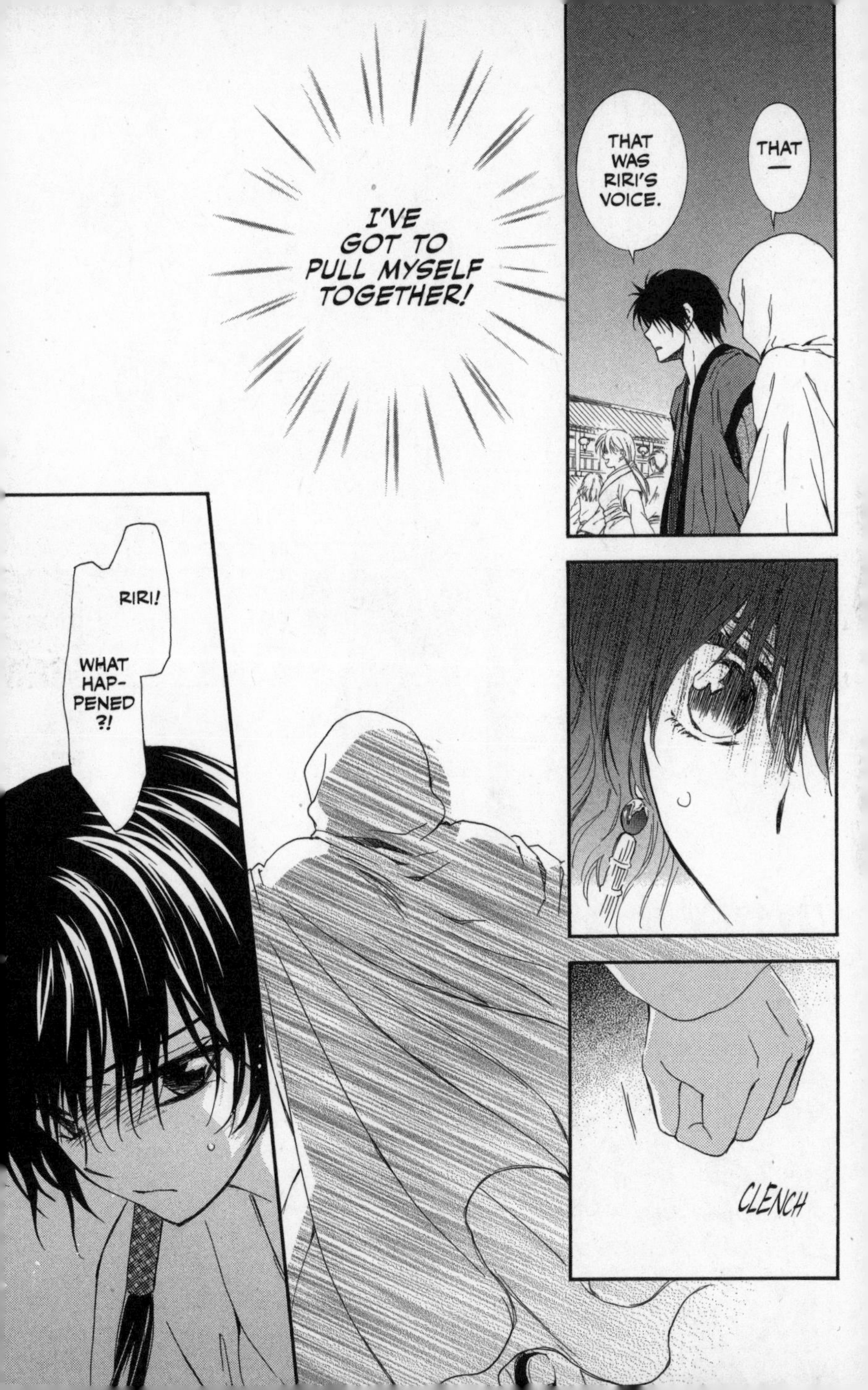
THAT—
THAT WAS RIRI'S VOICE.
I'VE GOT TO PULL MYSELF TOGETHER!
CLENCH
RIRI!
WHAT HAP-PENED?!

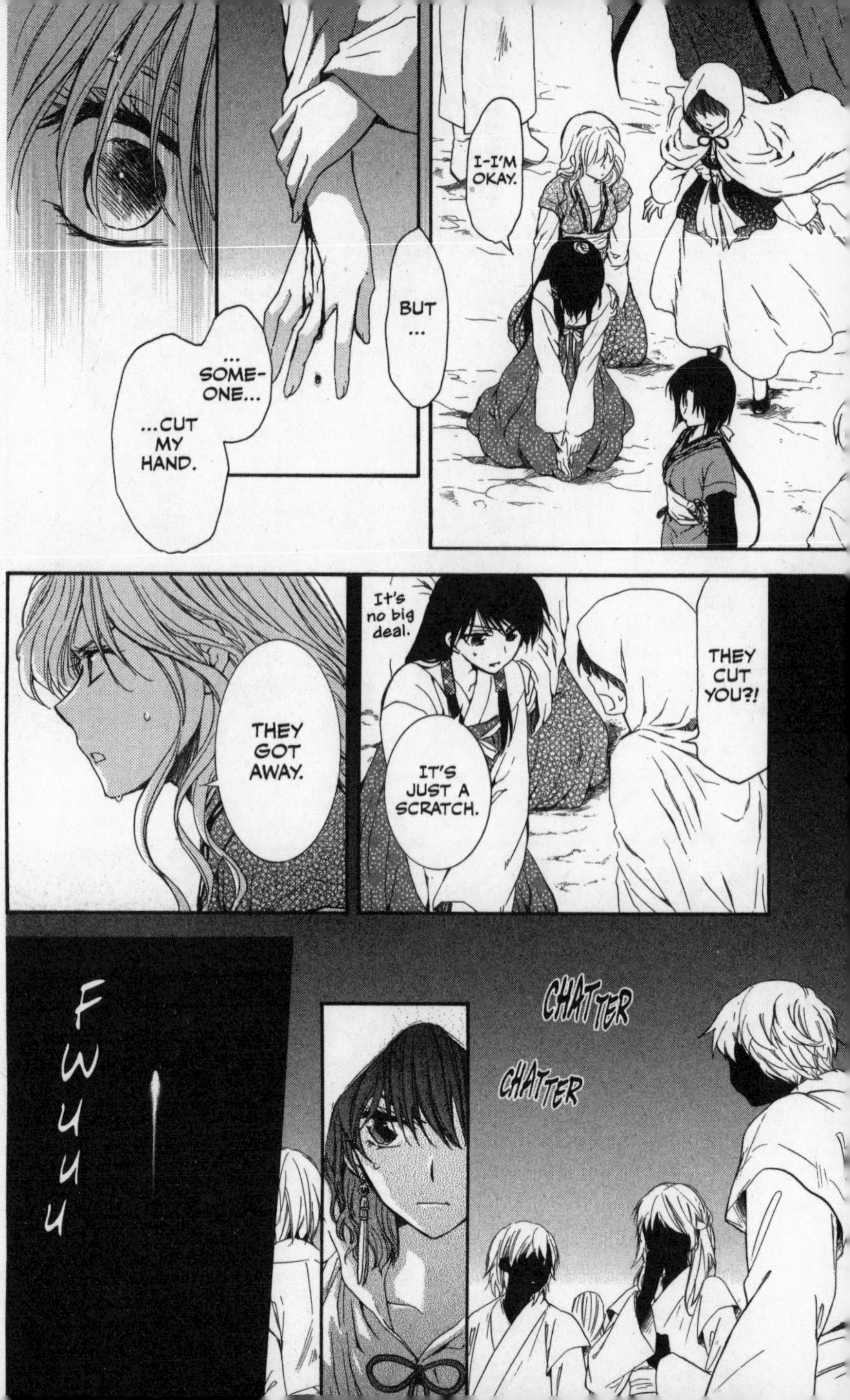
I-I'M OKAY.
BUT ...
... SOME-ONE...
...CUT MY HAND.
THEY CUT YOU?!
It's no big deal.
IT'S JUST A SCRATCH.
THEY GOT AWAY.
CHATTER
CHATTER
FWUUUU

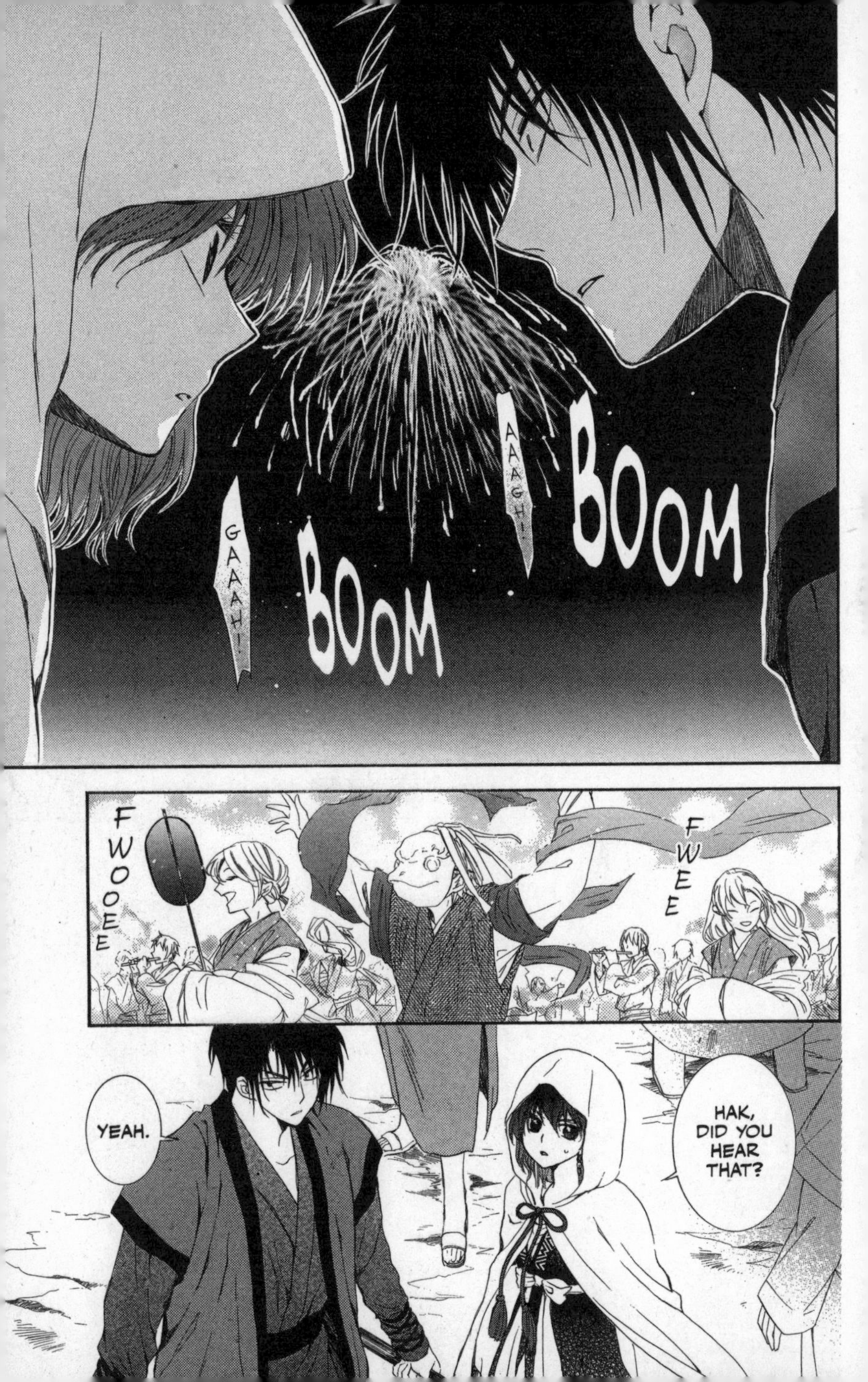
BOOM
AAAGH!
BOOM
GAAAH!
FWEE
FWOOEE
HAK, DID YOU HEAR THAT?
YEAH.

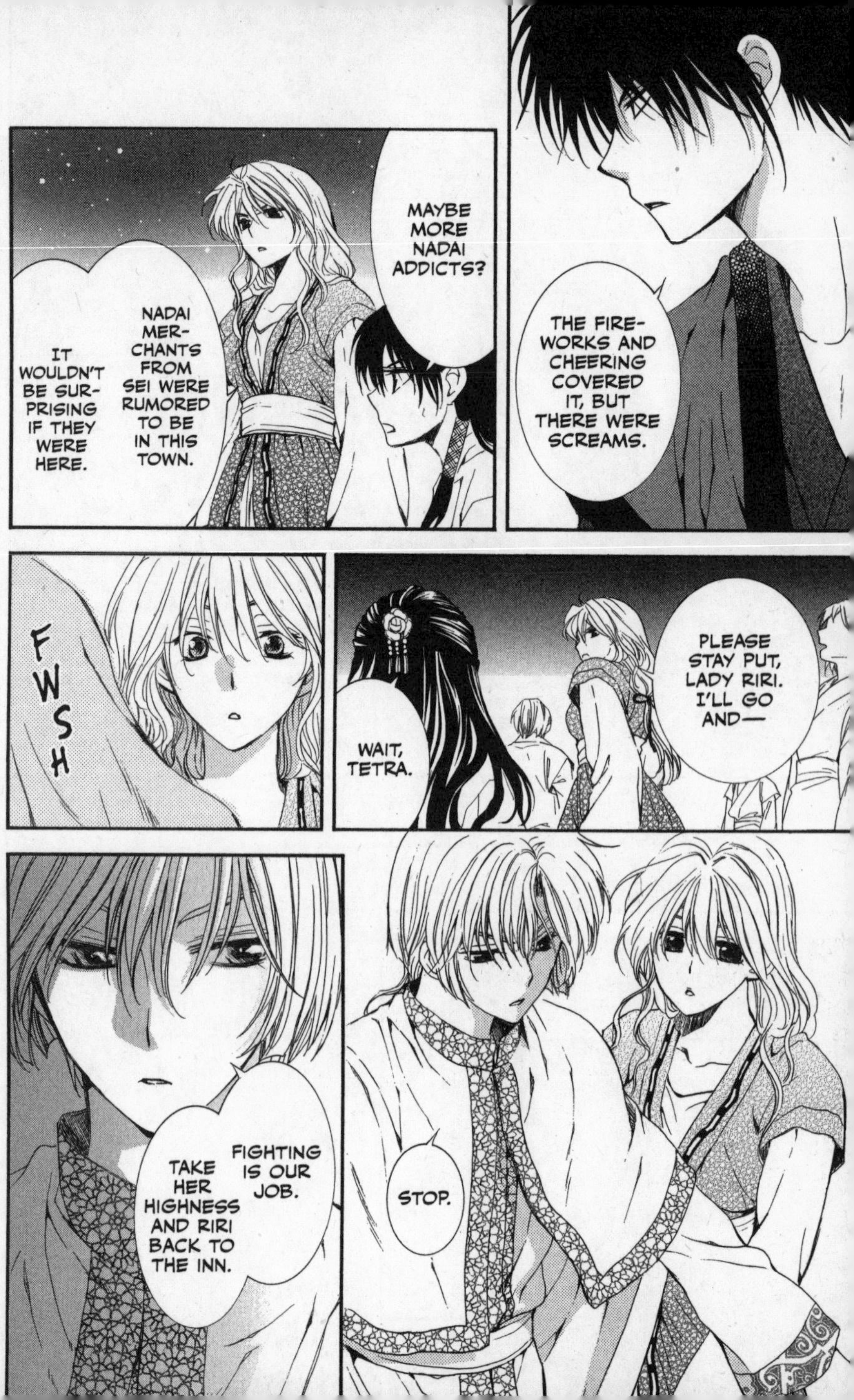
THE FIRE-WORKS AND CHEERING COVERED IT, BUT THERE WERE SCREAMS.
MAYBE MORE NADAI ADDICTS?
NADAI MER-CHANTS FROM SEI WERE RUMORED TO BE IN THIS TOWN.
IT WOULDN'T BE SUR-PRISING IF THEY WERE HERE.
PLEASE STAY PUT, LADY RIRI. I'LL GO AND—
WAIT, TETRA.
FWSH
STOP.
FIGHTING IS OUR JOB.
TAKE HER HIGHNESS AND RIRI BACK TO THE INN.

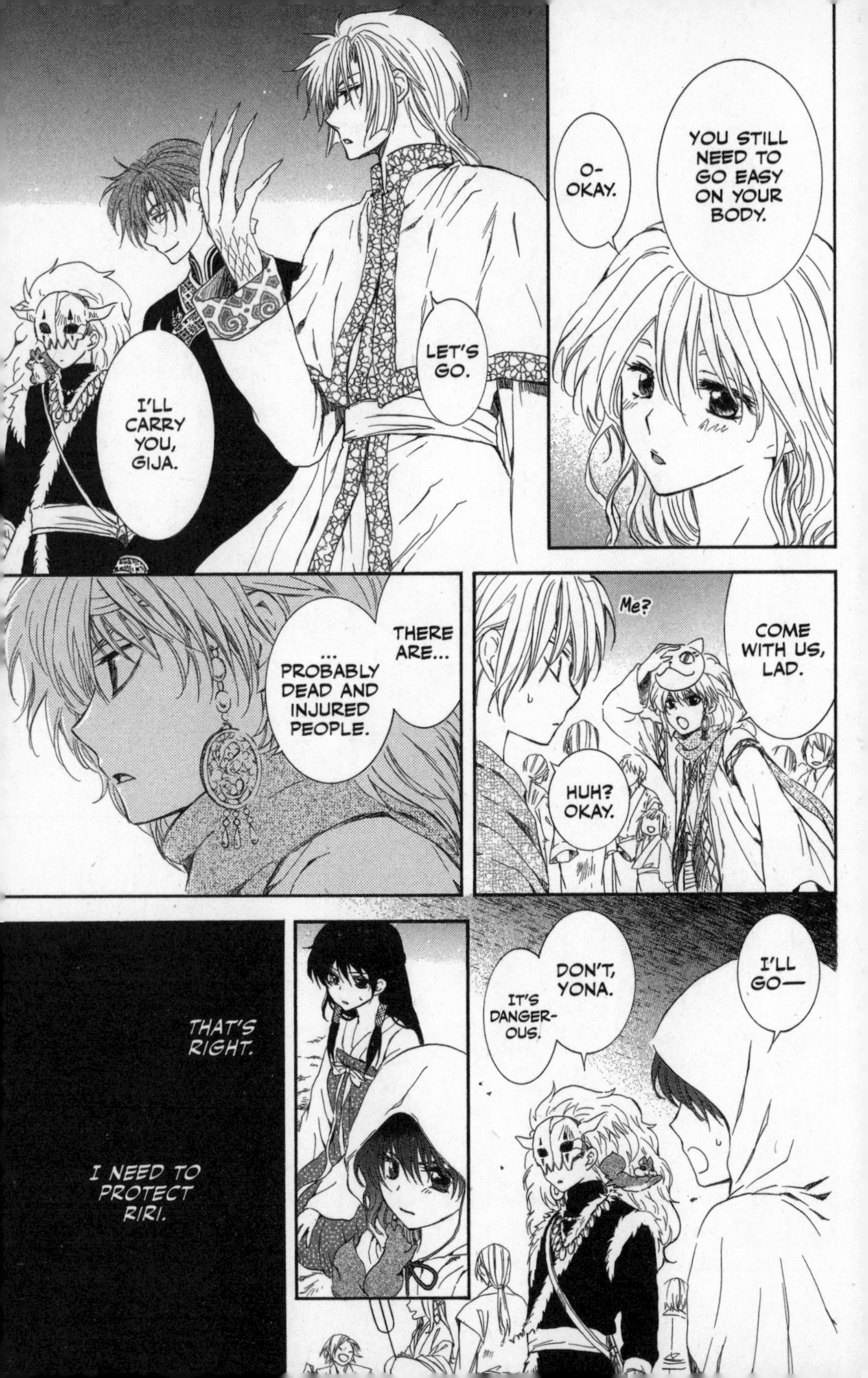
YOU STILL NEED TO GO EASY ON YOUR BODY.
O-OKAY.
LET'S GO.
I'LL CARRY YOU, GIJA.
COME WITH US, LAD.
Me?
HUH? OKAY.
THERE ARE... ...PROBABLY DEAD AND INJURED PEOPLE.
I'LL GO—
DON'T, YONA.
IT'S DANGER-OUS.
THAT'S RIGHT.
I NEED TO PROTECT RIRI.

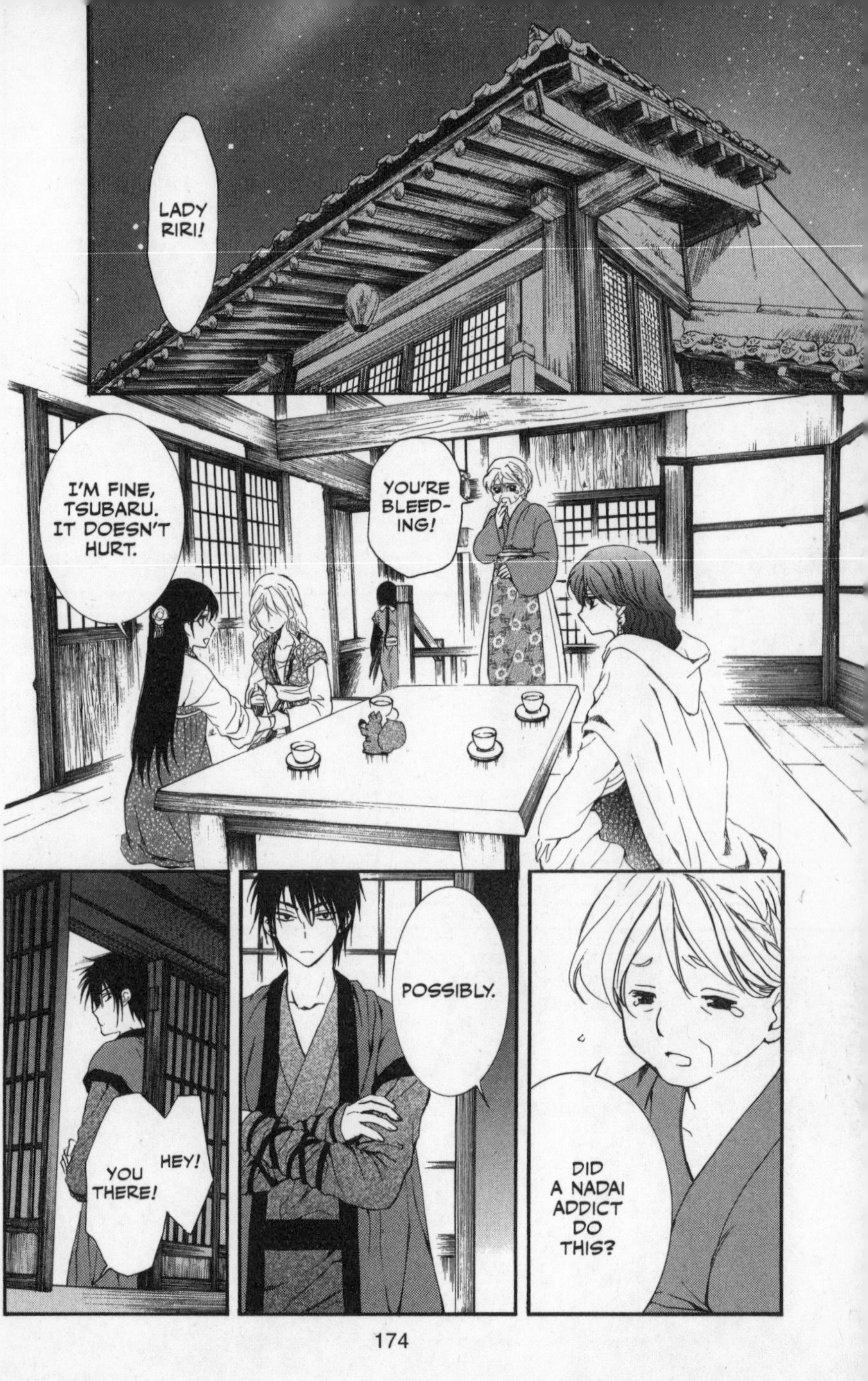
LADY RIRI!
YOU'RE BLEED-ING!
I'M FINE, TSUBARU. IT DOESN'T HURT.
DID A NADAI ADDICT DO THIS?
POSSIBLY.
HEY!
YOU THERE!

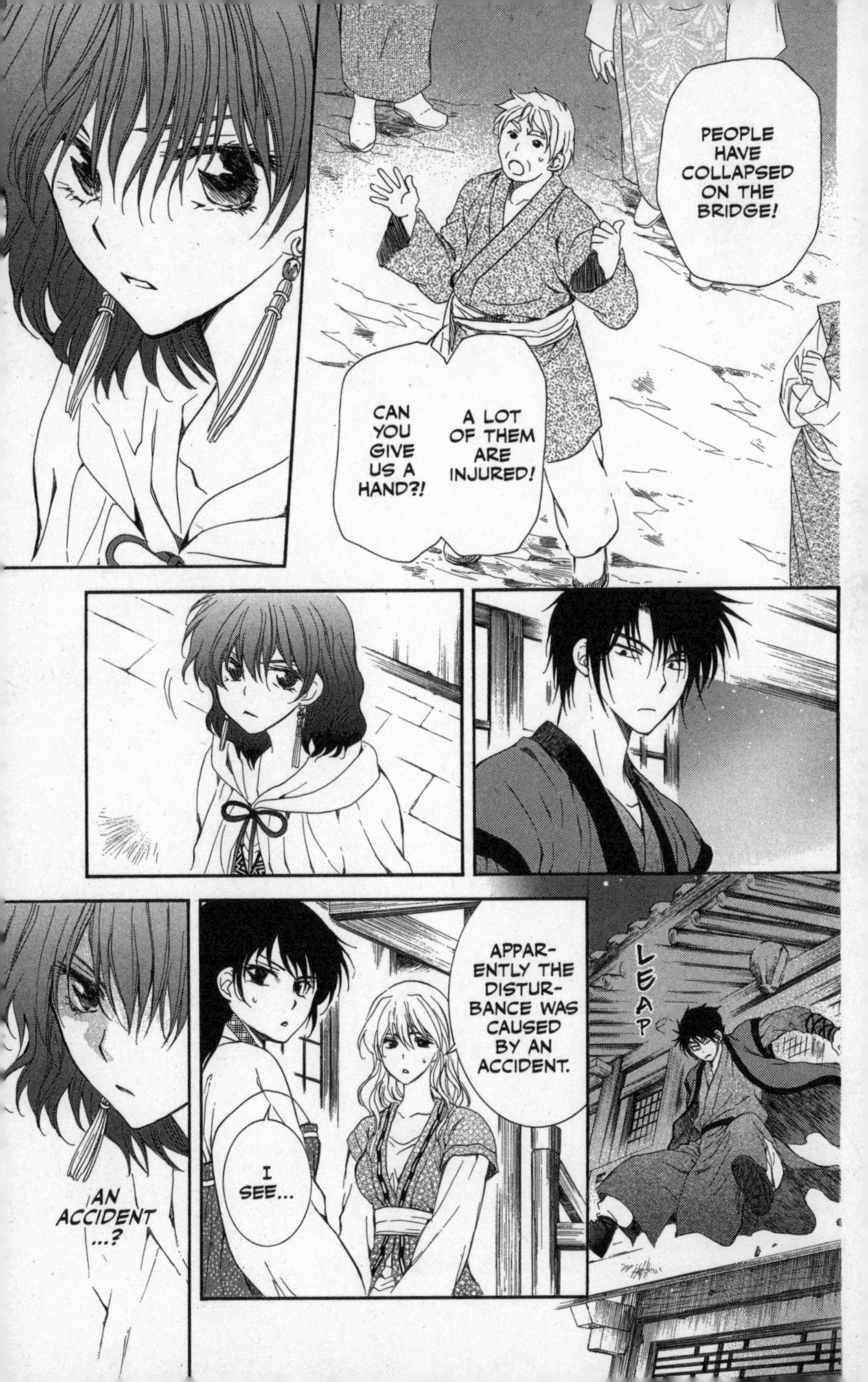
PEOPLE HAVE COLLAPSED ON THE BRIDGE!
A LOT OF THEM ARE INJURED!
CAN YOU GIVE US A HAND?!
LEAP
APPAR-ENTLY THE DISTUR-BANCE WAS CAUSED BY AN ACCIDENT.
I SEE...
AN ACCIDENT ...?

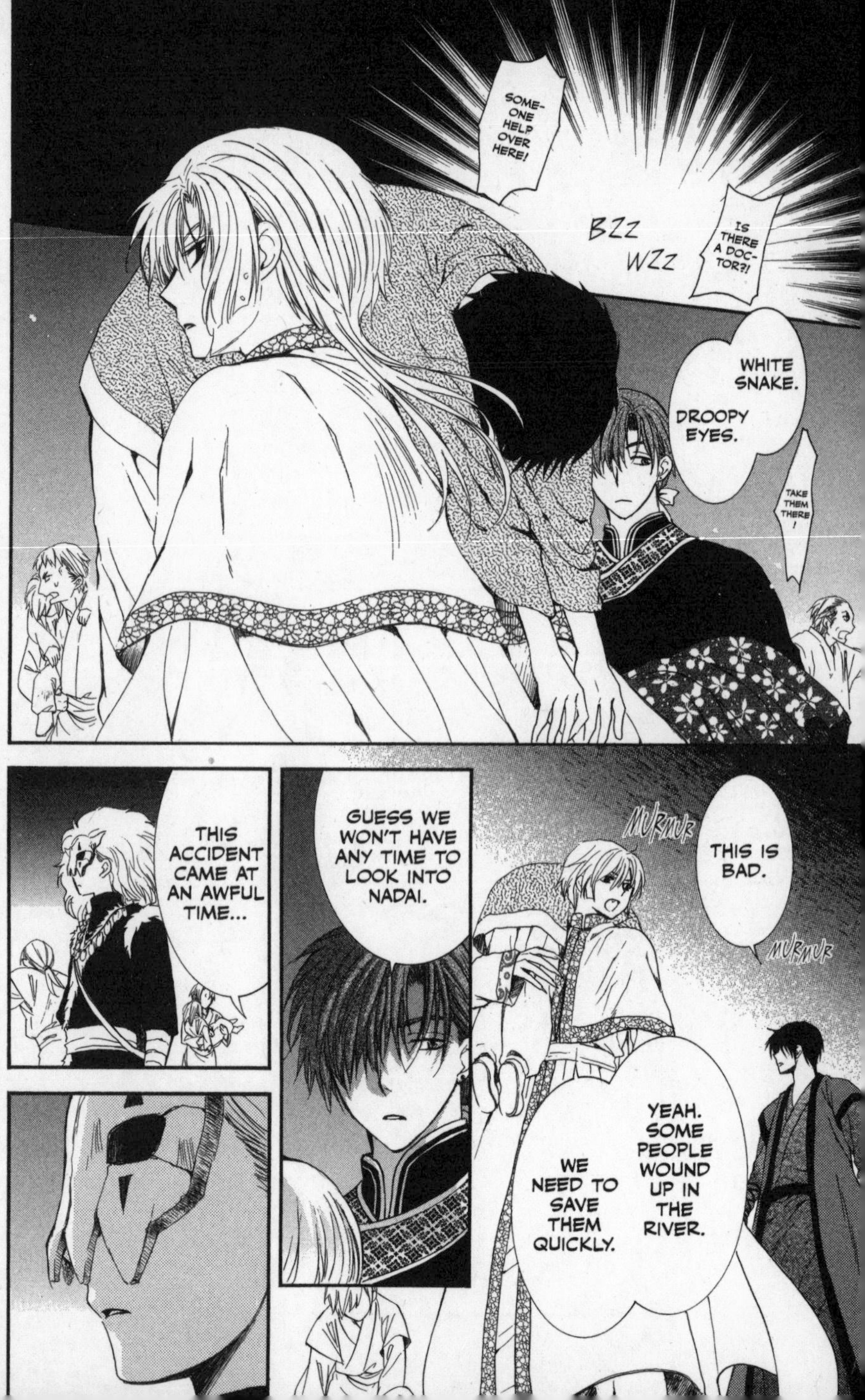
IS THERE A DOC-TOR?!
BZZ WZZ
SOME-ONE HELP OVER HERE!
WHITE SNAKE.
DROOPY EYES.
TAKE THEM THERE!
MURMUR
THIS IS BAD.
MURMUR
YEAH. SOME PEOPLE WOUND UP IN THE RIVER.
WE NEED TO SAVE THEM QUICKLY.
GUESS WE WON'T HAVE ANY TIME TO LOOK INTO NADAI.
THIS ACCIDENT CAME AT AN AWFUL TIME...

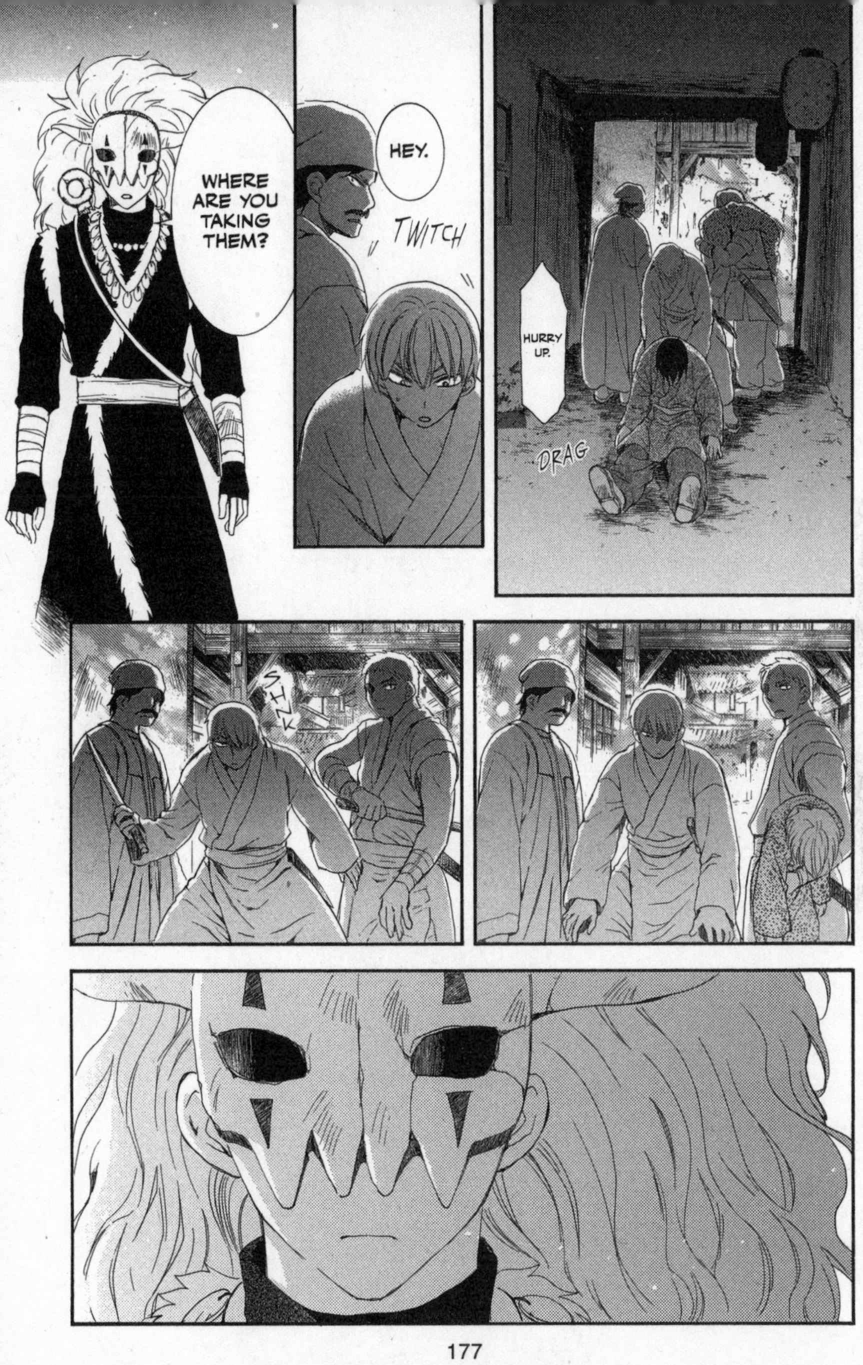
HURRY UP.
DRAG
HEY.
TWITCH
WHERE ARE YOU TAKING THEM?
SHNK

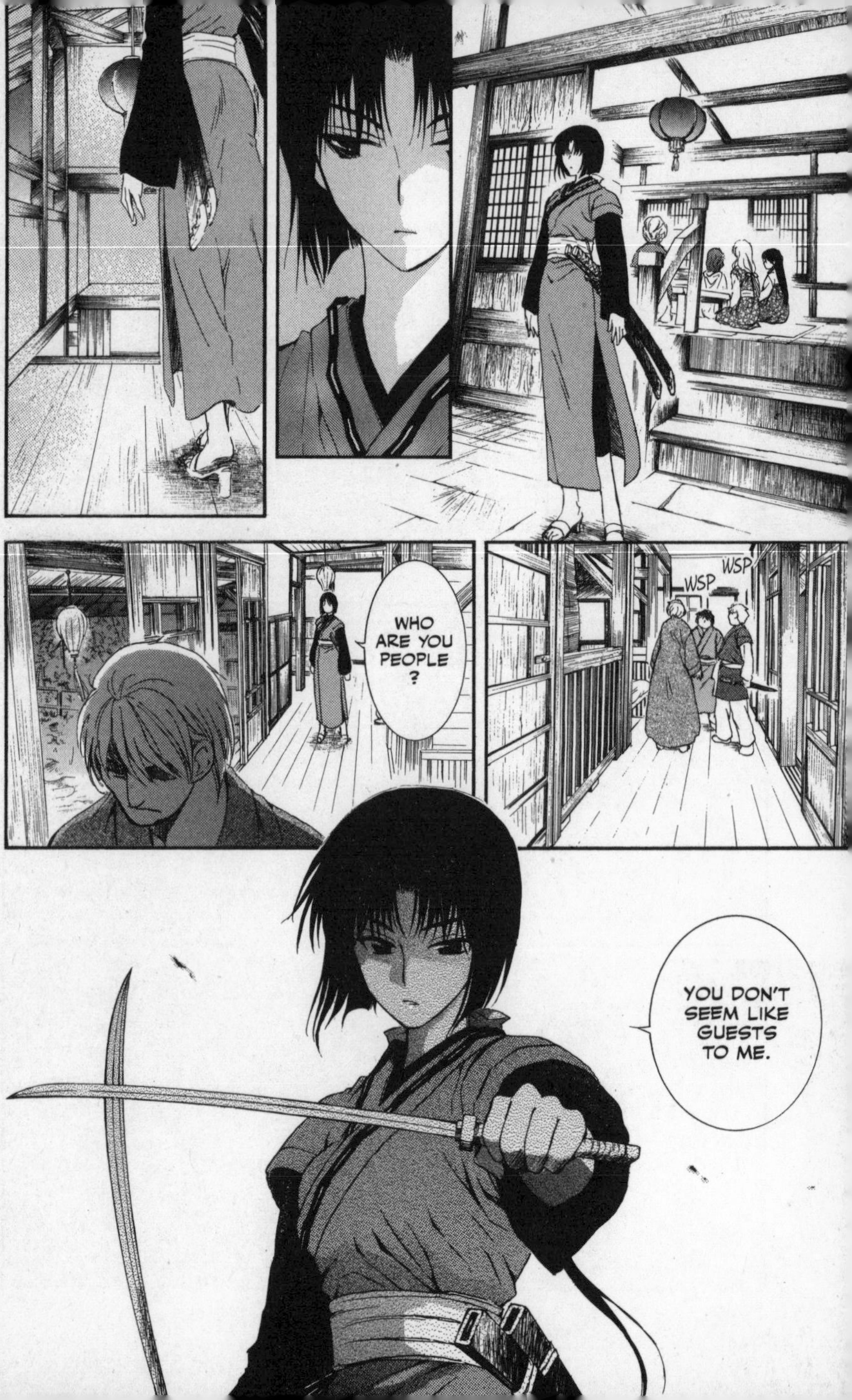
WSP
WSP
WHO ARE YOU PEOPLE?
YOU DON'T SEEM LIKE GUESTS TO ME.

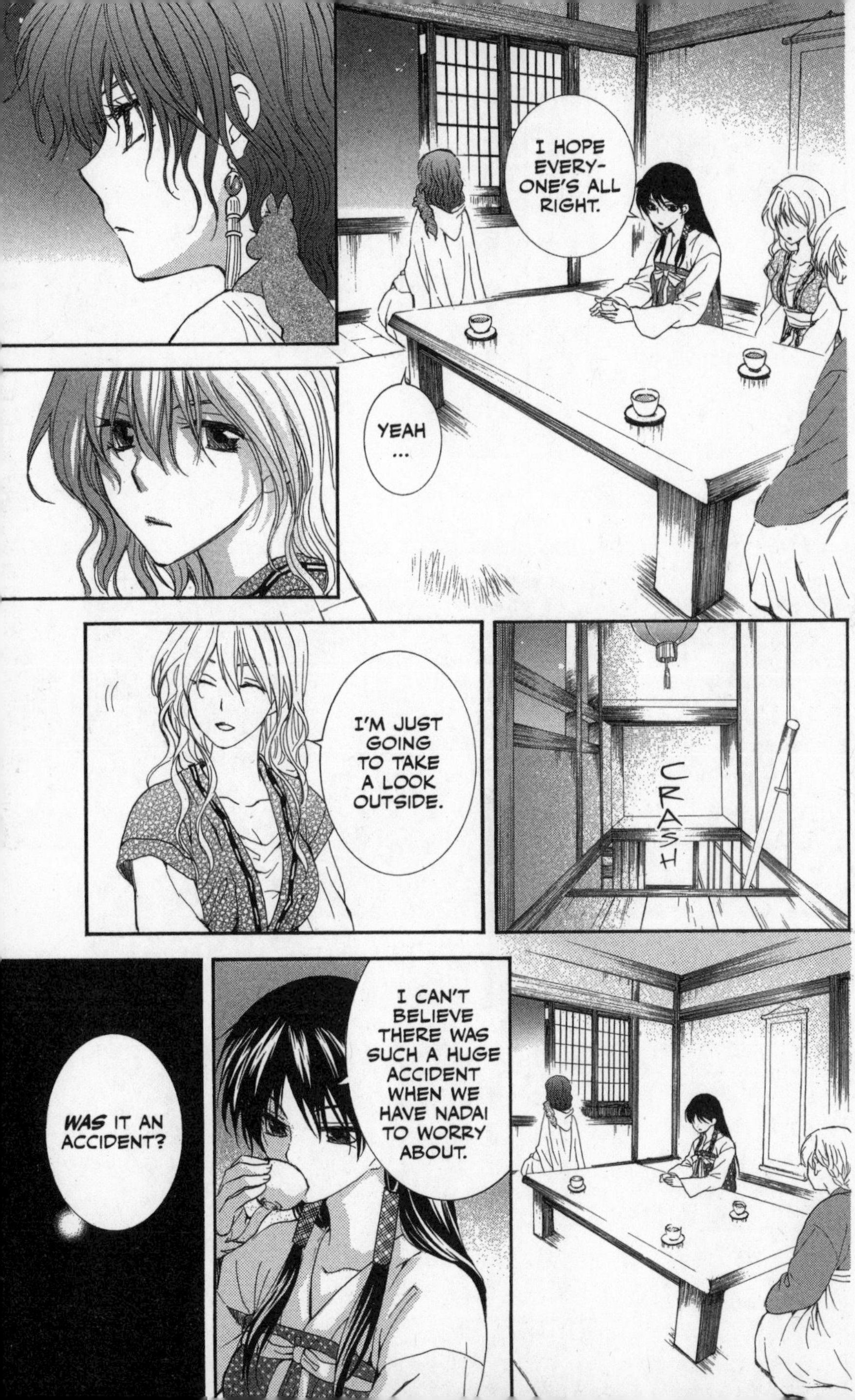
I HOPE EVERY-ONE'S ALL RIGHT.
YEAH ...
CRASH
I'M JUST GOING TO TAKE A LOOK OUTSIDE.
I CAN'T BELIEVE THERE WAS SUCH A HUGE ACCIDENT WHEN WE HAVE NADAI TO WORRY ABOUT.
WAS IT AN ACCIDENT?

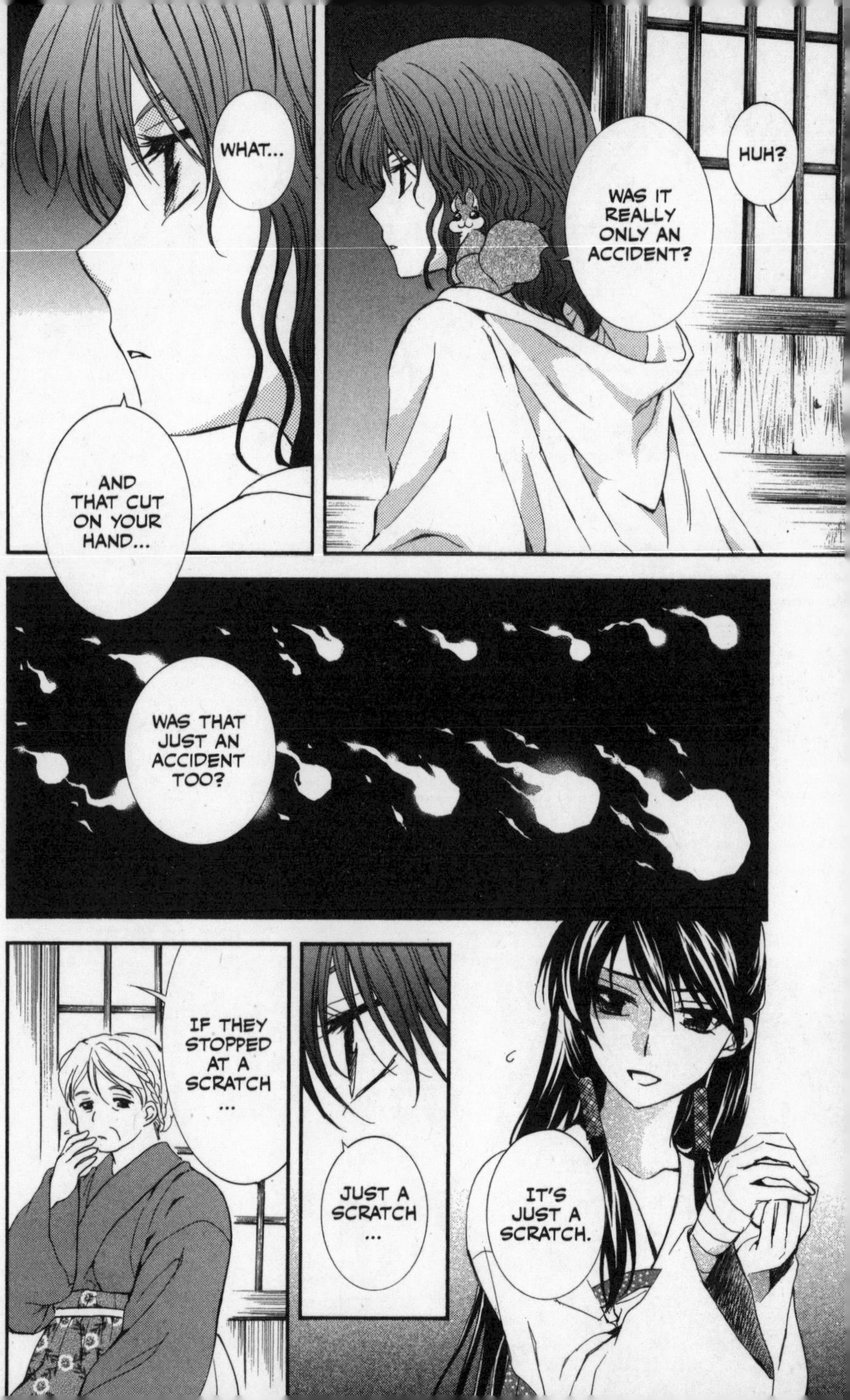
HUH?
WAS IT REALLY ONLY AN ACCIDENT?
WHAT...
AND THAT CUT ON YOUR HAND...
WAS THAT JUST AN ACCIDENT TOO?
IT'S JUST A SCRATCH.
JUST A SCRATCH ...
IF THEY STOPPED AT A SCRATCH ...

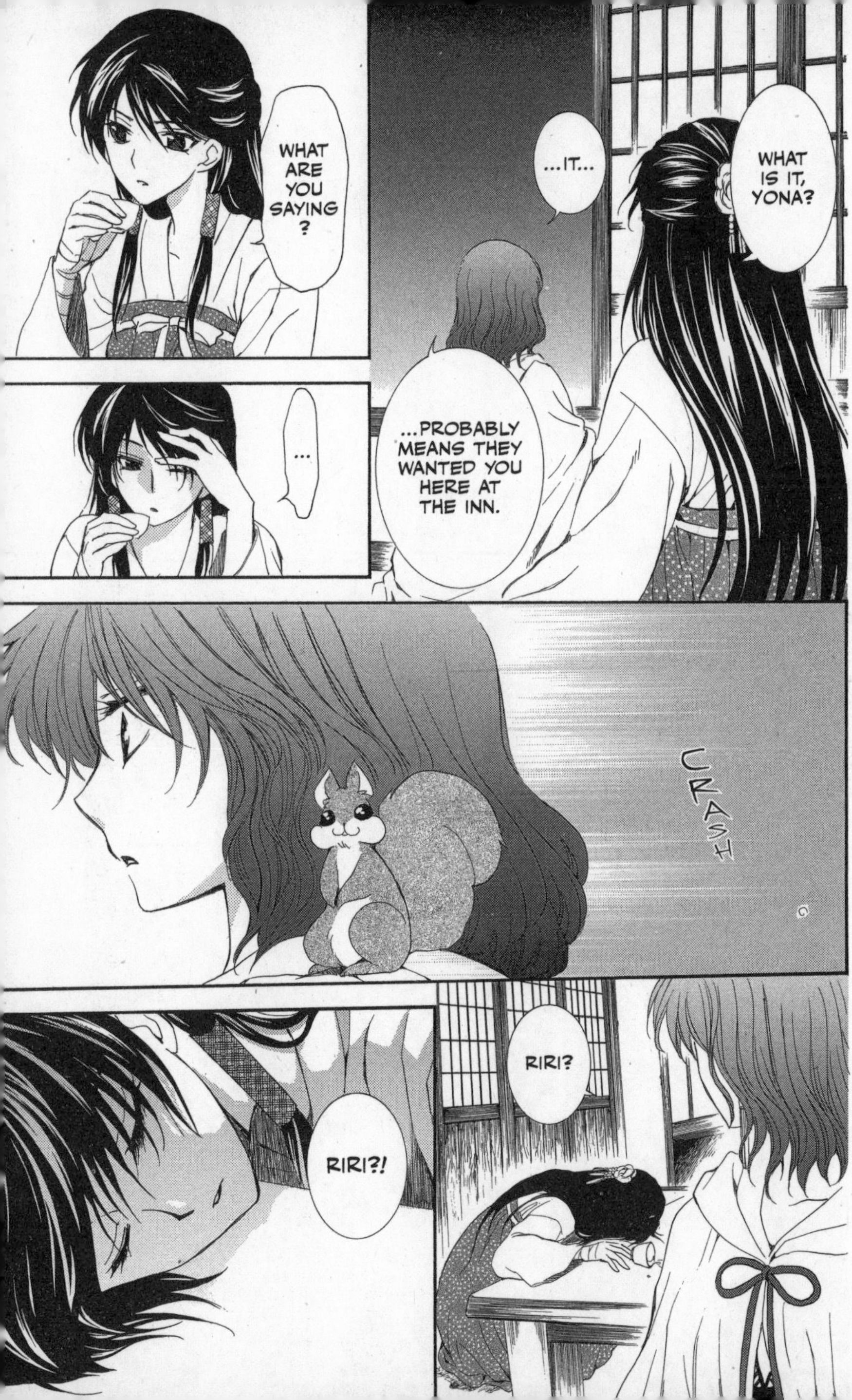
WHAT IS IT, YONA?
...IT...
...PROBABLY MEANS THEY WANTED YOU HERE AT THE INN.
WHAT ARE YOU SAYING?
...
CRASH
RIRI?
RIRI?!

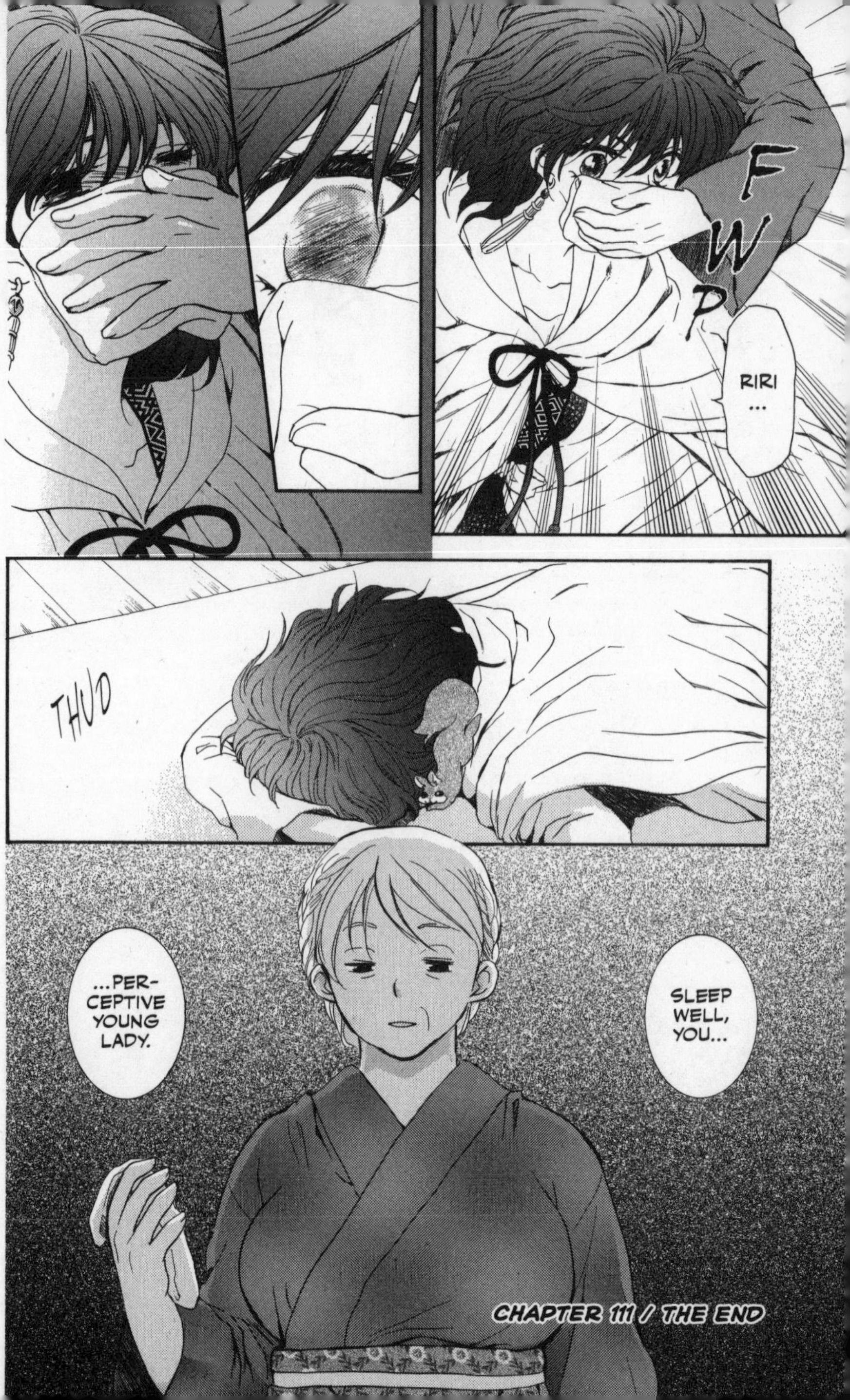
FWP
RIRI ...
THUD
SLEEP WELL, YOU...
...PER-CEPTIVE YOUNG LADY.
CHAPTER 111 / THE END

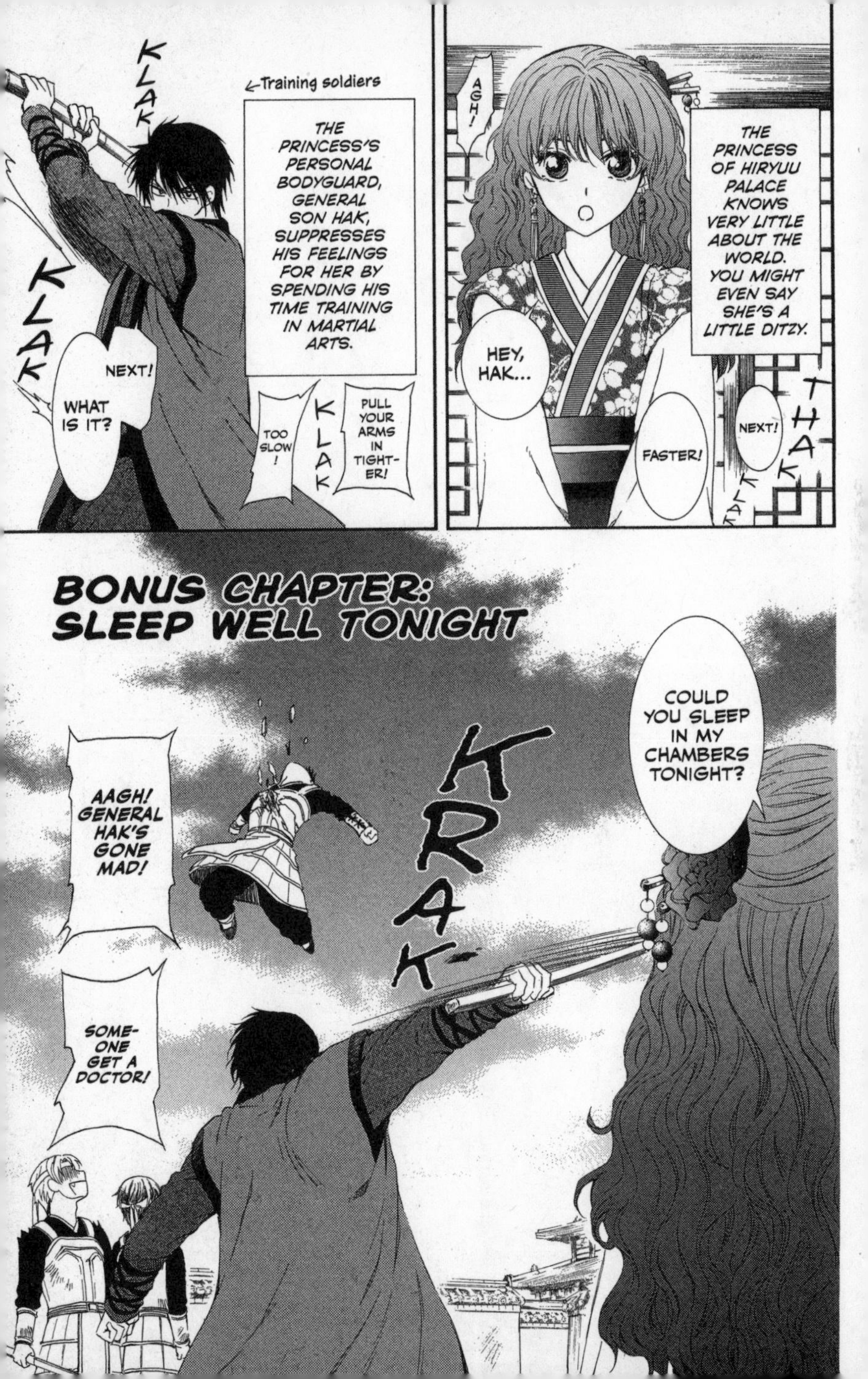
THE PRINCESS OF HIRYUU PALACE KNOWS VERY LITTLE ABOUT THE WORLD. YOU MIGHT EVEN SAY SHE'S A LITTLE DITZY.
AGH!
HEY, HAK...
THAK
NEXT!
KLAK
FASTER!
←Training soldiers
THE PRINCESS'S PERSONAL BODYGUARD, GENERAL SON HAK, SUPPRESSES HIS FEELINGS FOR HER BY SPENDING HIS TIME TRAINING IN MARTIAL ARTS.
PULL YOUR ARMS IN TIGHTER!
KLAK
TOO SLOW!
KLAK
NEXT!
WHAT IS IT?
KLAK
BONUS CHAPTER: SLEEP WELL TONIGHT
COULD YOU SLEEP IN MY CHAMBERS TONIGHT?
KRAK
AAGH! GENERAL HAK'S GONE MAD!
SOME-ONE GET A DOCTOR!

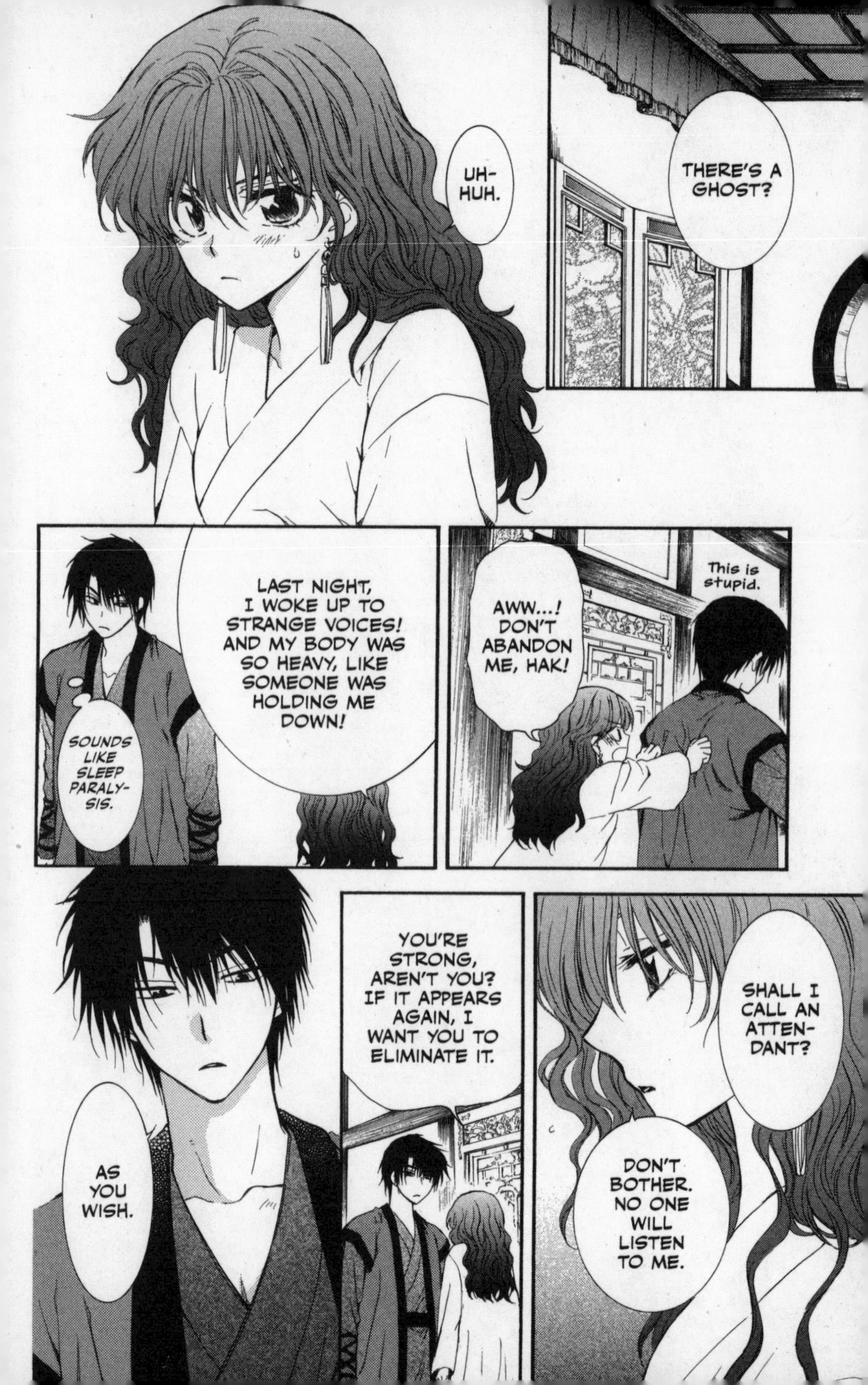
THERE'S A GHOST?
UH-HUH.
AWW...! DON'T ABANDON ME, HAK!
This is stupid.
LAST NIGHT, I WOKE UP TO STRANGE VOICES! AND MY BODY WAS SO HEAVY, LIKE SOMEONE WAS HOLDING ME DOWN!
SOUNDS LIKE SLEEP PARALYSIS.
SHALL I CALL AN ATTENDANT?
DON'T BOTHER. NO ONE WILL LISTEN TO ME.
YOU'RE STRONG, AREN'T YOU? IF IT APPEARS AGAIN, I WANT YOU TO ELIMINATE IT.
AS YOU WISH.

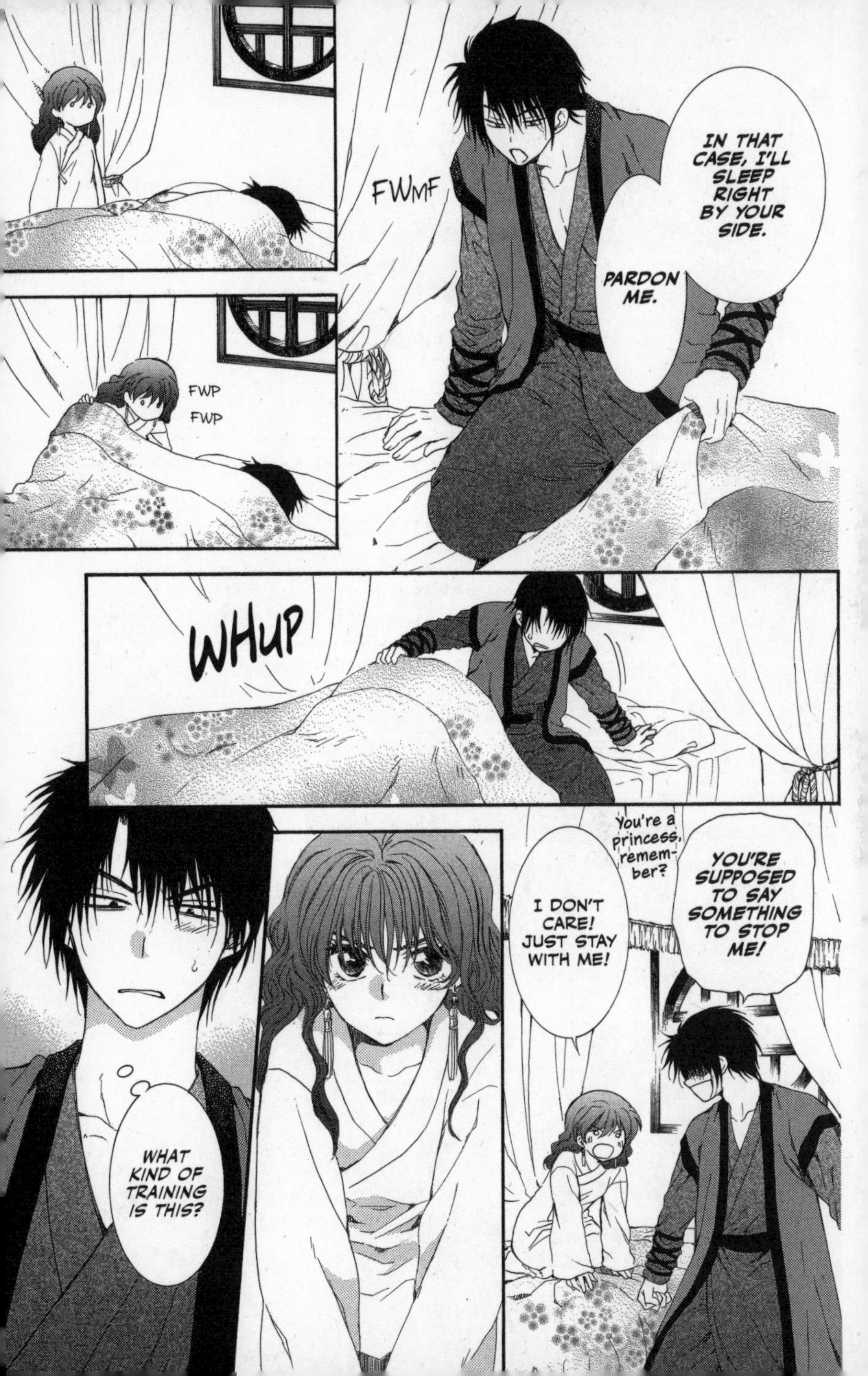
IN THAT CASE, I'LL SLEEP RIGHT BY YOUR SIDE.
PARDON ME.
FWMF
FWP
FWP
WHUP
YOU'RE SUPPOSED TO SAY SOMETHING TO STOP ME!
You're a princess, remember?
I DON'T CARE! JUST STAY WITH ME!
WHAT KIND OF TRAINING IS THIS?

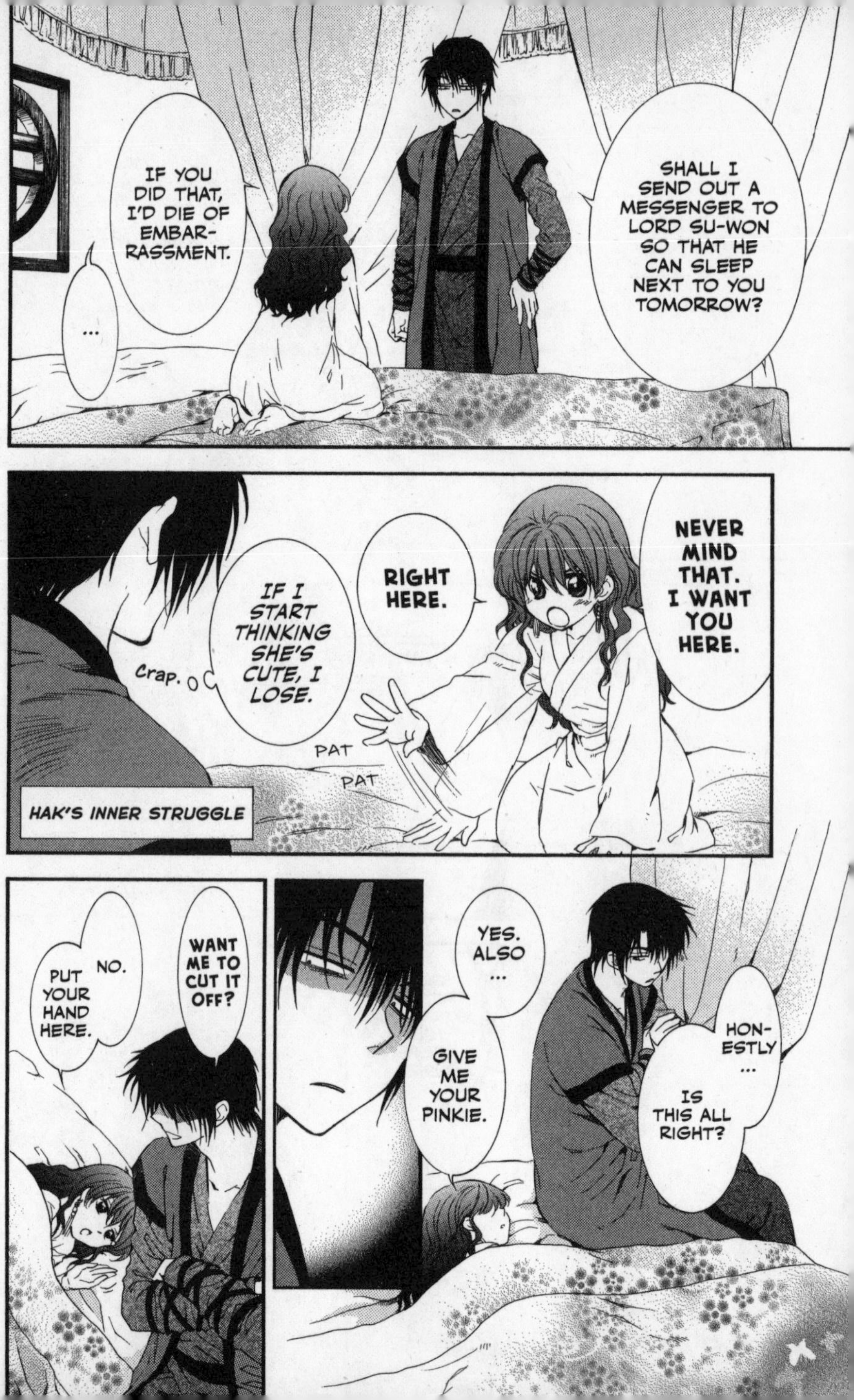
SHALL I SEND OUT A MESSENGER TO LORD SU-WON SO THAT HE CAN SLEEP NEXT TO YOU TOMORROW?
IF YOU DID THAT, I'D DIE OF EMBAR-RASSMENT.
...
NEVER MIND THAT. I WANT YOU HERE.
RIGHT HERE.
PAT
PAT
IF I START THINKING SHE'S CUTE, I LOSE.
Crap.
HAK'S INNER STRUGGLE
HON-ESTLY ...
IS THIS ALL RIGHT?
YES. ALSO ...
GIVE ME YOUR PINKIE.
WANT ME TO CUT IT OFF?
NO.
PUT YOUR HAND HERE.

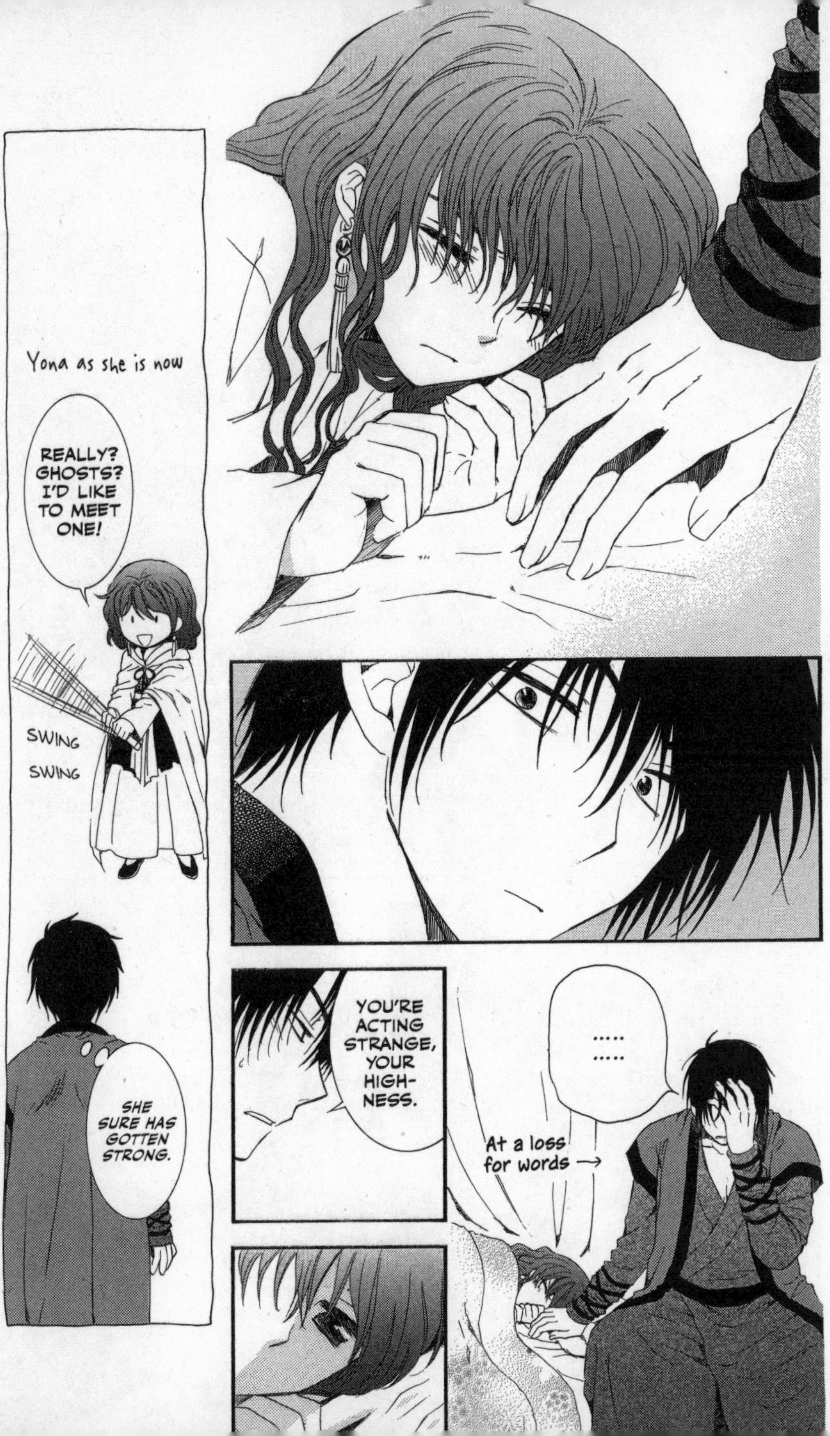

.....
.....
At a loss for words →
YOU'RE ACTING STRANGE, YOUR HIGHNESS.
Yona as she is now
REALLY? GHOSTS? I'D LIKE TO MEET ONE!
SWING
SWING
SHE SURE HAS GOTTEN STRONG.

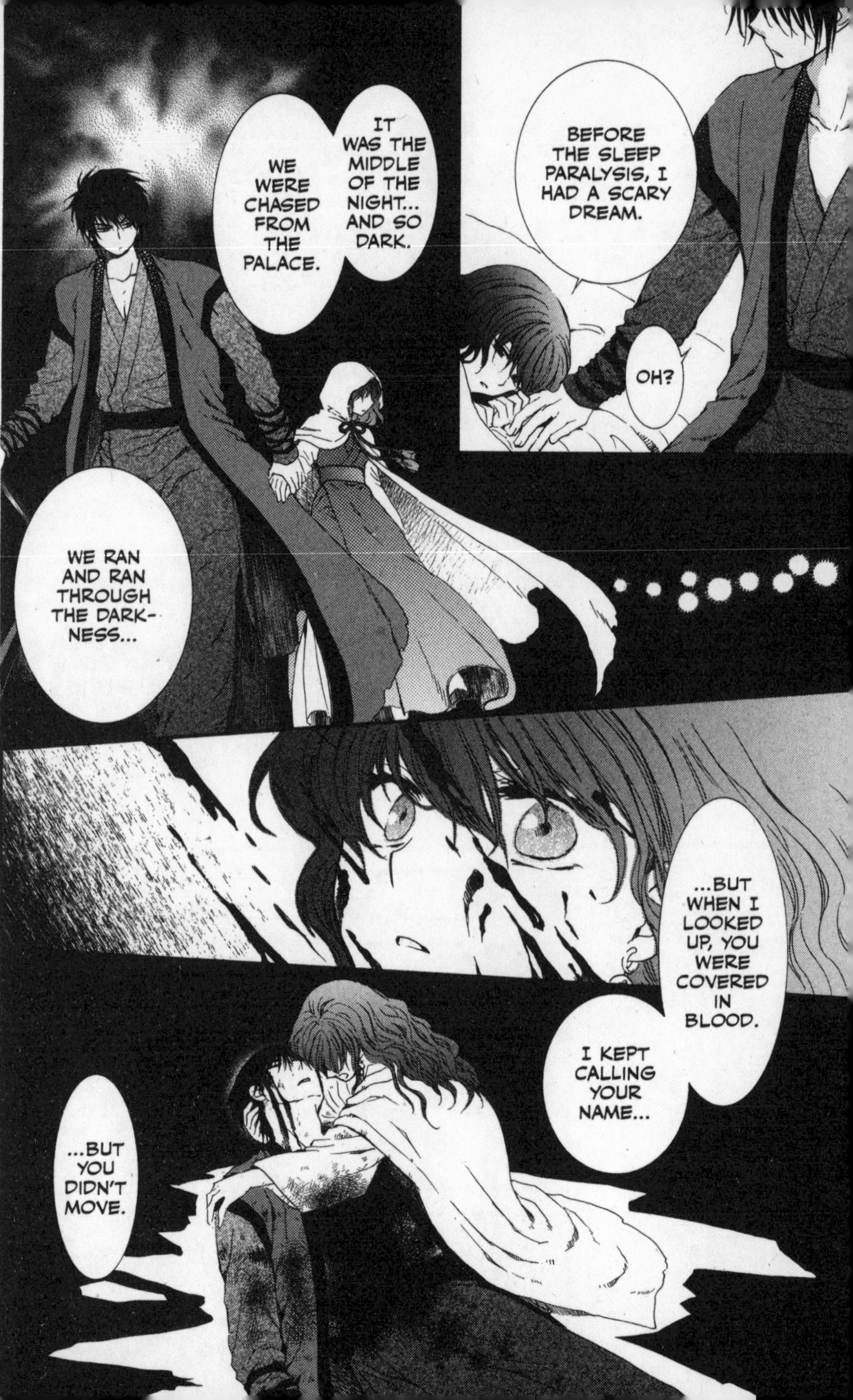
BEFORE THE SLEEP PARALYSIS, I HAD A SCARY DREAM.
OH?
IT WAS THE MIDDLE OF THE NIGHT... AND SO DARK.
WE WERE CHASED FROM THE PALACE.
WE RAN AND RAN THROUGH THE DARK-NESS...
...BUT WHEN I LOOKED UP, YOU WERE COVERED IN BLOOD.
I KEPT CALLING YOUR NAME...
...BUT YOU DIDN'T MOVE.

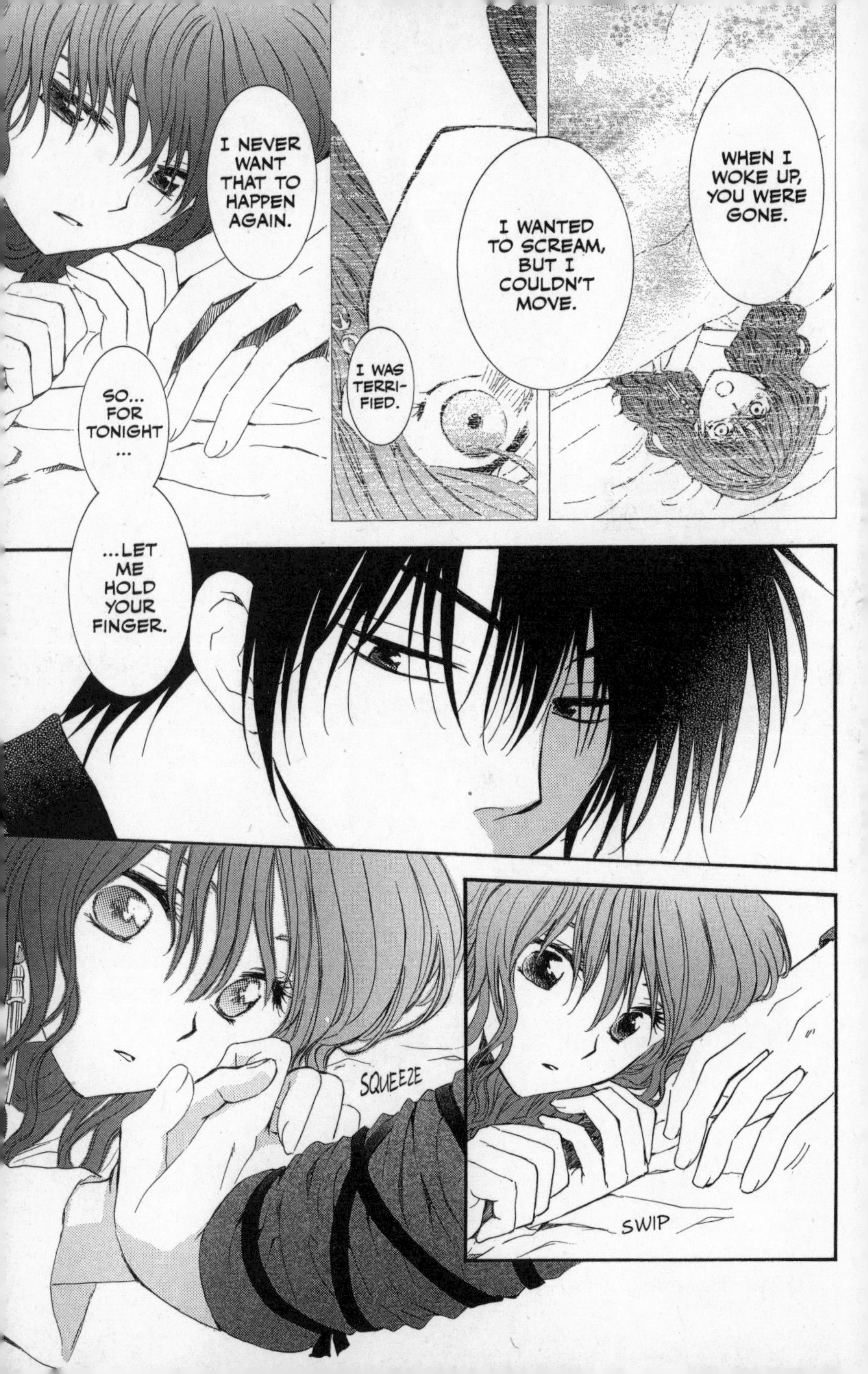
WHEN I WOKE UP, YOU WERE GONE.
I WANTED TO SCREAM, BUT I COULDN'T MOVE.
I WAS TERRI-FIED.
I NEVER WANT THAT TO HAPPEN AGAIN.
SO... FOR TONIGHT...
...LET ME HOLD YOUR FINGER.
SWIP
SQUEEZE

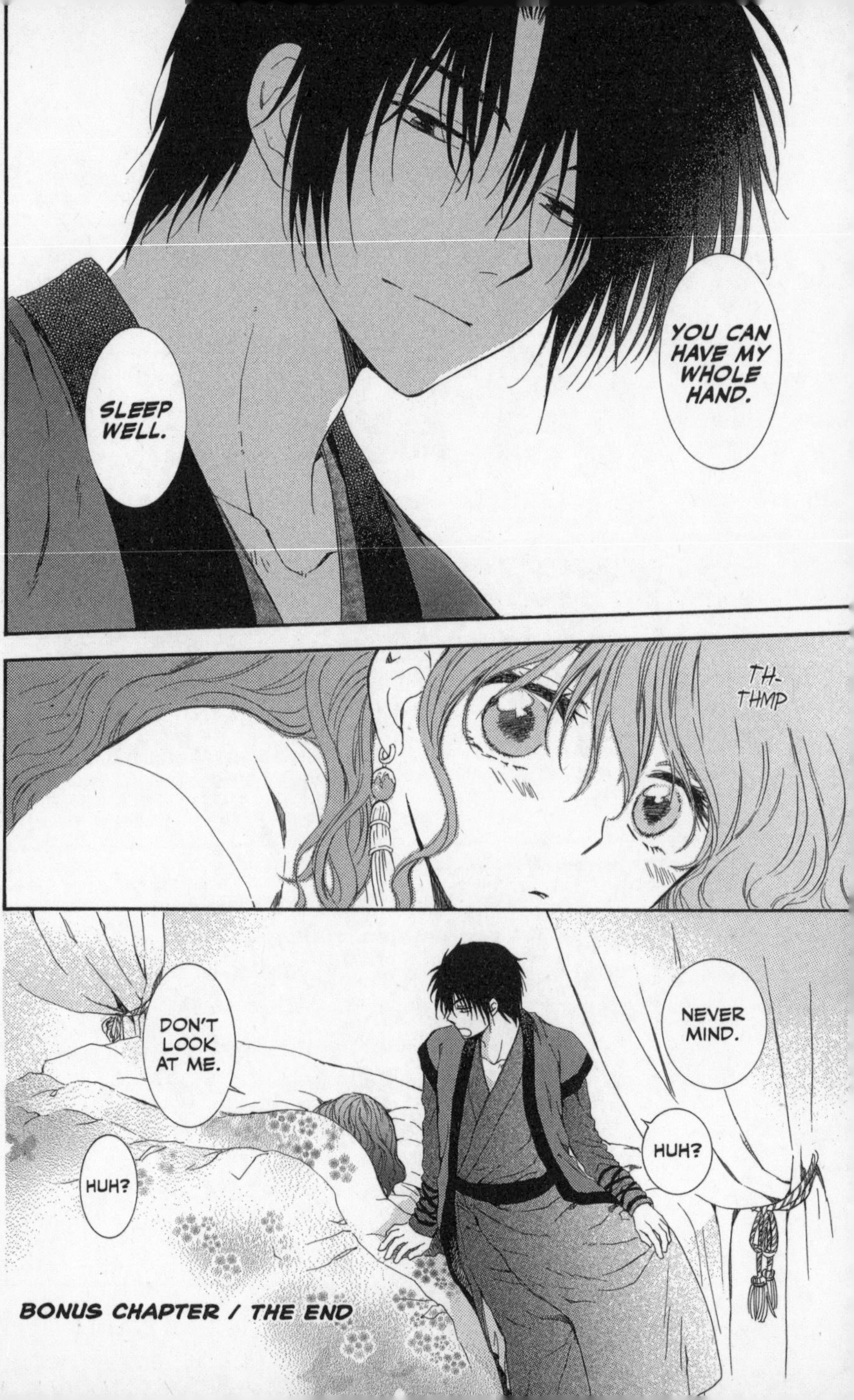
YOU CAN HAVE MY WHOLE HAND.
SLEEP WELL.
TH-THMP
NEVER MIND.
DON'T LOOK AT ME.
HUH?
HUH?
BONUS CHAPTER / THE END

I wasn't planning on doing a series of solo illustrations for the covers, but I feel like it worked. This time, it's Sinha. Who should I go with next time?

—Mizuho Kusanagi

Born on February 3 in Kumamoto Prefecture in Japan, Mizuho Kusanagi began her professional manga career with _Yoiko no Kokoroe_ (The Rules of a Good Child) in 2003. Her other works include _NG Life_, which was serialized in _Hana to Yume_ and _The Hana to Yume_ magazines and published by Hakusensha in Japan. _Yona of the Dawn_ was adapted into an anime in 2014.

YONA OF THE DAWN
VOL. 19
Shojo Beat Edition

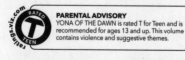

STORY AND ART BY
MIZUHO KUSANAGI

English Adaptation/Ysabet Reinhardt MacFarlane
Translation/JN Productions
Touch-Up Art & Lettering/Lys Blakeslee
Design/Yukiko Whitley
Editor/Amy Yu

Akatsuki no Yona by Mizuho Kusanagi
© Mizuho Kusanagi 2015
All rights reserved.
First published in Japan in 2015 by HAKUSENSHA, Inc., Tokyo.
English language translation rights arranged with
HAKUSENSHA, Inc., Tokyo.

The stories, characters and incidents mentioned in this publication
are entirely fictional.

Printed in the U.S.A.

Published by VIZ Media, LLC
P.O. Box 77010
San Francisco, CA 94107

10 9 8 7 6 5 4 3 2 1
First printing, August 2019

PARENTAL ADVISORY
YONA OF THE DAWN is rated T for Teen and is
recommended for ages 13 and up. This volume
contains violence and suggestive themes.

VIZ MEDIA
viz.com

Shojo Beat
shojobeat.com